INVENTED KNOWLEDGE

Invented Knowledge

False History, Fake Science and
Pseudo-Religions

RONALD H. FRITZE

REAKTION BOOKS

For Jeremy Black
Gentleman, Scholar, Facilitator and Friend

Published by Reaktion Books Ltd
33 Great Sutton Street
London EC1V 0DX, UK
www.reaktionbooks.co.uk

First published 2009
Reprinted 2009

Printed and bound CPI Antony Rowe, Chippenham, Wiltshire

British Library Cataloguing in Publication Data
Fritze, Ronald H., 1951–
    Invented knowledge: false history, fake science and
    pseudo-religions
    1. History – Errors, inventions, etc.
    2. Common fallacies
    3. Conspiracies
    4. Geographical myths
    5. Fraud in science
    I. Title
    001.9'6

ISBN: 978 1 86189 430 4

Contents

Introduction

> Man is an historical animal with a deep sense of his own past,
> and if he cannot integrate the past by a history explicit and true,
> he will integrate it by a history implicit and false.
>
> GEOFFREY BARRACLOUGH (1956)[1]

On 1 December 1862 Abraham Lincoln told the Congress of the United States, 'Fellow-citizens, we cannot escape history.'[2] He was right. The United States was embroiled in its Civil War, the nation's greatest crisis and its deadliest war. Every day Lincoln and his congressional colleagues experienced history and made history. He could say the same thing to the entire population of this world of ours if he could talk across the ages. We too live and make history every day. Sadly, Lincoln could just as well have said, 'Fellow-citizens, we cannot escape pseudohistory.' Pseudohistorical conspiracy theories had helped to bring on the war he was fighting. In the Northern states a widespread belief in the existence of the Slave Power Conspiracy caused people to fear that Southern slaveholders were plotting to destroy civil liberties and enslave poor whites. In the South many people believed that Northern Republicans were conspiring with radical abolitionists to foment a massive slave uprising that would end with barbaric slaves murdering hapless whites in their beds or worse. Both of these pseudohistorical misperceptions helped to fuel the fires of war.

The epoch of antebellum and Civil War America gave rise to a spate of pseudohistory, a sign that unprecedented physical uncertainty about the outcome of widespread political and military conflict was spilling over into the intellectual climate of the age. Americans began to reappraise the history of their tormented land, a reappraisal ripe for wild speculation stretching back into time. Consider the myth of the mound-builders of prehistoric America. According to this myth, a lost white race had settled North America in ancient times and built a glorious civilization whose sole remains were the many mounds scattered across the eastern United States. Tragically the savage ancestors of the Red Indians (Native Americans) invaded the land of the white men and destroyed the mound-builders.

The wilderness reclaimed the land. This mound-builder myth is widely thought to have contributed to inspiring a new religion, the Church of Jesus Christ of the Latter-Day Saints, whose members are better known as the Mormons.[3] If so, it was not the first or the last religion inspired by pseudohistory. The mound-builder myth also provided a convenient justification for the dispossession of the Native Americans from their lands. Other pseudohistorical myths told of Prince Madoc's discovery and settlement of America during the Middle Ages and his peoples' transformation into the fabled Welsh Indians. Tales of the Ten Lost Tribes of Israel or other ancient Hebrews wandering the Americas were added to the mix (see chapter Two). These are amusing stories at the least, and the large numbers of books on those topics from that era attest to their widespread popularity.

Things have not changed all that much from Lincoln's time. We cannot escape pseudohistory or pseudoscience either. The only difference is that today there are more pseudohistorical and pseudo-scientific ideas and more media for disseminating those ideas than just books. The delivery system for pseudohistorians and pseudo-scientists of all stripes now encompasses a charlatan's playground of film, television, radio, magazines and the internet. An especially influ-ential example of the role of media in disseminating pseudohistorical and pseudoscientific ideas is the late night radio show *Coast to Coast* AM, created and hosted for many years by Art Bell, although most of the hosting is currently done by George Noory. The list of past guests on the show's website contains the names of a good number of people discussed in this book.[4] During the spring of 2008 Hollywood and the film industry made its contribution to the corpus of pseudohistory. *10,000 BC* told the story of some primitive mammoth-hunters being oppressed by slave-raiders from an advanced pyramid-building civil-ization at the close of the Ice Age. It was a story inspired by Graham Hancock, Charles H. Hapgood and their fellows (see chapter Five). Even more excitingly, Harrison Ford returned to the silver screen in *Indiana Jones and the Kingdom of the Crystal Skull*, set in the 1950s. Indiana Jones fights Soviet Communists for control of the mysterious Crystal Skull, an artefact from a lost civilization that possesses awe-some powers. In fact the crystal skull is no man-made artefact at all, but the actual skull of an alien from another world, possibly another dimension and, of course, those aliens taught our ancestors the funda-mentals of civilization. The new movie is in the best traditions of the Indiana Jones series but an article on crystal skulls in a recent issue of *Archaeology* has provided convincing evidence that they are all modern fakes or hoaxes.[5] Then there is *Bloodline*, a documentary film by Bruce Burgess, which claims that Jesus Christ married Mary Magdalene and they had children whose bloodline has survived down to the present.[6] If this sounds like *The Da Vinci Code*, that is because it is rooted in the same pseudohistorical sources.

The Da Vinci Code, one of the most successful novels of the new century, was based on a premise derived from pseudohistory. Unlike Bruce Burgess, Dan Brown, the author of *The Da Vinci Code*, freely admits that his novel is a work of fiction, something many fans of the fiction refuse to accept. Dozens of books appeared to debunk all or parts of the history portrayed in *The Da Vinci Code* and some manage to combine good scholarship with clear writing. Still they have had little effect on those willing to believe in conspiracy theories about the descendants of Jesus and nefarious activities by the Christian church. Not that Brown has much reason to feel aggrieved about any of that. His legion of eager fans have helped to make *The Da Vinci Code* a huge bestseller with well over 60 million copies sold. The people who did feel aggrieved were Michael Baigent, Richard Leigh and Henry Lincoln, authors of *The Holy Blood and the Holy Grail* (1982), a book that claims the marriage of Jesus Christ and Mary Magdalene and the survival of their bloodline is historical fact. Brown clearly got his premise for *The Da Vinci Code* from *The Holy Blood and the Holy Grail* and that did not sit well with Baigent and Leigh. In March 2006 they filed a copyright infringement suit in Britain against Brown's publisher Random House. The judge found against Baigent and Leigh because they stated that *The Holy Blood and the Holy Grail* was non-fiction, a statement many professional scholars would have disputed. Because writers of fiction frequently borrow from non-fiction works for background, Baigent and Leigh's claim of copyright infringement was invalid. They appealed but lost again and found themselves facing legal bills for £3 million ($6 million).[7] Clearly there is big money in pseudohistory.

Pseudohistory and pseudoscience are not just represented by blockbuster films and bestselling books. The shelves of new and used bookstores are laden with many less successful works of pseudohistory, particularly in the New Age or Occult sections. Some titles manage to make their way into the history sections. Meanwhile the magazine racks display copies of pseudohistorical magazines like *Atlantis Rising*, *World Explorer/Adventures Unlimited* and *Ancient American* in cosy but incongruous proximity to the venerable *Archaeology* magazine and debunking periodicals like *Skeptic* and *Skeptical Inquirer*. A recent Scholar's Bookshelf catalogue lists a new book, *The End of Eden: The Comet that Changed Civilization* by Graham Phillips, which claims that around 1500 BC the comet 12P/Pans-Brooks made a close approach to the earth. The earth passed through the comet's tail and that resulted in a chemical entering the earth's atmosphere. An outbreak of warlike behaviour and monotheism occurred soon after. The aggression was caused by the chemical, the monotheism by the awesome spectacle of the comet in the sky. The late pseudohistorian Immanuel Velikovsky must be happy that someone has paid him the compliment of imitating his hypotheses: either that, or fretting that a copyright infringement suit cannot be filed from the great beyond. Another Scholar's Bookshelf catalogue offers *The Atlas of Atlantis and Other Lost Civilizations: Discover the History and Wisdom of Atlantis, Lemuria, Mu, and Other Ancient Civilizations* by Joel Levy. The title of the book speaks for itself.[8] For fans of quirky books, it is all good fun.

Pseudohistory and pseudoscience have aspects that are definitely not good fun. Denial of the Holocaust has been a growing phenomenon since the end of the 1970s. By the 1990s the aggressiveness of Holocaust deniers had become severe enough to arouse the concern of many scholars. At its December 1991 meeting the Council of the American Historical Association broke a longstanding policy of not certifying historical facts and passed a short but emphatic resolution that stated: 'The American Historical Association Council strongly deplores the publicly reported attempts to deny the Holocaust. No serious historian questions that the Holocaust took place.'[9] Soon after Deborah Lipstadt, a professor of history at Emory University, brought out *Denying the Holocaust: The Growing Assault on Truth and Memory* in 1993.[10] One of the people that Lipstadt identified as a Holocaust denier was the British writer David Irving. Irving took umbrage and filed a libel suit against her and her British publisher, Penguin Books, in 1996. The suit was filed in Britain, where the law places the burden of proof on the person accused of making the allegedly libellous statement. In the US the case would have never made it into a courtroom since the burden of proof in American law rests firmly on the person claiming to have been libelled. Unfortunately for Irving, Lipstadt and Penguin Books stood their ground and proved that Lipstadt's statements about Irving were true. In April 2000 the judge ruled that Irving had distorted research and was a Holocaust denier, an anti-Semite and a racist. This judgment left Irving with an enormous bill for all of the parties' legal expenses and financially devastated him. Nor were Irving's troubles over.

Many European countries have laws prohibiting Holocaust denial and some had outstanding indictments against Irving. On 11 November 2005, while Irving was visiting Austria, local authorities arrested him for Holocaust denial based on an arrest warrant from 1989. The

Austrians tried him, found him guilty, and sentenced him to three years in prison. In the end he served about ten months of his sentence from February to December of 2006. Some opponents of Holocaust denial worried that Austria's action would transform Irving into a martyr. Clearly Irving paid a heavy price for his Holocaust denial but earlier he had reaped substantial benefits. The example of his legal troubles has also done nothing to dampen down the persistence and the spread of the pseudohistory of Holocaust denial that runs rampant in the Middle East.

Holocaust denial has come to make strange bedfellows of neo-Nazis and Iranian militants – perhaps not all that strange. Reza Pahlavi, the Shah of Iran (1878–1944) was an admirer of Adolf Hitler. Pseudohistory often lends itself as a tool of racism, religious fanaticism and nationalistic extremism (see chapters Three and Four). The Nazis had their own pseudohistorical mythology of an Aryan super-race which they attempted to bolster with all sorts of pseudo-historical and pseudoscientific research.[11] Tamil nationalism in India is less heinous but it is based on a belief in the historical reality of the lost continent of Lemuria, once the home of a great ancient Tamil civilization.[12] Indiana Jones's adventures with Nazi archaeologists in *Raiders of the Lost Ark* and *Indiana Jones and the Last Crusade* are not pure fantasy. The Nazis did want to get possession of sacred artefacts like the Spear of Destiny that pierced the side of Christ. Pseudohistory is out there and an educated person can and should be able to identify it. But how? Get to know the territory of the study of history, both its rightful and its dubious claims.

What is pseudohistory or pseudoscience? That is a tricky question with elusive answers cast on the shifting sands of scholarship, taste and fashion. An easy answer would be to follow the lead of Justice Potter Stewart, who confessed the difficulty of defining obscenity, but said, 'I know it when I see it.' The real place to start defining pseudohistory is to answer the classic question, what is history? That, however, is also a vexed question for people living in a post-modernist age. A simple and elegant definition for history 'is a true story about the human past'.[13] The problem is that pseudohistorians insist that their ideas and writings are true stories about the human past. Critical scholars, of course, disagree. So how can a person know what is truth and fact, and what is lie and error in history, or science for that matter? The answer is evidence, including its quality and quantity. Evidence can take the form of documents from the past, old maps, artefacts, archaeological remains and scientific findings with implications for history. Another answer is the use of objective and empirical methods to analyse and evaluate the evidence.

Objective scholars with an honest agenda view evidence without bias or preconceptions, or at least they try hard to guard against them as far as it humanly possible. Pseudohistorians usually approach their subjects with preconceptions, perhaps even a hidden agenda based on the desire for royalties or reputation. They know going in what happened or think they do and so they look for the evidence to prove it. As a result pseudohistorians pick and chose their evidence. They ignore what contradicts their ideas and only use the evidence that bolsters their case. Objective, classically trained historians try to look at all the available evidence and seek to develop an interpretation or analysis that encompasses the entire body of evidence in all its complexity.

It is important to make the distinction between pseudohistory and pseudoscience on the one hand and bad, inaccurate or obsolete history and science that has been disproved, discredited or discarded on the other. During the Middle Ages the geocentric theory of the universe was the orthodox worldview and part of the mainstream of existing knowledge. Someone who argued for a geocentric solar system at the present time using the trappings of academic scholarship would be viewed as using pseudoscience, as would anyone advocating a flat earth theory. For the sixteenth-century Spanish chroniclers, accepting that Atlantis had existed was a reasonable position. While some sixteenth-century scholars expressed scepticism about the existence of Atlantis, many educated, reasonable and respectable people believed it existed and no one considered them to be crackpots or purveyors of fake knowledge. Even the irrepressible Ignatius Donnelly's classic *Atlantis: The Antediluvian World*, which is widely considered to be the first great work of pseudohistory, was actually moderately reasonable in its conclusions and evidence based on existing knowledge in 1882. The problem with pseudohistorians and pseudoscientists is that they often base their theories on disproved, discredited and discarded scholarship. Some such obsolete works, such as Donnelly's *Atlantis*, are continuously republished and have never gone out of print. Other tens of thousands of similar books and articles lurk on the shelves of libraries and used bookstores waiting to be rediscovered and reused. These writings are all wonderful resources for researching intellectual history and the history of science and culture. But they also await the attentions of the naive, the undiscriminating, the biased or prejudiced, the cynical and the unscrupulous who will utilize them as the raw materials of new works of pseudohistory and pseudoscience. As such, these discarded works of science and history form a 'cultic milieu' for the continuing production of works of pseudohistory and pseudoscience.

Long ago the sociologist Colin Campbell pointed out the existence of a 'cultic milieu' based on the fact that cults are ephemeral, loosely structured and rather individualistic organizations that follow a belief system. The adherents or fans of certain pseudohistorical ideas or hypotheses match that definition of cult as well. Just as cults are in a constant process of beginning, thriving and dying out, so do pseudohistorical ideas arise, reach a level of popular acceptance and fade away. But as new cults arise roughly as fast as old cults decline, so new variations of pseudohistorical ideas rise up as older ones lose their popularity. Sometimes Atlantis is all the rage, then the focus shifts to catastrophism and on to ancient astronauts, Chinese discoveries of pre-Columbian America or *Da Vinci Code* types of ideas about the bloodline of Jesus Christ. The point is that while individual cults come and go, there are always cults around. Clearly the same observation applies to pseudohistory and pseudoscience. Pseudohistorical ideas are always present even though individual ideas rise and decline in popularity.

The existence of a cultic milieu of pseudohistory also means that there is a stockpile of cultic beliefs or pseudohistorical ideas along with related books, writings and other artefacts available to provide starter material for new ideas. Adherents of Christian Identity mined the detritus of British-Israelism to develop their ideas and later added concepts from studies of UFOs to the mix (see chapter Five). Atlantologists frequently return to Ignatius Donnelly's books on Atlantis even though they are well over a hundred years old. Obsolete and antiquated scholarship is reshuffled and recombined with older pseudohistorical works to create new ideas and hypotheses or often simply to reinvent even older semi-forgotten pseudohistorical ideas. As fast as historians, archaeologists and scientists debunk pseudohistorical hypotheses, new ones emerge out of the cultic milieu like rejuvenated heads on a hydra.[14] In 1986 Kendrick Frazier, editor of *Skeptical Inquirer*, cited 'a sharp plunge' in books about pseudohistory and pseudoscience citing Immanuel Velikovsky and Erich von Däniken as prime examples. He thought psychics, astrology, health fads and fringe medicine would become the new challenge for sceptics. Although those topics remain perennially popular, clearly Frazier did not foresee Michael Baigent, Gavin Menzies or Graham Hancock among others coming on to the stage of popular culture and the cultic milieu with remarkable success.[15]

Pseudohistory and pseudoscience are modern phenomena. Their subject matter may be ancient or even primordial and their sources may date back to the beginning of recorded history but pseudohistory and pseudoscience are largely products of the last quarter of the nineteenth century onward. It is the conditions of modern society that have made their existence possible. The Darwinian revolution in science shattered the traditional Christian worldview of a 6,000-year-old history with its six-day creation of a fixed natural world and humanity. Modern science replaced that neat but circumscribed picture with a slowly changing universe of incomprehensible size whose origins stretched back into the deep time of an unimaginably old prehistory. Modern science did not simply discredit the Christian worldview: increasingly rapid developments in scientific knowledge meant that it disproved its own existing theories and replaced them with better ones. The same developments occurred in historical studies, particularly in ancient history where the rise of academic archaeology armed with empirical methods and new scientific techniques was pushing knowledge of the human past further and further back in time. All of this activity created the stockpile of discarded and discredited scientific theories and historical ideas that form the cultic milieu of pseudohistory and pseudoscience.[16]

Modern industrial society made mass education possible and necessary. By the beginning of the twentieth century most people in Western industrial societies were functionally literate. Industrialized printing made cheap books and magazines available. The rise of free public libraries made books and magazines even more readily available although early librarians often acted as censors. Still the mass culture of cheap books and widespread literacy created the possibility for subcultures to develop as various groups of people used the readily available knowledge for their own often undisciplined purposes. Inevitably some of these subcultures would focus their interests and even their worldviews on pseudohistorical and pseudoscientific topics. It has been suggested that the unorthodox, often irrational and sometimes spiritual beliefs arising from pseudohistory and pseudoscience serve as a substitute for traditional religion. It has also been suggested that the genres of popular fiction known as science fiction, horror and fantasy have inspired various pseudohistorical and pseudoscientific theories. One recent study has plausibly credited some of H. P. Lovecraft's horror tales from the 1920s and '30s about primeval aliens visiting the earth and creating life with inspiring the theories of Erich von Däniken and others that alien space-travellers visited the earth in prehistoric and historic times and were viewed as gods.[17]

Pseudohistorians differ from historians in other ways based on the flawed methodologies that they use. Pseudohistorians use the terms 'legend' and 'myth' interchangeably. Scholars view myth and legend as distinct concepts. A myth is an invented story which is used allegorically or tropologically to explain some natural event or phenomenon or some aspect of the human condition or psyche. A legend is a story about the past that has some basis in real historical events although it is often distorted with the passage of time.[18] Many pseudohistorians treat myths as legends and argue that myths literally describe distant historical events – a very ancient practice called euhemerism. The term comes from the Greek scholar Euhemerus (c. 300 BC) who argued that the myths of the Greek gods were actually the record of the acts of ancient kings. This apparent rationalizing of the Greek myths caused the great literary scholar Callimachus of Cyrene (c. 270 BC) to attack Euhemerus as a blasphemer against the gods. Modern scholars continue to attack latter-day euhemerists as blasphemers against historical or scientific truth.

Pseudohistorians, much like defence attorneys on television melodramas, tend to confuse the distinction between possibility and probability in their arguments even though there is a clear difference between the two. Something is possible when it could happen or could have occurred, however unlikely that event might actually be. For something to be probable, it must be likely that it occurred or could happen. So it is possible someone will buy me a lottery ticket tomorrow that will turn out to be a big winner. On the other hand, it is probable that I will go to work tomorrow at my office on campus, if it is a work day. By the same token, it is possible that Chinese explorers reached the Americas and colonized them while circumnavigating the globe in the process. Based on the reliable evidence available, however, it is highly probable that they did no such thing.

Another difference between history and pseudohistory is the nature of debates and disagreements among the players on the intellectual and pseudo-intellectual stages. Historians debate one another on a different plane than the back-alley venue for debates between historians and pseudohistorians. Historians certainly have their disagreements over interpretations. Sometimes they can be acrimonious. But, almost always, the basic facts are not in dispute. Historians agree that a man named Henry VIII was the king of England from 1509 to 1547. They agree about the main events or achievements of his reign. When they enter into debate they disagree over the significance, the consequences or the quality of those events or achievements. On the other plane pseudohistorical debates focus on basic facts: did certain events occur or not occur, did some places exist or not exist or did particular individuals or groups live or not live? Was there an Atlantis? Did a Scottish lord named Henry Sinclair and some Templar hold-outs settle in America before Columbus? Was the Holocaust a historical event or a hoax? Did intelligent extraterrestrials visit the earth during prehistory or antiquity and jump-start humanity and civilization? Are the Anglo-Saxon peoples descendants of the Ten Lost Tribes of Israel?

Pseudohistorians, pseudoarchaeologists or pseudoscientists exhibit other traits that set them off from mainstream scholars. Those traits have recently been catalogued by the classicist and historian Garrett Fagan. Pseudohistorians cling to outdated and obsolete scholarship or ideas or they distort viable scientific theories beyond any reasonable point. Numerous expert examinations have proven the Kensington Runestone to be a hoax but latter-day pseudohistorians continue to claim it is an authentic artefact of a medieval Norse presence in Minnesota. Zecharia Sitchin persists in claiming that asteroids are the remains of a planet that was pulled apart or exploded whereas scientists no longer believe asteroids were part of a destroyed planet.[19] Pseudohistorians disparage professional academics as stodgy and close-minded but whenever possible they solicit the support of any reputable scholar they can find or at least drop their names. Immanuel Velikovsky and Charles H. Hapgood both sought Albert Einstein's support for their respective catastrophist hypotheses and provide a good example of this behaviour (see chapter Five). Pseudohistorians make huge claims for their hypotheses. Gavin Menzies has the Chinese treasure fleets visit almost every part of the world. Immanuel Velikovsky asserted that the earth almost collided with Venus on two occasions and later with Mars, close encounters that caused great upheavals and global devastation. Meanwhile he cut five centuries out of ancient Egyptian and Greek history. To support such arguments pseudohistorians comb through evidence from many disciplines – history, geology, linguistics, biology and archaeology among others – but they use it without regard to context or standard interpretations. They focus on the anomalies in the evidence rather than what the preponderance of the evidence reveals to a reasonable researcher.[20] Pseudohistory is about sensationalistic topics: lost continents, lost tribes, the end of the world, the return of ancient astronauts or gods, vast conspiracies enduring over centuries or every conceivable Old World people or nation managing to get to the Americas before Christopher Columbus and still managing to keep it a secret except for some chatty Vikings in their sagas. Many pseudohistorians are obsessive about their subject and biased in their methods. That is when they are sincere. Others may be cynical about their pseudohistory and so are willing to say or write anything that sells whether they believe it or not. Still it can be great fun, sells books and movie tickets and is a great way to make a potentially lucrative living.

Some methodological comments about the book that follows need to be made. It is a selective rather than a comprehensive or exhaustive study of pseudohistory. Comprehensiveness would have required a much larger book. Exhaustiveness would have made it many volumes. The six chapters of this book look at various aspects of pseudohistory. Chapter One begins with what is probably the oldest theme in the annals of pseudohistory, Atlantis. The original and most famous lost continent has inspired myriad pseudohistorical hypotheses by the beguiled, hoaxers, cultists, nationalists and racists. People coming to America before Columbus is another perennial topic of pseudohistorians. All sorts of nationalistic, ethnocentric and racial motivations lie behind these hypotheses of pre-Columbian exploration and colonization, discussed in chapter Two. Chapters Three and Four look at how pseudohistory has inspired some racist religions: Christian Identity and the Nation of Islam. Chapter Five is a case study of the interconnections and mutual influences that have occurred among a select group of pseudohistorians. Finally a case study of the Black Athena controversy comprises chapter Six and shows that a thin and fuzzy line can separate academic history from pseudohistory. Unfortunately considerations of length have meant that topics such as Holocaust denial, Egyptomania, Afrocentricism and Nazi pseudohistory have only been mentioned in passing if at all.

Many groups espousing pseudohistorical ideas use the Bible as a source for some of their beliefs. Generally they take the biblical narrative very literally. For Immanuel Velikovsky the Ten Plagues of Egypt, the Exodus and the Conquest of Canaan were events that occurred just as the Bible describes them. His goal was to provide a naturalistic and scientific explanation of the miraculous phenomena described in the Books of Exodus and Joshua. Unlike Velikovsky, most biblical scholars do not think that definite dates can be assigned to those events or other aspects of the early history of the Hebrews or Israel, that the events happened as described or that they necessarily happened at all. The scholarly debate over the historical basis of the Old Testament narratives is not something that most pseudohistorians take cognizance of.

It should be pointed out that theory and hypothesis are not used as interchangeable terms. Theory is only used for a scientific concept that is broadly accepted as correct by scientists based on a broad array of evidence and research. Plate tectonics is a theory, as is evolution. The term hypothesis is used to designate historical or scientific concepts or interpretations that have been suggested but are not broadly accepted as correct, if they ever will be. Pseudohistorical concepts and interpretations are hypotheses by their nature.

Finally the term pseudohistory is used throughout the book with occasional references to pseudoscience or pseudoarchaeology. Some writers refer to pseudohistory as 'fringe history' or 'alternate history'. Apparently 'fringe' or 'alternate' are not considered to be as judgemental or pejorative as the term pseudohistory. Pseudohistorians prefer to use terms like 'forbidden history' to describe their works and, as is well known, forbidden fruit tastes the sweetest as well as being able to convey the knowledge of good and evil that comes from truth. The problem is that most pseudohistory is manifestly not true. Miguel de Cervantes observed in *Don Quixote* that 'No history can be bad so long as it is true.'[21] Since pseudohistory is not true, it is fallacious history and sometimes even dangerous history. Some people will object to the term pseudohistory but the fact is that the term is accurate. Pseudo means false and pseudohistory is false history in that it is wrong factually and incorrect methodologically. I will conclude with the words of Mark Twain, 'It may be thought that I am prejudiced. Perhaps I am. I would be ashamed of myself if I were not.'[22]

CHAPTER I

Atlantis: Mother of Pseudohistory

The various opinions respecting the Island of Atlantis have no interest for us except in so far as they illustrate the extravagances of which men are capable. But it is a real interest and a serious lesson, if we remember that now as formerly the human mind is liable to be imposed upon by the illusions of the past, which are ever assuming some new form. BENJAMIN JOWETT (1874)[1]

Atlantis sleeps beneath the seas. But not reason alone, nor the apparatus of scholarship, will, in the end, serve to probe her ancient mysteries. LEWIS SPENCE (1925)[2]

Either Atlantis is an island in the Atlantic ocean or it is not 'Atlantis' at all. JAMES BRAMWELL (1939)[3]

Sometime around 1525 BC a small island in the Aegean Sea literally lay under a cloud of doom. It was the volcanic island of Thera and its volcano had begun one of its periodic eruptions. Most of the island's inhabitants had already abandoned their Bronze Age city, known to modern archaeologists as Akrotiri. They took all of their moveable valuables with them. Akrotiri, or Therassos, as it was probably called, was a major centre within the vast and profitable trading empire of Minoan Crete. Its population of 10,000–15,000 people compared favourably with other Minoan cities. Knossos, the biggest Minoan city on Crete, had a population of 20,000. Palaikastro and Mallia, other important Cretan cities, had populations of 18,000 and 12,500 respectively. Phylakopi, a Minoan trading post on the island of Melos, only had 2,000 inhabitants. The important contemporary Levantine city of Ugarit had about the same size population as Akrotiri. While cities of this size seem small by modern standards, they were the metropolises of the Bronze Age. Given its size and the richness of its buildings, Akrotiri was clearly a wealthy and important city in the maritime trading world of the eastern Mediterranean Sea.[4]

Unfortunately for its inhabitants, the island of Thera was and is located on a powder keg. Plate tectonics and the forces of continental drift make the region of the Aegean Sea and the eastern Mediterranean one of the most earthquake-prone areas on earth. Bronze Age Thera was roughly circular in shape. Its southwest quarter was indented by a bay formed by the caldera of an earlier volcanic eruption dating back to around 54,000 BC. The northwest quarter of Thera contained a smaller bay that was the remnant of the caldera of another explosive eruption that took place about 18,500 BC. To the southwest of this northern bay lay the cones of three volcanic peaks. Despite this forbidding skyline of three volcanoes Thera had remained quiet during the early Bronze Age. Its favourable location on the maritime trade routes transformed it into a thriving urban centre.

Thera's idyll came to an end as the pressures of the seismic forces beneath it reached a dangerous level. Unlike some volcanoes on the verge of a major eruption, Thera gave its inhabitants plenty of warnings that doomsday was at hand. A series of earthquakes struck the island with increasing severity. These caused the Theran population to flee in terror. It was a good thing that they did because the last quake was quite powerful and destroyed many houses. The volcanos also ejected a substantial amount of pumice that rained down on Akrotiri and filled its streets knee-deep with ash. For a time things quieted down on Thera, allowing some of its residents to return. They commenced cleaning up and repairing the damage. It took about a year to get the island back to functioning relatively normally again although whether the entire population returned is unclear. This respite from the fury of the volcanoes lasted between two and five years, but eventually the earthquakes resumed with stronger and stronger tremors. Once again the Therans began to abandon their homes. Then, as an added incentive for them to depart, the volcanoes began to spew steam, gas and sulphurous smoke over the island. More earthquakes shook hapless Akrotiri, causing considerable damage. At that point the few remaining workers threw down their tools and fled to the ships remaining in the harbour to make their escape via the sea. As the eruption continued the three volcanic cones disappeared and a growing crater opened up in their place. A fine white pumice began to mix with the steam escaping from the maw of the volcano and covered the island with a layer two centimetres thick. Then, for a second time, the eruption halted for a period as much as several months long. The volcano, however, was not done with Thera and Akrotiri. The next phase of the eruption began with a rain of pea-sized pumice that increased in size and eventually covered the island with a layer over a metre deep. Debris from the widening crater was also blown into the air by the pressures from within the volcano. It plummeted down on the island as a cloud of smoke and steam rose over Thera to an altitude of 35 kilometres.

The longer the eruption continued, the more the volcano's crater grew. Eventually seawater began to leak into the crater, causing it to eject vast quantities of wet ash. When the magma chamber beneath

Thera had emptied itself, gravity caused the volcano to collapse back into the chamber. This collapse opened the super-hot magma chamber to a flood of seawater, causing the eruption to enter its final phase. Explosions resulting from the collapse of the magma chamber could have been heard as far away as Egypt, Pakistan and southwestern England. As a result of the collapse a substantial part of pre-eruption Thera disappeared. In its place appeared a bay close to 500 metres deep in places and surrounded by a rim of cliffs that were the caldera left by the explosion. Such an immense displacement of solid materials and water through implosion and explosion, together with the accompanying earthquakes, created fierce tsunamis. These fanned out from devastated Thera and crashed into the coastline of Crete within half an hour of the great explosion. Crete and neighbouring Aegean islands suffered extensive damage. The eruption also created a massive ash cloud that the wind carried mainly to the southeast of Thera. Ash fell on eastern Crete and the coast of southwest Asia Minor, blighting the vegetation. Thera's eruption in approximately 1525 BC was four times more powerful than the legendary explosion of Krakatoa in 1883. The less well known but far more intense eruption of Tambora in Indonesia during 1815 was approximately the same size as Thera's. Together they represent the two most violent volcanic eruptions during the past four thousand years. Thera's eruption was so powerful that tsunamis and ash clouds terrorized Egypt and caused significant damage. Some writers have even suggested that Thera's eruption might have been responsible for some of the biblical Ten Plagues of Egypt along with the parting of the Red Sea and the accompanying destruction of Pharaoh's army.[5]

A dramatic and traumatic event like the eruption of Thera would have seared itself into the folk memory of the people of the Aegean and the eastern Mediterranean. In fact, for the past hundred years reputable historians and archaeologists have been suggesting that tales of the destruction of Thera provided Plato with the inspiration for his account of Atlantis. This approach to Plato's story historicizes Atlantis by attempting to find a historical reality behind various ancient myths or legends. The assumption that all legends have a historical foundation is called euhemerism and is named after the ancient Greek scholar Euhemerus (fl. 300 BC), who pioneered this approach.[6] While Thera remains the most favoured location for Atlantis, other writers have suggested Troy or the city of Sipylus near Smyrna in Asia Minor,[7] while some have credited the enigmatic trading city of Tartessos or Tarshish in Spain as the inspiration.[8] The trouble with this situation is that multiple historicized Atlantises all competing for acceptance leave a bewildered public asking, 'Will the real Atlantis please stand up?'

PLATO'S ATLANTIS

> Hence we may safely conclude that the entire narrative is due to
> the imagination of Plato, who has used the name of Solon and
> introduced the Egyptian priests to give verisimilitude to his story
> [of Atlantis]. BENJAMIN JOWETT (1874)[9]

There are many Atlantises. People have claimed and still are claiming to have found the lost continent in widely scattered locations
throughout the world and even off the planet. Every continent, except possibly Australia, and the bottom of the sea have been cited as
the location for Atlantis.[10] When Atlantis existed is also a debatable
topic with many, yielding variations from millions of years ago to
mere centuries before the time of Plato (c. 427–347 BC). The proposed nature of Atlantean civilization also varies immensely from
an advanced Stone Age society along the lines of the Aztecs and Incas
to a Bronze Age society to an extremely advanced super-scientific culture that in some versions had its origins off the earth. The extent of
Atlantis also ranges from a small island with a single city to a large
but lost continent with many cities and a vast empire. Furthermore,
some theories of Atlantis claim that Atlantis, or at least Atlanteans,
survive among us or in some hidden place. The proliferation of all of
these competing and contradictory Atlantises is truly astounding
considering that the myth of Atlantis can be traced back to a single
point of origin: Plato and his writings the *Timaeus* and the *Critias*.

Plato told the story of Atlantis in an introductory section of his
dialogue the *Timaeus*. This dialogue was basically a reflection on the
creator of the universe and the state of the natural and physical sciences of that era as Plato understood them. Critias tells the story of
Atlantis to Socrates. Plato goes into greater detail about the supposed
history of Atlantis in his next dialogue, the *Critias*. Once again Critias
narrates to Socrates and other companions the story of Atlantis and
its war with the original Athens of nine thousand years before the
time of Plato. Unfortunately Plato stopped working on the *Critias*
right at the moment when Zeus, the king of the gods, had gathered
the Olympian deities together to decide on the destruction of an increasingly immoral Atlantis.

Atlantis as Plato described it is the font and the foundation for all
other Atlantises. That circumstance makes it essential to provide an
accurate account of Plato's description of Atlantis. According to Plato,

> there was an island situated in front of the straits which are
> by you [the Athenians] called the Pillars of Heracles, the island

was larger than Libya and Asia put together and was the way
to other islands and from these you might pass to the whole of
the opposite continent which surrounded the true ocean, for
this sea which is within the Straits of Heracles is only a harbor,
having a narrow entrance, but the other is a real sea, and the
surrounding land may be called a boundless continent.[11]

In this section Plato tells his readers that Atlantis is an island located
just outside the straits of Gibraltar, the modern name for the ancient
Pillars of Hercules. Atlantis is not just any island, but a very large island, larger than Sicily or Crete or Cyprus, which would have been
the largest islands familiar to Plato and his contemporaries. In fact,
Plato states that Atlantis was bigger than Libya and Asia combined.
Just what he meant by this comparison is unclear. Some scholars suggest that Plato was referring to two of the three continents known to
the ancient Greeks: Libya (Saharan Africa) and Asia (the Middle East
and India). If so, Atlantis was a rather large continent not merely an
island. Plato, however, never refers to Atlantis as a continent so he
may have been using a more limited definition of the geographical
terms Libya and Asia. The ancient Greeks commonly referred to the
region of North Africa between Egypt and Cyrene as Libya. They
also sometimes called the area known as Asia Minor or modern
Turkey by the shorter name of Asia. Taken together, the combination
of these two regions would not amount to a continent-sized landmass, but it would constitute an island far larger even than Sicily, the
largest island in the Mediterranean Sea.

Plato specifically locates Atlantis just beyond the Pillars of Hercules which led to the Atlantic Ocean. While at various times the
geography of the ancient Greeks applied the name of Pillars of Hercules
to other locations in the Aegean region, in this case it Plato is quite explicit that he means the Pillars of Hercules that are now known as the
Straits of Gibraltar. Apparently the sea separating Atlantis from the
Pillars of Hercules was supposed to be very small and narrow, so much
so that Plato refers to it as a harbour. Beyond Atlantis lies a sea that is
a 'true ocean', by which Plato meant the world-encircling River Ocean
of ancient Greek geography. Across that ocean lay a massive continent
that surrounded the known world. Various other islands were scattered
across the River Ocean between Atlantis and the great continent.

Plato describes Atlantis as a large and expansionist empire: 'Now
in this island of Atlantis there was a great and wonderful empire
which had rule over the whole island and several others, and over parts
of the continent, and furthermore, the men of Atlantis had subjected
the parts of Libya within the columns of Hercules as far as Egypt,

and Europe as far as Tyrrhenia.'[12] Clearly the Atlantean empire was huge. Besides the island of Atlantis it included other islands in the Atlantic Ocean and parts of the surrounding continent. It also controlled the entire western basin of the Mediterranean Sea, including most of Italy and up to the frontiers of Egypt. The Atlanteans, however, were not satisfied with what they already possessed and wanted more land, riches and power. They decided to undertake the conquest of the rest of the Mediterranean in one great expedition that took place about 9400 BC. The Athens of that day rallied the neighbouring countries against the Atlantean threat. A hard-fought struggle followed in which Athens found itself deserted by its allies and left to fight on alone. Against prodigious odds, the Athenians persevered and ultimately prevailed over the Atlantean invaders. They not only preserved their independence along with the other lands of the eastern Mediterranean, but also proceeded to liberate the peoples of the western Mediterranean from the Atlantean yoke. It was the zenith of the fortunes of the first Athens.

Unfortunately, Athens' triumph was short-lived. An immense catastrophe struck both the victors and the vanquished in the ancient war. According to Plato's narrative,

> But afterwards there occurred violent earthquakes and floods; and in a single day and night of misfortune all your warlike men [of Athens] in a body sank into the earth, and the island of Atlantis in a like manner disappeared in the depths of the sea. For which reason the sea in those parts [where the Straits of Gibraltar and the Atlantic Ocean meet] is impassable and impenetrable, because there is a shoal of mud in the way; and this was caused by the subsidence of the island.[13]

In short, a combination of earthquakes and floods swallowed up the Athenian army and caused Atlantis to sink beneath the waves (not too far if the problem of the mud shoals is anything to go by).

The Atlantis of Plato was a Bronze Age civilization in its material culture and technology, no more, no less. In its scale, however, everything about Atlantis was gigantic. Its empire was vast and controlled territories that far exceeded the extent of those later empires of Persia, Alexander the Great and Rome. The island of Atlantis was also a cornucopia of natural resources that furnished most of the Atlanteans' material needs although they still maintained a flourishing import trade. The fertile soil of Atlantis produced many types of crops in great quantities. Animal life was abundant and the herds of Atlantean domestic animals prospered grazing on its verdant pastures.

The island even contained elephants, which would not have been out of the question since neighbouring North Africa was home to a now extinct type of elephant that persisted up to the time of Imperial Rome. For the Greeks of Plato's day elephants were somewhat of a novelty. The mines of Atlantis produced great quantities of all sorts of metals including the enigmatic orichalc which, as Plato put it, 'is now only a name'.[14] Most scholars think that orichalc was probably brass or some similar alloy using zinc, a rare metal in the ancient world. Orichalc is the only mysterious item possessed by the At-lanteans and it did not play a prominent role in their civilization or their warcraft. Instead, what the Atlanteans had were vast lands, huge cities and extraordinarily large armies and navies. The At-lantean army could field 840,000 soldiers and 10,000 chariots. Its navy could man its 1,200 warships with 240,000 crewmen. No other Bronze Age state could deploy more than a small fraction of Atlantis's military might.[15]

Plato also points out that the preternatural power and wealth of Atlantis was largely attributable to the divine origins of its rulers. The various Greek gods had divided up the regions of the earth among themselves. Poseidon, the god of the sea, received Atlantis. Some mortals were living on Atlantis at the time of the division, and Poseidon took a fancy to one of them, Cleito, the daughter of Evenor and Leucippe. Taking Cleito as his mistress, Poseidon set her up in a fortified love nest on a hill surrounded by three concentric moats of water and fortifications on the two rings of land and on the mainland bordering the outermost moat. It was a luxurious abode that had both hot and cold springs to supply its water. Poseidon and Cleito produced five sets of male twins. Each of the sons received a tenth of Atlantis to rule. The eldest of the eldest pair of twins was named Atlas, and he received the fortified palace of his mother as part of his portion. Poseidon also appointed him king over his other nine broth-ers. The sons of Poseidon and their descendants ruled Atlantis wisely, thanks to the blood of Poseidon that flowed in their veins. They also enjoyed an unbroken royal succession of eldest son after eldest son for many generations. Atlas's successors were the wealthiest monarchs that had ever ruled or were likely to rule any time in the future.[16] Unfortunately, over time the heritage of Poseidon became diluted as the Atlantean rulers intermarried with mere mortals. Instead of cultivating greatness of character and virtue the Atlanteans became materialistic and abandoned their traditional moderation for greed and uninhibited ambition. The power of Atlantis continued to grow but so did its degeneracy. Observing this depraved development Zeus, king of the gods, called together his fellow deities to consider what punishment ought to be inflicted on the arrogant Atlanteans.[17] That punishment turned out to be defeat in war and the destruction of Atlantis. Based on what Plato wrote, the divine ancestry of the Atlanteans was so diluted by the time of the war with Athens that it conferred no military advantage on them.

The basic elements above form the fundamental core of the Atlantis story as Plato gave it. First, Atlantis was a very large island in the Atlantic Ocean. Second, it possessed an extensive empire in the Atlantic which included the lands of the western Mediterranean region. Third, about 9400 BC, the Atlanteans fought a war of conquest with Athens and lost. Fourth, earthquakes and floods caused Atlantis to sink beneath the Atlantic over the course of a single day and night. Fifth, Atlantis was a Bronze Age civilization in its technology and material culture. The only extraordinary feature of the Atlantean state was its enormous size. It possessed vast territories, myriad and plentiful natural resources, great cities and an immense population with correspondingly mighty armies and navies. Sixth, the prosperity of Atlantis had its origin in the fathering of its ruling dynasty by the god Poseidon. Of course, anyone who starts to delve into the study of Atlantology will quickly learn that many theories about Atlantis deviate significantly from the basic outline that Plato provided in the *Timaeus* and the *Critias*. It is very important to keep in mind about all these divergent alternative versions of what, when and where Atlantis was, that, as the writer James Bramwell said best in 1938, 'Either Atlantis is an island in the Atlantic ocean or it is not 'Atlantis' at all.'[18] His observation applies equally to all of the other main features of Plato's story. It is also important to remember that ultimately there can really only be one Atlantis, assuming that Atlantis ever existed at all.

What is the evidence for the existence of Atlantis? As far as documentary sources go, the *Timaeus* and the *Critias* of Plato are the only ancient, independent sources to mention Atlantis. There are subsequent references to Atlantis by various ancient writers including Strabo, Diodorus Siculus and Plutarch but they all refer back to Plato's account. According to the two dialogues, there were earlier sources that described Atlantis. Critias, who appears in both the *Timaeus* and the *Critias* as the narrator of the story of Atlantis, is said to be the maternal great-grandfather of Plato. He states that he learned about Atlantis when he was ten years old from his grandfather, who was also named Critias. The elder Critias heard about Atlantis from the Greek sage and lawgiver Solon, who was a friend and relative of Dropides, the father of the elder Critias. According to Solon, he had travelled to Egypt where he visited the Saïs district in the Nile delta. There he met with the priests of the goddess Neith, an Egyptian counterpart to the Greek goddess Athena, the patron of Athens. Solon and the Egyptian priests entered into a discussion about antiquity. As the discussion progressed, the priests informed Solon that he and his fellow Greeks were completely ignorant of the truly distant past. They pointed out that various natural disasters had not only destroyed the Greeks' historical records on several occasions, but these catastrophes had caused enough disruption that the Greeks even lost the knowledge of writing itself. As a result the historical memory of the Greeks was relatively short. On the other hand, Egypt's location protected it from the most severe effects of catastrophes like floods and earthquakes. As a result Egypt had managed to preserve records from the most ancient times and so possessed access to a span of history that other societies like the Greeks had lost. On the columns of the temple of Neith at Saïs the story of Atlantis was written and the priests there shared it with Solon, who brought it back to Greece.[19]

Plato never finished the dialogue *Critias*. Stopping in mid-sentence, where he was taking the Atlantis story and what details he would have added to the narrative as presented in the *Timaeus* will remain a mystery that died with Plato. It can be assumed that the account of Atlantis in *Critias* would be largely an expansion on *Timaeus*. Why Plato left the *Critias* unfinished is also a mystery. There is much speculation about his reasons. It has been suggested that he left *Critias* unfinished on purpose although what that purpose might be seems unfathomable.[20] Later Sir Francis Bacon would leave his *New Atlantis* unfinished as a tribute or nod to Plato and his *Critias* but it is hard to see what artistic reason that Plato might have had for not finishing his book. Plutarch stated that old age and death were what prevented Plato from finishing the *Critias*. However, since the uncompleted *Laws* is generally considered to be his last work, it would appear that Plutarch was mistaken.[21] The twentieth-century classicist P.B.S. Andrews suggested that Plato stopped working on *Critias* out of embarrassment when he came to realize that he had badly misread Solon's Atlantis material. If he applied the correct reading to the *Critias*, it would contradict his *Timaeus* and make him look foolish.[22] A more common and persuasive explanation of Plato's failure to complete the *Critias* suggests that he simply wrote himself into a corner and found it impossible to finish. Plato conceived of the *Timaeus* and the *Critias* as part of a trilogy that would have included a third dialogue, the *Hermocrates*, the name of the fourth person attending the festive dinner with Socrates, Timaeus and Critias. The *Timaeus*, apart from the brief telling of the Atlantis story, provides a discussion of the creation of the universe, which is followed by a summary of Greek scientific conceptions of the physical and biological world. The *Critias* described the original and most ancient Athens as the ideal society envisioned by Socrates. Presumably, if the Atlantis story of the *Critias* had been completed, it would have told of noble Athens' triumph against impossible odds over the preternaturally powerful Atlantean empire. Although the subject of the *Hermocrates* was not explicitly stated, it would probably have dealt with the recovery of human civilization from the catastrophe that destroyed Atlantis and the primeval Athens to the time of Plato.[23] The fact that Plato had envisioned the *Critias* as the second part of a trilogy would negate any argument that it was ended in mid-sentence for artistic reasons. Instead it is more likely that he abandoned the project because it was not working out as he intended. In its place Plato turned to composing the *Laws* which discussed the concept of the ideal state using many historical examples.[24] The *Laws* was Plato's last work and he did not complete it before his death in 348 BC.

ATLANTIS AFTER PLATO

Is it not a wonderful thing that a few pages of one of Plato's dialogues have grown into a great legend, not confined to Greece only, but spreading far and wide over the nations of Europe and reaching even to Egypt and Asia? BENJAMIN JOWETT (1874)[25]

While Plato never finished his Atlantis story, his *Timaeus* and *Critias* were the beginning of the almost 2,500-year-long debate over Atlantis. Aristotle, Plato's most famous pupil, considered the Atlantis story to be a fiction created by his teacher's imagination. As he put it, 'Its inventor [Plato] caused it to disappear, just as the Poet [Homer] did with the wall of the Achaeans.'[26] Other Greek and Roman scholars such as Pliny and Strabo followed Aristotle's lead in taking a sceptical approach to the existence of Atlantis. Some, however, gave credence to Plato's story. Crantor (*c*. 335–375 BC), the first commentator on the *Timaeus*, believed that the Atlantis story was true. Unfortunately Crantor's commentary has been lost and what survives are fragments described and paraphrased by a much later commentator, Proclus (AD 410/412–485). Crantor's words are widely quoted in Atlantological literature as providing confirmation of the existence of Atlantis that is independent of Plato's account.[27] Supposedly Crantor confirms the existence of the Egyptian records of Atlantis that were written on the pillars of the temple at Saïs. Some modern writers have even asserted, without foundation, that Crantor either contacted the Egyptian priests by letter or travelled to Saïs himself. Instead, it is likely that Crantor did not even provide an independent confirmation of Plato's Atlantis story but Proclus' prose has been mistranslated and misconstrued to attribute to Crantor a direct knowledge of the Egyptian records about Atlantis. Proclus is actually referring to Plato's knowledge of the Egyptian historical records. Crantor did believe in the historical truth of the Atlantis story, but his belief assumed the literal truth of Plato's narrative of Atlantis. It was a leap of faith not shared by any other commentators on Plato between his time and that of Proclus, himself never a believer in a historical Atlantis.[28] Otherwise the only other ancient writer to give credence to the historical truth of Plato's account of Atlantis is Plutarch (c. AD 45–c. 120), although he is basically repeating Plato rather than supplying any new evidence.[29]

By the time of Proclus the Roman Empire was experiencing a deep crisis from which the eastern half would successfully emerge intact while the western succumbed to the invasions of various Germanic tribes. Culture and scholarship declined in western Europe along with the Roman state. Cosmas Indicopleustes (fl. AD 545), an Egyptian merchant turned Nestorian monk, regressively argued for a flat earth while maintaining that Plato's Atlantis story was a garbled remembrance of the biblical flood of Noah. Otherwise the clerical scholars of medieval western Europe took little interest in Atlantis. They did have access to some of Plato's Atlantis account since Chalcidius (fourth century) had translated the *Timaeus* into Latin. It was read throughout the Middle Ages and was actually the only work of Plato that was available to early medieval scholars in Latin translation.[30] For the medieval scholars Atlantis was simply a story embedded in the *Timaeus'* discussion of the creation and the nature of the universe.

The European discovery of (or encounter with) the Americas in 1492 and the years that followed created conditions in which interest in Atlantis was revived. According to the medieval worldview, which was a mixture of Judeo-Christian and Graeco-Roman concepts, there were three continents: Africa, Asia and Europe. These three continents were inhabited by the descendants of Ham, Shem and Japheth, the sons of Noah. All humans could trace their ancestry back to Adam, the first man. Furthermore, all humans had physical access to the saving teachings of Jesus Christ, even if they chose to reject that gospel message. The discovery of the Americas upset all of these cosmographic assumptions. South and North America were two continents not envisioned in the medieval worldview and were inhabited by humans who possessed no apparent connection to any of the sons of

Noah or to Adam. These humans also appeared to lack any access to the teachings of Christianity. How could these new lands and new peoples be fitted into the existing worldview of the Europeans?

During the sixteenth and seventeenth centuries many theories were put forward to explain the origins of the Native Americans and the place of the Americas in the history of geography.[31] Some writers turned to the concept of Atlantis and Atlanteans for an explanation. Beginning in 1553 Francisco López de Gómara (1511–1566?), secretary to Hernán Cortés and a historian of the Spanish conquest of the Americas, suggested that refugees from Atlantis had settled in the Americas. He partially based his theory on the idea that the Aztec word for water, 'atl', was connected to the name Atlantis. Gómara also left open the possibility that other ancient peoples had also helped to settle the Americas.[32] Two years later, in 1555, Augustín de Zárate (1514–after 1560), a treasury official, published the *History of the Discovery and Conquest of Peru*. Citing Plato (although somewhat inaccurately), he asserted that people could and did easily reach the islands of the West Indies and the American mainland from Atlantis, a huge continent that filled much of the basin of the North Atlantic Ocean prior to its sinking. At the same time he readily accepted that some of the people who settled Peru might have come from across the Pacific Ocean.[33] Pedro Sarmiento de Gamboa (*c.* 1532–1592) was a Spanish explorer and soldier who sailed to Mexico in 1555 and travelled on to Peru in 1557. He developed a strong fascination with the pre-Columbian history of the Americas. In his *History of the Incas*, written in 1572 but not published until 1906, he contended that Atlanteans had settled Peru while sailors from Ulysses' fleet had reached the Gulf of Mexico and stayed on to settle Mexico and Central America. He also identified the various Atlantic islands, including the Greater and Lesser Antilles, as remnants of Atlantis.[34] Gómara, Zárate and Sarmiento all believed Atlantis had played a greater or lesser role in the peopling of the Americas. Needless to say, they also believed in a historical Atlantis or Atlantic island, as it was sometimes called. Not everyone agreed with their conclusions, however, and the theory of Atlantean settlements in the Americas largely went out of favour by the seventeenth century. Unlike among the Spanish, the Atlantean-refugee theory never caught on in northern Europe, with writers such as Englishman Samuel Purchas and Frenchman Marc Lescarbot regarding Atlantis as a myth or an allegory.[35] The Jesuit missionary and scholar José de Acosta (1539/40–1600) thoroughly rejected the claim that all, or some, of the aboriginal peoples of the Americas were the descendants of Atlantean refugees. As he vividly put it in 1590,

Some very intelligent men speak of this [Atlantis] and discuss
it very seriously, but these are such absurd things, if one thinks
about them a little, that they seem more like fables or stories
by Ovid than history or philosophy worthy of the name . . .
Whether Plato wrote it as history or allegory, what I find obvious
is that everything he said about that island, beginning with the
dialogue of Timaeus and continuing to the dialogue of Critias
cannot be told as true except to children and old women.[36]

Acosta's skeptical rationalism prevailed over the adherents of the Atlantean refugee theory among most mainline scholars during the
seventeenth century and beyond.[37] An exception to this statement
was Gregorio García (d. 1627), a Spanish Dominican who worked in
Peru. He published his *Origen de los indios del nuevo mundo e Indias
occidentales* (Origins of the Indians of the New World and the West
Indies) in 1607. The book surveyed all the major theories about the
origins of the Native Americans. García considered both Plato's Atlantis story and that of the settlement of Atlantean refugees in the
Americas to be true. The problem is that he also believed all the other
theories about the origins of the Native Americans were true – even
when they contradicted each other.[38] Given the limitations of scientific and archaeological knowledge prior to the nineteenth century it
was almost inevitable that the careful and sensible logic of Acosta
would fail to eradicate the more flamboyant theories.

Some writers avoided the question of Atlantean refugees by
identifying the newly revealed Americas as the surviving remnant of
Atlantis itself. In other words, America was Atlantis and Atlantis was
America! Girolamo Fracastoro (1478–1553) first identified America
as a surviving residue of a much larger Atlantis in his epic poem
Syphilidis sive de Morbo Gallico (Syphilis or the French Disease) in
1530. Fracastoro was an Italian physician whose primary concern was
the origin of the sudden and serious outbreak of the previously
unknown venereal disease syphilis rather than Atlantology.[39] Other
writers either picked up on Fracastoro's Atlantis in America idea or
arrived at it independently themselves. Francisco López de Gómara,
in addition to advocating that the Native Americans were Atlantean
refugees, somewhat inconsistently also put forward the theory of
Atlantis in America in his *La historia de las Indias y conquista de
México* (History of the Indies and the Conquest of Mexico) in 1552.
A few years later, in 1580, the English scholar Dr John Dee (1527–
1608) labelled America as Atlantis on one of his maps.[40] Not everyone
found the Atlantis in America theory persuasive. Also writing in 1580,
the great French sceptic Michel de Montaigne (1533–1592) composed

his famous essay 'Of Cannibals' in which he rejected the idea that America was Atlantis or a remnant of it.[41] Needless to say, Acosta would have also rejected the concept of Atlantis in America since he viewed the entire Atlantis story as a preposterous fiction. But while the scepticism of Montaigne and Acosta may have dented the theory of Atlantis in America, they did not come close to suppressing it. In 1600 the renowned Richard Hakluyt in the dedicatory epistle to the third volume of the second edition of his *Principall Navigations* made reference to America as a western Atlantis.[42] Gregorio García in 1607 included the Atlantis in America in his *Origin de los indios*. His book discussed eleven major theories about the origins of the Native Americans and accepted all of them as true so, like his contemporary Gómara and many advocates of pseudohistorical theories from the nineteenth century onward, he was capable of simultaneously holding incompatible ideas without any sense of contradiction.[43]

Sir Francis Bacon (1561–1626) greatly popularized the concept of Atlantis in America by using it in his *New Atlantis*, written in 1610 although he left it unfinished. The book was finally published in its unfinished state in 1626 shortly after Bacon's death. In *New Atlantis* Bacon told of a ship sailing from Peru across the Pacific Ocean to Japan and China. During the voyage winds drove the ship north and obstructed their progress for a year at which point their provisions ran out. Facing disaster the ship came upon the unknown but Christian and cultured island of Bensalem, Bacon's new Atlantis. The travellers learn that the Bensalemites had traded with Atlantis in ancient times, 'Great Atlantis, that you call America'. Unfortunately a great flood devastated Atlantis, destroying its thriving civilization and trade. A remnant of the Atlanteans survived in the heights of the mountains and after the deluge began repopulating America but were reduced to the primitive state of the Native American tribes. Needless to say Bacon's account of Bensalem was a fable: no such island existed. Even in 1610 most educated people knew that, based on the accumulated state of geographical knowledge at that time, Bensalem could not exist. On the other hand, Bacon's comments about Atlantis being America have been accepted as plausible or true by some readers of *New Atlantis* ever since.[44] Like Plato, Bacon wrote about a lost land and left his account unfinished. Like Plato, Bacon created a fictional account that managed to become transformed into a historical fact in the realm of pseudohistory.

The Atlantis in America theory continued as a reasonably respectable theory for more than two hundred years. Englishman John Swan (fl. 1635) in his *Speculum Mundi* (second edition 1645) stated that America was part of Atlantis. John Josselyn (1608–1675), an

English natural historian and herbalist, wrote *An Account of Two Voyages* in 1674 which included a section titled 'Chronological Observations of America' in which he stated his belief that America was Atlantis and that the Carthaginian Hanno tried to sail there in 3740 Anno Mundi.[45] Atlantological theories concerning Atlantis in America received an important boost when the Spanish historian Andrés Gonzáles de Barcia (d. 1743) brought out a revised and expanded second edition of Gregorio Garcia's *Origen de los Indios* in 1729. It contained all of Garcia's theories and more while maintaining the contradictory credulity of accepting all of the theories as true just as Garcia had done.[46] Others continued to use Atlantean refugees or Atlantis in America theories to explain the peopling of the Americas. Scholars and philosophers engaged in the debate over the alleged inferiority of the Americas in comparison to the eastern hemisphere occasionally called on the existence or the non-existence of Atlantis or Atlantis in America to help support their arguments.[47] Even the illustrious German naturalist Alexander von Humboldt (1769–1859) advocated the Atlantis in America theory.[48]

Although the Atlantis in America theory dominated Atlantology prior to the middle of the nineteenth century, it had rivals. A significant number of scholars continued to take a literal approach to Plato's narrative and placed Atlantis in the Atlantic Ocean. The polymath Jesuit scholar Athanasius Kircher (1602–1680) in 1664 composed a map with a south-to-north orientation that pictured Atlantis as a large island between Spain and the Americas. It included a caption, 'The Egyptians and Plato's Account of the location of the long submerged island of Atlantis'. Kircher, a prodigious writer and known to his contemporaries as 'the master of a hundred arts' and to modern scholars as 'the last man to know everything', revived Cosmas' idea that the destruction of Atlantis comprised part of the great biblical flood.[49]

Other scholars argued for locations outside of the mid-Atlantic for Atlantis, often motivated by conscious or unconscious nationalistic biases. Olaus Rudbeck (1630–1702) taught medicine at the University of Uppsala during Sweden's brief era as a major European power during the last two-thirds of the seventeenth century and the early years of the eighteenth. Although an accomplished scholar of anatomy and medicine Rudbeck's interests shifted to antiquities and archaeology. Those interests transformed into an obsession as Rudbeck, using rudimentary scientific methods, developed the theory that Atlantis was the source of all other civilizations and that its location was Sweden in the region of Uppsala. He introduced his theory to the academic world in 1679 with the publication of the first volume of his *Atlantica*. By 1702 *Atlantica* had grown to four and a half volumes totalling 2,500 pages. Rudbeck does seem to have pondered the coincidence that his researches had ended up locating primordial Atlantis right where he lived. Although his conclusion strikes modern readers as farcical, *Atlantica* was widely read and respected among his contemporary European scholars including Pierre Bayle, Sir Isaac Newton, Gottfried Wilhelm Leibniz and Charles-Louis de Secondat, Baron de Montesquieu. With the abrupt decline of Sweden's imperial greatness during the first decades of the eighteenth century, Rudbeck's reputation faded into almost complete obscurity.[50]

It is important to remember that the fact that although Humboldt, Rudbeck and other scholars accepted the Atlantis in America theory or even the idea that Atlantis was a historical place located somewhere, it is not a sad testament to their naivete or their credulity. These were highly intelligent people who had a good basis for their beliefs. Going into the nineteenth century, the state of scientific, historical or archaeological knowledge was often spotty or inaccurate. Many topics had never been systematically researched and lots of things remained undiscovered. Scholars did not possess the information they needed to resolve issues about the historical existence of Atlantis. It is a great irony that just when the general public became interested in theories about the existence of Atlantis, scientific and archaeological discoveries appeared proving that the Atlantis of Plato almost certainly could not have existed. In 1882 American politician Ignatius Donnelly (1831–1901) published his *Atlantis: The Antediluvian World*, basing it on the latest scientific and historical scholarship available to him in Gilded Age Minnesota. Within ten to twenty years, advances in scholarship had undercut most of his arguments in favour of a historical Atlantis and Atlantology was largely relegated to the fringe world of pseudohistory.

IGNATIUS DONNELLY AND ATLANTIS

> The fact that the story of Atlantis was for thousands of years regarded as a fable proves nothing. There is an unbelief which grows out of ignorance, as well as a scepticism which is born of intelligence. The people nearest to the past are not always those who are best informed concerning the past. IGNATIUS DONNELLY (1882)[51]

Ignatius Donnelly has been rightly credited with starting the modern popular culture's craze for Atlantis but the French novelist Jules Verne gave him considerable help.[52] Prior to the second half of the nineteenth century discussions about Atlantis had been largely confined to scholars and writers possessing a traditional classical education. They would have encountered Atlantis during the course of reading Plato, particularly since the *Timaeus* was considered one of the more fundamental Platonic dialogues. That situation changed when Jules Verne (1828–1905) published his science fiction novel *Twenty Thousand Leagues under the Sea* in 1870. During the course of the novel Captain Nemo in his submarine *Nautilus* takes Professor Pierre Aronnax for a visit to the sunken ruins of Atlantis near an active undersea volcano. It is an extremely dramatic and evocative scene that captured and continues to capture the imaginations of Verne's readers. Verne was a highly popular author during his lifetime and continues to be widely read today with multiple editions of his more famous works still available in bookstores. *Twenty Thousand Leagues under the Sea* has also been adapted for comic books, cinema and television multiple times. Verne's novel is a popular culture classic that made Atlantis a household word along with the name of Verne himself. Verne brought the idea of Atlantis into the emerging popular culture of the industrial and urban West and its accompanying cultic milieu of esoteric beliefs about history and science.

Ignatius Donnelly was born in Philadelphia, the son of an Irish immigrant who had engaged in Herculean efforts to get a medical education only to die at the beginning of his career as the result of catching typhus from a patient. In consequence the young Ignatius Donnelly grew up poor. Like many urban Irish-Americans, he entered politics – in his case, the politics of Philadelphia. He met and courted Kate McCaffrey and in 1854 they married despite the wishes of both her parents and his mother. Soon after the marriage Donnelly decided to move to Minnesota with the goal of getting rich on the developing northern frontier. Arriving in Minnesota in 1856, he partnered in the Nininger City land development which collapsed the very next year along with the rest of the Minnesota land boom. Donnelly was left broke just when he thought he had gained the status of millionaire. Part of his problem as a businessman was that he had neither the taste nor the temperament for ruthless exploitation of or hard dealing with other people. While that characteristic hurt him as a businessman, it made him popular with his neighbours and would serve him well when he decided to enter Minnesota politics.

Initially it appears that Donnelly took up a political career to restore his fortunes. As a protégé of Alexander Ramsey, the Republican governor of Minnesota, Donnelly worked hard to become a loyal and dependable party stalwart. Ramsey appointed him as his lieutenant governor in 1859. In 1863 the Ramsey political machine secured Donnelly's election as a member of the United States House of Representatives, where he served until 1869. During most of that time he willingly and enthusiastically engaged in the various schemes of graft, corruption and favour-peddling associated with the pro-business Ramsey administration, along with most politicians of that era. Donnelly, however, had a conscience and by 1868 he broke with Ramsey and became a Democrat. Being a man of conscience, he sympathized with underdogs. Most boldly for the Minnesota of the 1860s and '70s Donnelly advocated equal treatment and educational opportunity for Native Americans and African-Americans. Changing political parties naturally cost him the support of Ramsey and without that support he had no political career, as he soon found out when he campaigned unsuccessfully for the United States Senate and the United States House in 1868 and 1870. At that point Donnelly reconciled with Ramsey and returned to the Republican party in 1870, but his career as a mainstream politician was basically over.

During the 1870s Donnelly took up farming with no great success. He also read voraciously and began to write books. His first book, *Atlantis: The Antediluvian World*, appeared in 1882 and was his most successful work. The next year he published *Ragnarok: The Age of Fire and Gravel*, which postulated that the earth had experienced a catastrophic near-miss with a gigantic comet in the distant past.[53] (Interestingly enough several years earlier Jules Verne had written a novel titled *Off on a Comet* (1877) based on a similar premise.) *The Great Cryptogram* of 1888 asserted that Sir Francis Bacon was really the author of Shakespeare's plays. A few years later, in 1891, he published *Caesar's Column* under the pseudonym of Edmund Boisgilbert. It was a dystopian novel of the future about a revolt of oppressed workers in 1988 bringing a painful end to grossly inequitable, urban industrial society that the US had become. The novel was a response to the rosy view of the future offered in Edward Bellamy's utopian novel *Looking Backward* (1888) and was very popular among reform-minded Americans and members of the labour movement during the 1890s. Other novels followed but none of them enjoyed the success and popularity of *Caesar's Column*.[54]

Donnelly also remained in politics, supporting the Grange movement, the Farmers Alliance and eventually Populism. He was an unwavering champion of the little man – both farmers and urban workers – which did not endear him to the monied interests and mainline politicians. His enemies pilloried him with nicknames like 'the wild Jackass of the Prairie', 'Ignominious Donnelly', 'the prince of crackpots' and 'Ignis Fatuus' (foolish or idiotic fire; will-o'-the-wisp). The controversial subject-matter of his books only played into the hands of his detractors. *The Great Cryptogram*, intended to be the culmination of Donnelly's writing career, flopped upon publication. Although it received hundreds of reviews and notices, virtually all were negative. The publisher sued Donnelly for the return of $4,000 in unearned royalties while parodies of the book appeared almost immediately.[55] That failure, however, is not the whole story of Donnelly's literary career.

Both *Atlantis: The Antediluvian World* and *Ragnarok* were successful books and reasonably well received at the time they were published. *Atlantis* enjoyed the greatest success and its sales were brisk enough that it had gone through 23 printings by 1890. It is a good read if its generally tendentious tone is overlooked. While the scholarly underpinnings of the book are clearly inadequate and erroneous by the standards of present-day knowledge, in 1882 *Atlantis* represented a reasonable albeit unorthodox speculation about the events of the distant past. It received many positive reviews and among its admirers was the British prime minister William Ewart Gladstone, who went so far as to write Donnelly a four-page letter about *Atlantis*.[56] Donnelly lived in an era before the advent of Alfred L. Wegener's theory of continental drift which was itself initially laughed at and marginalized. Geologists of Donnelly's time postulated the existence of all sorts of lost continents and extinct geographies. In the 1880s German biologist Ernst Haeckel and Austrian paleontologist Melchior Neumayer theorized about a land bridge connecting South Africa and India. The land bridge was given the name Lemuria by the English zoologist Philip Sclater. Lemuria would eventually be extended into the Pacific Ocean and become a Pacific version of Atlantis. This lost continent of the Pacific quickly attracted the attention of pseudohistorans and occultists who sometimes call it Mu instead of Lemuria.[57] In his *Atlantis*, Donnelly frequently cites the work of Alexander Winchell, one of the leading geologists of late nineteenth-century America. Winchell tried mightily to harmonize Christian theology with Darwinian evolution and for a time had some success. Advances in science rendered his theories untenable and he is now largely forgotten, but in 1882 he was a thoroughly respectable source for Donnelly to use.[58]

Initially the nineteenth-century explorations of the floor of the Atlantic Ocean also tended to support Atlantis theories like Donnelly's by revealing what appeared to be the remains of an submerged continent. Later researches disproved that conclusion. The same observation applies to Donnelly's use of archaeology and linguistics. During the late nineteenth century there was no radiocarbon dating to establish an accurate chronology and only a limited amount of archaeological exploration, which meant that Donnelly's ideas were at least possible given the state of contemporary knowledge. His linguistic arguments followed the common methodologies of Anglo-American scholars although the Germans, the leaders in that discipline, were pioneering different and more sophisticated methods. Few results of the new German scholarship had made its way to the English-speaking world by 1882 so Donnelly remained ignorant of important new ideas that would undermine his Atlantis theory. In the discipline of classics there was no unanimity on the historical or fictional nature of Plato's Atlantis – even today some reputable scholars still consider Plato's Atlantis story to have a greater or lesser historical element, although they are a minority, so Donnelly would still have company.[59]

Donnelly neatly summarized his claims and contentions in thirteen propositions listed at the beginning of *Atlantis: The Antediluvian World*:

1. That there once existed in the Atlantis Ocean, opposite the mouth of the Mediterranean Sea, a large island, which was the remnant of an Atlantic continent, and known to the ancient world as Atlantis.
2. That the description of this island given by Plato is not, as has been long supposed, fable, but veritable history.
3. That Atlantis was the region where man first rose from a state of barbarism to civilization.
4. That it became, in the course of ages, a populous and mighty nation, from whose overflowings the shores of the Gulf of Mexico, the Mississippi River, the Amazon, the Pacific coast of South America, the Mediterranean, the west coast of Europe and Africa, the Baltic, the Black Sea, and the Caspian were populated by civilized nations.
5. That it was a true Antediluvian world; the Garden of Eden; the Gardens of the Hesperides; the Elysian Fields; the Gardens of Alcinous; the Mesomphalos; the Olympos; the Asgard of the traditions of the ancient nations; representing a universal memory of a great land, where early mankind dwelt for ages in peace and happiness.
6. That the gods and goddesses of the ancient Greeks, the Phoenicians, the Hindoos, and the Scandinavians were simply the kings, queens, and heroes of Atlantis; and the acts attributed to them in mythology are a confused recollection of real historical events.

7. That the mythology of Egypt and Peru represented the original religion of Atlantis, which was sun-worship.

8. That the oldest colony formed by the Atlanteans was probably in Egypt, whose civilization was a reproduction of that of the Atlantic island.

9. That the implements of the 'Bronze Age' of Europe were derived from Atlantis. The Atlanteans were also the first manufacturers of iron.

10. That the Phoenician alphabet, parent of all the European alphabets, was derived from an Atlantis alphabet, which was also conveyed from Atlantis to the Mayas of Central America.

11. That Atlantis was the original seat of the Aryan or Indo-European family of nations, as well as of the Semitic peoples, and possibly also of the Turanian races.

12. That Atlantis perished in a terrible convulsion of nature, in which the whole island sunk into the ocean, with nearly all its inhabitants.

13. That a few persons escaped in ships and on rafts, and carried to the nations east and west the tidings of the appalling catastrophe, which has survived to our own time in the Flood and Deluge legends of the different nations of the old and new worlds.[60]

From that starting point Donnelly proceeded, in 38 chapters and close to 500 pages, to present a vast array of evidence supporting his various arguments for the existence of Atlantis. It has been pointed out that Donnelly argued his case like a lawyer rather than practising the scientific method of investigation.[61] Subsequent Atlantological writers have gone well beyond Donnelly in their embellishments of the revived Atlantis myth, adding supernatural elements, super-scientific knowledge or aliens from other planets. Still Donnelly established the basics of the modern myth of Atlantis: that it was the source of human civilization; the primordial inspiration for legends of an earthly paradise; its rulers became the inspiration for the gods of the ancients; and its cataclysmic destruction was the source for all legends of universal floods. In spite of the flaws of Donnelly's scholarship and the fact that advances in knowledge have rendered his *Atlantis* obsolete, he laid the foundations for the modern revival of Atlantism. After Donnelly popular culture took the Atlantis myth in a variety of directions while spiritual occultists made their own ethereal contributions to the pseudohistorical lore of Atlantis and other lost continents.

OCCULT AND SPIRITUALIST ATLANTIS

Indiana is not Atlantis. CHARLES PORTIS (1985)[62]

What do occultists, spiritualists and mystics have to contribute to the pseudohistorical lore of Atlantis and other lost continents? Quite a bit, actually. Unfortunately their provision of verifiable scholarly research on the subject of Atlantis has been nil. Still the writings and pronouncements of various practitioners of occult, spiritualist and mystic learning have added prodigiously to the cultic milieu associated with Atlantis.

Occultist interest in Atlantis began about the same time that Ignatius Donnelly's *Atlantis: The Antediluvian World* first appeared, in the writings of Helena Petrovna Blavatsky (1831–1891), one of the founders of Theosophy. Whether Madame Blavatsky influenced Ignatius Donnelly or vice versa, or whether the two worked independently of each other is a debatable point. What is not debatable is that Madame Blavatksy had a keen interest in Atlantis which ended up spreading from the Theosophical Society into other occult groups.

Madame Blavatsky, or HPB as she liked to style herself, was an adventuress extraordinaire although just exactly how extraordinaire is difficult to say.[63] Large segments of Madame Blavatsky's life are known only through her own personal testimony and that is most assuredly not completely reliable or credible. Born Helena von Hahn in Russia, she grew up in a privileged environment since her family belonged to the Russian nobility and were part of the intelligentsia. Her mother was novelist Helena Andreyevna, known as the George Sand of Russia, while her maternal grandmother was both an eminent botanist and a princess, Helena Pavlovna de Fadeev. Andreyevna died when the young Helena was only eleven years old and she went to live with Pavlovna. Growing up around such strong and accomplished women helped Madame Blavatsky to develop into a very independent-minded young woman, one prone to rebelliousness and nonconformity. At seventeen, she married Nikifor V. Blavatsky, the vice-governor of Yerevam in the Caucasus, who at forty was twice her age. She married, it is said, to spite her governess. The marriage gave Helena the surname that she would use for the rest of her life; otherwise it had little impact on her life. The Blavatskys never consummated the marriage and after a few months Helena Blavatsky began her life of travels, leaving the hapless Nikifor forever. Little is known about her life from 1848 to 1858, although she claimed to have met the Tibetan Master Morya at the London Exhibition in 1851. According to her own account Blavatsky made her way to Tibet where she studied for seven years with the mysterious Masters or Adepts, particularly the Masters Morya and Koot Hoomi. These superhuman teachers of esoteric knowledge would guide Madame Blavatsky for the rest of her life (or so she would claim) and their teachings formed the eventual basis for the beliefs of Theosophy.

During these years Blavatsky claimed at times to have had various lovers but just as frequently she would deny any such thing. In 1858 she visited Russia but soon left with an opera singer named Asgardi Metrovich. They remained a couple until 1871 when Metrovich was killed by an explosion on a ship sailing to Cairo. Blavatsky continued on to Cairo where she organized a seance business in 1872 with Emma Cutting, later Coulomb. Their enterprise quickly collapsed when their customers accused them of fraud – not an auspicious start for a spiritualist leader-to-be.[64] From Cairo Blavatsky made her way to Paris where in 1873 the Master Morya instructed her to move to New York City.

Post-Civil War America had an avid interest in spiritualism and one of the more interested Americans was Colonel Henry Steel Olcott (1836–1906), an expert on agriculture, a Civil War veteran and one of the men appointed to investigate the assassination of President Abraham Lincoln. When the war ended he became a lawyer of modest success. It was, however, a comedown from the excitement and responsibility he enjoyed as a soldier and government official. To fill a void in his vaguely unsatisfactory life he developed an interest in spiritualism, the practice of communicating with the spirits of the dead through mediums. Spiritualism was a common interest that brought Olcott and Blavatsky together for the first time at the Eddy farm in Chittenden, Vermont, on 14 October 1874, where members of the Eddy family had been exhibiting psychic powers. It appears that Blavatsky had heard of Olcott and went to Chittenden in the hope of meeting him. Olcott and Blavatsky immediately became close albeit platonic friends or, as Olcott put it, 'chums'. They soon occupied apartments near each other in New York City and spent much of their time in each other's company. Then on 3 March 1875 Olcott received a letter from the Master Tuitit Bey of Luxor. It was a precipitated letter which seemingly just materialized from a Master, although in some cases another party (in this case, Blavatsky?) served as an amanuensis for the Master sending the letter. Other letters would follow over the years to Olcott and others, although Tuitit Bey would be pushed aside by the Masters Morya and Koot Hoomi while additional Masters would joint the flow of enlightening correspondence. Letters containing instructions for Blavatsky, Olcott or their followers would apparently materialize in desk drawers or cabinets. It was interesting how often the instructions from the Masters coincided with the known desires and opinions of Madame Blavatsky.

On 7 September 1875 Blavatsky, Olcott and other like-minded acquaintances began the process of forming the Theosophical Society during a gathering in a New York apartment. Meanwhile Madame Blavatsky had already begun work on a massive guide to Theosophy, published in 1877 as the two-volume *Isis Unveiled*. She claimed that her book was heavily based on precipitated pages of a manuscript composed by the Masters. In fact it was the product of Blavatsky's synthesis, with considerable help from Olcott, of about a hundred books on occult topics. Frequently Blavatsky plagiarized rather than synthesized. The American Orientalist scholar William Emmette Coleman studied *Isis Unveiled* for three years and documented two thousand passages lifted from other people's books, a fact that calls into question Theosophical claims about the book's authorship by the Masters. Despite Coleman's revelations, *Isis Unveiled* was a success, although the infant Theosophical Society was struggling to survive.[65]

Isis Unveiled contains some references to Atlantis but nothing on the scale of Blavatsky's later writings. Mention of Atlantis appears only four times in a book of over a thousand pages. All four references simply comment on the reality of a historical Atlantis along the lines of that depicted in Plato's *Timaeus* and *Critias*.[66] Atlantis did not play any specific role in Blavatsky's doctrine at that time. Rather it is simply part of her attack on the modern separation of religion and science and Christianity in particular. The Platonic Atlantis of *Isis Unveiled* was a far cry from the occult Atlantis of the later Blavatsky and her followers.

Madame Blavatsky became a naturalized citizen of the United States in July 1878, but less than six months later, in December, she and Olcott would travel to India.[67] They hoped to revive the fortunes of Theosophy and, of course, letters from Masters Morya and Koot Hoomi told them to make the move. Blavatsky's time in India would influence her to formulate Theosophical doctrines with a more Eastern orientation. That eastward shift increased the Theosophical Society's attraction for native Indian converts even as it displeased Westerners who preferred to focus on Theosophy's roots in Western esotericism. By 1882 Blavatsky and Olcott set up their headquarters at Adyar near Madras, all the time guided by a steady stream of letters from Masters Morya and Koot Hoomi. Furthermore, Madame Blavatsky's old associate, a somewhat down and out Emma Cutting (now Coulomb), and her husband Alexis had joined the Theosophical Society's staff at Adyar as caretakers. The Coulombs resented the relatively menial positions provided by Blavatsky. Problems followed and eventually the Coulombs were fired for dishonesty. They got their revenge, however, by publishing letters from Madame Blavatsky that purported to show how they had colluded together to fake the precipitated letters from the Masters by building secret sliding doors in cabinets and other trickery.[68]

The Coulombs' revelations created a scandal and an independent investigation followed. Richard Hodgson of the Society for Psychical Research (SPR) arrived in India in September 1884 to study the precipitated letters associated with Madame Blavatsky and the Theosophical Society. Several months later he concluded that the precipitated letters and the existence of the Masters were a huge fraud perpetrated by Blavatsky and some confederates. According to Hodgson's assessment of Madame Blavatsky in his report, 'she has achieved a title to permanent remembrance as one of the most accomplished, ingenious, and interesting impostors of history'.[69] Supporters of Theosophy and Madame Blavatsky have rejected Hodgson's report ever since. Some have claimed that the sliding doors had been built without Madame Blavatsky's knowledge while she was away from Adyar on a trip. One hundred years later, in 1986, Vernon Harrison, an expert in the authentication of documents and forgery, published an article in the *Journal* of the Society for Psychical Research that repudiated Hodgson's report as biased and methodologically flawed. He expanded the article into a monograph of 108 pages that was published by the Theosophical University Press.[70] It is important to note that Harrison only disputes Hodgson's contention that Madame Blavatsky was the author of the letters from the Masters, commonly know as the Mahatma letters. Harrison does not rule on the authenticity of the letters as the precipitated compositions of the ethereal Masters. Whether Madame Blavatsky wrote the letters or not, certainly something dubious was going on since the supposedly aloof and serene Masters seemed to get involved in the squabbles of the Theosophical Society in a frequent and most unbecoming manner and would continue to do so.

Colonel Olcott sent Madame Blavatsky to Germany in 1885 in an attempt to get her out of the glare of the Coulomb scandal. She used the forced leisure to write her other massive work, the two-volume *Secret Doctrine*, which presented a series of far-fetched ideas unsupported by any reliable historical or scientific research. It was published in 1888.[71] Madame Blavatsky describes in the first volume, *Cosmogenesis*, how the universe has evolved and in the second volume, *Anthrogenesis*, how humanity has evolved. The *Secret Doctrine* also shows how Madame Blavatsky's time in India had caused her to move from the predominantly Western esotericism of *Isis Unveiled* to a more Eastern and Buddhist esotericism. It is the book where Blavatsky presents a full-blown occult Atlantis along with other lost continents, and it has influenced other occult and spiritualist groups ever since.[72]

Blavatsky's new Atlantis is far removed from the Platonic Atlantis of *Isis Unveiled* and is an important link in her scheme of human evolution. Unfortunately the factual basis for Blavatsky's book is nonexistent. She claimed to have received her information during trances in which the Masters or Mahatmas of Tibet communicated with her and allowed her to read from the ancient *Book of Dzyan*. The *Book of Dzyan* was supposedly composed in Atlantis using the lost language of Senzar but the difficulty is that no scholar of ancient languages in the 1880s or since has encountered the slightest passing reference to the *Book of Dzyan* or the Senzar language. Claiming to have used these sources, Madame Blavatsky described how the world would go through seven eras, each associated with a root race. Each of these root races was further divided into seven sub-races except for the first two root races. The first root race came to the earth from the moon and were ethereal spirits who began to gather physical material around their insubstantial cores. They inhabited an area called the 'Imperishable Sacred Land' which may not have been a strictly physical location.[73] Next came the second root race which lived on the arctic continent of Hyperborea. While sexless, the second race had physical bodies but were referred to as 'boneless', which would indicate they were somewhat like jellyfish.[74] After Hyperborea sank below the sea the Pacific continent of Lemuria arose and took its place. The Lemurians formed a third and rather strange root race of apelike hermaphrodites who reproduced by laying eggs, had four arms and an eye in the back of their heads. Their development of true bodies took place about 18 million years ago during the evolution of the Lemurian sub-races. Then disaster struck the Lemurians – they discovered sex and brought down upon themselves the wrath of the Theosophical gods. Lemuria suffered a rain of fire and sank back into the Pacific Ocean. Meanwhile, Atlantis arose about 850,000 years ago to form the home of the fourth root race.[75]

Unlike the first three root races, the Atlanteans were quite human except that they were bigger, more intelligent and generally better than humans of the present era. They invented aeroplanes and electricity and spread their civilization to other parts of the world, including Egypt and the Yucatan in Central America. Many of the Near Eastern pyramids, various Druid temples and some Mesoamerican ruins are remnants of Atlantean culture. But Atlantis too eventually suffered an apocalyptic catastrophe. Earthquakes destroyed that continent and it slipped under the sea about 11,000 years ago, just as Plato described.[76]

Humans known as Aryans are the fifth root race and its first sub-race arose in Central Asia. Anglo-Saxons are the fifth sub-race while Blavatsky suggested that the sixth sub-race was in the process of evolving in North America. The sixth and seventh root races were yet to come and new continents would also arise, such as Nuatlantis, which would arise from the depths of the South Atlantic some point in the future. In the years after Blavatsky's death in 1891 other Theosophists, particularly Annie Besant (1847–1933) and W. Scott Elliot, have added considerable detail to Blavatsky's outline of the world's prehistory along with much detail about the earlier root races and the lost continents of Lemuria and Atlantis.[77] They used the same ethereal sources as Blavatsky such as 'astral clairvoyance', that is, direct mental communication with those holy and very informative Mahatmas and their library of Senzar books. Blavatsky's version of Atlantis attributed precocious scientific knowledge to its inhabitants, a characteristic that has appeared over and over in Atlantological books, both fictional and those purporting to be non-fiction.

Blavatsky's use of Atlantis and other lost continents in the cosmology of Theosophy was adopted or imitated by other occult and spiritualist groups. It is not surprising that the splinter movement of Anthrosophy adopted belief in an occult Atlantis since it was a direct offshoot of Theosophy. Rudolf Steiner (1861–1925) founded Anthrosophy in 1913. He was born in the Austro-Hungarian Empire and studied philosophy despite his father's wish that he become a civil engineer. During his late teens Steiner met two men who served as his spiritual guides: the herbalist Felix Kotgutski and an unnamed individual who Steiner simply called 'The Master'. These men, particularly 'The Master', set Steiner firmly on the path of combating the rampant materialism of nineteenth-century industrial society while synthesizing science and religion into a harmonious whole. They encouraged Steiner to continue his studies and in 1891 he earned a doctorate from the University of Rostock. When he reached the age of 40 Steiner began to lecture publicly about his philosophical ideas, clairvoyance and his access to the mystic Akashic Records. His lectures were popular and quickly led to his appointment in 1902 as general secretary of the newly formed German chapter of the Theosophical Society. Steiner, however, found that Madame Blavatsky's increasing emphasis on Eastern esoteric traditions was unsatisfactory and inappropriate for a Western following. That disagreement ultimately led to his break with Theosophy and the formation of the Anthrosophical Society in 1913.[78]

Steiner did not attract the sort of controversy and scandal that seemed to follow Madame Blavatsky. He also managed to accomplish some genuinely positive things with his system of Waldorf Schools, his Campbell Villages for the education of mentally disabled children, his methods of organic gardening and his holistic approach to medicine.[79] Anthrosophic cosmology continued to be based largely on Blavatsky's theosophical doctrines with some additions and corrections from Steiner.[80] Steiner also developed an interest in Rosicrucianism in the years before his break with the Theosophical Society, but his ideas about Rosicrucianism do not seem to have been based on any accurate knowledge of or close acquaintance with historic Rosicrucianism.

Twentieth-century Rosicrucians claim to be part of a tradition of esoteric knowledge stretching back to antiquity and beyond. Historic Rosicrucians from the sixteenth through the eighteenth centuries had no interest in Atlantis, other lost continents or cosmologies going back millions of years involving weird and questionably human races.[81] While Atlantis was a topic of discussion for scholars of the sixteenth, seventeenth and eighteenth centuries, the concept of the lost continent of Lemuria or Mu was undreamed of until the last quarter of the nineteenth century. Lost continents only became an important aspect of Rosicrucianism lore in 1907 with the foundation of the Rosicrucian Fellowship at Columbus, Ohio, by Max Heidel, a Danish astrologer and student of Rudolf Steiner. Other Rosicrucian societies sprang up in the United States at the same time or after the appearance of the Rosicrucian Fellowship: Societas Rosicruciana in America (1907), a schism from Masonry; Fraternitas Rosae Crucis (1922) and the Ancient Mystical Order Rosae Crucis or AMORC (1925). All of these groups adopted what were originally Theosophical beliefs about Atlantis, prehistory and cosmology although they altered those ideas to suit their own purposes.[82]

Another occult practitioner with an interest in Atlantis was Edgar Cayce (1877–1945). Born in Hopkinsville, Kentucky, and possessing an education only to seventh grade (age 13), he was a psychic who from a state of trance provided medical advice. Basically Cayce would go to sleep on a couch and in that state would deliver advice, predictions about the future and information about the unknowable past. When he awoke he would have no memory of his pronouncements, which in the case of his medical advice were generally accurate and effectual. They also demonstrated knowledge which Cayce apparently did not possess. Cayce also believed in reincarnation even though it conflicted with the traditional Christian beliefs that he also held. Because people were reincarnated, according to Cayce, he could access their past lives during his trances and tell them about what he learned. Cayce claimed to have been reincarnated many times and had previously been an Atlantean, a Persian ruler and an ancient Greek chemist from Troy among others. It was the knowledge from his Greek chemist persona that enabled him to make his healing suggestions. He also suggested that people's ailments often stemmed from problems that had occurred in their previous lives.

Theosophy taught the existence of Akashic Records which listed and catalogued everything that had occurred since the beginning of the universe. They are stored in the ether or space known to Hinduism and Buddhism as the fifth element or *Akasha*. Adepts or masters with psychic powers could access the Akashic Records and teach others to access them. Many occult practitioners from Madame Blavatsky onwards, including Rudolf Steiner, claimed a greater or lesser ability to consult the Akashic Records. Edgar Cayce told people that while he was in one of his trances his spirit would travel to the Akashic Records and read what he needed to know about the past and the future. Between 1923 and 1944 Cayce did life readings from 1,600 people, 700 of whom had lived previous lives on Atlantis. It has been pointed out that the actual portion of people who led earlier lives on Atlantis may be much higher since Cayce's life readings accessed previous lives that bore relevance to the current problems of the individuals having the readings done.[83] Taken together these readings purported to reveal a detailed history of Atlantis and human prehistory. According to Cayce, millions of years ago spirits lived on the earth that would periodically inhabit physical bodies. After a while the spirits had become so accustomed to living in physical bodies that they became trapped. Over time some of these spirits evolved into human beings, which occurred about 10.5 million years ago. These humans created the first civilization on Atlantis, which possessed advanced technology including access to vast supplies of energy that came from tapping into the power from crystals. Atlanteans also developed air travel, lasers, atomic energy and sophisticated means of communication.[84] Cayce may have been the first person to credit Atlanteans with using mysterious crystals for energy, something that various Atlantologists, some science fiction writers and the makers of Disney's *Atlantis: The Lost Empire* incorporated into their own work.

The problem for the primeval world of Atlantis was that Atlanteans were split into two groups: the Children of the Law of One and the Sons of Belial. The Children of the Law of One followed the spiritual values and teachings that were the heritage of human beings from their spiritual and divine beginnings. In contrast the Sons of Belial engaged in greed and materialism and lived out of balance. They even mated with strange creatures and produced hybrid monsters. Soon these monsters and other large and savage creatures reminiscent of dinosaurs were threatening the survival of humanity. The Atlanteans decided to use their advanced technology of bombs and death days to destroy the monsters. Alas for the Atlanteans, their weapons did more than kill the dinosaurs. The huge explosions caused volcanos to erupt, the continents of Atlantis and Lemuria to break up with parts sinking into the sea, the earth to change its axis and the north and south poles to shift their locations. This cataclysm took place about 50,722 BC and resulted in many Atlanteans seeking refuge in other lands. Their memories of the first Atlantis became the basis for the worldwide legends of a primordial Garden of Eden or Paradise, although apparently they only remembered the good things and forgot the rampaging dinosaurs and other monsters.

Atlantis recovered from the disaster and flourished for a second time between 50,000 and 28,000 BC. It continued to develop more sophisticated technology, which included what appear to have been forms of radio, television, radar and anti-gravity. Cayce's descriptions of some Atlantean technology are simply incomprehensible. The conflict between the Children of the Law of One and the Sons of Belial also continued. One of the major issues of their conflict involved the exploitation of the so-called 'Things', a group of sub-humans. The Sons of Belial wanted to use the 'Things' as slaves while the Children of the Law of One want to uplift the 'Things' to be fully human. Atlanteans of this era also acquired a high level of psychic power along with a deep knowledge of the natural world and the universe. While the Children of the Law of One used this knowledge for good, the Sons of Belial abused it. Overall Atlanteans were sinking into spiritual corruption. Then about 28,000 BC a phase of massive storms, eruptions of volcanoes and widespread flooding occurred. Cayce claimed that this second destruction of Atlantis was the same event as the Great Flood of the Bible. It resulted in Atlantis breaking up into several even smaller islands. Whether this calamity was a natural phenomenon or the result of Atlanteans' misuse of their technology is unclear. In the aftermath some Atlanteans again migrated to other lands, particularly the Americas, to escape the consequences.

Despite the ravages of this second tribulation, Atlantis survived and entered its third and final phase of existence from 28,000 to 10,000 BC. Sadly, the conflict between the Children of the Law of One and the Sons of Belial continued. While Atlanteans continued to expand their technological knowledge, their moral and spiritual nature continued to deteriorate. The Sons of Belial persisted in using technology recklessly and for depraved ends, especially the mysterious power crystals or 'firestones', the great power source of Atlantis. Misuse of the power crystals brought on a series of earthquakes that caused the remnant of Atlantis to sink under the waves of the Atlantic Ocean. Only a few scattered islands remained, the peaks of Atlantis's highest mountains.

Cayce did predict that part of Atlantis would rise again in 1968 near the island of Bimini in the Bahamas. Interestingly from an Atlantological point of view, in 1968 explorers discovered the so-called Bimini Road under the waters off Bimini. Believers in Atlantis claim the stones are ruins of the lost Atlantis while geologists consider them to be a natural phenomenon. Supporters of Cayce claim that the discovery of the Bimini Road is proof of his prophetic abilities. Of course, it was his prophecy that pointed searchers eager to find evidence of Atlantis to Bimini. Some might argue that it is highly possible that the wish became father to the thought. It is important to recall that Cayce also predicted the return of Jesus Christ in 1998, an event that would be accompanied by another series of titanic earthquakes that would alter the earth's landscape once more.[85] That said, Cayce found and his followers continue to find in Atlantis a potent warning for their fellow Americans to avoid the mistakes and sins of the Atlanteans.

Atlantis and its Pacific counterpart Lemuria continue to play a significant role in the beliefs of various occult groups. Some people believe that Mount Shasta is inhabited by the descendants of Atlantean or Lemurian refugees. The source for this belief is a novel by Frederick Spencer Oliver titled A Dweller on Two Planets (1894). It purports to be a memoir by Phylos the Tibetan, a claim that has been taken to be literally true by some believers in the occult. In 1936 they organized themselves into the Lemurian fellowship. Fifty years later, like-minded persons staged the New Age event called the Harmonic Convergence in 1987 at Mount Shasta. Over the years there have been sightings on Mount Shasta of mysterious white robed figures. Are they Atlanteans or Lemurians? Occultists say yes, but sceptics point out that various contemporary occultists have wandered the slopes of Mount Shasta in their own ceremonial white robes while performing purported Atlantean or Lemurian rituals. These latter day Lemurian imitators are the source of the sightings.[86]

Another recent manifestation of Atlantis and the Occult is the case of jz Knight (b. 1946) and her Atlantean soulmate Ramtha. It is perhaps no coincidence that Knight was born in Roswell, New Mexico, as Judith Darlene Hampton (Knight was her third husband's name).[87] Raised in poverty, Knight suffered emotional and sexual abuse during her childhood and lacked the financial resources to attend college under conditions conducive to academic success. She dropped out after one year and sought emotional and economic security in the first of a series of marriages. During her second marriage she experimented with pyramid power during which she experienced an encounter with the 35,000 year-old Atlantean Ramtha. He ultimately proved to be the man that Knight had been looking for her entire life. Ramtha spoke through JZ Knight and advocated the empowerment of women. Hoping to promote the Atlantean's teachings, Knight formed the Ramtha School of Enlightenment. The School enjoyed considerable success financially. Actress Shirley McLaine became a follower of Ramtha and came to believe that she had been a brother of Ramtha during a previous life on Atlantis. Knight's second and third husbands, Jeremy Wilder and Jeffrey Knight, each in turn tried to exploit the success of Knight and the Ramtha School of Enlightenment for their own personal gain. The stability of the marriage with Jeffrey Knight was further undermined by his being a practising homosexual. In the end, Knight was left with Ramtha, the only man who had never let her down and who literally knew her from the inside out. He also provided her with a very good living.[88] But is Ramtha an authentic contact with the ancient past, a delusion or a con game? Clearly most people would consider Knight's claims to be preposterous. One can safely assume that the people paying for the services of the Ramtha School of Enlightenment are reasonably well satisfied with their vicarious encounters with Ramtha's version of Atlantis. The manifestations of Atlantis are legion.

THE ATLANTIS OF POPULAR CULTURE

> The world, like a child, has readily, and for the most part
> unhesitatingly, accepted the tale of the Island of Atlantis.
> BENJAMIN JOWETT (1874)[89]

In 2001 the Walt Disney Picture Company made its contribution to popular culture's images of Atlantis when it brought out the animated feature film *Atlantis: The Lost Empire*. The Disney story begins thousands of years in the past with the destruction of Atlantis by an explosion and an immense tidal wave. Although this Atlantis is located in the distant past, it was not a Bronze Age culture, but far more advanced. Its inhabitants possessed flying machines, electricity and advanced medicine. Although it was an ancient super-civilization, that could not save it from the cataclysm and Atlantis disappeared, or so it seemed. Atlantis was certainly not forgotten. Men looked for it through the ages but failed to find it. The one true guide to finding Atlantis was an ancient book called *The Shepherd's Journal* which told the story of Atlantis's destruction and the location of its survivors. Many sought *The Shepherd's Journal* as the first step to finding Atlantis and its treasures. A deleted scene from the Disney film shows a Viking ship searching for Atlantis using *The Shepherd's Calendar* but a sea-monster guarding Atlantis sinks the ship. The story moves forward to 1914 where the guileless Milo Thatch works in a junior position at the Smithsonian Institution. Milo is an altruistic scholar of Atlantis and dreams of rediscovering the lost continent and the secrets of its advanced technology. Unfortunately Milo suffers from the usual fate of dreamers of Atlantis – he is the object of derision. Someone, however, does take Milo seriously. His grandfather's old friend, wealthy Preston B. Whitmore, offers to finance an expedition to take Milo in search of Atlantis.

The expedition travels on a giant submarine named the *Ulysses*, reminiscent of Captain Nemo's *Nautilus* from *Twenty Thousand Leagues Under the Sea*. It is manned by a large, heavily armed company led by Commander Lyle Tiberius Rourke. He provides Milo with *The Shepherd's Journal* which Whitmore's people had recently recovered in Iceland. The submarine *Ulysses* is a necessity in the search for Atlantis because the lost city is located in a vast subterranean chamber beneath the sea that can only be reached through an underwater tunnel. Upon the expedition's arriving at the tunnel, a huge lobster-like robot attacks and destroys the *Ulysses* along with most of its crew. Milo, Rourke and a surviving remnant escape to the subterranean chamber where after a series of adventures they encounter a band of Atlanteans, who take them to meet their rather inhospitable king Kashekin Nedakh. The king wants Milo and his companions to leave immediately but his beautiful young daughter Kida (who is actually thousands of years old) has taken a liking to Milo and persuades her father to give the strangers permission to stay.

Disney's *Atlantis* is a shadow of its former glory. Its inhabitants have forgotten how to read their ancient script and how to work their high-tech machines. For Milo, Atlantis appears to be an isolated utopia but to the intrepid Kida it is boring and stultifying. She recognizes that her fellow Atlanteans have lost their creative spark and have degenerated. For her, the outsiders are not a threat, they instead might be a means for Atlantis to be rejuvenated. Meanwhile Atlantis precariously exists next to a dormant volcano – only one threat to the lost empire.

King Kashekin is right to be suspicious of the outsiders. Except for Milo, Rourke and the others are mercenaries who merely seek to acquire the Heart of Atlantis, a mysterious power source, whatever the cost to the Atlanteans. Kida becomes merged with the Heart of Atlantis and Rourke takes her captive along with the Heart of Atlantis. As he attempts to carry Kida to the surface, Milo attacks him with a force of Atlanteans and a group of the crew of the *Ulysses* whose consciences have caused them to take Milo's side. Milo reactivates some of the forgotten Atlantean flying machines. After a fierce battle Rourke is killed and Milo and his friends free Kida and return her to Atlantis just in time for the power of the Heart of Atlantis to save the lost city from the fury of the newly awakened volcano. With the threats to Atlantis successfully countered, Milo's friends return to the surface loaded with gifts of Atlantean treasure. They promise to keep the existence of Atlantis a secret. Milo decides to stay behind with the lovely Kida so that he can translate the writings of the Atlanteans and help them to recover their forgotten knowledge. And they all lived happily ever after. Keep in mind: it's a Disney movie.

Disney's Atlantis is just one version of the popular culture's image of the lost continent. It exhibits the standard features of a super-civilization that existed in the distant past on an Atlantic island that sank beneath the sea in a great disaster resulting from the misuse of the Heart of Atlantis as a weapon. Despite the massive tidal wave, Atlantis actually survived, thanks to the Heart of Atlantis's powers. At the beginning of the film, Plato is quoted for verisimilitude, ' in a single day and night of misfortune, the island of Atlantis disappeared into the depths of the sea'. The quote only says that Atlantis disappeared, not that it was totally destroyed. Lo and behold, Atlantis did survive as the lost empire Milo found. Disney, however, misleadingly quotes Plato by failing to indicate deleted text with ellipses. The unedited quote reads:

> But afterwards there occurred violent earthquakes and floods;
> in a single day and night of misfortune all your [Athens'] war-
> like men in a body sank into the earth and the island of Atlantis
> in like manner disappeared in the depths of the sea.[90]

Whereas the Disney version of the quote implies the possibility of Atlantis surviving, the full quote clearly indicates that both the Athenian army and Atlantis suffered annihilation as a result of earthquakes and floods.

Of course, Disney Pictures was hardly the first to suggest that Atlantis survived in some manner. Arthur Conan Doyle's novel *The*

Maracot Deep (1929) has a party of scientists exploring the depths of the ocean. They encounter a highly advanced city of Atlantis protected by a dome. Numerous other science fiction novels have used similar plot lines. Marvel Comics created Namor the Submariner, ruler of a submerged and technologically sophisticated underwater Atlantis. Most recently the television series *Stargate Atlantis* has spun off from *Stargate SG1*, which in turn spun off the film *Stargate*. The premise of *Stargate Atlantis* is that Atlantis was a super-scientific city built several million years ago by the Ancients, an incredibly advanced race of humans. They moved Atlantis to the Pegasus Galaxy but after coming under deadly attack, they hid Atlantis under the ocean and fled back to earth around 10,000 years ago. The story of this migration to and from the planet in the Pegasus Galaxy evolved into the legend of Atlantis. Perhaps the most quirky example of the super-civilization of Atlantis surviving catastrophe genre of fiction is the film *Alien from LA* (1987) starring supermodel Kathy Ireland in a doomed attempt to cross over into an acting career. Ireland plays Wanda Saknussem, a nerdy student (remember this is science fantasy!), searching for her missing father, archaeologist Arnold Saknussem. Her father has been attempting to prove that a spaceship named *Atlantis* crash landed into the depths of the earth thousands of years ago and that there may be survivors. After undergoing a series of adventures Wanda manages to reach Atlantis, where the inhabitants continually debate whether a surface world exists and if it is inhabited. Hence, in an amusing twist, Wanda becomes the alien from LA for the Atlanteans. During the course of her adventures, Wanda develops into a supermodel although not because of any Atlantean super-science. *Alien from LA* is based on a cute, offbeat idea but unfortunately was not carried out well in terms of the writing or the acting. Despite these flaws the film clearly demonstrates the continuing fascination with Atlantis in popular culture.

Popular culture also maintains a view of Atlantis that is a bit more faithful to Plato's account. In this version Atlantis is an ancient super-civilization which has become flawed by megalomania and greed. It was eventually destroyed as a result of its evil behaviour. *The Lost Continent* (1900) by C. J. Cutcliffe Hyne is a classic example of this genre as well as one of the best fictional depictions of Atlantis. Hyne's Atlantis is a great empire with colonies scattered around the earth. Unfortunately a beautiful but evil woman named Phorenice has gained control of Atlantis through some vaguely described supernatural powers. Tyranny and oppression follow. The hero of the novel, aptly named Deucalion (the name of the Greek equivalent of Noah), returned from the colony of Yucatan to find his homeland in bondage to Phorenice, who seeks to make him her unwilling spouse. The Atlantean priesthood rebels but the despotic queen defeats them. Her triumph, however, is short-lived as the priests have set in motion cosmic forces that will sink Atlantis beneath the waves and destroy Phorenice in the process. Deucalion escapes to the east taking the memory of Atlantis and remnants of its civilization with him and the legend of Atlantis is born once again.

Another example of the Atlantis as a destroyed super-civilization is the film *Atlantis, the Lost Continent* (1961). Unfortunately this Atlantis movie was not one of the film industry's better efforts and became notorious for its retreading of easily recognizable footage, props and sets from other films ranging from *Quo Vadis* to *Forbidden Planet*. The story begins with a young Greek fisherman named Demetrios rescuing a mysterious young woman, the sole survivor of a shipwreck. The beautiful maiden turns out to be Princess Antillia (a name fraught with Atlantological connotations) from the land of Atlantis, a kingdom located across the seas far to the west. Antillia being pretty and Demetrios being male, he agrees to take her home, an arduous voyage. Unfortunately, upon returning Antillia to her homeland the Atlanteans prove to be neither grateful or hospitable. Demetrios finds himself enslaved and forced to work in the mines of Atlantis. It turns out that the Atlanteans have been raiding their neighbours for slaves and the mines of Atlantis are a model of diversity with Greeks, Norsemen, sub-Saharan Africans and Native Americans among the population of slaves. All of them are delving the earth for the crystals that the Atlanteans use for their power source and for ray-guns. Azor, the high priest of Atlantis (played by Edward Platt, who would go on to acting fame as the befuddled Chief in *Get Smart*), seeks to lead Atlantis in the preemptive annihilation of its enemies and the conquest of the world. Atlantean civilization is wondrous with advanced medicine and submarines but it also abuses its scientific knowledge. Besides their plan to use deadly ray-guns to achieve world domination, the Atlanteans also engage in hideous, Nazi-like experiments that create extremely strong creatures with human bodies and bull's heads, just like the Minotaur of Greek mythology. All this tampering with power crystals and monstrous humans makes Atlantis a society significantly out of balance with arrogance and cruelty in the ascendant. The inevitable earthquakes and volcanic eruptions follow these abuses since the Atlanteans need to be punished for tampering with Mother Nature. Demetrios manages to escape the sinking of Atlantis along with others of the diverse slaves. They also return to their native lands and take with them tales that evolve into the legend of Atlantis. Like the Atlantis of Hyne,

Demetrios' Atlantis is destroyed and it is not going to rise again. On the other hand, popular culture's fascination with Atlantis and other lost continents continues unabated and shows no sign of sinking out of sight.

CONCLUSION

> Let us beware how we blend doubt with certainty, and falsehood with truth. We have abundant proofs of the great changes and revolutions the globe has undergone, without appealing to tradition or fable.
> The greatest of these revolutions would be the disappearance of the Atlantic land [Atlantis], if it were true that this part of the world ever existed. It is probable that this land consisted of nothing else than the island of Madeira. VOLTAIRE (1765)[91]

It is probably safe to say that Atlantis and to a lesser degree Lemuria and other lost continents have become a permanent part of popular culture, pseudohistory and the cultic milieu. As L. Sprague de Camp and Willy Ley have so evocatively put it: 'If one were asked to pronounce a magical name, a single word known to every listener, a word of splendor and of mystery, a word which means many different things to many different people, that word would and could only be: Atlantis.'[92] While these words were written long before the appearance of the internet, a series of simple online searches will bear out their enduring truth. A search of Google using 'Atlantis' as the term yields 28.8 million hits. Using the same term on Yahoo produces 44.9 million hits. Searching Amazon.com's books section just using 'Atlantis' delivers 18,644 hits. WorldCat on FirstSearch provides 10,000 results when 'Atlantis' is used in a keyword search. Clearly a large portion of the items listed by these searches have nothing to do with Atlantis the lost continent. Instead they refer to a space shuttle, resorts, casinos and a host of other things which amply prove that 'Atlantis' is indeed 'a magical name'. Meanwhile, estimates for the number of books that have been written about Atlantis range from 2,000 to 20,000 titles with the actual number probably lying somewhere in the middle.

One does not have to go far or wait long to stumble across some manifestation of Atlantis in popular culture. In the magazine racks of chain bookstores it is common to find the periodical *Atlantis Rising*, which is full of articles about the existence of the lost continent. Other magazines like *Ancient American: Archaeology of the Americas before Columbus* and *World Explorer* frequently publish articles supporting or assuming the existence of Atlantis or Lemuria. In contrast magazines like *Archaeology, Skeptic* and *The Skeptical Inquirer* from time to time bring out articles debunking various aspects of Atlantology. On the bookshelves of the same bookstores a browser in the History section or the New Age section will often find titles dealing with Atlantis in whole or in part. Some debunk but more argue for the historical existence of Atlantis. Over in the fiction section, both general and science fiction/fantasy, novels dealing with Atlantis continue to appear. *Atlantis* by David Gibbins appeared in a hardcover edition in 2005 with the mass-market paperback coming off the presses a year later. It involves a scientific expedition seeking Atlantis in the Aegean but along the way getting pulled into terrorist machinations and uncovering a conspiracy to conceal the existence of Atlantis. It is the type of light reading that during its lifetime in print often graces the book kiosks of airports.

For those who prefer watching to reading, television offers plenty of Atlantis fare. *Stargate Atlantis* enjoys a good run on the Science Fiction Channel and will certainly continue to be broadcast as reruns long after the producers stop making new episodes. Documentaries about Atlantis are periodically aired on the long-running BBC series *Horizon*, the Public Broadcasting Network, the Discovery Channel, the History Channel, the Learning Channel, the Travel Channel and even the Science Fiction Channel. The History Channel series *Digging for the Truth* kicked off a season with a two-hour Atlantis show in 2006. Besides the usual Atlantis background with Plato's account and other standard lore, this episode included a segment on the Cyprus–Atlantis project of Robert Sarmast, a new wrinkle on the quest for Atlantis's location.[93] The Science Fiction Channel also produced a documentary titled *Quest for Atlantis* in 2006, hosted by Natalie Morales, that concentrated on Robert Sarmast's theory. Basically Sarmast suggests that Atlantis was located on a basin which now lies under a mile of water off the coast of the island of Cyprus. In the prehistoric era of the Ice Ages the Mediterranean Sea did not exist. Instead the basin of the Mediterranean was a series of inland lakes or seas. Cyprus was not then an island but was connected to the mainland of Asia Minor by exposed land including the basin that Sarmast has identified as Atlantis. Sarmast's entire theory is based on finding correspondences between Plato's description of Atlantis and the topography of the submerged basin. Not a single artefact has been found to support Sarmast's circumstantial contention although he claims to have located an area which is the actual circular city of Atlantis, including its acropolis. He hoped to acquire proof positive by sailing a rented scientific vessel with advanced underwater imaging equipment to the location of the alleged circular city. The *Digging for the Truth* documentary included a chronicle of that expedition which included in its crew an apparently enthusiastic and sympathetic geologist who had been brought along to verify and to interpret the scientific data from the imaging equipment. As Sarmast's ship approaches its goal the tension mounts and just when the sensors reach the target area, the equipment crashes without warning. Some might be inclined to view this equipment failure in a conspiratorial light, à la *The X-Files*, but the producers of *Digging for the Truth* kindly did not do so. The problem for Sarmast is that he's got a rented ship and his time is running out. There is only enough time to make a second run at the target area. It too does not go well and imaging is only done for a portion of the alleged circular city. Still Sarmast thinks the images look promising for proving his theory. Unfortunately the hitherto sympathetic geologist turns killjoy and declares the underwater formation to be natural and not man-made. Shades of the Bimini Road! At this point, some viewers of the documentary, including me, were feeling a bit sorry for Sarmast. After all, his equipment either malfunctioned or only produced partial results. Now he's got to return his rented ship and that geologist has pronounced the ruins of that circular city to be natural geological formations. A lot of people might have felt somewhat embarrassed or sheepish if they found themselves in Sarmast's position but he remained undaunted through it all. The imaging done of the target location was only a partial survey and there is plenty of room for ruins in the remaining area. *Digging for the Truth* graciously forbore from pointing out that Sarmast's expedition was a failure and had done nothing to prove the existence of Atlantis. Lest anyone feel too sorry for Mr Sarmast, ask this, how many young guys get to be the focus of a couple of documentaries on prime-time television hosted by someone as good-looking as Natalie Morales, or Josh Bernstein, for that matter? Meanwhile, fans of Atlantis need to be patient and wait for the lost continent's next inevitable appearance on the big screen of the movie theatres.

Clearly Atlantis is an enduring and marketable commodity that appeals to many different types of people. When it comes to the subject of Atlantis, many people would fully agree with the sentiment of Fox Mulder in *The X-Files* when he acknowledged to his partner Scully, 'I want to believe'. It is a phenomenon that I have observed personally. In June 2007 I gave a lecture on a cruise in the Mediterranean concerning the island of Santorini and its Atlantis connection. I talked about how the general consensus of scholars was that the story of Atlantis was a myth invented by Plato and that he was not describing a historical place or real events. At that same time I also pointed out that many scholars accepted the possibility that the titanic eruption of Thera during the Bronze Age left memories that would later inspire Plato's story of Atlantis. That night a man from our dinner group, who had attended the lecture, told me how disappointed he and another man sitting next to him had been to learn that Atlantis never existed. As L. Sprague de Camp has noted:

> Atlantis provides mystery and romance for those who don't find ordinary history exciting enough, and can be readily turned to account to point a moral lesson–in fact, any of many different and contradictory moral lessons.
>
> But most of all, it strikes a responsive chord by its sense of melancholy loss of a beautiful thing, a happy perfection once possessed by mankind. Thus, it appeals to that hope that most of us carry around in our unconscious, a hope so often raised and as often disappointed, for assurance that somewhere, some time, there can exist a land of peace and plenty, of beauty and justice, where we, poor creatures that we are, could be happy. In this sense Atlantis . . . will always be with us.[94]

He's right. The serious study of the ancient history of the Bronze Age, of prehistory or of archaeology can be heavy going for the non-professional. The arcana of ancient languages, the painstaking excavation of an archaeological site, the details of the technologies of radiocarbon dating and dendrochronology are all important and exciting in their own way but they lack the drama of primordial wars, archaic magic, ancient catastrophes and primeval superhumans. These are exactly the sorts of things that writers supporting the existence of Atlantis offer their readers although without much in the way of verifiable and ultimately convincing evidence. Atlantis sells.

Do Atlantological writers actually believe what they are writing? Surely they would all answer with a resounding and somewhat indignant yes! Those who are of a more cynical cast of mind, however, will have their doubts. Writers of science fiction and fantasy use Atlantis in their writings but they are not believers. One author who dabbled in the Atlantis theme was H. P. Lovecraft (1890–1937). Lovecraft is best remembered as a writer of short stories that combine elements of the macabre, horror, fantasy and science fiction. His tales of grotesque races of non-humans who ruled the earth during distant and forgotten epochs are reminiscent of the cosmologies of the occultists such as Madame Blavatsky. In 1920 he tried his hand at a tale related to Atlantis when he wrote 'The Temple'. It tells of a German submarine's encounter with the ruins of an unknown civilization beneath the waters of the Atlantic Ocean. A ruined temple turned out to still be occupied by some sort of supernatural presence and on that eerie note the story ends. Lovecraft also used facets of the myths of Atlantis and Lemuria in his stories 'Dagon' (1917) and 'The Call of Cthulhu' (1926) which both involve the reemergence of submerged land with the remains and still living inhabitants of ghastly prehistoric civilizations.[95] But Lovecraft was no believer in Atlantis. For him it was a convenient bit of unconventional lore that lent itself to his style of short story. As he explained to Elizabeth Toldridge on 20 November 1928: 'Extravagant theorists like Lewis Spence try to prove that both Europe & America were peopled in migrations from a sunken Atlantis, but I greatly doubt if any mid-Atlantic continent has existed since ages vastly anterior to man. If any vast inhabited land areas have sunk, it has been in the *Pacific*. I have used the sunken-land motif often in fiction – it fascinates me.'[96]

Some years later Lovecraft was even more emphatic in a letter written to Frederic Jay Pabody on 19 June 1936 when he proclaimed, 'I feel sure that the Platonic Atlantis is sheer myth.'[97] This is not to portray Lovecraft as a hardheaded sceptic who happened to write weird short stories. He held some quirky and unorthodox opinions and ideas but belief in Atlantis was not one of them.

Lovecraft's friend and correspondent Robert E. Howard, best known as the creator of the fictional character Conan, is rather a different story. Atlantis appeared in Howard's fiction but more as a backdrop than a main setting. Howard created another character, Kull, a barbarian from Atlantis. Seeking his fortune, Kull travelled to civilized lands and fought his way to the kingship of Valusia. Howard's fictional Atlantis was the home of wild barbarians, not a primeval super-civilization. Conan lived during the Hyborian Age, which was long after the sinking of Atlantis and came from Cimmeria, a northern barbarian land. Howard indicates that the hardy Cimmerians were the descendants of barbarian refugees from Atlantis. Where did Howard get these ideas? It has been suggested that Howard derived some of his ideas from reading Madame Blavatsky's *Secret Doctrine* and Lewis Spence's works on Atlantis although neither author is found among his surviving books.[98] Opinions vary among Howard scholars as to whether he believed in a historical Atlantis or not. Some maintain that he considered the prehistory presented in his Kull and Conan stories to be simply the product of his imagination.[99] But as Howard's 1928 letter to Harold Preece shows, Howard did believe that an Atlantis like Kull's homeland had existed in the distant past. As he put it, 'About Atlantis – I believe something of the sort existed, though I do not especially hold any theory about a high type of civilization existing there – in fact, I doubt it.' He goes on to echo the ideas of Lewis Spence about the Cro-Magnons being Atlantean refugees. In these beliefs, it has been suggested that Howard was reflecting the Aryanism and the blurring of history and fiction that pervaded the worldviews of various people, including the Nazis, in the years between the two world wars.[100] In the present Clive Cussler, a prolific author of adventure novels which frequently utilize archaeological themes in their plots, clearly believes or wants to believe in the possibility of a historical Atlantis. His novel *Atlantis Found* is based on the premise that a comet struck the earth in 7120 BC and wiped out the existing civilizations. Those destroyed civilizations provided the basis for the Atlantis legend. The acknowledgments for the book include thanks to Donald Cyr, Graham Hancock and Charles Hapgood, who mainstream scholars consider to be purveyors of questionable fringe scholarship. A postscript indicates that all sorts of people reached the Americas by sea in the centuries and the millenia prior to 1492.[101]

Believers in Atlantis are not all that rare in modern industrial society, as the thriving market for books and documentaries about the lost continent demonstrates. During the 1980s some anthropologists conducted a series of surveys of college students' beliefs about various pseudoscientific and pseudohistorical topics.[102] One question asked students from Connecticut, Texas and California if Atlantis was the home of a great civilization. In Texas and California about 30 per cent of the students surveyed answered yes, while almost 40 per cent of Connecticut students answered yes. A large portion of the students were undecided about how to answer the question – in Texas and California about 30 per cent, in Connecticut 20 per cent. Surprisingly a significant portion of the students had never heard of Atlantis, in Texas about 20 per cent while in California and Connecticut it was 15 per cent. Only questions about the Shroud of Turin and Europeans visiting America before the Vikings received similar high percentages of 'never heard of it' responses. What is most notable is that more college students believed in Atlantis than didn't – roughly one-third were believers while a quarter were sceptics. Close to half of the students surveyed were either undecided about Atlantis or had never heard of it. Sadly these results bear out the observation of the seventeenth-century philosopher Thomas Hobbes that, 'between true science and erroneous doctrine, ignorance is in the middle'.[103] Belief in Atlantis among American college students was alive and well during the mid-1980s and there is no reason to believe that the situation has changed between then and now. Obviously colleges seeking to teach critical thinking and the debunking of pseudohistory, pseudoscience and pseudoarchaeology have their work cut out.

One might ask what is the harm of believing in Atlantis and other lost continents? In most cases such beliefs are relatively harmless. Most believers in Atlantis are fairly casual and vague about their beliefs. They accept that Atlantis existed in about the same way that they would accept that ancient Sumer existed in ancient Iraq or that a civilization called Great Zimbabwe once thrived in southern Africa. They do not know much about the topics. Their beliefs have no real impact on their day-to-day lives except possibly as entertainment. For the Theosophists and other occultists Atlantis has a greater importance since it forms an integral part of their religious worldview. Most occultists are harmless people, often with good educations and comfortable incomes. Some are active in efforts to deal with various social problems. Hardened sceptics will grant that Henry Steele Olcott, Annie Besant and Rudolf Steiner were well-intentioned people who did some good things. Judgements of others like Madame Blavatsky and Charles Webster Leadbeater are liable to be considerably harsher. Occult religions are particularly prone to attract charlatans and opportunists.

Fallacious beliefs can also be turned to foul purposes. The rise of Nazism in Germany had strong connections with groups professing occult, pseudohistorical and pseudoscientific ideas that the Nazis incorporated into their own reprehensible ideologies. They identified Atlantis as the original homeland of the Aryans and committed financial and intellectual resources to trying to prove it.[104] Atlantis was only a piece of the Nazi jigsaw puzzle of pseudohistory but it was a crucial piece. Fanaticism and hate can corrupt anything and Atlantis is no exception. At a less intense level many proponents of the existence of Atlantis and other lost continents promote the same vague anti-intellectualism that characterizes the world of pseudohistory and pseudoscience in general. Yes, Atlantis can be fun and even sort of sexy, but the Atlantean rock with the cute and harmless Disney character sitting on it may, when turned over, reveal an ugly Nazi.

Who's on First? The Pseudohistory of the Discovery and Settlement of Ancient America

Some people say that the New World was known a long time ago
and its exact location written down, and all knowledge of it lost.
GONZALO FERNÁNDEZ DE OVIEDO (1535)[1]

Inform me, Whence the Tawny People came?
Who was their Father, Japhet, Shem, or Cham?
And how they straddled to th'Antipodes,
To look another World beyond the Seas?
And when, and why, and where they last broke ground,
What Risks they ran, where they first anchoring found?
NICHOLAS NOYES (1702)[2]

It all began on 28 July 1996, the day of the hydroplane race known
as the Tri-City Water Follies on the Columbia River.[3] It took place at
Columbia Park in Kennewick, Washington. Two college students,
Will Thomas and Dave Deacy, decided to skip paying the entrance
fee and sneak into the race-grounds by going around the fence and
wading up the Columbia River. While wading in the shallow water,
Thomas noticed a round stone and thought he would pull a joke on
Deacy by claiming it was a skull. The joke, however, was on Thomas.
When he pulled the stone out of the river bottom it really was a human
skull. Surprised by their find, the two young men ultimately informed
the police of their macabre discovery but not before they finished
watching the boat race. When the police arrived they took charge of
the skull and called in county coroner Floyd Johnson. The Tri-City
area of Kennewick, Richland, and Pasco has a combined population
of over 160,000 people, but it is divided between two counties. As a
result Benton County coroner's office does not have the resources
and forensics laboratories depicted in various CSI television series.
Instead Floyd Johnson called upon a local freelance archaeologist
named James Chatters, who served as a sometime deputy coroner
and provided expertise in forensic anthropology.

The Kennewick skull proved to be perplexing. Chatters thought the bones appeared to be quite old, that is, the pre-Columbian or before-1492 type of old. The problem was that the skull exhibited the sort of physical traits that forensic anthropologists associate with the skulls of white people of European descent. Since it was entirely possible that the weathering of the bones had made them seem much older than they really were, Chatters initially thought they were probably the remains of a nineteenth-century pioneer.[4] Meanwhile further searching of the area of the Columbia River where the skull had been found revealed more bones, in fact almost an entire skeleton. An inspection of the pelvic bones disclosed a dense object embedded in it. The object appeared to be some sort of stone spear point. One suggestion was that the stone point provided evidence that Native Americans had killed the pioneer. The problem was that the style of the stone point was Cascadian, a type of spear point that had been in use 5,000–9,000 years ago but not in historic times. That circumstance gave renewed credence to Chatters' initial hunch that the skeleton might be thousands of years old. He decided that the skeleton needed to be radiocarbon dated to determine its actual age. The skeleton just might turn out to be an important archaeological find. Unfortunately for Chatters and Johnson the local newspaper had published stories about the finding of the skeleton which aroused the interest of local Native Americans.

Native Americans are sensitive about the mistreatment of the skeletal remains of their ancestors by researchers, scientific institutions and museums. The bones of some 200,000 Native Americans had been stockpiled, mostly during the late nineteenth and early twentieth centuries, in the collections of various universities and museums. Graves were robbed or the corpses of Native American warriors killed on the battlefield were decapitated by the US army to build up the collections. Many early professional anthropologists engaged in collecting activities of a dubious moral and ethical nature. Even the great Franz Boas, renowned for his humane and sensitive approach to the study of anthropology, participated in bone-collecting. The Native Americans had become outraged by these bone-collecting practices. Many of them viewed it as an insult to their religious beliefs which required the respectful treatment of their ancestor's bones, lest the wrath of the vengeful spirits of the dead be aroused. Others simply considered it disrespectful of their humanity.[5] As a result Native Americans and their supporters had worked hard to get the Native American Graves Protection and Repatriation Act (NAGPRA) enacted in 1990. The new law required that Native American skeletons be returned to the appropriate tribes for reburial. It also set rules for the study or the reburial of any Native American remains that might be discovered in the future. NAGPRA, however, contained some rather vague sections that could be interpreted differently depending on one's predilections. Needless to say, the predilections of white anthropologists and archaeologists interested in the prehistory of North America could be and often were quite different from the wishes of the members of many tribes of Native Americans. A find like the skeleton of the Kennewick Man provided just the sort of issue that would pit the desires of scientific archaeology against the religious beliefs of Native Americans.

The Umatilla tribe of the Columbia River valley began demanding the reburial of the bones by the early morning of 29 July based on the preliminary newspaper reports mentioning 'some apparently worn-down teeth'. On the next day, Tuesday 30 July, the *Tri-City Herald* published a story that suggested that the bones probably belonged to an early white settler. Undeterred, an Umatilla leader, Armand Minthorn, asked for a second opinion with the paradoxical demand, 'Find out what it is; just don't do any study.'[6] Some of the Native Americans did not trust Chatters, or any scientific archaeologists for that matter. They also had some political clout. The bones had been found in an area under the jurisdiction of the Army Corps of Engineers. While the local Army Corps archaeologist had initially been cooperative with Chatters and Johnson, Native American pressure on higher ranking officials brought the Army Corps around to their point of view. The Army Corps was engaged in cleaning up the Hanford Nuclear Facility also located in Benton County and the nation's most contaminated nuclear site. Cooperation from the Umatilla and other local tribes was crucial and, in the big picture of the Army Corps, it was the Hanford clean-up that counted, not some old bones found in the Columbia River at Kennewick.[7]

Meanwhile Chatters had sent samples of the bones to the University of California Riverside for radiocarbon dating. After receiving preliminary numbers on 26 August, the laboratory at UC-Riverside informed Chatters that the bones dated to 9,330–9,580 years old. That made the Kennewick bones one of the oldest intact skeletons ever found in North America. It also reignited the efforts of the Umatillas and other tribes to get the Kennewick Man reburied. They claimed that he was obviously Native American since any skeletal remains dating before 1492 must by definition be Native American in ethnicity.[8] The fact that the features of the Kennewick skull were not at all similar to those of historic Native Americans was irrelevant to their definition of what constituted a Native American. This assumption ignores the testimonies of the Norse sagas that some Norse colonists died at Vinland and so were buried in pre-Columbian North America. In another way, the features of the Kennewick Man were highly relevant. Many Native American tribes claim to be autochthonous, meaning they have always lived in their traditional tribal lands from the time of creation onward. Archaeological evidence does not support their claims but the response of the Native American radicals is to question the validity of the scientific findings or to claim that archaeologists are mistaken, incompetent or liars with a nefarious political agenda. In the case of the neighbouring Umatilla, who claim to be autochthonous to the Columbia River valley, the solution was to get Kennewick Man's remains buried in the ground – untested and unstudied – as soon as possible. The Umatilla also assert that their traditional religion demands such reburials as a sign of respect and a way to keep the spirit of the bones from becoming angry. For them, any study of Native American remains is a desecration.

Besides the problem of the great age of the Kennewick bones, Chatters aroused controversy by describing the bones as 'caucasoid', a term of physical anthropology that has been avoided more and more by recent scholars because of its racial connotations. In fact Chatters did not use the term inaccurately in its technical sense. It appears that Kennewick Man was most physically similar to the prehistoric people who became the Jumon culture that occupied Taiwan and Japan in prehistoric times and were also the ancestors of the Ainu and the Polynesians. These people were technically caucasoids as the science of physical anthropology defines the term. Unfortunately the use of the term 'caucasoid' also prompted all sorts of ill-informed and unfounded speculations about prehistoric visits and colonizations of the Americas by Europeans. Such stories appeared in the media and further angered the Umatilla and neighbouring tribes. They, in turn, put pressure on the Army Corps.

The Army Corps demanded that Floyd Johnson and Chatters hand over Kennewick Man's remains. Johnson and Chatters complied on 2 September 1996. Quickly the Umatilla and four other neighbouring tribes claimed the Kennewick remains under the provisions of NAGPRA. In a display of uncharacteristic swiftness, on 17 September 1996 the Army Corps announced its intention to turn the bones over to the Native American tribes for reburial. Fearing the loss of Kennewick Man for scientific study, eight prominent anthropologists specializing in human origins in the Americas filed suit at the US Magistrate's Court in Portland, Oregon, to prevent the repatriation and reburial of Kennewick Man and, instead, to require the Army Corps to do further scientific studies of the bones. Litigation began on 24 October 1996. Meanwhile dozens and dozens of other individuals and

65

groups filed claims for the Kennewick Man's remains. Most of these claims were dismissed because the claimants lacked legal status to make any claim. One claim, however bizarre its pseudohistorical and pseudoscientific claims, proved to have considerable staying power.

The Asatru Folk Assembly joined the litigation of the eight anthropologists by filing their own claim to Kennewick Man on 24 October 1996. Founded by Stephen McNallen as the Viking Brotherhood in 1971, the group's name changed in 1974 to the Asatru Free Assembly, which disbanded in 1986. Undaunted, McNallen refounded the group as the Asatru Folk Assembly in 1994. Basically the Asatru are attempting to revive the worship and lifestyle of the ancient peoples of Scandinavia and northern Europe – the religion and culture of Norse mythology. They also believe that Europeans visited the Americas and settled there during prehistoric times on a number of occasions; hence the basis of their claims to Kennewick Man as an ancestor. While they exhibit a certain quirky charm and although mainstream adherents eschew racism of any kind, some elements of the Asatru have been connected with the racist neo-paganism that emerged from the Christian Identity movement. In the world of obfuscating post-modernism that rejects science and empirical research as pathways to the truth, or at least a closer approximation of the truth, the Asatru's religious claim was every bit as good as the Umatilla except that it was neither politically correct nor backed by the behind-the-scenes politics of cleaning up the Hanford Nuclear Facility.[9]

The Kennewick Man case dragged on for years. Even the Clinton administration got involved, whether out of the politics of political correctness or the politics of nuclear waste is unclear. On 1 April 1998 the Army Corps turned Kennewick Man over to the US Department of the Interior, an ironic day for such a decision. Then, on 6 April 1998, the Army Corps 'stabilized' the site where Kennewick Man had been discovered by dumping hundreds of tons of dirt and debris on it, all at taxpayers' expense. Ostensibly done to protect the site from looters, this action effectively destroyed the site for future archaeological research. Otherwise, the Federal Government's strategy changed from acting in haste to engaging in one delaying tactic after another. The plan produced results when the Asatru Folk Assembly dropped its litigation on 14 January 2000 due to running out of money. There is also some reason to suspect that they may have achieved their real goal, which was to garner publicity and name recognition for their group.

Interior Secretary Bruce Babbitt joined the fray by ruling on 26 September 2000 that Kennewick Man was Native American by ignoring any scientific evidence while giving full faith and credit to Native

American oral traditions and some questionable assumptions about the extent of tribal territories at the time Kennewick Man was alive. Further legal action by the lawyers for the eight anthropologists stopped that move. As a result the government resumed its delaying tactics. Government tests on the remains were done slowly, and the results proved inconclusive or methodologically unsound. More strangeness inserted itself when self-proclaimed Polynesian chief J. P. Siofele attempted to file a claim in Kennewick Man on 26 July 2001. The court rejected Siofele's claim within a month as untimely even though it was based on the scientific evidence of a Polynesian affiliation for Kennewick Man that was far superior to the factual basis of the claims of the Umatilla and the other tribes.

By the middle of 2002 the Federal magistrate John Jelderks had grown weary of the US Justice Department's delays, and subsequent legal decisions had started to go against the government defendants. On 29 August 2002 Jelderks ruled that NAGPRA did not apply to Kennewick Man and that the Army Corps of Engineers had violated the National Historic Preservation Act by burying the Kennewick site, and consequently he gave permission for the scientists to study the remains of Kennewick Man. Various appeals against the ruling by the government and the tribes followed, including the Polynesian chief Siofele. These legal actions continued into 2004 when on 4 February the Ninth Circuit Court of Appeals upheld Jelderks' ruling in favour of the scientists. Tribal requests for a rehearing were rejected and on 22 July the Justice Department announced that it would not appeal the Kennewick Man case to the US Supreme Court. On 6 July 2005 the scientists were finally allowed to study Kennewick Man, slightly more than three weeks before the ninth anniversary of the discovery of the skull by Thomas and Deacy. One result of the close examination of the bones was a definitive finding that Kennewick Man had been deliberately buried. Chatters had suggested that Kennewick Man might have died away from his group and been inadvertently and quickly covered by mud and silt of the Columbia River.

The saga of Kennewick Man is not over. On 9 January 2006 East Benton County Museum opened a new Kennewick Man exhibit and *Time* magazine featured him on its 13 March 2006 cover. The actual remains of Kennewick Man still reside in the care of the Burke Museum of Natural History and Culture at the University of Washington where their condition is periodically inspected. Both Native Americans and the Asatru remain interested in Kennewick Man and continue to pray over his bones. The struggle for the bones also continues as US Representative 'Doc' Hastings has sponsored legislation permitting the study of ancient remains while Senators Byron Dorgan and

John McCain have sponsored attempts to amend NAGPRA to favour
the Native American activists' position of defining all pre-1492
human remains as Native American without any necessity for testing
or study.[10] Meanwhile the academic study of the prehistoric peopling
of the Americas remains in a currently glorious state of confusion.
The dominant Clovis First theory of human origins in the Americas
is collapsing in the face of an accumulation of contradictory evidence. In scholarly terms it is a time of transition at the end of which
a new and more accurate paradigm or theory will emerge. But if the
Native American activists prevail the realignment of the study of
American prehistory will be stalled, leaving the topic in a vacuum
that will be filled by the Asatru and other beliefs based on pseudohistory and pseudoscience.

THE SETTING

It is easier to refute what is false about the Indians' origin than to
discover the truth. JOSÉ DE ACOSTA (1590)[11]

Pseudohistorical hypotheses about the history of the Americas before
1492 fall into two basic and somewhat interconnected categories or
questions. One question is how and when humans first came to live in
the Americas and who they were. The second question is: did other
Old World people discover the Americas before Columbus, who were
they and when did they do it? Both of these questions are the subjects
of legitimate historical, archaeological and scientific research, but they
have also been the nursery of voluminous pseudohistorical speculations starting virtually in 1493 and continuing unabated ever since.

The study of human origins in the Americas is currently in a state
of flux and turmoil, as the controversy surrounding the Kennewick
Man skeleton shows. The once preeminent Clovis First Theory,
which had dominated North American archaeology for close to seventy years, has disintegrated as a result of accumulating contradictory
evidence. In 1932 a site near Clovis, New Mexico, revealed the existence of a Palaeo-Indian hunting culture that emerged abruptly about
11,000 years before the present and had spread rapidly across North
America. The Clovis First Theory claimed that Ice Age nomads migrated out of Alaska or the lowlands of Beringia, now submerged
under the Bering Sea. As the glaciers of the Ice Age began to recede,
an ice-free corridor opened up between the Cordilleran Ice Sheet of
the Rocky Mountains and the Laurentide Ice Sheet of eastern Canada.
Nomadic hunters from Alaska or Beringia made their way down this
corridor, possibly following wandering herds of mammoths or other

Ice Age mega-fauna. Once they made their way out of the passage between the glaciated regions and entered the warmer lands to the south, the newcomers discovered that they had reached a hunter's paradise. It was crowded with massive herds of mammoth, bison and other grazing animals which had not learned to be wary of humans. These nomadic hunters were the Clovis culture who hunted many of the Ice Age mega-fauna to extinction within less than a thousand years of their arrival in North America. At that point Clovis culture evolved into the Folsom and other cultures while they rapidly peopled the entire western hemisphere.[12]

The Clovis First Theory possessed a coherence, clarity and simplicity that made it an attractive explanation of how the Americas came to be inhabited by humans. Also helpful to the acceptance of the theory was that at first the available archaeological research generally tended to support it. Unfortunately, over time, further research accumulated that called the Clovis First Theory into question.[13] Findings in genetics, linguistics and archaeology contradicted the Clovis First timeline by suggesting that humans had been living in the Americas longer than the theory allowed. The collapse of the Clovis First Theory, however, has not yet resulted in the rise of a new master theory explaining the peopling of the Americas. Despite the qualms of some die-hard Clovis First adherents, archaeological evidence from both North and South America indicates human occupation dates back to at least 15,000 years ago, which is 3,000 or 4,000 years longer than the Clovis First chronology. Just when, where or how humans first arrived in the Americas remains murky. No reliably dated archaeological evidence has been found earlier than 15,000 years ago, but genetic and linguistic theories suggest that humans must have first arrived at least 30,000 years ago or longer. It has been suggested that crucial archaeological evidence lies submerged under the sea along the present-day coastline of Alaska and western Canada. The melting of the Ice Age glaciers raised the sea level and covered what was once dry land.

For now no scholarly consensus exists regarding the first peopling of the Americas. The study of the prehistory of the Americas has been left in as confused a state as it had been prior to the rise of scientific archaeology and anthropology during the second half of the nineteenth century. The idea of walking across the Bering landbridge still continues to beckon to some scholars since geographically and genetically it makes the most sense. Modern Native Americans are genetically most closely related to Asiatic peoples of Siberia. The problem is to determine when people could have walked into North America from Alaska – it clearly had to have taken place earlier than the 11,000 years ago of the Clovis First Theory. Other scholars have postulated that humans sailed down the western coast of Canada in small boats during the Ice Age.[14] The evidence for their passage now lies beneath the Pacific Ocean since sea levels have risen as the glaciers of the Ice Age have waned. More controversial is another hypothesis which claims that people from the Solutrean culture from Europe sailed across the North Atlantic of the Ice Age, probably between 27,000 and 20,000 years ago, bringing the elements of what would become the Clovis culture with them. Archaeological sites from the Clovis culture are most common in the southeastern United States, which lends circumstantial credence to the hypothesis. Dennis Stanford of the Smithsonian Institution and Bruce Bradley of Colorado have proposed the Solutrean hypothesis, but so far other archaeologists and anthropologists have not been supportive.[15]

The problem for all of these theories is that existing archaeological evidence is too sparse to fully support any of them or can be given alternative or contradictory interpretations. The archaeological evidence from South America is particularly confusing. Some of the artefacts and human remains recovered from archaeological sites along the west coast seem to indicate affinities with Australasian peoples. Other artefacts and human remains from Brazil seem to indicate connections with prehistoric Africa. Materials from the archaeological site at Pedra Furada in Brazil have produced dates ranging from 20,000 to 50,000 years ago although these findings have not been found reliable by most archaeologists. Nor have most archaeologists seriously considered the possibility that South America might originally have been peopled by settlers from Africa or Australasia.[16] Doubt and uncertainty loom over the academic study of the peopling of the Americas.

BEFORE COLUMBUS

> The ancients considered the Pillars of Hercules the head of navigation and the end of the world. The information the ancients didn't have was very voluminous. Even the prophets wrote book after book and epistle after epistle, yet never once hinted at the existence of a great continent on our side of the water, yet they must have known it was there, I should think. MARK TWAIN (1869)[17]

Controversies and wild theories about the discovery and peopling of the Americas began soon after Christopher Columbus completed his first voyage by returning to Spain in 1493. Once people realized that the Americas were a previously unknown land and not part of Asia, they began to give other people credit for the discovery besides Columbus. As the great nineteenth-century German naturalist and explorer Alexander von Humboldt caustically observed, 'There are three stages in the popular attitude toward a great discovery; first, men doubt its existence, next they deny its importance, and finally they give the credit to someone else.'[18] In Columbus' case, besides the Ice Age settlers of the Americas and the Norse of Leif Ericsson, there are hundreds of other theories proposing various individuals from the Old World who reached and even settled the Americas before him. Ancient Egyptians, Phoenician traders, wandering Greeks, fleeing Trojans, shipwrecked Romans, Buddhist missionaries, Chinese refugees, marauding Mongols, medieval Arabs and Mandigo merchants from Africa are just some of the many groups and individuals who supposedly beat Columbus to the Americas.[19] The first and second editions of *Pre-Columbian Contact with the Americas across the Oceans: An Annotated Bibliography*, compiled by John L. Sorenson and Martin H. Raish, between them list over 6,000 items dealing with that topic and they do not claim to be exhaustive.[20] Furthermore, new writings about pre-Columbian visitors and settlers continue to appear since the second edition of the bibliography was published in 1996. Mainstream archaeologists and historians usually consider such works to be suspect and in many cases just plain ridiculous. Many of these works can be safely classified as pseudohistory. They try to present themselves as real historical works, but their research and interpretations are badly flawed, making their conclusions false or at least highly dubious.

The first of the attempts to deprive Columbus of the credit for discovering the Americas appeared during his lifetime. It also appears that Columbus may have indirectly caused the problem. He was a Genoese foreigner and a poor governor, both of which aroused considerable resentment among the Spanish in Hispaniola. The situation was not helped by Columbus's steadfast insistence that Hispaniola and the other islands were simply outlying parts of Asia, not a new world. Furthermore, Columbus had struck such a good deal for his share of the wealth generated by his discoveries that the Spanish crown could not afford to honour the agreement. Litigation followed for years and the Spanish government was anxious to promote any story that detracted from Columbus's claims of priority of discovery.[21]

The story of the Unknown Pilot was probably the earliest attempt to deprive Columbus of the credit for first reaching the Americas. A widespread dislike of Columbus appears to have helped it to spread initially. It has since proved to be a very persistent tale that still continues to make appearances in books dealing with the discovery of the Americas, even some that purport to be scholarly treatments. Many versions of the 'Unknown Pilot of Columbus' story have circulated and they vary greatly in their details. Reduced to the basic common elements, the story tells how a trading vessel in the Atlantic was blown off course to the west by a great storm which lasted many days. There in the far western waters the survivors landed on an unknown island which was inhabited by naked people. The sailors then attempted to return to Europe but since they did not know the best route for taking advantage of the winds and the currents they remained at sea for a dreadfully long time. When they eventually reached land most of the crew had died from lack of food and water and the few survivors were beyond recovery. All but one of the survivors, an unknown pilot, died quickly. Christopher Columbus, a close friend of the last survivor, took him in and nursed him. Grateful for this hospitality, the dying man gave Columbus sailing directions and a chart to the location of the islands that had accidentally been discovered during the ill-fated voyage. It was on the basis of this secret information that Columbus formulated his own 'Enterprise of the Indies'.[22]

The details of the various 'Unknown Pilot' stories differ without affecting the core of the story. Sometimes the ship is travelling from Spain or Portugal to England and/or Flanders. In other cases the destination was Madeira, the Canaries or Guinea. The dying crew returned variously to Graciosa or Terceira in the Azores, Madeira or Porto Santo, or the Canaries. Meanwhile, the unknown pilot is called an Andalusian, a Basque, a Galician or a Portuguese. The early Peruvian historian Garcilaso de la Vega goes so far as to give the 'Unknown Pilot' a name, Alonso Sanchez, and a specific hometown, Huelva.[23]

Apparently rumours of the existence of the 'Unknown Pilot' began to circulate with Columbus's first landing in the Americas. Bartolomé de las Casas reported that the story was being widely discussed when he first arrived in Hispaniola in 1502. It first appeared in print in Gonzalo Fernández de Oviedo's *Historia general y natural de las Indias* in 1535 although he rejected it. Later Las Casas included the story in his unpublished *Historia de las Indias* and took the ambiguous attitude that while the story was probably not true, it was certainly possible. Other Spanish chroniclers repeated and embellished the story. Furthermore, knowledge of the 'Unknown Pilot' story was not confined to the Hispanic world. Sir Thomas Herbert, an Englishman, mentioned it in his *A Relation of Some Yeares Travaile . . .* in 1634 while advocating Price Madoc of Wales as the first discoverer of America.[24] The passage of time did not diminish the credibility of the 'Unknown Pilot' story. It almost seemed to increase it.

The story, however, has never gone unchallenged. Oviedo definitely dismissed its veracity while Las Casas doubted it. Ferdinand, the youngest son of Christopher Columbus, was naturally a leading six-teenth-century debunker of stories that detracted from the glory of his father's achievement. His biography of his father claimed that the sup-posed unknown pilot was actually named Vicente Dias, a Portuguese seaman who had made several unsuccessful voyages of exploration with Luca de Cassano into the western Atlantic around 1452.[25]

Debate over the story continued over the intervening centuries although it gradually lost credibility. The Spanish crown never at-tempted to use the story during its legal battles with Columbus' heirs over the cancellation of his lucrative concessions in the newly dis-covered lands. Although it would have worked in the crown's favour, it apparently was not given any credence. If the story had been true, it would also have meant that all of Columbus's geographical re-search and theories about the possibility of sailing west to reach Asia were a deception used to hide his secret, true destination. Finally, in 1942, Samuel Eliot Morison in his biography *Admiral of the Ocean Sea: A Life of Christopher Columbus* pointed out that the winds and the currents of the Atlantic would not allow a ship to be storm-blown in the manner of the 'Unknown Pilot' story. In Morison's opinion, the true source of the story lay with the rumour-mongering malcon-tents among Spain's first colonists in the New World who disliked Columbus.[26] These arguments would seem to have provided a final negative answer to the mystery of the 'Unknown Pilot' but that was not to be the case.

The debate flared up again in 1976 with the publication of the Spanish historian Juan Manzano Manzano's *Colón y su Secreto: El Predescubrimiento* which appeared in a second edition in 1982. In Manzano's opinion one of the surest proofs that Columbus had se-cret information was his unshakeable certainty that something lay in the west within reasonable sailing distance. Contrary to Morison, Manzano also claims that it was quite possible for a sailing ship to be blown to the West Indies by a storm while using the high seas route known as the *volta de Mina* from Guinea to Portugal. It was on just such a voyage that the supposed ship of the 'Unknown Pilot' was fatefully and fatally blown west. Once Columbus gained possession of the secret he used it at crucial junctures to persuade the doubting Ferdinand and Isabella to support him or to encourage the Pinzon brothers to keep sailing west for a little while longer. Manzano's argu-ment provides an extremely detailed interpretation of the events of Columbus' career, based throughout on the assumption of an 'Un-known Pilot'. In spite of such elaborate arguments, however, various and serious problems remain. The traditional version of Columbus formulating his 'Enterprise of the Indies' out of his own research and imagination continues to fit the known facts better than any reliance on an 'Unknown Pilot' as the true source of his inspiration.[27]

Columbus' death in 1506 did not end the controversies over who first discovered the Americas, rather it caused them to proliferate. Columbus's heirs became locked in a legal struggle with the Spanish crown over the titles and revenues associated with his discovery. In response historians loyal to the Spanish crown churned out claims that ancient Spaniards led by their king Hespero, Carthaginians and even Atlanteans had reached and settled the Americas long before the upstart Columbus.[28] The Venetians also waded into the controversy. As the home of the intrepid Marco Polo and possibly the greatest trading city of Europe, Venice was justifiably proud. Unfortunately, by the sixteenth century that fabled city's fortunes were waning. Venetians were also jealous of the favourable notice that Columbus's discoveries had earned for his hometown of Genoa, a longtime rival of Venice. So in 1558 Nicolo Zeno, the scion of an elite Venetian family, published a book. It purported to be a first-hand account by two of his ancestors of explorations that they had made to North America during the 1390s in the company of a mysterious northern potentate named Prince Henry Sinclair, almost a full century before Columbus. The tale was obviously a hoax but it has resurfaced time and time again in the writings of various supporters of pre-Columbian exploration theories.[29]

Other European powers, envious of Spain's American empire, put forward their own nationalistic claims about pre-Columbian explorers. The French king Francis I sarcastically complained that he would liked to see where Adam's will had divided the world between Spain and Portugal as those two countries had done with the assistance of the pope in the Treaty of Tordesillas in 1494. So to give legitimacy to French interloping in the Americas, scholar Guillaume de Postel claimed that ancient Gauls had sailed to the Americas. The Gauls later abandoned the new land because they thought it was too much of a wilderness.[30]

The English concocted their own theory of pre-Columbian discovery of America in which they credited a Welsh prince named Madoc, a younger son of the Welsh ruler Owen Gwynedd. Madoc made two or three voyages to the Americas in 1170 and after. Upon his father's death Madoc's older brothers engaged in civil wars that ravaged Wales. To escape the carnage Madoc sailed across the western ocean where he found an unknown and habitable land. Leaving a settlement of 120 people, he returned home to recruit more colonists. There he fitted out a fleet of ten vessels and returned to join the first group. Some accounts even mention a third voyage.[31]

Details of the history of Madoc's supposed colony are fragmentary, confused and contradictory. Various parties have put forward a wide assortment of claims as to where Madoc landed: Mobile, Alabama; Florida; Newfoundland; Newport, Rhode Island; Yarmouth, Nova Scotia; Virginia; various points in the Gulf of Mexico and the Caribbean Sea including the mouth of the Mississippi River, the Yucatan, the Isthmus of Tehuantepec, Panama and the northern coast of South America; various islands in the West Indies and Bahamas along with Bermuda; and the mouth of the Amazon River. Madoc's actual route is, of course, unknown. Some think that he followed a northern route similar to that of the Vikings. Most supporters of the Madoc story, however, propose a southern route utilizing the same winds and currents used by Columbus in his voyages.

Almost pure speculation dominates what Madoc and his followers did once they reached the New World. The most fully developed version of the Madoc story has the prince and his followers landing in Mobile Bay in Alabama. The later Spanish explorer Hernando de Soto observed mysterious ancient fortifications in Mobile Bay and for true believers Madoc made an obvious candidate for the builder. From Mobile Bay the Welsh moved northward to the region of Chattanooga, Tennessee, where they built more fortifications, such as those at Fort Mountain, Georgia and the Old Stone Fort at Manchester, Tennessee. The explanation for all this moving and fortifying by the Welsh is the implacable hostility of the neighbouring tribes of Native Americans. Continuing to move north, the beleaguered Welsh fought and lost a climatic battle at Sand Island on the Ohio River by Louisville, Kentucky. From there the greatly weakened remnant of the Welsh fled westwards. Travelling up the Missouri River they developed into an allegedly culturally and physically distinct tribe, the Mandans.[32]

The historiography of the Madoc myth is a complicated affair. It first appeared in a manuscript history of Wales written by the Welsh antiquary Humphrey Llwyd which was completed around 1559. Llwyd had access to old Welsh chronicles and writings, no longer extant, which makes his account the oldest surviving report of Madoc's western voyage. The manuscript went through several hands until another Welshman, John Dee, read it and used the Madoc legend in his manuscript 'Title Royal' of 1580 to help justify English claims to some of North America. That document, in turn, inspired Sir George Peckham to write his *True Reporte* published in 1583. Peckham's *True Reporte* was the first printed work to mention

Madoc and used the story to argue for the primacy of England's claims to the Americas. David Powel quickly followed with *A Historie of Cambria* in 1584, largely based on the manuscript work of Humphrey Llwyd.[33]

One of the great problems for supporters of the historicity of Madoc's voyage is that no definite mention of it occurs before Humphrey Llwyd. Madoc's contemporaries in the twelfth century are silent about his activities. One later Welsh poet, Maredudd ap Rhys, wrote a poem around 1440 in which he described a Madoc, son of Owen Gwynned, as a great sailor. While Mareddud's poem mentions no voyage to a western land, it does indicate that a seafaring Madoc tradition existed by the fifteenth century. It appears that medieval Flemish visitors to Wales circulated an earlier but now lost romance of Madoc throughout western Europe. Whether this lost romance included a western voyage is not known. These lost tales of Madoc are probably the source for claims by Dee, Peckham and others that Madoc discovered America.[34]

Although the sixteenth-century English were interested in the Madoc myth primarily as a means to strengthen their claims to territory in North America, interest continued into the seventeenth century and beyond. Sir Thomas Herbert in 1634 continued to argue for the priority of Madoc over Columbus as the discoverer of America in *A Relation of Some Years Travaile, Begunne Anno 1626 . . .*[35] Others followed with their own retellings of the Madoc myth. Supposed sightings of Welsh Indians kept interest in Madoc stimulated through the eighteenth century. Even the revelation by John Evans's mission to the American West in 1792 that no Welsh Indians seemed to exist failed to diminish belief in Madoc's voyage to America. It was Thomas Stephens's prize essay for a Welsh literary competition in 1858, *Madoc – An Essay on the Discovery of America by Madoc ab Owain Gwynedd* (later published in 1893), which finally demolished the serious historical basis for the Madoc myth.[36]

Despite Thomas Stephens's work, popular belief in the Madoc myth has continued into the twenty-first century. Reuben T. Durrett (1824–1913), the founder and president of the Filson Club of Kentucky, wrote *Traditions of the Earliest Visits of Foreigners to North America* in 1908 as a publication of the club. It focused mainly on the Madoc myth and while Durrett did not firmly endorse the historical truth of Madoc's voyage he remained highly sympathetic to the possibility. His contemporary Benjamin Franklin De Costa, the leading authority on pre-Columbian explorers of the Americas, did believe in Madoc. Later, in 1950, Zella Armstrong revived the cause of the Madoc myth with her book *Who Discovered America: The Amazing Story of*

Madoc, which argued forcefully for the existence of Madoc's voyage and colony. Inspired by such writings, the Virginia Cavalier Chapter of the Daughters of the American Revolution, at the urging of the forceful amateur historian and curator of Fort Morgan, Hatchett Chandler, got involved in the Madoc myth in 1953 by erecting a marker commemorating the Welsh prince's supposed landing at the site of Fort Morgan in Mobile Bay, Alabama. Richard Deacon followed up in 1966 with *Madoc and the Discovery of America*, which provided another detailed defence of Madoc's historicity. Even Gwyn A. Williams's highly scholarly study from 1979, *Madoc: The Making of a Myth*, which maintained a sympathetic but sceptical tone throughout, concluded on a credulous note.[37]

Meanwhile the story of Madoc's voyages to America and his establishment of a colony there led to persistent and widely believed travellers' tales of encounters with Welsh-speaking Indians in various parts of North America, starting in the sixteenth century and continuing until the end of the nineteenth century. It seemed quite reasonable that some of the Native Americans might be descendants of Madoc's people. Such a belief was further encouraged by the coincidental occurrence of words with similar sounds and meanings in Welsh and various Native American languages.

Reports of Welsh Indians were rumoured among both the English and the Spanish who visited North America during the sixteenth century. The reliability of these stories is highly questionable, however, since the supposed witnesses seldom spoke Welsh themselves. One of the most famous accounts was that of David Ingram of Barking, Essex, who reported encountering Indians using Welsh words in 1568. He had been marooned along with a hundred others on the coast of the Gulf of Mexico by the famous seaman John Hawkins after the disastrous fight with the Spanish at San Juan d'Ulloa. Miraculously Ingram and two others managed to travel across country for twelve months to what is now New Brunswick. There a French ship picked them up and returned them to England.[38]

The first Welshman to claim to have encountered Welsh Indians was the Reverend Morgan Jones. While travelling in the Carolinas in 1666, some Tuscarora Indians called Doegs captured Jones and planned to execute him. But when Jones inadvertently spoke Welsh they became excited and spared him. Jones's experience contained all the basic elements of what would become the typical story of encounter with Welsh Indians. A Welshman is captured by Native Americans and faces imminent death which is averted when the Indians discover that their captive speaks their language, Welsh. Another important element is that the Welsh Indians belong to an unidentified or unidentifiable group of Native Americans, which made future confirmation of their Welshness difficult or impossible. Still Morgan Jones's story was widely repeated and republished with greater or lesser embroidering of the facts over the years.

Other stories of Welsh Indians followed, although by the early eighteenth century their locale had moved from the rapidly civilizing East Coast to the more remote central Mississippi and upper Missouri river valleys. Even the famous frontiersman Daniel Boone (1734–1820) believed in Welsh Indians and claimed to have met blue-eyed Indians he considered to be Welsh. From the mid-1750s onwards more detailed accounts than Boone's accumulated. In 1764 the Welshman Maurice Griffith and some Shawnee Indians were captured and threatened with death by a tribe of white Indians. Griffith, of course, saved the day by speaking Welsh. About the same time Captain Isaac Stewart was captured by ordinary Indians but through good fortune, a travelling Spaniard ransomed Stewart along with a Welshman named John David. Their party crossed the Mississippi River and proceeded up the Red River where they encountered some Welsh-speaking Indians. For a change, these Indians did not threaten anyone with death. But they did tell stories of how their ancestors had crossed the seas and landed at Florida. They also displayed some parchment rolls with writing on them.

All these stories along with many others created a virtual Welsh Indian fever among the members of London's Welsh community, an already highly nationalistic group. So in 1792 they sent young John Evans to North America to find the lost Welsh Indians. Arriving in St Louis Evans aroused the suspicions of nervous Spanish officials who were worried about the British attempting to lay claim to the Louisiana Territory or turning the Indians against them. By 1793 Evans had joined the frontier trader James Mackey on an expedition up the Missouri River. After several years of adventures, including a period of residence with the Mandan tribe, Evans returned to St Louis. From there he sadly reported to his supporters in London that no Welsh Indians existed.

John Evans's report still did not settle the question of Welsh Indians. Die-hard Welsh nationalists believed that the Spanish had bought off Evans and caused his true findings about Welsh Indians to be suppressed. This conspiracy theory still survives among supporters of the reality of the Madoc myth. Even when the famous Lewis and Clark expedition of 1804–6 failed to find any evidence of Welsh Indians, some people continued to believe in their existence. A contemporary of Lewis and Clark's and the author of *Historical Sketches of Louisiana* (1812), Major Amos Stoddard maintained that

Lewis and Clark had simply missed the Welsh Indians by following the wrong tributary of the Missouri River. As a result stories of Welsh Indians continued to be reported and believed throughout the nineteenth century. The frontier painter George Catlin lived some months among the Mandans during his travels through the American West during 1829–38. He was convinced that they were descended from the Welsh.

By the beginning of the twentieth century belief in the existence of Welsh Indians was no longer respectable. The myth had been discredited by hard facts too many times. So the entry on 'Welsh Indians' in F. W. Hodge's two volume *Handbook of Indians North of Mexico*, which was published by the Bureau of American Ethnology of the Smithsonian Institution in 1910, took a completely sceptical position on the question.[39] Over the course of time, as the historian Bernard De Voto has calculated, thirteen real tribes have been identified as Welsh along with five nonexistent named tribes and another three unnamed tribes.[40] Besides the Mandans, the tribes of the Delaware, Cherokees, Comanche (Padoucas), Conestogas, Creeks, Hopis, Modocs, Navajo, Omans, Senecas, Shawnees and Tuscaroras all bore the honour of being considered the descendants of Madoc's settlers. In spite of all the contrary evidence the myth of Welsh Indians has stubbornly remained a supposed historical truth in the popular consciousness. It even appeared as fact in some school textbooks of American history well into the twentieth century.

Just as nationalism motivated the early promoters of the Madoc myth, ethnic pride had motivated other advocates of pre-Columbian discovery theories. Scandinavian Americans bitterly resented the celebration of the 400th anniversary of Columbus's discovery of America in 1892. One manifestation of that resentment was the hoax involving the Kensington Runestone. Its supporters claimed that it provided evidence of a supposed Norse expedition to the interior of North America during the mid-fourteenth century. From the very beginning scholars have declared the Runestone to be a fake. As a result it almost sank back into oblivion but Hjalmar R. Holand championed its cause in 1907 and spent the next half-century trying to get it accepted as an authentic Norse artefact. In 1948 he was rebuffed by the experts of the Smithsonian Institution, who also concluded it was a hoax. Other devastating scholar attacks followed but Holland and his followers remained unfazed. The Runestone still continues to attract believers. It is an interesting phenomenon, by the way, that artefacts allegedly proving medieval Norse settlements in the US are almost always clustered in areas with large populations of Scandinavian ancestry.[41]

In fact Scandinavian Americans were right. Norse voyagers did reach North America about the year 1000. The Icelandic sagas accounts of Leif Ericsson's colonization of Vinland in North America, widely thought to be fiction by late nineteenth-century scholars, have been proved to be historically correct by indisputable archaeological evidence. The archaeological discoveries first made by Helge Ingstad and his wife Anne Stine Ingstad in 1960 at L'Anse aux Meadows on Newfoundland have revealed a Norse settlement, which might even be the settlement established by Leif Ericsson. Convincing evidence of sustained trade between the Greenland Norse and the native peoples of the eastern coastal lands of sub-Arctic Canada has also been accumulating in various archaeological sites. Unfortunately none of these discoveries has enhanced the credibility of the story of the Kensington Runestone in the slightest degree.[42]

In the twentieth century theories about pre-Columbian explorers from sub-Saharan Africa have arisen and found a ready audience among African-Americans. Similar theories about ancient Egyptians have been around for much longer.[43] According to most writers on the subject the two main periods for African visits to the Americas before 1492 occurred during the Olmec era in Mexico from c. 1500 to c. 300 BC and during the fourteenth and fifteenth centuries.[44] The African visitors to the Olmecs were supposedly the inspiration for the great stone heads known by the archaeological nickname of 'babyfaces'. White diffusionist writers such as James Bailey and Constance Irwin assume that black Africans came to the Americas as slaves or mercenaries of the Phoenicians.[45] The black scholar Ivan van Sertima, however, contends in his writings that the blacks were ancient Nubians who had conquered Egypt and ruled it as the 25th dynasty from 750 to 650 BC. They came to Mexico as the leaders of the expeditions which included Egyptians and Phoenicians. Once in Mexico the Nubians managed to make themselves part of the Olmec ruling elite.[46] The fourteenth- and fifteenth-century visits involved the Mandingo and Songhay peoples of West Africa visiting the medieval Americas for trade and colonization. The Harvard professor of Slavic languages, Leo Wiener, pioneered this theory in the early 1920s and Van Sertima revived it in 1976.[47]

Evidence for these African visits comes from several sources. One is the transfer of African plants to the Americas or vice versa. Tobacco, cotton and maize (or corn) have been cited as evidence for such transatlantic contacts but have been discredited as genuine pre-Columbian transfers. The evolution of cotton does seem to prove that contact took place between the Old World and the Americas. But that contact took the form of seeds drifting from the Old World to the Americas in the distant past rather than humans carrying the cotton plants on their voyages. Certainly the chronology of domestic cotton and corn growing in the Old World and the Americas does not support the existence of African contacts with pre-Columbian America.[48] Supposed negroid skeletal remains of pre-Columbian provenance are also not widely accepted as genuine or convincing evidence. Races are not that distinct skeletally. The pre-Columbian Negro skeletons may simply be Native American skeletons.

The purported representations of negroid people in pre-Columbian statues and pictures may actually be just the depiction of Native Americans with seemingly negroid features. It also may be some artistic convention that is not yet understood. Some diffusionist scholars, however, prefer to see true black Africans in these presentations. Alexander von Wuthenau, a German expatriate living in Mexico, is the great advocate of using the artistic evidence of portraiture to prove contacts between the Americas and the Old World. In his *Unexpected Faces in Ancient America: The Historical Testimony of the Pre-Columbian Artist* (1975) he sees the presence of all sorts of Old World peoples, including black Africans.[49] Most scholars remain sceptical of this sort of evidence since much remains to be learned about the artistic conventions of the ancient Americans. Some Native Americans had negroid features but had never been in contact with Africans. Various types of physiognomies can be found distributed in all races, which weakens the impact of Von Wuthenau's evidence.

Oral traditions and legends have been cited to prove the occurrence of Mandingo voyages to medieval America. The problem is that the king of Mali who supposedly sponsored these voyages, Abubakari II, is a rather shadowy figure. Abubakari II (or Abu Bakr) was the grandson of Sundiata (fl. first half of the thirteenth century), the founder of the dynasty of mansas (rulers) of Mali. Abubakari II was also the brother of Mansa Musa (d. 1332?), the most famous ruler of medieval Mali. A paucity of reliable documentation makes it impossible to compile an accurate listing of the mansas of Mali with the actual years of their reigns. The great North African historian Ibn Khaldun (1332–1406) does not even credit Abubakari with having reigned as a mansa of Mali. Other sources and oral traditions place him as a mansa during or before the years *c.* 1307–11.[50] According to these same oral traditions Abubakari thought that there were lands on the other side of the Atlantic Ocean. So in 1307 he sent out an expedition of about four hundred ships to find out what lay across the sea to the west. Only one of those ships returned and it reported that an enormous and powerful current had carried off the others to

81

the west before land had been sighted. Undaunted, Abubakari gathered an even bigger fleet, according to some reports numbering over two thousand ships, and prepared to sail west with himself in personal command. In 1311 (or 1307) he appointed his brother Kankan Musa (i.e., Mansa Musa) as regent and then departed. He was never heard from or seen again.[51]

The story of Abubakari II is based on oral traditions passed on by the West African griots, who specialized in learning and narrating the oral history of their people. Research has shown that the griots' historical narrative is often accurate, even remarkably accurate, although not invariably so. Many questions exist concerning the historicity of Abubakari's voyage. First, was Abubakari ever a mansa of Mali? That is by no means certain. Second, why was his fleet so suspiciously large? Two thousand ships, even if they were dugout canoes or reed boats with crews of only four to ten people, is still a very large expedition to sail off into the unknown. It just does not ring true. Third, supporters of African voyages to pre-Columbian America, such as Ivan Van Sertima, claim that many such voyages were made. But even the legends of Abubakari belie that contention. Instead, to Abubakari and his people the western Atlantic was a great mystery. There was no memory of previous African voyages to guide them. That does not seem credible if so many earlier voyages took place. It would appear that the story of Abubakari probably has less basis in historical events than the fictional travels of Sir John Mandeville during the European Middle Ages.

Some people have constructed pre-Columbian discovery theories not because of national or ethnic pride, but apparently because they simply enjoy a good, bizarre story that upsets the more mundane, accepted theories. It is more fun to believe that the ancient Egyptians reached the Americas and brought those lands the benefits of their civilization. After all, Egyptians had pyramids and so did the ancient peoples of Central America. So obviously the Egyptians taught pyramid building to the Native Americans. Such theories ignore the fact that Egyptian pyramids were tombs while Central American pyramids were platforms for temples. They also ignore the chronological problem that virtually 2,000 years separated the Pyramid Age in Egypt from the building of the first pyramids in Central America.[52]

Bizarre theories have abounded in spite of such problems. Harold Gladwin, a talented amateur archaeologist, sullied a previously pristine record for scholarship when in 1947 he suggested, on the basis of no convincing evidence, that a fleet of Alexander the Great's made its way across the Pacific Ocean and so brought higher civilization to the benighted Native Americans. His theory is so outlandish that some scholars have suggested that it was actually an elaborate practical joke on his friend the archaeologist A.V. Kidder, a suggestion that Gladwin supporters hotly deny.[53] From the mid-1970s to the 1980s Barry Fell, a retired marine biologist from Harvard University, has waded into the field of bizarre archaeological theories with a series of books that suggest that ancient Celts, Egyptians, Phoenicians, Libyans and Hebrews all visited and settled in North America in the centuries prior to the birth of Christ. His theory primarily relies on supposed inscriptions that Fell and his supporters claim to find in profusion all across the eastern US.[54] Professional archaeologists and geologists, however, do not consider the inscriptions to be man-made, let alone readable. Instead they present evidence to show that the supposed inscriptions are merely scratches on rocks produced by glaciation, erosion and weathering. They also point out Fell's propensity to cite as solid evidence such well-known archaeological frauds as the Davenport Tablets.[55] Such flawed scholarship did not prevent Fell's books from outselling more reputable works by mainstream scholars nor does it prevent television shows such as *Terra x* and *In Search Of* from citing him as an expert, a status professional archaeologists indignantly deny him. He is hardly alone.

FIRST PEOPLE?

> Can it still be asked from whence came the men who people America?
> VOLTAIRE (1764)[56]

> Great question has arisen from whence came those aboriginal inhabitants of America? THOMAS JEFFERSON (1787)[57]

All of the hypotheses about pre-Columbian visits that have been discussed so far speculate about Old World peoples visiting the Americas prior to 1492. In all cases the visitors encountered native peoples already living there. Columbus mistakenly called these people Indians, a name that has persisted ever since. The presence of these Native Americans raised the questions of how they got to the Americas, when they arrived and where they came from. Various scholars and writers have attempted to answer these questions for over four hundred years and no definitive answers have emerged, so inevitably a wide assortment of pseudohistorical and pseudoscientific explanations have been put forward. It is important to remember that at the time many of these conjectures were first suggested they were not all that outlandish given the state of historical and scientific knowledge prior to the middle of the nineteenth century. Since then most of these hypotheses have been discredited by sound researches in archaeology, science and history and they have entered the cultic milieu of pseudohistory.

The discovery of the Americas revived interest in the story of Atlantis with some people speculating that the Native Americans were Atlantean refugees. Others went further and identified North America as Atlantis or a remnant of Atlantis with the Native Americans as the survivors of the cataclysm that devastated the lost continent.[58] Beliefs in the Native Americans as Atlantean refugees and in Atlantis as America moved from learned culture to popular culture as advances in science and history discredited the Atlantis myth. Other hypotheses about Indian origins appear in the wake of Columbus' voyages. One of the earliest and most persistent hypothesis claimed that Native Americans were descendants of Carthaginian colonists. Gonzalo Fernández de Oviedo y Valdés first proposed it in 1535, basing his contention on the mistaken belief that Aristotle credited the Carthaginians with the discovery of a great island in the Atlantic Ocean about 590 BC. Oviedo's hypothesis quickly attracted other Spanish supporters such as Alejo Vanegras de Bustos, whose *Primera parte de las differencia de libros q ay en el universo* (1540) claimed that both Phoenician and Carthaginian settlers were responsible for populating the Americas. Francisco López de Gómara, secretary to Hernán Cortés and chronicler of the early Spanish empire in the Americas, added a new aspect to the Carthaginian hypothesis in his *Historia general de las Indias* (1552). He suggested that the Carthaginian explorer Hanno discovered the Americas during his explorations down the west coast of Africa around 490 BC.[59]

The Carthaginian hypothesis proved popular among Spanish writers and was picked up by writers from other nations. The Portuguese explorer and historian Antonio Galvão in 1555 wrote a history of the exploration of the world that mentioned the Carthaginian settlement of the Americas in 590 BC.[60] It was an obvious choice for early modern Europeans to suggest the Carthaginians as the discoverers and settlers of the Americas. They were an intrepid seafaring people and their great city of Carthage was founded in 814 BC by Phoenicians from the city of Tyre, another accomplished seafaring people. Early modern Europeans would have been very familiar with the Carthaginians because of their epic wars with Rome from 264 to 165 BC. At the same time, because detailed knowledge about the Carthaginians was not available, they were also a mysterious people which actually made them more plausible as the ancestors of Native Americans. Other Spanish writers repeated the Carthaginian hypothesis of Oviedo: Vanegras de Bustos and López de Gómara along with that undiscriminating enumerator of theories about pre-Columbian visitors, Gregorio García, whose *Origen de los indios del nuevo mundo e Indias occidentales* appeared in 1607. Later in the seventeenth century some Spanish historians such as Juan de Torquemada rejected the Carthaginian hypothesis because they doubted whether any ancient people of the Mediterranean Sea had any knowledge of the Americas.[61]

Non-Spanish writers, such as French scholar Robert Comte in 1644, also began to advocate the Carthaginian hypothesis. In 1671 the English geographer John Ogilby (1600–1676) repeated Comte's assertions. Another Englishman, traveller John Josselyn (fl. 1638–1675), gave the Carthaginian Hanno credit for reaching America, although he was a strong supporter of the idea that Tartars discovered and populated the Americas.[62]

The Carthaginian hypothesis broadened into Canaanite and Phoenician variants. The first scholar to suggest that the Native Americans were the descendants of Canaanites was Mexican writer Juan Suarez de Peralta (*c.* 1536–1591). His *Tratado del descumbrimiento de las Indias*, written in 1580 but not published until 1878, suggested multiple origins for the Native Americans that included the Carthaginians and Canaanites. The importance of a Canaanite origin hypothesis was that, due to the Biblical curse on Ham and Canaan, it provided a justification for the Spanish enslaving the Native Americans. In his *History of New France* (1609) the early seventeenth-century French historian Marc Lescarbot considered the possibility that Canaanites fled from their Israelite conquerors and settled in America. In 1612 English writer William Strachey reached the same conclusions. Both writers cite idolatry and the practice of cannibalism among the natives of North America as evidence of Canaanite ancestry, since the Canaanites had engaged in, or were alleged to have engaged in, such practices. Finally Cotton Mather, in his book *The Serviceable Man* of 1690, also suggested that Canaanites came to America to escape the invasion and conquest of their land by Joshua and the Children of Israel. He also argued that as the descendants of Ham and Canaan Native Americans were subject to the Biblical curse. Therefore the wars of the English settlers against the tribes of New England and their displacement were justified. In the twentieth century supporters of the Canaanite origin hypothesis rightly tended to merge it with the Phoenician origin hypothesis since both groups belonged to the same basic ethnic and cultural group. Needless to say, the biblically based Canaanite origin theory has no basis in archaeological evidence.[63]

In some cases writers appear to have incorrectly used the terms 'Carthaginian' and 'Phoenician' interchangeably, a practice that has continued to the present. When writers properly distinguish between the Phoenicians and Carthaginians the general pattern has been to attribute any supposed voyages before 600 BC to the Phoenicians and those after 500 BC to the Carthaginians. Carthage barred the ships of all other cities and peoples of the Mediterranean basin from sailing through the Straits of Gilbraltar about 509 BC and that blockade may have included ships from the Phoenician mother country. After that date only Carthaginian ships would have had access to the waters of the Atlantic and the opportunity to reach the Americas.

The Spanish scholar Andrés González de Barcía Carballido y Zúñiga revived the hypothesis of a Phoenician discovery and settlement of the Americas when he published his revision of Gregorio García's *Origen de los indios del nuevo mundo* in 1729. From then on Phoenician visitors and colonists became a standard part of the fringe scholarship of ancient American history. In 1781 the French scholar Antoine Court de Gebelin speculated that the Phoenicians were in cordial contact with Native Americans before 2000 BC, a chronological impossibility in light of the more accurate dating of modern archaeology. Other Phoenician hypotheses followed in the nineteenth century, including Sir George Jones's *An Original History of Aboriginal America* (1843) and John B. Newman's *Origin of the Red Man* (1852).[64]

In 1872 the most enigmatic of the supposed Phoenician artefacts came to light – the Paraíba Stone. A man named Joaquim Alves da Costa claimed to have found, near the Paraíba River in Brazil, a broken stone that had an inscription in a strange alphabet carved on it. After transcribing the inscription, Costa sent the copy to Rio de Janeiro for study. Brazil had no experts in ancient Semitic languages but the conscientious naturalist Ladislau Netto took up the assignment, learned Hebrew, ultimately determining that the writing on the stone was Phoenician, and then translated it. His translation described how ten ships with Phoenicians from Sidon sailed from Ezion-Geber and around Africa in 534 BC. Storms blew some of them west to the coast of Brazil, where they carved the inscription. Immediately the French scholar Ernest Renan attacked the Paraíba inscription as a fake and others soon joined him. By 1885 the hapless Netto felt compelled to publish a retraction of his original conclusions and even suggested five possible suspects for composing the hoax. Despite this setback and the fact that Costa disappeared with the stone, some people continued to believe in its authenticity. No accredited scholar ever saw the stone at first-hand. Even the original location of the find was in great doubt since Brazil has two different Paraíba regions. Still, the story of the Paraíba Stone continued to attract believers.[65]

During the 1960s Cyrus Gordon, a respected professor of Semitic languages and an ardent diffusionist, revived the Paraíba Stone's claims to authenticity. Basically Gordon asserted that the Paraíba inscription contained Phoenician grammatical constructions unknown in 1872. These same constructions were originally used during the 1870s to argue against the stone's authenticity. Subsequent research during the twentieth century, Gordon said, revealed that the anomalous grammatical usages in the Paraíba Stone were genuine. Other equally qualified specialists disagree with his conclusions and continue to declare the Paraíba Stone a hoax. That judgement remains the opinion of archaeologists and historians in general.[66]

Most hypotheses of Phoenician voyages to the Americas had them crossing the Atlantic Ocean to get there, but not all. In 1892 Thomas Crawford Johnston joined supporters of a Phoenician presence in the Americas. He gave the story a new aspect in 1913 with his book *Did the Phoenicians Discover America?* He claimed that the Phoenicians of King Hiram I sailed down the Red Sea, over the Indian Ocean and across the Pacific Ocean to reach the Americas.[67]

The Phoenician hypothesis continued to attract many supporters during the twentieth century in addition to Cyrus Gordon. One was Joseph Corey Ayoob, who in 1951 privately published *Were the Phoenicians the First to Discover America?* That work reappeared in a second edition in 1964 and was followed by another study of the Paraíba Stone in 1971. Reaching a much wider audience was the popular writer Charles M. Boland. In his book *They All Discovered America* (1961), he included a chapter that claimed Phoenicians visited America prior to 480 BC and again in 480 BC, 310 BC and 146 BC. The problem was that he was talking about the closely related Carthaginians. Frederick J. Pohl, in his *Atlantic Crossings before Columbus* (1961), also conflates the Phoenicians with the Carthaginians. In contrast Constance Irwin's *Fair Gods and Stone Faces* (1963) carefully distinguished between Phoenician and Carthaginian voyages to America. Her hypothesis claims that Phoenician traders, accompanied by Negro slaves, reached Mexico about 800 BC and helped to stimulate the rise of the Olmec civilization. Unfortunately, while 800 BC was the earliest date for artefacts from Olmec archaeological sites examined by 1963, subsequent research pushed back the beginning of Olmec civilization to 1500 BC, well before the possibility of Phoenician influence. Irwin also suggests that refugees from Tyre, who fled during the siege by Nebuchadnezzar of Babylon from 587 to 574 BC, came to the Americas and further stimulated the native civilizations of Mesoamerica. Cyrus Gordon's *Before Columbus: Links between the Old World and Ancient America* (1971) reached

the same basic conclusions as Irwin and supplied further archaeological and linguistic evidence of Phoenician visits. A few years later
James Bailey in *The God-Kings and the Titans* (1973) followed Irwin
in asserting the presence of Phoenician colonies in pre-Columbian
America. Barry Fell, an advocate of an ancient Celtic presence in
America, also believes that Phoenicians visited the Americas and
supplies supposed linguistic and archaeological evidences for their
presence in his bestselling *America BC* (1976). Unfortunately, in Fell's
case, the specifics of the arrival dates and the routes followed by these
alleged Phoenician settlers and traders are much vaguer than those of
Irwin and Bailey. Still, all these writers show that the hypothesis of
Phoenician visits and colonies is very much alive and well.

The Phoenicians and Carthaginians were probably the greatest
sailors of the Mediterranean. Their ships were capable of oceanic
travel, and archaeological evidence has been discovered that indicates
they reached the Azores. Just how much they really knew about geography and navigation will never be known for sure. Their jealously
guarded secrets have been lost forever in the ravages of war and time.
Technically it is possible that the Phoenicians and Carthaginians
reached the Americas, but no archaeological evidence has yet been
discovered to prove the contentions of Irwin, Gordon, Bailey, Fell and
others. Since even the fleeting Norse presence in Vinland left definite
archaeological remains at L'Anse aux Meadows in Newfoundland, it
seems logical that the allegedly more extensive Phoenician and
Carthaginian presence would have left similar evidence. The absence
of such remains is strong circumstantial evidence that the Phoenicians and Carthaginians never reached the Americas.

During the sixteenth century many hypotheses claimed that the
biblical Hebrews or ancient Jews were the ancestors of all or some of
the aborigines of the Americas. There are several variations on the
Hebrew-origin hypothesis. One contentious aspect concerned the extent of the role played by Hebrew immigrants. Some writers claimed
that all Native Americans were descendants of Hebrew settlers, but
others believed that the Hebrews had settled among a preexisting
population of aboriginal peoples and were assimilated. For example, one theory pointed out that servants of King Solomon travelled
to his mines in Ophir for gold and located Ophir in America. Some
of these Hebrews remained behind and either completely populated
the land of Ophir or merged with its original inhabitants. Most
supporters of the Ophirite hypothesis favoured the latter view.[68]

Other theories claimed that various Hebrew groups fled to the
Americas as refugees from war and persecution. The most famous
hypothesis identified the Ten Lost Tribes of Israel as the ancestors

of the Native Americans. The biblical kingdom of Israel consisted of ten of the twelve tribes of Israel. It came under attack by the warlike Assyrian Empire and in 722 BC the Assyrian king Sargon II overran Israel, captured its capital of Samaria, and carried off 30,000 captives. According to 2 Kings 17:6 and 23, 'the king of Assyria captured Samaria and carried the Israelites away to Assyria, and placed them in Halah, and on the Habor, the river of Gozan, and in the cities of the Medes . . . So Israel was exiled from their own land to Assyria until this day.' For many people, this event marked the end of the Ten Tribes of Israel. The neighbouring peoples of Media and Assyria simply absorbed them into their own populations, and the exiles lost their religious and ethnic identity. The apocryphal book of 2 Esdras 13:40–45, however, supplied the following intriguing information, indicating that the Ten Tribes were not finished at all, they were merely lost or hiding.

> These are the ten tribes that were led away from their own land into captivity in the days of King Hosea, whom Shalmaneser the king of the Assyrians led captive; he took them across the river, and they were taken into another land. But they formed this plan for themselves, that they would leave the multitude of nations and go to a more distant region, where mankind had never lived, that there at least they might keep their statutes which they had not kept in their own land. And they went in by the narrow passages of the Euphrates river. For at that time the Most High performed signs for them, and stopped the channels of the river until they had passed over. Through that region there was a long way to go, a journey of a year and a half; and that country called Arzareth.

According to 2 Esdras, the Ten Lost Tribes would reappear during the last days of the world. Endless speculations arose as to where the Ten Lost Tribes were and what they were doing. *Arzareth* literally means 'another land', but what land? Various places in Africa, Asia and Europe have been suggested as possible sites. The European discovery of the Americas provided yet another possible candidate for Arzareth – that 'more distant region, where mankind had never listed'. The Ten Lost Tribes hypothesis remains the most popular of the Hebrew origin hypotheses from the sixteenth century onwards.[69]

Other hypotheses focused on the surviving remnant of the twelve tribes of the Hebrews, the king of Judah and its successors. Jerusalem, the capital of Judah, fell in 586 BC to the armies of Babylon and its inhabitants were carried away. Most of the survivors or their descendants eventually managed to return to their homeland, but some writers suggest that some refugees fled to the Americas and became the ancestors of the Native Americans. That belief is the foundation of *The Book of Mormon*. Mormons traditionally believed that the peoples described in *The Book of Mormon* populated all of the Americas. Recent Mormon scholarship has scaled back those claims and only credits the Hebrews with populating Mexico's Isthmus of Tehuantepec.[70] Other writers have speculated that Hebrew or Jewish refugees came to America after the destruction of Jerusalem by the Romans in AD 70. Another possibility involves survivors of the Bar Kochba revolt in AD 135. Other traumatic events that might have transformed the Jews into refugees are the various barbarian invasions of the Roman empire during the fifth century or the Islamic invasion of the eastern and southern Mediterranean coasts during the seventh century. Generally the later in time a Hebrew group supposedly reached the Americas the less it would have been responsible for populating those continents. These later Hebrew immigrants would have instead formed enclaves or colonies within the existing societies of the Native Americans.

One question that arises is why the Hebrews have been such popular and perennial candidates as ancestors of the Native Americans. The eminent anthropologist Robert Wauchope attributes this popularity to the widespread knowledge of the ancient Hebrews that the Bible makes possible. Prior to the rise of modern anthropology the Hebrews were by far the best-known ancient people in an ethnographic sense. Furthermore, as the English writer John Ogilby pointed out in 1671, traumatic events of the ancient world scattered the Hebrews or Jews far from their ancestral homeland. European travellers grew accustomed to finding Jews in all sorts of seemingly out-of-the-way places, including the Americas. Therefore when they encountered strange customs and practices among the indigenous peoples they visited, they naturally used their knowledge of the biblical Hebrews as the measure for comparison. Lacking valid theoretical concepts of anthropology these European observers were unable to distinguish among shared cultural traits that were the result of parallel evolution and independent invention and those that might have resulted from possible cultural diffusion. If a Native American tribe practised a custom such as circumcision it was commonly and erroneously assumed that they had Hebrew antecedents or contacts in the past.[71]

Despite the high profile of the ancient Hebrews in European consciousness the first Europeans to explore or settle in the Americas after 1492 did not turn to Hebrew hypotheses of Indian origins. The first known reference may be in *The Decades of the New World* by Peter Martyr de Anglería (*c.* 1455–1526), who stated that Christopher Columbus thought Hispaniola was the land of Ophir. That suggestion opened up the possibility that the natives were descended from Hebrew visitors. Spanish writers, however, did not advocate Hebrew origin hypotheses until the last quarter of the sixteenth century. The first person definitely to promote the Ten Lost Tribes version of the Hebrew origins hypothesis was Johannes Fredericus Lumnius of the Low Countries in his *De extremo Dei Iudicio vocationes* (About the Summoning of the Final Judgment of God) of 1567 and *De vicinitate extremi judicii Dei et consummationis saeculi* (About the Nearness of the Final Judgment of God and the Fulfilment of the End of Days) of 1594. Although not widely circulated, Lumnius established the theological foundations of the Ten Lost Tribes hypothesis. Following 2 Esdras, he claimed that they escaped the Assyrians and settled in America. The French scholar Gilbert Genebard followed Lumnius in the same year with his *Chronographia*, which also supported the Ten Lost Tribes hypothesis.[72]

Although the eminent Bartolomé de Las Casas and other Spanish scholars rejected the Hebrew origins hypothesis, some Spanish scholars studying the natives of Mexico found it a reasonable explanation of supposed similarities between Hebrew and Native American customs. Diego Durán, Juan Suárez de Peralta (*c.* 1536–1591), and Juan de Tovar closely studied the aborigines of Mexico and found interesting parallels with the Hebrews. Writing about 1580, both Peralta and Durán pointed out how similar the story of the Ten Lost Tribes' escape from the Assyrians to the land of Arzareth was to the Aztec legends of wandering from their homeland of Aztlan. Other scholars put forward their own versions of the Hebrew origins hypothesis. An interesting twist on the Ten Lost Tribes hypothesis appeared in 1681 in the book *Tratado único y singular del origen de los indios occidentales de Perú, México, Santa Fé y Chile* (A unique and singular tract about the origin of the West Indians of Peru, Mexico, Santa Fe and Chile), written by Diego Andrés Rocha (*c.* 1607–1688), a Jesuit and canon lawyer, to show why the Native Americans behaved poorly. Although he believed that Native Americans had ancestry from early Spanish visitors, he believed they were largely descended from Tartars and Hebrews, which accounted for their wildness.[73]

Jose de Acosta and other eminent scholars rejected the possibility of Native Americans being descendants of Hebrews. As Acosta sensibly asked: 'How can it be, when the Jews have been so assiduous in preserving their language and ancient customs, to the point that in every part of the world where they live today they differ from the rest, that in the Indies alone they have forgotten their ancestry, their law, their ceremonies, their Messiah, and finally all their Jew-ishness?'[74] Good sense arguments have never stopped absurd theories, and the Hebrew origin hypothesis was no exception. Instead it spread to northern Europe. In 1644 the Jewish community of Amsterdam was rocked by the report that Antonio de Montezinos (Aaron Levi) had discovered the Ten Lost Tribes in the Spanish province of Peru. Montezinos claimed that while travelling in the region of Quito he and his Native American guide Francisco confided in each other that they were practising Jews. Emboldened by this information, Fran-cisco led Montezinos on a seventeen-day journey into the wilderness. At an unknown river Francisco made a signal and some white people started to cross the river. Although the cautious white people would not allow Montezinos to cross the river into their land, he learned that they were Hebrews of the tribe of Reuben. The whites were on friendly terms with the native tribes in the area and had converted many of them to Judaism. Together they were plotting to overthrow the Spanish. Needless to say, Montezinos' news was greeted with en-thusiasm and apocalyptic musings. Menasseh Ben Israel, the great rabbi of Amsterdam, used Montezinos' story to persuade Oliver Cromwell and other Puritan leaders of the short-lived English re-public to allow Jews back into England. More importantly, Mon-tezinos' story spread far more widely than any of the earlier tales about Native Americans being descendants of the Ten Lost Tribes. From that point the Ten Lost Tribes hypothesis firmly entered the popular consciousness of Western society and has remained strongly ensconced ever since.[75]

James Adair, the eighteenth-century historian of North Ameri-can Indians, was another great popularizer of the Hebrew origins hy-pothesis, and others followed in the early nineteenth century. Elias Boudinot and Ethan Smith were early nineteenth-century American writers who accepted the truth of the Ten Lost Tribes version of the Hebrew origins hypothesis. They also probably deeply influenced the thinking of Joseph Smith, Jr, the founder of Mormonism. Other writ-ers, such as Anne (or Barbara) Simon in her *The Ten Tribes of Israel Historically Identified with the Aborigines of the Western Hemi-sphere* (1836), accused the early Spanish priests and officials of sup-pressing evidence that the Native Americans were of Hebrew ancestry. Edward King, Viscount Kingsborough, also supported the Hebrew origins hypothesis and agreed with Simon's suspicions. The Ten Lost Tribes hypothesis has managed to find committed backers ever since.[76]

Other versions of the Hebrew origins hypothesis have not had such long careers or such large followings in popular culture, with the exception of the adherents of *The Book of Mormon*. One interesting hypothesis concerns the burial site and supposed Hebrew inscriptions found at Bat Creek, Tennessee during the late nineteenth century. In 1894 Cyrus Thomas, a Smithsonian Institution archaeologist, identified the Bat Creek site as a Cherokee burial ground. That identification has been challenged in the twentieth century by various writers including the irrepressible Cyrus Gordon, professor of Semitic languages. They claim that the Bat Creek inscription is Hebrew and related to the Bar Kochba rebellion that took place during AD 135 in Roman Judea. Gordon attempted to bolster the theory by pointing out that the Bat Creek inscription ties in quite nicely with various finds of Roman and Bar Kochba coins in the Kentucky and Tennessee area. Unfortunately, experts consider these finds to be fakes. Gordon's willingness to consider the possibility that these inscriptions were made by refugees from the defeat of the Jewish Revolt in AD 70 does not help his case because the arguments against it are almost as strong as those against the Bar Kochba rebellion.[77]

The Hebrew origins hypothesis continues to attract new supporters. Professional archaeologists and anthropologists, on the other hand, completely dismiss it in all its versions. They insist that no convincing evidence of pre-Columbian Hebrew visitors has yet been found, and strongly feel that none ever will, because no such visits took place. Still the romance and mystery associated with the Ten Lost Tribes as well as other aspects of the history of the Jewish people have made the Hebrews prime candidates for being pre-Columbian visitors to and settlers of the Americas, at least in the realm of popular culture. It is an odd fate for an ancient people never well known for being seafarers.

Some Spaniards, such as Pedro Sarmiento de Gamboa, claimed that Ulysses and his Greeks visited and even settled in the Americas so it was inevitable that someone would propose that Trojans also visited the Americas. The leading advocate of the Trojan origin theory was English adventurer Thomas Morton (*c.* 1590–1647), who wrote *New English Canaan; or New Canaan, Containing an Abstract of Three Books* in 1637. Morton claimed to discern Latin and Greek words in the languages of the native tribes of New England. That combination of languages caused him to suspect that the Trojans were the ancestors of the Native Americans since supposedly the Trojans would have used both Latin and Greek. If Aeneas and his Trojan refugees could wander the Mediterranean until they eventually settled down in Italy, why could later Trojans led by their leader Brutus not have fled war-torn Italy for the Americas? In 1729 Spanish historian Andrés González de Barcía Caballido y Zúñiga added the

Trojan-origin hypothesis to his revision of Gregorio García's 1607 work on Native American origins. The problem is that no archaeological evidence backs up Morton's hypothesis, which was pure speculation backed up by a few dubious linguistic parallels.[78]

The early years of the nineteenth century saw the appearance of the Hindu origins hypothesis. Hindus did not stand high in the historical consciousness of Europeans and were not known as a seafaring people so they were not considered to be possible visitors or settlers of the Americas. That changed in 1820 when the American lawyer and amateur archaeologists Caleb Atwater (1778–1867) published *Descriptions of the Antiquities Discovered in the State of Ohio and Other Western States* as part of the first volume of the *Transactions* of the American Antiquarian Society. In this work Atwater identified Hindu settlers as the mysterious mound-builders of North America. The artefact that convinced Atwater of this Hindu connection was a Native American vase with three faces on it called the Triune Vessel. Atwater claimed that the three faces were the Hindu gods Brahma, Vishnu and Shiva. Soon after, Judge John Haywood of Tennessee echoed Atwater's Hindu hypothesis in his *The Natural and Aboriginal History of Tennessee* in 1823. Because Hindu immigrants were not really the mound-builders and no other evidence accumulated to sustain the theory, it died out in the face of competition from more plausible theories.[79]

The Hindus, however, were not permanently retired as pre-Columbian visitors to the Americas. The German traveller, naturalist and anthropologist Alexander von Humboldt (1769–1859) noted strong resemblances between the Hindu and Mexican calendars. In 1866 the French architect Eugene-Emmanuel Viollet-le-Duc (1814–1879) pointed out similarities between the design of ancient Mexican buildings and the architecture of certain buildings in southern India. These and other writers saw correspondences between the trio of Mexican gods Ho-Huitzilopochtli-Tlaloc and the three Hindu deities Brahma-Vishnu-Shiva.[80] The leading twentieth-century exponents of Hindu contacts with the Americas were Gordon Ekholm of the American Museum of Natural History and Robert Heine-Geldern. Both men were respected prehistorians and supporters of the hypothesis that various contacts took place between ancient America and East and South Asia, particularly China. They believe that the Hindus learned of the existence of the Americas from Han Chinese merchants, who had already visited the Mexico. Hindu merchants, besides trading with Southeast Asia, followed the Chinese to the Americas. Ekholm and Heine-Geldern think that these visits by Hindus of India and Indochina probably took place around 700. They cite many cultural parallels as evidence, such as the lotus motif used by both cultures in decorations, and the common shape of Maya and Cambodian pyramids. Other scholars have long suggested that the similarities between the games of patolli in Mexico and parchisi in India provide strong evidence for contact. The problem is that many of Ekholm and Heine-Geldern's parallels are too far apart chronologically to convince other scholars that diffusion of culture occurred. Sceptics suggest that independent invention or parallel evolution provides a more plausible explanation of these cultural similarities. These scholars also point to the curious selectivity of this supposed cultural diffusion. No useful plants or animals were exchanged and the Hindus failed to teach Native Americans to adopt the wheel for hauling heavy loads. Cultural exchanges were limited to art when many other useful items could easily have been exchanged. Given the weakness of such circumstantial evidence, most scholars believe that Hindus did not reach the Americas in the era before Columbus.[81]

Early European visitors to the Americas also made the obvious observation that Native Americans looked East Asian. Speculations about Chinese visits and settlements in the Americas began with Antonio Galvão in 1555 when he pointed out that the ancient Chinese were great sailors and that the natives of the West Indies bore a strong physical resemblance to the Chinese.[82] Others followed his lead during the sixteenth century and in 1607 Gregorio García enshrined the idea along with a host of other hypotheses about pre-Columbian visitors to the Americas in his *Origen de los indios de el nuevo mundo, y Indias occidentales*. García also lumped the Chinese together with the Tartars, Scythians and Siberians as ancestors of the Native Americans.[83] Meanwhile in 1590 the Jesuit scholar and missionary José de Acosta had published his *Natural and Moral History of the Indies* which speculated that Old World peoples had reached the Americas by land. He suggested that they walked over some sort of land-bridge connecting Asia and North America or that they had to cross only a narrow strait. Acosta thus anticipated Semën Dezhnëv's discovery of the Bering Strait in 1648 by some sixty years.[84] Such speculation turned attention to the Tartars, Siberians and Scythians, terms used by European writers for the peoples living closest to this land-bridge or strait, as the likely ancestors of the Native Americans. The peoples of Siberia became better known in the last hundred years and were increasingly seen as both distinct ethnically and culturally distinct from the Chinese but with affinities to the Native Americans. This information coalesced into the venerable Bering land-bridge theory of the peopling of the Americas, which although under challenge has yet to be replaced by a more plausible alternative.[85] Meanwhile speculation about Chinese visitors, settlements and cultural contributions to pre-Columbian Native American cultures has continued unabated for the last four centuries and has even recently come to the forefront of the fringe ideas about the past.

THE CHINA SYNDROME

> Timaeus remarks that the greatest offence in the writing of history is falsification; he therefore advises all those whom he has convicted of making false statements to find some other name for their books, and call them anything they may choose, but not history . . . I would agree with him that truth must play the dominant role in works of this kind . . . if history is deprived of the truth, we are left with nothing but an idle, unprofitable tale. POLYBIUS (c. 146 BC)[86]

In 2002 a new player entered the arena of speculations about the first peopling of the Americas and other pre-Columbian explorations. His name was Gavin Menzies and his book was *1421: The Year China Discovered America* (if you bought it in the United States) or *1421: The Year China Discovered the World* (if you bought it in Great Britain). Menzies claims that during 1421 a fleet of Chinese ships sailed around the world and visited every part of it but western Europe and the Mediterranean basin. In some places they even established colonies. China's Ming dynasty, in particular Emperor Zhu Di, sponsored these voyages under the leadership of a Turkish eunuch admiral named Zheng He (Cheng Ho). Between 1405 and 1433 seven expeditions sailed from China.[87] It is the sixth expedition of 1421–2 that forms the focus of Menzies' book. Zheng He did not accompany this expedition for its entire voyage because he was back in China during 1422. Menzies starts from that known fact and speculates that the rest of the great fleet sailed throughout the world exploring and colonizing. One fleet commanded by Yang Qing left before the main fleet under the overall command of Zheng He. Yang Qing's mission was to take astronomical readings that would be useful for determining longitude. Later Zheng He followed with the main fleet. At Sumatra he divided the expedition into four parts before entering the Indian Ocean. Staying behind with the smallest portion of the ships, Zheng He took care of diplomatic business in Southeast Asia and returned to China.

The other three parts of the fleet were left under the respective commands of the eunuchs Hong Bao, Zhou Man and Zhou Wen. Travelling together, the three eunuchs sailed around the Cape of Good Hope with a mighty squadron of 75 to 90 great treasure ships.

Making their way up the west coast of Africa the Chinese reached the Cape Verde Islands, where they established a settlement. At that point Zhou Wen sailed west and reached Hispaniola and Cuba while Hong Bao and Zhou Man went to South America. After leaving settlers on the Caribbean islands Zhou Wen sailed up the coast of North America and following the winds and the currents his fleet looped its way around the North Atlantic, missing Europe and the Maghreb and making its way back to Cape Verde. After presumably checking in with the new Chinese colony, Zhou Wen voyaged west once more to Hispaniola, Cuba and up the eastern seaboard of the present day US. This time the Chinese continued to sail north and made their way into the Davis Strait between Greenland and Baffin Island. The intrepid Zhou Wen and his wooden ships managed to circumnavigate Greenland and reached Iceland. From there the Chinese fleet cruised along the northern coast of Russia and Siberia and passed through the Bering Strait on its way back to China. Thus Zhou Wen rounded an icebound northern Greenland and navigated the treacherous Northeast Passage over a century before Europeans even thought to look for it. He also managed to accomplish what European seamen would fail to do until Baron Nils Nordenskjold negotiated the Northeast Passage in a steam-powered metal ship in 1878–9.

Meanwhile Hong Bao and Zhou Man continued to travel south along the eastern coastline of South America. Reaching the Straits of Magellan they managed to sail through successfully into the Pacific Ocean, preceding Magellan by a century. On the Pacific side of the strait they separated with Hong Bao heading south and Zhou Man heading north. Hong Bao reached the South Shetland Islands off the Antarctic Peninsula. From there his fleet sailed east utilizing the winds of the Roaring Forties and the currents of the West Wind Drift. Stopping at Heard and Kergualen Islands, Hong Bao and his ships eventually reached western Australia. The stalwart Chinese seamen proceeded northward through the Sunda Strait between Sumatra and Java and made their way home to China.

Zhou Man covered even more territory in his voyage. His flotilla worked its way up the west coast of South America using the Humboldt Current. When it turned west and became the South Equatorial Current, the Chinese followed the prevailing winds and currents which took them to both New Zealand and Australia. Passing through the Torres Strait and the Molucca Passage, Zhou Man's ships sailed east of the Philippines and caught the great Kuroshio Current. They used it to cross the North Pacific back to North America. Cruising down the western coast of North and Central America, the adventurous Chinese left some settlers. They then caught the South Equatorial Current, revisited Australia and at long last returned to China. Zheng He's commanders had managed to visit every part of the world but Europe. Although they failed to conquer the Northwest Passage, they mastered the Straits of Magellan and the Northeast Passage. Zhou Man accomplished the first circumnavigation of the earth while Zhou Wen not only discovered North America and circled Greenland, he also managed to circumnavigate Africa and circumnavigated the Eurasian landmass as well. All three of the admirals rounded the Cape of Good Hope some seventy years before Bartolemeu Dias while Hong Bao visited the icy wastes of Antarctica. If Menzies is to be believed these three eunuchs make the pantheon of European explorers – Columbus, Gama, Magellan, Drake, Cook and others – look like prepubescent boys.

But is Menzies to be believed? *1421* is written as a sort of amalgamation of a historical narrative, travelogue and detective story with Menzies telling of the voyages of the Ming fleet, his own travels in search of the evidences of their voyages and the wonderful things that he found. It is a compelling story of adventure and discovery which draws the reader into it quite effectively. Basically Menzies purports to present an overwhelming amount of cartographic, documentary, astronomical and archaeological evidence that proves his contentions. He also lays claim to special knowledge based on his years of service as a Royal Navy officer and a commander of a submarine, a quality that mere academics could not hope to possess. Professional historians, archaeologists and scientists, however, find Menzies' assertions about the Ming explorations not simply improbable but absurd and completely unfounded on any convincing or credible evidence. Various scholars have presented point by point refutations of Menzies' major points or have performed detailed dissection and exegesis on portions of his book to show how Menzies' evidence miserably fails to prove his contentions. Various scholars have declared him to be incompetent or dishonest or both.[88] *1421* continues to sell despite being almost universally trashed by scholars. It has become a bestseller and is the outstanding success story of pseudohistorical literature. Was the success of *1421* luck, genius or something else entirely?

Every author has a story of how their book got started or how it developed into its final form. These stories are a form of autobiography and as such possess an aura of first-hand authenticity but, like much autobiographical writing, the role of after-the-fact revision and invention can loom very large. In the introduction to *1421* Menzies tells of visiting the John Ford Bell Library at the University of Minnesota around 1990 and viewing its wonderful map of Zuane

Pizzigano from 1424 with its mysterious islands of Santanazes and Antilia. After studying the map he became convinced that Santanazes and Antilia represented the real islands of Guadaloupe and Puerto Rico, which meant that someone had reached the Caribbean at least 75 years before Christopher Columbus. Menzies initially suspected that that someone was the Portuguese and took a trip to the archives of the Torre do Tombo in Lisbon for confirmation. His first speculation proved to be wrong. Since he remained absolutely convinced that his identification of Santanazes and Antilia was correct, this left Menzies groping about for a society in the early fifteenth century that was capable of great feats of oceanic navigation. Working his way through a mental catalogue of global history during the early fifteenth century, he considered various existing states and empires and eliminated them one by one. When he had finished that process only one candidate remained, the China of the early Ming dynasty. At that point, he set out to prove it and thus began the odyssey of research and discovery that culminated in the publication of *1421*.[89]

Later statements by Menzies, his agent and his publisher present a very different picture of the genesis of *1421*. Instead of an exciting tale of a preternaturally visionary and talented amateur scholar embarking on a quest that should result in a major revision of world history, which established and obfuscating professional scholars would doggedly resist, something more contrived and manufactured emerges.[90] In fact, *1421* as published is actually only a small but subsequently expanded section of the *1421* manuscript Gavin Menzies originally wrote. Menzies and his wife Marcella traveled to China for their silver wedding anniversary. While they toured the Forbidden City and its architectural wonders, the date of 1421 kept coming up as when major buildings were erected and institutions were established. This seeming significance of the year 1421 fascinated Menzies, and he decided to write a book about that year in China and the rest of the world. Of course the flurry of activity culminating in 1421 might simply be a reflection of the fact that the Yongle emperor moved the imperial capital to Beijing that year to better defend the northern frontier. When Menzies compared early Ming China with England in 1421, it was clear that China was the bigger, more populous, richer and more sophisticated society.[91] After working and researching for years Menzies produced a huge manuscript of 1,500 pages, but his agent Luigi Bonomi considered it unpublishable. Bonomi, however, was intrigued by a small section of the manuscript in which Menzies presented his hypothesis concerning Admiral Zheng He's lieutenants exploring the world in 1421. He suggested that Menzies refocus his book on those voyages. Menzies agreed but also asked Bonomi to rewrite the first three chapters for him. Bonomi did the rewrites since Menzies was 'not a natural writer'. More importantly Bonomi and Menzies decided to use the media to ignite publishers' interest in the manuscript. Bonomi contacted the firm Midas Public Relations about getting a major newspaper to do a story on Menzies and his 1421 hypothesis. Meanwhile Menzies hired a room at the Royal Geographical Society to announce his book and perhaps generate controversy which would in turn generate publicity. Soon the British *Daily Telegraph* brought out a long article featuring Menzies and his idea about the Chinese voyages. It also lured all sorts of media and publishers to attend Menzies' talk at the Royal Geographical Society. Bonomi's strategy was to create a bidding war for Menzies' book among publishers. His strategy worked extremely well. He and Menzies were even able to meet with a number of publishers prior to the Royal Geographical Society talk. Bantam Press, a division of Transworld, were particularly impressed by Menzies. They offered him £500,000 for the world rights for 1421. Bonomi and Menzies were ecstatic. They had a large and reputable publisher willing to print their book which could only enhance its credibility. It was quite an accomplishment for a self-taught amateur historian who had left school at fifteen.[92]

The problem remained that Menzies' manuscript was only 190 pages and was in need of further rewriting and expansion to transform it into a blockbuster bestseller. Eventually it would reemerge from that process as a 500-page book and the story of that transformation provides a fascinating look at the process of manufacturing a bestseller. Bantam Press thought Menzies' book possessed tremendous potential but it suffered from being poorly written and presented. According to Menzies, what they said in a more diplomatic form was, 'You know, if you want to get your story over, you've got to make it readable, and you can't write, basically.' The manuscript also needed expansion. Supposedly 130 people worked on the manuscript including a ghost writer named Neil Hanson. The research, however, remained Menzies'. With all those people working on the manuscript, apparently not a single one engaged in any fact checking nor was an expert academic consultant brought in to give an opinion on the quality of Menzies' research and scholarship. The result was an engagingly written but sensationalistic book that garnered scathing reviews from scholars.[93]

One of the more severe critics of 1421, Felipe Fernández-Armesto, a professor and a well-respected expert in the history of exploration, suggested that Menzies was 'either a charlatan or a cretin'. Fernández-Armesto is also an author with Transworld. When asked about his negative opinion of *1421*, an unabashed Sally Gaminara, publisher for Transworld, commented, 'Well, maybe he'd like to have the same commercial success himself.' Apparently revenue stream trumps considerations of factual accuracy, literary merit and intellectual integrity.[94]

Like many purveyors of pseudohistorical hypotheses Menzies craves to associate his book with the approval of mainstream scholars. His acknowledgments for *1421* lists dozens of scholars but when the Australian TV show *Four Corners* contacted twelve of them, the investigators found that most had provided Menzies with 'very limited' help or actually disagreed with his contentions. Kirsten Seaver, a scholar of early Arctic exploration and the author of a book that definitively proves the Vinland Map to be a hoax, believes that Menzies manipulated her and other scholars. She wrote to Menzies requesting that he not acknowledge her, but he claims that he never received the letter. Later, in an interview with the *Sunday Times*, Menzies cited Seaver's scholarship and used it to bolster his interpretations in ways that had no connection to anything that she had actually written or said. When contacted by a reporter from the *Sunday Times* Seaver repudiated Menzies' claims. At that point he threatened to sue her for libel if she did not write a letter of retraction to the *Sunday Times*. He even provided her with a copy of the letter he wanted her to write, or rather to sign and mail. His publishers, however, told him not to sue so he dropped the matter.

Transworld marketed *1421* on the basis that Menzies, as an ex-naval officer, possessed technical expertise in seamanship and navigation that academic scholars lacked. As Sally Gaminara of Transworld put it, 'It was Gavin's love and use of maps which persuaded us that there was something unusual, a contribution he could make to the whole issue.' Others, however, vehemently question Menzies' navigational skills and his interpretations of maps. Captain Phil Rivers, a master mariner, has pointed out numerous factual errors on Menzies' part and even wrote a small book *'1421' Voyages: Fact and Fantasy* in 2004; he was not alone. Highly critical reviews and articles along with several websites have been set up to debunk Menzies' *1421*.

Despite this scholarly opposition or perhaps in part because of it, *1421* has been a sensational success for Transworld and William Morrow, the American publisher. Well over a million copies have been sold, including translations into dozens of languages, and the book continues to sell. Of course Transworld and William Morrow spent considerable amounts of money on promoting *1421* in order to achieve that result. Menzies and his book have received massive amounts of publicity which only served to boost sales. Prestigious universities from Harvard to Oxford to Lisbon to Melbourne have invited him to speak, which Menzies claims 'doesn't happen unless professors in those universities think I'm right'. Faculty at universities which have invited Mamoud Ahmedinajad, George W. Bush, Ann Coulter, David Horowitz or Al Sharpton to speak might find Menzies' assumption that a speaking invitation equals a faculty endorsement of the speaker's ideas to be problematic. The Public Broadcasting System even produced a two-hour documentary about *1421*. It first aired on 21 July 2004. The first hour of the show provided a straightforward rendition of Menzies' hypothesis which was a plus for Menzies. Unfortunately for him, the second hour was devoted to letting various Chinese scholars dissect and criticize his ideas mercilessly. The price of publicity can sometimes include intense public humiliation but it also allowed Menzies to claim the imprimatur of a PBS documentary about his book. Menzies set up a website for *1421* and has invited readers to contribute evidence to support his hypothesis. They have obliged him by sending in thousands of items of information, virtually all of which experts emphatically dismiss as worthless, irrelevant or misconstrued. Critics of Menzies and *1421* complain of the public relations machine that continues to hype interest in the book and which has created an almost cult-like quality to the followers of the website. Clearly the *1421* phenomenon is very much alive and well.

Other books backing Menzies' hypothesis have started to appear. *The 1421 Heresy: An Investigation in the Ming Chinese Maritime Survey of the World* by Anatole Andro came out in 2005 and purports to have found evidence in European documents that proves Menzies' hypothesis. *The Island of the Seven Cities: Where the Chinese Settled When They Discovered America* by Paul Chiasson appeared in 2006. He claims to have discovered the remains of pre-Columbian Chinese settlements on Cape Breton Island in Canada. Needless to say, Gavin Menzies is delighted by the backing that Andro and Chiasson give to his hypothesis. Academic historians, however, find Andro's and Chiasson's books to be every bit as incorrect and wrong-headed as *1421*. As was the case with *1421*, formal complaints have been made to have librarians reclassify Chiasson's book as fiction not history. Meanwhile, the ever-enterprising Menzies has concocted a new hypothesis that China actually explored earlier than Zheng He. Kublai Khan sent fleets out to explore the world with Marco Polo as a passenger on those voyages and mapping their discoveries, something he neglected to mention in his famous *Travels*. One persistent complaint against Menzies' hypothesis of the 1421 voyages is that the Chinese had somehow managed to miss

Europe while exploring the rest of the world. So he has corrected that omission by writing a new book *1434: The Year a Magnificent Chinese Fleet Sailed to Italy and Ignited the Renaissance*, which appeared in mid-2008. He has also suggested that the Chinese sailed up the Thames and visited London! But for some unfathomable reason no contemporary chronicler bothered to record these events, which could not have been anything other than astonishing to those Europeans who experienced the alleged Chinese visits.

1421 is the most successful book of pseudohistory to appear since Ignatius Donnelly's *Atlantis: The Antediluvian World* over a hundred years earlier. The difference between the two books is that when Donnelly wrote his research had some scientific and historical credibility based on the state of knowledge at that time. Menzies' hypothesis and research has withered under the light of intelligent and informed criticism from the very beginning. His success has been the result of an extensive publicity and marketing campaign that ignored established scholarship and expert opinion in favour of sensationalist and unwarranted speculation at every step of the way. Adroit use of the internet and various media outlets also served to keep *1421* in the public consciousness and to foster a loyal and credulous following of readers. Menzies maintains, 'The public are on my side, and they are the people who count.' A reflective person, in contrast, has to ask, does *1421* really advance the state of proven and reliable knowledge about the trans-oceanic exploration of the world, or has it just generated a lot of heat (and cash for Menzies and his publishers) without providing any corresponding light? For now, it is yet another entry in the vast body of books and hypotheses about people who reached America before Christopher Columbus.

Mudpeople, Satan's Spawn and Christian Identity: Racist Cosmogonies and Pseudohistory, Part I

Vain wisdom all, and false Philosophie:
Yet with a pleasing sorcerie could charm.
JOHN MILTON[1]

INTRODUCTION

The terminology of racist invective is vast and often quite ancient. It is also growing. Late twentieth-century America added some curious terms to this unsavoury lexicon: mudpeople, ZOG, white devils and icepeople/sunpeople are all words or phrases with definite racist implications. Although these words took on their racist meanings during the twentieth century they are based on visions of the nature of human origins that go back to the beginnings of humanity, or rather the beginning of the supposed different forms of humanity. The motivations behind the formulation of these racist theories of human origins are readily understandable even if their conclusions are aberrant and odious. Humans are concerned with knowing who they are. We all want an identity as individuals and as a society or as a group within a society or the world itself. Individuals want to know about their family's past. Societies and groups want to know their collective history. The further they can go back with their histories, the better. If the search for identity can be traced back to creation or the beginning of recorded history that is best of all.

The word for the study of the origins of the universe, and along with it humanity, is cosmogony. Various cultures and religions have had their cosmogonies and the biblical account of creation found in Genesis is the foundation for Jewish, Christian and Islamic cosmogonies. All these religions share a belief in a single creation or monogenesis and that all humans are the descendants of Adam and Eve and later of Noah and his sons. This circumstance means that humanity is a single species and that God is equally concerned with the ultimate welfare of all humans, or at least all believers. In all three of these world religions the concept that some races are inferior or superior has no place. Judaism, Christianity and Islam all teach that humankind is one, a unity and equal in worth.

Unfortunately some people have managed throughout history to twist and to pervert this basic message that humans are one species and that we are all in this earthly existence together. Some fringe groups have used traditional religious teachings along with history and archaeology in an inappropriate or even heretical way to prove that some humans are innately superior and good while others were created inferior and evil. Even scientific evolutionary theory has been marshalled on a number of occasions to prove the superiority of one group of humans over another. This chapter will look at one group, Christian Identity, which has used unorthodox versions of Christian cosmogony and prehistory as a form of pseudohistory to validate its prejudices about other groups or races. A following chapter will look at the unorthodox cosmogony and prehistory of the Nation of Islam. These groups have tapped into an existing pool of sometimes centuries-old spurious scholarship in science and history to justify their conclusions.

DAKOTA DEATH TRIP

> It was religion that gave birth to the Anglo-American societies. This must always be borne in mind. Hence religion in the United States is inextricably intertwined with all the national habits and all the feelings to which the fatherland gives rise. This gives it a peculiar force.
> ALEXIS DE TOCQUEVILLE[2]

On 13 February 1983 outside Medina, North Dakota, US marshals attempted to serve a misdemeanour warrant on Gordon Kahl, a combat veteran of World War II then in his early sixties. The warrant concerned Kahl's violation of his probation from his conviction for failure to pay his federal income taxes. Unfortunately Kahl, his son Yorie and their friends David Broer and Scott Faul were armed and resisted. In the gunfight that followed two marshals were killed and several others were wounded, one very seriously. Yorie Kahl was also seriously wounded. At the end of the shootout Gordon Kahl approached the already mortally wounded deputy US marshal Robert Cheshire and shot him twice in the head. After seeing that Yorie received medical attention, Kahl fled from North Dakota. A massive federal manhunt followed. Somehow Kahl made his way to Texas, where he had worked off and on, and finally to Arkansas. There Leonard Ginter helped Kahl hide from the authorities. In the second week of March Ginter arranged for Kahl to stay on the farm of

Arthur Russell outside Mountain Home. Kahl stayed there until 30 May when he returned to Ginter's home near Smithville. The FBI received word of Kahl's whereabouts on 2 June and the next day they surrounded the Ginter house with other law enforcement officers. Although they managed to get Ginter and his wife out of the house without violence, the operation ended tragically. Gene Matthews, the sheriff of Lawrence County, entered the Ginter house on his own initiative and exchanged shots with Kahl. Apparently both men received mortal wounds. Matthews managed to get out of the house but later died of his wounds. Meanwhile lawmen poured bullets into the house, which caught fire. Kahl's badly burned body was found later with a bullet in the head.

Gordon Kahl was an unlikely public enemy. As an elderly veteran with extensive combat experience he seemingly epitomized the 'band of brothers' mystique and the values of the World War II generation and the American heartland. The same thing could be said of those who gave Kahl shelter in Arkansas. Ginter was a 63-year-old retired carpenter while Arthur Russell was 74 and Ed Udey was 70. What they all had in common, however, was a visceral dislike of the US government and its income tax. What turned these men into geriatric revolutionaries? Ultimately the answer is their connections with and acceptance of the beliefs of the religious movement known as Christian Identity. Gordon Kahl had long associations with the Posse Comitatus, an offshoot of Christian Identity. Members of the Posse, along with adherents of the related Aryan Nations and the Covenant, Sword and Arm of the Lord groups, either sympathized with Kahl or actively aided him. Ginter and Kahl first met through Posse Comitatus. The belief system of Christian Identity was what motivated all of these men and those groups in their hatred and resistance toward the US government.[3]

CHRISTIAN IDENTITY

> You may charge certain persons not to teach any different doctrine, nor to occupy themselves with myths and endless genealogies, which promote speculations rather than the divine training that is in faith.
> TIMOTHY, 1:3–4.

Christian Identity is an unorthodox movement that has amalgamated several pseudohistorical ideas about human origins into their theology of Christianity. Those ideas have been used to produce a system of beliefs that justifies anti-Semitism and racism while presenting an apocalyptic vision of the present and near future. Adherents of

Christian Identity have three distinct beliefs about human origins. First, they believe that the whites of the British Isles along with western and northern Europe are the descendants of the Ten Lost Tribes of Israel. Since Identity Christians are whites whose ancestors came from those regions, this belief has the implication that they are part of God's chosen people and are direct biological descendants of Adam. They are created in God's image as was Adam and are capable of salvation. Second, they believe that non-white humans have their origins in pre-Adamic races and are not descendants of Adam. These pre-Adamites are inferior to whites and are incapable of accepting Christianity and being saved. They are also minions of Satan and are called mudpeople. The belief that non-whites are of pre-Adamic origin, inherently inferior and without souls is a powerful justification for racism and white supremacy. To practice tolerance and integration is tantamount to collaborating with the Devil and his rebellion against God. Third, Christian Identity teaches that Jews are the seed of Satan, his biological descendants. They claim that Satan sexually seduced Eve through the serpent in the Garden of Eden and the result was the birth of Cain. After killing Abel the evil Cain departed for the land of Nod where he took a wife from among the pre-Adamic people dwelling there. The children of that marriage and their descendants are the Jews of modern society. Such a lineage directly links the Jews to Satan biologically and makes them his followers and allies in the titanic struggle with God and his faithful. Anti-Semiticism becomes an article of faith in support of God's cosmic plan, not a prejudice in the worldview of Christian Identity. Jews are literally the Devil's children and therefore are irredeemably evil and implacable enemies of the godly Identity Christians. Making this potent mix of choseness, racism and anti-Semiticism even more dangerous is Christian Identity's belief that the end of the world is very near. The final cosmic battle of good and evil has commenced for them and it is not all that clear that the good will triumph. Defeat will mean the extinction of the white Adamic race because for believers in Christian Identity the Apocalypse is a race war between the white descendants of the Ten Lost Tribes of Israel and the demonic Jews and their sub-human pre-Adamite minions.

Christian Identity envisions a grim and violent worldview. Most people learning about Christian Identity express astonishment that late twentieth-century America could have produced such a hate-driven perversion of Christianity. The intellectual and ideological foundations of the beliefs of Christian Identity have a convoluted root system that leads back to all sorts of pseudohistory and other faux and discredited scholarships.

FROM TEN LOST TRIBES TO SATAN'S SEEDLINE

> For the time is coming when people will not endure sound teaching,
> but having itching ears they will accumulate for themselves teachers
> to suit their own likings, and will turn away from listening to the
> truth and wander into myths. TIMOTHY, 4:3–4.

The biblical Hebrews were God's chosen people, chosen, that is, to produce the Messiah, the redeemer of humanity. According to the biblical narrative they were the descendants of the patriarch Abraham, his son Isaac and Isaac's son Jacob, who was given the name Israel. Jacob and his wives Leah and Rachel along with their maidservants produced twelve sons; they were the beginning of the Children of Israel. Each of the twelve sons founded one of the twelve tribes of the biblical Hebrews.[4] After the Children of Israel conquered the land of Canaan they divided the land among themselves. Since the tribe of Levi served as priests for the Hebrews they did not occupy a specific territory. The Hebrews still continued to have twelve non-priestly territorial tribes because Manasseh and Ephriam, the two sons of Joseph, were raised to tribal status. But in the process of blessing the Twelve Tribes, the patriarch Jacob gave the greater blessing to Ephriam, the younger son of Joseph, rather than the eldest, Manasseh. As Jacob put it, 'He [Manasseh] also shall become a people, and he also shall be great; nevertheless his younger brother [Ephriam] shall be greater than he, and his descendants shall become a multitude of nations.'[5]

Once the united monarchy was established over the Hebrews, they enjoyed prosperity under their kings, David and Solomon. It was not, however, a completely happy union and the northern tribes were resentful of domination by the tribe of Judah. When Solomon died in 925 BC, his son Rehoboam behaved with sufficient arrogance to goad the northern tribes into rebellion. As a result from 924 BC there was a divided monarchy with the northern kingdom of Israel and the southern kingdom of Judah. Israel lasted as an independent kingdom until the years 745–722 BC when Assyria came to dominate the region and ultimately captured Samaria, the capital of Israel in 722 BC. At that point the Assyrians carried off thousands of the Israelite elite into exile and replaced them with foreigners. Judah survived until the Babylonian sieges of Jerusalem in 597 and 586 BC led to the exile and Babylonian captivity of the Judaean elite.

The difference between Judah and Israel was that while some of the Judaean exiles eventually returned to Judah and restored the Temple in Jerusalem, those from Israel never returned. Not only did the exiled Israelites never return, they became the legendary Ten Lost

Tribes of Israel. An incredible amount of lore developed around the Ten Lost Tribes. Where did they go? What was their place in God's providential history? Who were they now? Myriad lands were identified as the dwelling place or places of the Ten Lost Tribes. Many peoples have been identified as the descendants of the Ten Lost Tribes, including the Native Americans, the Lemba people of southern Africa and the Japanese imperial dynasty. Various prophetic roles have been assigned to the Ten Lost Tribes. Hundreds of books are devoted in whole or in part to the Ten Lost Tribes, but what is really known about them?[6]

Very little reliable information exists about the Ten Lost Tribes. The Assyrian king Shalmanessar V invaded the northern kingdom of Israel in 724 BC and besieged the capital of Samaria. He died in 722 BC but his successor Sargon II completed the reduction of the city that same year and carried away close to 30,000 captives. According to 2 Kings 17:6 and 23, 'the King of Assyria captured Samaria and he carried the Israelites away to Assyria, and placed them in Halah and on the Habor, the river of Gozan, and in the cities of the Medes . . . So Israel was exiled from their own land to Assyria to this day.'[7] In the ancient world, an exiled people would usually be absorbed into the population around them and eventually lose any distinctive religious or ethnic identity. Such an assimilation was almost certainly the fate of the exiled members of the elite of the northern kingdom of Israel, the Ten Lost Tribes. Over time, however, they became the objects of considerable prophetic and apocalyptic speculation, especially after the fall of Jerusalem and the commencement of the Babylonian Captivity in 586 BC. Several of the Old Testament prophetic books spoke of God gathering the scattered remnants of both the kingdoms of Israel and Judah together as one harmonious nation.[8]

The apocryphal book of 2 Esdras 13:39–40 (or 4 Ezra) added some intriguing details about the fate of the Ten Lost Tribes which claimed that they continued to survive as a distinct and separate people.

> And as for your seeing him [the Messiah] gather to himself another multitude that was peaceable, these are the ten tribes which were led away from their own land into captivity in the days of King Hoshea, whom Shalmaneser the king of the Assyrians led captive; he took them across the river, and they were taken to another land. But they formed this plan for themselves, that they would leave the multitude of the nations and go to a more distant region, where mankind had never lived, that there at least they might keep their statutes which they had not kept in their own land. And they went in by the

narrow passages of the Euphrates river. For at the time the Most High performed signs for them, and stopped the channels of the river until they passed over. Through that region there was a long way to go, a journey of a year and a half; and that country is called Arzareth [another land].

In these passages, the writer of 2 Esdras 13 is articulating a common legend among the Jews of the Hellenistic and Roman era, that the Ten Lost Tribes survived as a discrete people somewhere. Furthermore, they not only survived, they would be returning home as the end of the world approached.

> Then they dwelt there until the last times; and now, when they are about to come again, the Most High will stop the channels of the river again, so that they may be able to pass over. Therefore you saw the multitude gathered together in peace. But those who are left of your people, who are formed within my holy borders, shall be saved. Therefore when he destroys the multitude of the nations that are gathered together, he will defend the people who remain. And then he will show them very many wonders.

Scholars think that a Jew living in the immediate aftermath of the Jewish War of AD 66–73 and the Roman destruction of the Temple in Jerusalem in AD 70 wrote the section of 2 Esdras containing chapter 13 and the material on the Ten Lost Tribes. He was not alone in his beliefs. Flavius Josephus in his *Antiquities of the Jews*, which was completed in AD 93/4, also discusses the Ten Lost Tribes. Largely following the biblical narrative he describes the people of the Northern Kingdom as lawless, impious and so deserving of God's punishment through the agency of the Assyrians. Later he states that the Ten Tribes did not participate in the return from the Babylonian Captivity but instead continued to dwell beyond the Euphrates River.[9]

From that point the legend of the Ten Lost Tribes grew. When the Ten Tribes failed to march in support of Simon Bar Kochba's rebellion (and his widely accepted claims to be the Messiah of the Jews) of AD 132–5 against Rome, it started a long debate among the rabbis. Meanwhile travellers began to report encounters and sightings of the Ten Lost Tribes in various parts of Africa and Asia. These reports continued through the Middle Ages and beyond. Some accounts described the Ten Tribes as vassals of Prester John, the great Christian potentate of Asia, or later Africa. When Mongol armies began their depredations of Russia and Eastern Europe they were identified as the fearsome hordes of Gog and Magog, who would be loosed on the earth during the Last Days. Other rumours linked the Mongols with the Ten Lost Tribes and in the process caused some people to fuse the Ten Lost Tribes with Gog and Magog. Meanwhile speculations within Islam, particularly the Ottoman Turks, about the Ten Lost Tribes allying themselves with Jewish Messiahs or Christian crusaders continued during the fifteenth, sixteenth and seventeenth centuries. The great fiasco of Sabbatai Sevi (1626–1676), the apostate Messiah, in 1665–6 included all sorts of rumours of formidable armies of the Ten Lost Tribes marching on Palestine to join him and also to punish persecutors of the Jews. It also brought an end to any further significant occurrences of Jewish Messianism.[10]

The discovery of the Americas opened up new vistas for seekers of the Ten Lost Tribes. Various people speculated that all or some of the tribes of Native Americans were descendants of various Jewish refugees, including the Ten Lost Tribes. Of particular significance, in 1644 a report by Antonio de Montezinos reached the Jews of Amsterdam. He claimed to have encountered the tribe of Reuben in the jungles of Peru. Menasseh ben Israel, the great rabbi of Amsterdam, used Montezinos' story to persuade Oliver Cromwell to readmit the Jews to England. This episode contributed greatly to spreading knowledge of the legend of the Ten Lost Tribes.[11] Sightings of one or more of the Ten Lost Tribes in various places all over the globe have continued ever since.

According to prophecies and legends the Ten Lost Tribes are supposed to play an important role in the fulfilment of God's plans for the end of this world. They are a remnant of God's Chosen People, the Hebrews of the Old Testament, the Children of Israel. It is a unique status, one that other people might envy or wish to share. That, in fact, is the fundamental motivation behind the rise of British Israelism and later Christian Identity. Throughout the history of Christianity, various peoples and countries have laid claim to be God's new favourites. John Aylmer, later a bishop, proclaimed early in the reign of Elizabeth I that 'God is English'. Later Puritans in both Old and New England would compare themselves to the ancient Israelites and claim the status of being the newly chosen people of God. All of this talk about Israelites was meant to be taken in a metaphysical or spiritual sense. It was the British Israelites who first claimed a direct biological link to the Children of Israel.

Richard Brothers (1757–1824) was the first to teach and write about the idea of the British and other Europeans being a 'Hidden Israel', unaware of their biological Jewish descent. Although he was born in Newfoundland, Brothers came to England as a child and joined the Royal Navy as a midshipman when he was fourteen. In 1783 he gained the rank of lieutenant but was discharged with half-pay later that year due to the ending of the war associated with the American Revolution. At that point Brothers began to behave in an increasingly erratic manner. Living in boarding houses, in 1789 Brothers began to object to taking the oath required to receive his half-pay. He also came to believe that God had commissioned him for some great purpose so he began to prophesy. In the melange of his predictions, he actually managed to predict correctly the deaths of Louis xvi of France and Gustav iii of Sweden. Both monarchs died violently at the hands of their subjects. Brothers' various unpaid landlords and local officials remained unimpressed and instead focused their ire on his voluntary impecuniousness.

When the French Revolution began in 1789 English people watched it unfold with mixed feelings of bewilderment, fear, expectation and admiration. The 1790s were a decade of religious ferment as great events in temporal affairs were assumed to presage great events in the spiritual realm. In 1793, a year that virtually began with the execution of Louis xvi, Brothers described himself as a 'nephew of the Almighty', which supposedly meant that he was a descendant of one of Jesus Christ's brothers or sisters. By the end of 1794 Brothers was beginning to publish his prophecies. He claimed that hidden Jews lived throughout Europe and that he was a descendant of King David. Proceeding from this information, Brothers predicted that he would be revealed as a Hebrew prince and proclaimed ruler of the earth on 19 November 1795. The scattered Hebrews would be led back to Palestine and they would begin rebuilding the Temple in 1798. Brothers also stated that upon his revelation as the ruler of the world, George iii of Britain was to turn over his crown to him. That was a sensitive claim to make since Britain had been at war with Revolutionary France since February 1793. The execution of Louis xvi had made George iii especially sensitive about the possibility of losing his throne while various groups in the British Isles sympathized with the French Revolution and republicanism. So on 4 March 1794 officials arrested Brothers on suspicion of treason. An investigation followed. By 4 May the authorities had placed Brothers in a private lunatic asylum. There he remained confined until 1806 when his friend and disciple John Finlayson secured his release. Brothers lived the remainder of his life on the charity of friends and believers in his prophecies. Finlayson allowed him to live in his house from 1815 to Brothers' death from cholera in 1824. During these years Brothers continued to publish his prophecies, which included the explicit linking of the British with the Ten Lost Tribes. Despite all his peculiar beliefs and behaviour Brothers had managed to attract a following. A member of parliament, Nathaniel Brassey Halhed of Lymington, spoke in the House of Commons in favour of Brothers but got no support from his fellow MPS. As his rather specific prophecies failed to come true, Brothers' supporters for the most part drifted off. His proto-British Israel theories anticipated the later appearance of British Israelism but do not appear to have had any appreciable influence on the later movement.[12]

The real beginning of British Israelism can be found in the writings of John Wilson. Wilson was an Irish weaver with an attraction to both radical politics and pseudohistorical ideas based on spurious and problematic scholarship. In 1840 he published *Lectures on Our Israelitish Origins*. Originally a slight book of 144 pages, it had grown to 452 pages by the appearance of the posthumous fifth edition in 1876. Wilson wrote articles and lectured on his theories of British Israelism up to his death in 1871. Basically he argued that the Ten Tribes of the northern kingdom of Israel had migrated from the Middle East to Europe. There they founded various nations, particularly the Anglo-Saxon and Germanic peoples. The tribe of Ephriam had settled in Britain and this made the British preeminent due to the patriarch Jacob's promises to Ephriam. Wilson asserted all biblical prophecies to Israel referred to the Ten Tribes except those that dealt expressly with the Jews of the southern kingdom of Judah. Furthermore, the Hebrew blood of the descendants of Judah, the modern Jews, had been greatly diluted through marriages with non-Hebrews over the centuries. Why Wilson apparently thought the blood of the Ten Tribes of Israel had not been similarly diluted is unclear.

The evidence that Wilson used to trace the wanderings of the Ten Tribes employed simplistic phonetic similarities instead of real philology. Using this approach, Wilson claimed that hundreds of English words derived from Hebrew. Place-names enshrined the passing through or settling of one or another of the Ten Tribes so that Denmark became associated with the tribe of Dan while Succoth, a place in the Trans-Jordan region of Palestine associated with the tribe of Gad, became the root of Scots, hence Scotland. Writing in the middle two quarters of the nineteenth century, Wilson contended that the various Germanic peoples of Britain, the Netherlands, Germany and Scandinavia were all closely related and possessed a common destiny. This belief connected nicely with the prevailing assumptions of racial Anglo-Saxonism and Teutonism that dominated during that era.[13]

Wilson's writing laid the foundations of British Israelism. During the 1870s adherents of British Israelism began to form associations.

Some British Israelites supported Wilson's Teutonist approach but, in the end, the anti-Teutonism of the Anglo-Israel Association prevailed in 1878 when it absorbed its pro-Teutonic rival. That result was almost inevitable given the anti-German drift of British opinion after 1870 and the unification of Germany. Great Britain found itself facing an extremely capable challenger for world power. Germany threatened British primacy in industrial productivity, naval power and imperial domination. British Israelism, always a highly patriotic and nationalistic movement, shared the concerns of greater British society about the potential German threat.[14]

Edward Hine (1825–1891) was the next prominent British Israelite writer to arise after John Wilson. Besides being staunchly anti-German, his writings and activities helped to spread British Israelism to the United States. Calling himself a disciple of Wilson, Hine claimed that he became converted to British Israelism in 1840 during his early teenage years as a result of hearing Wilson lecture. Hine, however, did not take up an active role writing and lecturing on British Israelism until much later in 1869 towards the end of Wilson's life. Hine also introduced some significant revisions. He confined the descendants of the Ten Lost Tribes solely to Britain except that he accepted that Manasseh was located outside of Britain in the United States. This connection meant that the United States and Britain constituted the entire non-Jewish remnant of scattered Israel in both genealogical terms and in terms of prophetic destiny. Together with the surviving Jews they constituted 'All Israel' and the two groups would resettle Palestine and so fulfil biblical prophecy. Meanwhile Hine added the twist of identifying the Germans as the descendants of the Assyrians. Apparently, like the Ten Tribes of Israel, their Assyrian conquerors and oppressors also migrated from the Middle East. Eventually these wandering, warlike, and militaristic Assyrians settled down to become warlike and militaristic Germans.[15]

Considering the growing connections between British and American culture during the nineteenth century it was to be expected that British Israelism would make its way to the United States and Canada. The career of Joseph Wild (1834–1908) provides a good example of this phenomenon. He was born in Lancashire and at the age of sixteen started itinerant preaching as a Primitive Methodist. About 1856 he emigrated to the United States where he preached to and served various congregations in both the United States and Canada. Earning his DD at Ohio Wesleyan University in 1870, he was called to a church in Brooklyn in 1872. After three years passed, Wild was scheduled to be moved to another church. Not wanting to leave Brooklyn he accepted a call from the Union Congregational Church of Brooklyn where he stayed until 1881. After that he moved to the Bond Street Congregational Church in Toronto where he stayed. In his efforts to better understand the Bible Wild came across the British Israel writings of John Wilson during the 1850s. He found that they provided him with new and convincing insights into biblical prophecy and it would appear that he brought these ideas with him when he moved to North America. After studying the relationship of British Israelism to the Bible for twenty years, Wild began to lecture on the subject himself in 1876. Along the way he also developed an interest in pyramidology, the belief that the Great Pyramid of Giza incorporated all sorts of prophetic information in its dimensions, which he in turn incorporated into his British Israelite beliefs. Sometime between 1876 and 1879 Wild also came into contact with Edward Hine's version of British Israelism and incorporated Hine's ideas into his *The Ten Lost Tribes*, first published in 1879.

Wild followed Hine in identifying England with the tribe of Ephriam and the United States with Manasseh. He also identified the British monarchy as the heirs of King David of Israel. In his account, which is not unique to Wild, the prophet Jeremiah fled the Babylonian conquest of the southern kingdom of Judah. With him he took the daughters of Zedekiah, the last king of Judah, and the artefact known as Jacob's Pillar (or pillow). It is supposed to be the stone that the patriarch Jacob used for his headrest when he dreamed about his ladder of angels ascending and descending from Heaven. Sailing to Ireland via Egypt on a Danite ship, Jeremiah and the daughters of Zedekiah settled among the Danites already living there. The daughters married into the Danite/Irish royalty and from there spread the Davidic bloodline into Scotland and England. Jacob's Pillar became known as the Stone of Destiny or the Stone of Scone and was moved to Scotland, later to England by conquest (and recently back to Scotland). Wild also included a plentiful amount of pyramidology in his book, relating it all to contemporary events, circa 1879. Wild, however, made no effort to found a British Israel movement in the United States.[16]

The founder of an American movement of British Israelism was Charles Adiel Lewis Totten (1851–1908). He was the son of James Totten, who had risen from captain to brigadier-general in the Union army during the course of the Civil War. Graduating from West Point in 1873 Totten was commissioned a second lieutenant in the artillery corps. Promoted to first lieutenant in 1874, he saw action in the Bannock War of 1878 and the campaign against the Chiricahua in 1881. After 1881 he served in various posts in the New York, Rhode Island and Connecticut area until he resigned from the army in 1893 to pursue his biblical research. It was during 1883 that Totten developed an interest in British Israelism and began to publish on the subject. His writings attracted the attention of both Piazzi Smyth and Edward Hine in England. Smyth later wrote an introduction to one of Totten's books. When Edward Hine came to North America during 1884–8, to lecture and proselytize for British Israelism, he spent part of that time with Totten in New Haven, Connecticut.

Totten was a prolific writer on many subjects. Besides British Israelism, he wrote on military science, athletics, the metric system and various topics from the Bible including the Flood, Joshua bidding the sun to stand still and the Nativity. His bibliography of British Israel writings is somewhat confusing due to his practice of giving later editions of a book a different title. Like other British Israelists he developed an interest in pyramidology. For later British Israelists and adherents of Christian Identity, Totten was the academic jewel in their crown and he is referred to as 'Professor Totten of Yale'. In truth, Totten was not a regular member of the Yale faculty. He was simply an army officer assigned to Yale University as a professor in the military science program during the years 1888–92.[17] Totten helped to spread the ideas of British Israelism through his writings and his periodical *Our Race*, all of which were published by the Our Race Publishing Company of New Haven, Connecticut.

The proselytizing efforts of Hine and Totten had an impact and British Israel ideas spread to various places in the United States and Canada. British Israelism was a belief that could fit comfortably into the late nineteenth and early twentieth centuries' values as an age of imperialism. These years were the apogee of the British Empire and the time when the USA attained status as a world power along with a little empire of its own. It was an era when scientific racism held sway. British Israelism provided a religious explanation for the success of Britain and the USA. They were an integral part of God's chosen people and British Israelism linked them to this destiny biologically as well as spiritually. It was a comfortable place to be – if you were a member of the Chosen.

British Israel ideas diffused through the USA and Canada and retained an active following in Britain that remained reasonably vital through the 1920s. It is important to keep in mind that British Israelism was not a mass movement. At its height the British Israel World Federation only had around 5,000 members although they were a well-to-do and bookish group. Members with a scholarly bent produced a myriad of more or less redundant books on aspects of British Israelism. In the US Totten published his own books in multiple editions. The British Israel writer W. H. Poole, a Canadian, published his almost 700-page *Anglo-Israel or the Saxon Race Proved to be the Lost Tribes of Israel in Nine Lectures* in 1889 and it was widely read. All of this contributed to the creation of a milieu of pseudohistorical scholarship that has remained embedded in various recesses of popular culture ever since. Wild, Totten and other British Israelists were very concerned about biblical prophecy and its fulfilment. For them, the final days of the world would arrive when the Twelve Tribes of Israel would be reunited in the Holy Land of Palestine. All Israel would be formed. They lived in an age when the Ottoman Empire that controlled the region of the Middle East was declining. Britain had a presence in that region through having acquired controlling interest in the Suez Canal in 1875 and effective control of Egypt from 1882. That put Britain (or Ephriam from a British Israel point of view) right next to Palestine, the ancient land of Israel. At some point the Jews would be restored to their homeland in Palestine along with Britain and the USA. The Jews would then be converted and the final battles would be fought with the looming colossus of the Russian Empire but All Israel would win in the end. As Joseph Wild put it in 1879, 'The Jews, England, and the United States from this [their reunification as the Twelve Tribes] and henceforth are one in interest, policy, and destiny.'[18]

It is important to remember that British Israelism never developed into a separate denomination. Its ideas could be grafted on to a person's existing denominational affiliations. In England British Israelists were also loyal members of the Church of England although some Anglican clergy periodically attacked these beliefs. In the United States and Canada various Protestants, particularly Methodists and those of an evangelical nature, were attracted to British Israelism. Charles Fox Parham, the founder of Pentecostalism, took up British Israelism as did J. H. Allen (1847–1930), who founded the Church of God (Holiness). Allen served prominently in the British Israel World Federation and wrote *Judah's Sceptre and Joseph's Birthright* in 1902. *Judah's Sceptre* became a classic of British Israel writing, appearing in many editions, and is still available today. Other groups would follow the British Israel path such as Herbert W. Armstrong and his Worldwide Church of God. Armstrong became a British Israel adherent during the 1920s and eventually published the oft revised and reprinted *United States and Britain in Prophecy* in 1942. Initially its prophetic message was concerned about World War II and the struggle with fascism. Later editions took up themes of the Cold War struggles and events such as the United States–Iran Hostage Crisis of 1979. Armstrong never adopted the anti-Semitic stance that some British Israel groups drifted into, which eventually culminated in the Christian Identity movement. After his death in 1986 scandal and dissension rocked the Worldwide Church of God. By 1995 the church's leader Joseph W. Tkach repudiated Armstrong's controversial doctrines, including British Israelism, as non-biblical.

Charles Adiel Lewis Totten died in 1908 and his magazine *One Race* ceased publication in 1915. This situation left British Israelism without a handy venue for publication until A. A. Beauchamp, a Boston printer, stepped in to be the movement's publisher. In 1918 he began to publish the monthly magazine *Watchman of Israel*, later renamed *New Watchman*. By 1919 Beauchamp was publishing a list of sixteen titles related to British Israelism and pyramidology including reprints of Joseph Wild and J. H. Allen's principal works.[19] One of the steady contributors to *Watchman of Israel* was Reuben H. Sawyer (1866–?) of Portland, Oregon, a Christian pastor. Like J. H. Allen, he was active in the British Israel World Federation. British Israelism, however, was not Sawyer's only interest. From 1921 to 1924 he was active in the Oregon Ku Klux Klan. Sawyer's activities with the Klan marked the beginning of the American branch of British Israelism's drift into increasing anti-Semiticism. Sawyer introduced the idea of the Sephardic Jews being the only good and authentic Jews while the Ashkenazic Jews were evil, false Jews. Meanwhile, in 1924 A. A. Beauchamp shifted his principal interests to Christian Science. The *New Watchman* and Beauchamp's publishing company became Christian Science outlets while British Israelism in the United States was once more left adrift.[20]

British Israelism began as a philo-Semitic movement but in its Christian Identity guise became virulently anti-Semitic. This transformation might seem puzzling at first but it is readily explicable. The philo-Semiticism of the British Israelists was actually extremely fragile even though it might seem to be a bedrock assumption of the movement. British Israelists believe they are God's chosen people along with the Jews. They also believe that, jointly with the Jews, they will reoccupy the land of Israel as a prelude to the Second Coming. The problem is that the joint occupation of the land of Israel is to be a Christian occupation. It requires the mass conversion of the Jews to Christianity for the prophecy to be fulfilled. If the Jews did not convert, disappointment, frustration, and eventually anger would be sure to follow. During the early sixteenth century Martin Luther had looked for Jewish conversion during the early years of the Reformation which would serve as a harbinger of the Apocalypse. When it failed to occur he shifted to a very anti-Semitic stance. The same pattern occurred with British Israelism and the Jews. During World

War I, on 9 December 1917, British general Edmund Allenby captured Jerusalem from the Ottoman Turks. For the British Israelists the leader of the Ten Tribes, Ephriam (England), had reoccupied Israel according to biblical prophecy. Some Jews started to return to Israel and apocalyptic hopes were high. Unfortunately for the British Israelists the returning Jews did not convert to Christianity. In fact many of them were Zionists and came into conflict with the British occupation government of Palestine. British Israelists observing these developments were dismayed and disillusioned. Their once positive feelings toward Jews started to drift in an increasingly negative direction. Enthusiasm for philo-Semiticism faded among British Israelists by the late 1920s, just as anti-Semiticism was growing in strength in Europe and North America. Beginning in the late 1920s the American branch of British Israelism took a distinctly anti-Semitic and right-wing turn, an evolution that would ultimately lead to Christian Identity after 1945. The main figure of British Israelism in America during these years was Howard B. Rand, who somewhat indirectly and unconsciously introduced right wing conservatism into the movement.

Howard B. Rand (1889–1991) was born the son of British Israelist adherents and lived in Haverhill, Massachusetts. Michael Barkun, the leading historian of the Christian Identity movement, considers Rand to be the bridge between British Israelism and Christian Identity. After graduating from law school Rand practised law along with some sidelines in insurance and the construction businesses. By 1927 he was active in the British Israel World Federation and in 1930 started to organize the Anglo-Saxon Federation of America, publishing a monthly newsletter called the *Bulletin* which later became a magazine with slick paper titled *Destiny*. Rand was trying to create a national British Israel organization in the United States and in the process made alliances with various right-wing individuals. William J. Cameron (1878–1955) and Rand met in 1930 at a British Israel convention in Detroit. Cameron already held strongly anti-Semitic views. He had been the editor of Henry Ford's newspaper, the *Dearborn Independent*, from 1921 to 1927 and had been closely involved with the writing and publication of its notorious and highly controversial 'International Jew' series. Cameron continued to work as Ford's public relations person until the early 1940s. His membership in the Anglo-Saxon Federation of America also provided Rand with contacts with Cameron's numerous right-wing acquaintances and their financial resources. Thanks to the work of Rand and Cameron during the 1930s the ideas of British Israelism were disseminated on the national level. They also transformed the movement in the USA into an organization with many right-wing members who held anti-Semitic and racist prejudices. By the end of World War II Rand had for some time lost interest in maintaining the Anglo-Saxon Federation of America and it collapsed. It was from the remnants of Rand's organization that Christian Identity emerged in southern California.[21]

After 1945 the British Israelists in southern California came under the influence of Gerald L. K. Smith (1898–1976), a former associate of Huey Long of Louisiana and the premier anti-Semite in post-World War II America. Under his guidance the right-wing segment of British Israelism in America was transformed during the 1950s and 1960s into Christian Identity. Whether Smith, who was more interested in political rather than religious matters, was a Christian Identity believer is unclear. There is no doubt that he had close associations with Wesley Swift (1913–1970), the most influential Christian Identity minister prior to 1970. In common with many Christian Identity figures Swift was also involved in Ku Klux Klan and anti-Communist activities.

Another prominent Christian Identity leader was William Potter Gale (1917–1988). Gale served on General Douglas MacArthur's staff (no haven of liberal thought) during World War II and helped to organize Filipino guerillas to fight the Japanese. At the age of 27 he became the youngest lieutenant-colonel in the US Army but had to retire in 1950 at the age of 33 due to his war injuries. According to his own account Gale learned about British Israelism through the writings of Charles Totten. Like Swift he engaged in various right-wing activities including the founding of the Christian Defense League sometime between 1957 and 1964, theft of dynamite and a plot to assassinate Martin Luther King, Jr. Along with Swift he came under investigation by the attorney-general of California for his involvement in paramilitary activities, including the Christian Defense League. Gale founded the Posse Comitatus in 1969/70, an organization that recognized no government above the county level. He advocated tax resistance for which he was convicted on federal charges in 1987. He died of emphysema in 1988 at the age of 71 while appealing his conviction. Another follower of Smith was Richard Girnt Butler (1918–2004), who reactivated the Christian Defense League. In 1973 he moved to Idaho and set up the Church of Jesus Christ Christian along with a training compound/fortress for Posse Comitatus. Swift, Gale, Butler and others formulated the mix of ideas and doctrines that constituted Christian Identity.[22]

CHRISTIAN IDENTITY AND HUMAN HISTORY

We do not understand the glorious state of Adam, nor the nature of his sin, nor the transmission of it to us. These are matters which took place under conditions of a nature altogether different from our own and which transcend our present understanding.

The knowledge of all this is useless to us as a means of escape from it; and all that we are concerned to know is that we are miserable, corrupt, separated from God, but ransomed by Jesus Christ, whereof we have wonderful proofs on earth. BLAISE PASCAL[23]

Christian Identity combined beliefs in British Israelism, the existence of pre-Adamic races and the Jews as Satan's children. Identity Christians were white from western and northern European ancestries, particularly the British Isles. They were God's chosen people, descendants of the Ten Lost Tribes and members of the Adamic race. They possessed souls and could believe in God. But to British Israelism the followers of Christian Identity added strongly racist and anti-Semitic elements. If the whites of western and northern Europe were the Adamic race, and so were inherently superior, conversely other humans were innately inferior or even Satanic. Christian Identity writers made arguments to that effect based on a variety of pseudo-historical sources.

Christian Identity's argument for the inferiority of non-white peoples is based on the concept of pre-Adamism. Biblical sources teach the unity of all humans. Adam is the ultimate father of all the peoples of the earth. Furthermore, the universal flood later destroyed all of sinful humanity except for Noah and the extended family of his three sons Shem, Ham and Japheth and their wives. Once again the common ancestry and basic equality of all humankind is affirmed. Racists find this Christian idea of the unity and equality of humanity to be highly inconvenient to their worldview. Therefore they are quite interested in any reconstruction of human origins that denies a common ancestry and biological unity for the human species.

Pre-Adamism, the idea that some humans lived on the earth before the creation of Adam, is one of the concepts that Christian Identity adopted. The idea that other worlds existed before Adam's creation has a long history, particularly in medieval Jewish thought. This early Jewish theory, however, speculated that God had created earlier worlds and destroyed them for their sins. Nothing from these earlier creations survived in the present world.[24] The discovery of the Americas in 1492 with their population of hitherto unknown humans shook the assumptions of the existing medieval worldview with its single creation of Adam or monogenesis. How did the Native Americans fit into the family of Adam's descendants, or did they? Most European writers produced speculative theories that linked the

Native Americans to Adam. Some did not. Paracelsus proposed the idea of a Double Adam. God created one Adam for the Old World and another for the Americas but this theory imputed no superiority to one creation or the other. Such speculations opened the door to pre-Adamism.[25] The book of Genesis contains some material that strongly implies that other peoples were living on the earth when Adam and Eve were created. When Cain murdered his brother Abel God placed a mark on him to prevent anyone from killing him as a criminal. At that time, however, only Adam and Eve should have been present, so why did Cain need to be marked? Afterwards Cain travelled to the land of Nod, east of Eden, married and founded a city. Who was around for him to marry and to populate his city?

As the sixteenth and seventeenth centuries progressed various vague and clandestine theories about pre-Adamism circulated among free thinkers. The first person who dared to publish a detailed speculation about pre-Adamism was the French Huguenot Isaac La Peyerère (1594–1676).[26] La Peyerère was writing on pre-Adamism as early as 1643 but did not publish until 1655 when his *Praeadamitae* and his *Systema theologicum ex praeAdamitarum hypothesi* appeared. These works were translated into other languages, including English where they appeared respectively as *Men Before Adam* (1656) and *A Theological System upon That Presupposition That Men were before Adam* (1655). La Peyerère argued that all humans but the Jews were pre-Adamites and that God had created Adam and his Jewish descendants to carry out the purposes of sacred history and bring salvation for all humanity. Part of his pre-Adamite theory included the denial that Noah's flood was universal, rather it was confined to Palestine. According to La Peyerère everyone would ultimately be saved. His writings aroused the wrath of the Roman Catholic Church and he was forced to convert to Catholicism, recant and write refutations of his own ideas, apparently somewhat half-heartedly. La Peyerère's approach to the text of the Bible was critical and he treated it like any other historical document. His work helped to promote scepticism and was a milestone in the evolution of the higher criticism of the Bible. It also provided an apparently respectable scholarly foundation for other speculations about pre-Adamites.

From the late seventeenth century until the mid-nineteenth century, scientific endeavours revealed more and more evidence that indicated an age for the earth that was far longer than the biblical chronology of six thousand years. In fact remains of humans far older than six thousand years were being discovered. How could this deep time, which grew from tens of thousands of years to hundreds of thousands and eventually to millions of years and beyond, be reconciled to the chronology of the Bible? Evolutionary theories were challenging the biblical account of creation and the problem became more acute after the publication of Charles Darwin's *Origin of Species* in 1859. Various efforts were made to harmonize the biblical narrative with new scientific discoveries. Unfortunately some of these harmonizing theories imbibed deeply of the scientific racism and ethnic prejudices of the nineteenth century. The basic idea was that there was a pre-Adamite creation or creations sometime in the distant past that was followed ultimately by the creation of Adam in God's image according to the biblical chronology. This approach opened the way to classifying humans into different species, which in turn could provide scientific justification for racial and ethnic prejudices.[27]

These alternative harmonizing theories of human origins had several basic variations. In one version God created humans multiple times over a long period of time. Multiple creations are referred to by the term polygenesis. God's first creation would have been the Negroes. They were the first humans created after God had created the other animals and so they were closer to being animals than other humans. After that God created the other increasingly intelligent and sophisticated races. The process culminated with the creation of Adam, the progenitor of the white race. Another approach involved the creation of the animalistic and dark pre-Adamites at some point in the primordial past and then about six thousand years ago God created Adam and the white race. The other races represented various degrees of interbreeding between the two species of pre-Adamitic and Adamic races. A third variant had God create the Negro race and then it was allowed to evolve. At a certain point God allowed Adam and his white descendants to emerge from this evolutionary morass. This theory equated divine creation with an ongoing process of biological and cultural evolution. With few exceptions, most theories of human origins that involved pre-Adamism were predicated on assumptions of white supremacy and black inferiority. In turn the emerging Victorian sciences of race provided a powerful affirmation of racial prejudice. During the years from around 1850 up to about 1920 various writers in the South of the USA used pre-Adamite theories in ways that linked science and Christianity to justify inequality for African-American slaves and freedmen.

Pro-slavery Southerners generally preferred the biblical story of Noah's curse on Ham as a religious justification for slavery. This approach preserved a single creation or monogenesis and the idea of a universal flood destroying all people but Noah and his family. It was orthodox and traditional which allowed its supporters to take the biblical narrative literally.[28] Some Southern writers, however, followed the lead of La Peyerère and rejected biblical literalism by accepting the existence of pre-Adamites. According to this rather unorthodox reinterpretation of Biblical history, God created the pre-Adamites along with the rest of the animals. That creation took place some indeterminate but lengthy amount of time before the creation of Adam. Pre-Adamites were not created in God's image like Adam and his descendants and so they lacked souls and the ability to accept Christianity and be saved. As with the other animals, God gave Adam dominion over the pre-Adamites, a circumstance that provided a powerful justification for slavery and white supremacy. The anti-black Southern writers also put forward the claim that the serpent who tempted Eve was actually a pre-Adamite, who also served as an agent of Satan. Accounts vary as to whether the serpent or *Nachash* was a Negro or a Mongolian type of pre-Adamite. *Nachash* is the Hebrew word translated as serpent in the Genesis account but these nineteenth-century Southern commentators suggested spurious alternate meanings or Hebrew homonyms that implied that the serpent was actually a pre-Adamite. Later Christian Identity writers have adopted this interpretation of *Nachash* into their belief system. As a result Eve's temptation becomes a sexual seduction and in some accounts Cain is the result of that original sin. Cain later grows up and murders his brother, or rather half-brother, Abel. Afterward he goes into exile and became the ruler of the pre-Adamites living in the Land of Nod. Their bloodlines mix and Cain's vastly superior bloodline raises up the pre-Adamites somewhat. These Southern pre-Adamite theorists also vary somewhat in their accounts. One version has the interbreeding of Cain and the Negro pre-Adamites producing the Mongoloid races, who were superior to blacks but inferior to whites. Others have Cain settling with a preexisting Mongoloid race of pre-Adamites. The common denominator is that the white Adamic race is manifestly superior and possesses a God-given right of dominion over all other races. All these writers agree that the great and original sin is race-mixing or miscegenation. After all, for these anti-black Southern writers, the pre-Adamites are separate creations and distinct species so that intermarrying with them would be an abomination to God.[29]

Unfortunately, according to the argument of these anti-black authors, the Adamites continued to commit the great sin of miscegenation and that is why God sent the flood of Noah as a punishment. A universal flood, however, presented the pre-Adamite theorists, along with later Christian Identity writers, with a problem – how to explain pre-Adamite survival. One suggestion by Samuel A. Cartwright, which appeared in *DeBow's Review* in 1860, proposed that Noah took pure-blooded pre-Adamic blacks on to the Ark along with all the other animals. After the universal flood's end Ham was made the overseer of the *Nachash* or black race represented by Canaan, who was Ham's ward, not his son.[30] A more popular answer was to localize the flood to the Tarim Basin in Central Asia. That area was the dwelling place of the Adamic race and there in antediluvian times they merrily mated with their pre-Adamic neighbors living outside the basin and so angered God. In reaction he sent a flood that filled up the bowl of the Tarim Basin and obliterated all the Adamic people and their mixed-race offspring except for faithful Noah and his family. After the flood, Noah and his sons spread out over the earth and resumed that natural dominion of the Adamic race over the pre-Adamites. But Noah's descendants had still not learnt their lesson about miscegenation. Ham's son Mizraim founded a white Egypt but the Egyptians intermarried with black Africans and the decline of the great Egyptian empire followed. During Reconstruction some Southern pre-Adamite theorists even argued that God had destroyed the slave regime of the antebellum South because of the sin of miscegenation. Northern writers, like the geologist Alexander Winchell, took a less biblically based approach and argued that God first created the pre-Adamic blacks and set an evolutionary process of improvement into motion. The end result was the appearance of a superior Adam from whom the white races descended. Blacks remained biologically inferior in a separate branch of human evolution. This approach preserved monogenesis and white supremacy but it found little favour with either anti-black Southerners or later Christian Identity writers. It also got Winchell fired from Vanderbilt University.[31]

The writings of La Peyerère and the nineteenth-century pre-Adamite theories provided a rich stock of pseudohistorical and pseudoscientific literature for British Israelite writers of the early twentieth century and Christian Identity writers in the late twentieth century to draw upon. The pyramidologist David Davidson in 1927 followed the Southern pre-Adamists by writing the speculative *A Connected History of Early Egypt, Babylonia, and Central Asia* which credited Cain with setting up a mixed-race civilization east of the Tigris River. Mrs Sydney (Ellen) Bristow went even further in the same year in her *Sargon the Magnificent*. She identifies the historical Mesopotamian ruler Sargon as Cain, who settled among the non-white Babylonians and through his vastly superior Adamic traits raised them to be a mighty but evil empire stretching from Britain to China. For Bristowe the Mongoloid and Asiatic peoples are the descendants of Cain's intermarrying with black Babylonians. Davidson and Bristowe's ideas had wide currency among their contemporary

British Israelists even though these Cain theories were not necessarily central to British Israel concerns. Their ideas would later deeply influence Christian Identity writers.[32]

A premier Christian Identity writer like Wesley Swift basically adopted the racist pre-Adamite theories with very little alteration. The various races of the world are pre-Adamic blacks or the results of race-mixing while the whites of North America and Europe are the beleaguered Adamic race. Swift and others like William Potter Gale had added one significant embellishment. They have developed a fusion of *Paradise Lost* and *Star Wars*. God's angels and archangels patrolled the universe in spaceships but as the Adamic race was about to be created Satan started his civil war in the Heavens. He and the rebel angels used pre-Adamite blacks as their minions but to no avail. The Archangel Michael and a mighty armada of spaceships defeated them and the rebel survivors fled to the earth. At that point God commanded the Archangel Michael to hold up his attack so that Satan could fulfill his destiny on earth. Meanwhile the Archangel Michael stands guard over the earth with others known as the Watchers. In this version of primordial history the pre-Adamites are a Satanic creation.[33] All in all, the concept of pre-Adamism adopted by Christian Identity provides a powerful religious justification for the racial prejudices of the adherents of the movement. It is no wonder that Christian Identity is to a large degree the Ku Klux Klan at prayer.

The idea of the Jews as the seedline of Satan is the unique and original contribution of Christian Identity to the pseudohistory of human origins. Compared to British Israel beliefs and the view of non-whites as the descendants of pre-Adamic races, its intellectual pedigree is quite recent. Jews have suffered persecution for thousands of years. Scattered among other cultures and religions, they stand apart from the larger society in the practice of their religion and culture. That separation assures that they periodically experience persecution because they are different. The twentieth century witnessed some of the most intense outbreaks of anti-Semitism. Nazis dehumanized the Jews as an evil race and slaughtered millions of them in the Holocaust but other cultures have their own versions of anti-Semitism and Christian Identity's is possibly the most virulent since it identifies the Jews as the demonic progeny of Satan.

Logically Christians and Muslims should both have a positive attitude toward Jews. The roots of Christianity and Islam lie in Judaism. What faithful Christian or Muslim could disparage Father Abraham, King David or the Prophet Isaiah because they were Jews? None. So how does a faithful Christian anti-Semite justify ill-feelings toward Jews? One strategy that is commonly used by British

Israelites and Identity Christians along with secular anti-Semites is to depict modern Jews as adulterated or false Jews. One contention is that while living in the land of Israel, ancient Hebrews intermarried with their neighbours – the Edomites, the Canaanites and the Hittites. Jewish blood became very watered down and the diaspora of the Jews among the peoples of the Mediterranean, the Middle East and Europe with accompanying intermarriage further diluted it. Such mongrelized Jews would logically be inferior to the supposedly more pure-blooded descendants of the Ten Lost Tribes. Another argument suggests that there are true/good Jews, the Sephardim, and false/bad Jews, the Ashkenazim. Sephardic Jews may have experienced some adulteration of their blood but they were basically acceptable. Ashkenazic Jews are impostors, really descendants of the nomadic Khazars, a Turkic-Iranian people, who converted to Judaism during the eighth century. These Ashkenazim are dishonest and scheming people and not even Jewish in a biological sense. As such, they definitely do not have any affinity with the true Israelites of the descendants of the Ten Lost Tribes. In fact these false Jews are the world conspirators of the *Protocols of the Elders of Zion*. Furthermore, this division of good Jews/bad Jews allows some Christian Identity believers to take a respectful attitude toward the abstraction of biblical and Sephardic Jews while justifying their loathing for Ashkenazic Jews, who form the great majority of Jews, living in the USA.[34]

The idea that Satan has fathered human offspring is as old as the existence of Satan himself. Such diabolical children would pose a grave danger to normal humans and the existence of a few particularly sadistic or perverse people certainly fuels the belief that demons walk among us. It is not all that common, however, to identify a specific group as the Devil's children in a historical (or rather, pseudohistorical) narrative. About 1800 the Irish parliamentarian Francis Dobbs speculated that a non-Adamic race had been spawned as a result of Satan seducing Eve at the fall.[35] A few years later, in 1826, the predestinarian Baptist minister David Parker (1781–1844) wrote a pamphlet titled *Views of the Two Seeds* which suggested that Eve had given birth to two seedlines. God planted the good seedline and his chosen people were descended from it. Satan planted the evil seedline and wicked people were descended from it, starting with Cain.[36] Traditionally Cain had nothing to do biologically with Hebrews, Jews or anyone else since any Cainites would have been destroyed in Noah's flood. At the same time, biblical tradition also viewed Cain as someone who had introduced much wickedness into human existence. Certainly that is the view that Mrs Sydney Bristowe took in *Sargon the Magnificent*, which identifies Cain with the historical

Sargon of Akkad as the creator of a vast and malevolent empire. Her historical theories remain very popular with British Israelists and Identity Christians.

Michael Barkun has traced the rise of Christian Identity in the period after World War II. By no later than 1960 the Christian Identity writer Conrad Gaard had made the link between Satan and his descendants, the Jews of modern times. The simplified version of this theory is that Satan impregnated Eve at the fall of man with Cain. Obviously this means that Cain is Satan's son, not Adam's, which serves to explain Cain's evil nature. Furthermore, if the modern Jews are the descendants of Satan's son Cain, that explains the alleged evil nature of the Jews and justifies any animosity that Identity Christians hold toward them. The Jews are supposedly on this earth to help carry on Satan's war with God, they are the primary agents of a gigantic, cosmic, Satanic conspiracy that is being played out in the present. Barkun points out that Wesley Swift and Bernard Comparet, another prominent Christian Identity figure, might have developed the idea of the Jews being the children of Satan before Gaard but this cannot be documented because so many of their writings and sermons are not dated. What is certain is that this ferociously demonizing view of the Jews is an almost universally agreed upon doctrine of Christian Identity. William Potter Gale vigorously promoted the idea. At present the second generation Christian Identity writer Dan Gayman's pamphlet *The Two Seeds of Genesis 3:15* (1978) is prominently listed on the website of Kingdom Identity Ministries.[37] The only competing theory of Jewish identity in the Christian Identity movement is the idea that the modern Jews are the false Jews. They are frauds who claim to be part of the bloodline of authentic Jews but in fact are mongrel descendants of Canaanites and Edomites. Or, even more heinous, the modern Jews are the descendants of the nomadic Khazars, who converted to Judaism but possess no biological connection to the ancient Hebrews. Furthermore Khazars are allegedly a particularly loathsome group of barbarians with aggressive and greedy traits they have passed on to their pseudo-Jewish descendants. Although versions of the Khazar theory had been circulating since about 1900, the current Khazar theory came to prominence among Christian Identity ministers through their reading of prominent Jewish writer Arthur Koestler's somewhat fanciful book *The Thirteenth Tribe* which appeared in 1976. While Koestler wrote the book to celebrate Judaism, Christian Identity writers used it to bolster their derogatory theories about the origins of modern Jews.

Obviously these differing theories of Jewish origins are not particularly compatible. Still Christian Identity writers are perfectly content to espouse them simultaneously and are not at all worried about seeming contradictions. Any theory that depicts the Jews negatively, whether they are the demonic progeny of Satan or frauds who have usurped the status of God's chosen people, is quite agreeable to Identity Christians. Their worldview is anti-Semitic and any pseudohistorical theory that justifies that world view is all right with them.[38]

APOCALYPSE WHEN?

> Fanaticism is to superstition what delirium is to fever, and what fury is to anger. The man who has ecstasies and visions, who takes dreams for realities, and his imaginings for prophecies, is an enthusiast. The man who backs his madness with murder is a fanatic. VOLTAIRE[39]

Christian Identity adherents live in a world where as white Europeans they are God's chosen people. Unlike the triumphalist view of the British Israelists during the late nineteenth and early twentieth centuries, when the Ephriamite British Empire comfortably controlled much of the world, including the Holy Land after 1918 with the Second Coming imminent, Identity Christians consider themselves to be surrounded by the worldly might of Satan and his demonic followers. Christian Identity developed during the era of the Cold War when a Christian coalition of the USA and its allies faced the godless Soviet Union or, in the minds of many religious right-wingers, Gog and Magog. The racism and anti-Semitism of the people who were attracted to Christian Identity caused them by the 1960s to see domestic developments within the USA as equally threatening. The Civil Rights movement, the rise of a pro-Israeli foreign policy and other momentous social changes of the 1960s provided the first generation of Christian Identity ministers with ominous evidence that things were going horribly wrong in the USA. Enforcement of civil rights laws meant that the inferior pre-Adamites of the coloured races, the so-called mudpeople, were being treated as equals. The way to widespread miscegenation lay wide open and mass destruction could not be far behind if the examples of Noah's flood and the defeat of the Confederacy were paid proper heed. Support for the state of Israel by the USA meant that the government was aiding the Devil's children, the false Jews, and so forwarding the ancient and vast conspiracy of Satan. It did not take long for some Identity Christians to conclude that the US government was under the control of the Jews. It was a Zionist Occupation Government or ZOG, one that was opposed to God and his chosen people, the descendants of the Lost Tribes. Obviously the supporters of Christian Identity considered themselves to be beleaguered and surrounded at home and abroad.

Christian Identity, like many fundamentalist evangelicals and British Israelites, believes that the end of the world is at hand. Its vision of the final struggle between the godly and the Satanic, however, is comparatively more bleak and pessimistic. Mainstream fundamentalist evangelicals believe that when the last days of the world arrive there will be a colossal struggle between good and evil but good will assuredly triumph. While this struggle will be worldwide, its greatest battle, Armageddon, will center on the historic land of Israel. Generally evangelicals believe that an event called the Rapture will occur prior to the commencement of the Tribulation and the last great battle of Armageddon. The Rapture is an event in which Christ appears in the heavens and true believers, both living and dead, will assume spiritual bodies and rise up to join him. Through the Rapture, true believers are allowed to miss the Tribulation, a seven-year period of horrible and widespread suffering during which Satan/Anti-Christ will rule the earth. The Tribulation will end when God leads his heavenly hosts and destroys the forces of Satan at the great and final battle of Armageddon. Following the biblical account, the traditional teaching of the Christian churches has been that believing Christians would be on earth and suffer through the Tribulation with everyone else. Therefore, although the theory of the Rapture is held by many conservative evangelicals, liberal Christians, Roman Catholics and old-line Protestant denominations dismiss it as unbiblical. In fact the idea of the Rapture is of relatively recent origin. John Nelson Darby (1800–1882), a Plymouth Brethren minister and founder of the Darbyite branch of the movement, is usually credited with conceiving of the Rapture. The idea, however, did not catch on widely among evangelicals until Hal Lindsey wrote his *Late Great Planet Earth* in 1970, which incorporated the Rapture into his scenario for the end of the world.[40]

Christian Identity, while extremely conservative, rejects the Rapture although it embraces the Tribulation. Identity Christians believe that there will be no Rapture and that true Christians will experience the Tribulation and will play an important part in helping God to fight Satan's cosmic conspiracy at Armageddon. Furthermore, they do not locate the climatic battle in Palestine or the territory of the biblical land of Israel. Christian Identity believes that the land of Israel is located wherever the true Children of Israel, the chosen people, dwell. Since the whites of North America are the descendants of the Ten Lost Tribes and they live in North America, that is where Armageddon will occur. The anxious atmosphere of the Cold War deeply influenced much apocalyptic speculation after 1945 which included identifying the Soviet Union with the barbaric and godless hordes of Gog and Magog. Christian Identity accepted all that anti-communist imagery but added the demoralizing twist that the US government was not an ally against evil, rather part of the Satanic conspiracy. The Zionist Occupation Government (ZOG) controlled the United States.[41]

Threatened by invasion, internal subversion and a corrupt and coopted government, what were Identity Christians to do? Their answer was to arm themselves, prepare for the coming war and head for the wilderness, in other words, survivalism. Survivalism is the practice of living a largely self-sufficient existence in some isolated spot with family, a few friends and lots of guns. The general public views survivalists as somewhat eccentric people who don't like urban life, are pioneer wannabes or environmentalists who also happen to be gun-nuts. The religious motivation of many survivalists is ignored in the media reports. In fact the Aryan Nations' compound in Idaho, the Covenant, Sword and Arm of the Lord compound in Arkansas, and the homesteads of people like Randy Weaver were closely associated with Christian Identity. From the point of view of Identity Christians, their tragedy and their frustration is that they know that the Apocalypse is near but that knowledge has been suppressed among the general population of Americans. Most people are unaware, oblivious or uncomprehending of the danger from Satan and his minions and their coming race war.[42]

What makes Christian Identity's view of the end of the world grim and pessimistic is its dualistic tendencies. Many Identity writers seem to feel that there is a very close balance of power between good and evil, or God and Satan, and that their final conflict could go either way.[43] It is a worldview that inclines those Identity Christians engaged in survivalism to be quick to shoot when confronted by the FBI, the AFT or the US marshals, as the incidents involving Gordon Kahl and Randy Weaver demonstrate. Survivalist and paramilitary activities also tend to draw the attention of the Federal and state governments. Survivalists with children run into problems about living conditions or schooling. Others refuse to pay taxes like Gordon Kahl. Some engage in borderline to fully fledged violations of firearms laws. A few even talk about forcibly overthrowing the Zionist Occupation Government, a threat, if repeated often enough, that will cause concern in the Federal government. Even fewer Identity Christians go on to actually engage in violence.

New religious movements sometimes organize a defence/police type of paramilitary force. Mormons had their Danites while the

Nation of Islam has their Fruit of Islam. Christian Identity has two defence forces, a real but defeated one and a mythical and therefore undefeatable one. The real but defeated force was known as the Order, a revolutionary group of white racists with Christian Identity ties that operated during the early 1980s. The Order was also known as the Brüder Schweigen or Silent Brotherhood, a name that betrays a romanticization of Nazism.[44] Robert J. Matthews (1953–1984) founded the Order in September 1983 at his home in Metaline Falls, Washington. The Order hoped to precipitate an Aryan uprising against the US government which would also become a race war against Jews and blacks. While the plans of the Order were vast in terms of their goals, it is important to remember that it was a very small group of people, numbering about forty at the height of its membership. Financing their activities through armoured car robberies, the Order successfully accumulated several million dollars. In June 1984 they assassinated the aggressively anti-racist talk-radio host Alan Berg, who also happened to be Jewish. Such activities drew the attention of the FBI who quickly managed to infiltrate the Order. On 8 December 1984 they tracked down Richard Matthews at Whidbey Island on the Washington coast where he died in his burning house during the course of a gun-battle with the FBI. By the spring of 1986 the entire Order had been arrested, tried and sent to prison. Although a few other organizations have followed the pattern of the Order, most notably the Aryan Revolutionary Army which was suppressed in 1997, most Christian Identity adherents and other right-wing racists have acquiesced into fantasies of resistance rather than pursuing the reality.[45]

The Phineas Priesthood served as the fantasy of resistance. Richard Kelly Hoskins invented the idea in his 1990 book *Vigilantes of Christ*. He derived the concept of a Phineas Priesthood from various biblical passages (Numbers 25:6–13 and Psalms 106:29–31); they were a group that served as the protectors of true Christians, that is, Identity Christians. They would also punish sinners and a big sin for Identity Christians would be race-mixing. According to the myth inspired by Hoskins, the Phineas Priesthood was such an ultra-secret and incorruptible organization that the FBI would never be able to penetrate it. Of course, the fact that the Phineas Priesthood did not exist in a physical sense probably had something to do with the FBI's failure to infiltrate it. Hoskins even identified various historical people as Phineas Priests, a list that included Robin Hood, John Wilkes Booth, Jesse James, Gordon Kahl and Robert Matthews. Being deceased, they were all beyond FBI interrogation. Hoskins also drew the parallels that Phineas Priests were to true Christians as kamikazes were to the Japanese or Zionists were to the Jews.[46] In fact it could be more appropriately argued that Phineas Priests served the same role for Christian Identity that the Golem filled for persecuted Jews – a fantasy protector.

The FBI's success in infiltrating right-wing racist groups engaged in crime and sedition has made Identity Christians and their close associates ultra-cautious about plotting and reinforced their already paranoid worldview. Besides fantasizing about fictional Phineas Priests, some people in the Christian Identity movement and the racist right began to advocate leaderless resistance. What they meant was that committed individuals or lone wolves would carry out sponta- neous terrorist acts against targets of opportunity. Such an approach needed no organization that the FBI could penetrate and destroy. Leaderless resistance was the ultimate in revolutionary anarchy. Ob- viously the strategy of leaderless resistance is the logical consequence of a weak revolutionary movement that has been steadily compro- mised by infiltration and collaborators. Weakness does not neces- sarily mean harmless and Timothy McVeigh's bombing of the federal building in Oklahoma City in 1995 shows the horrific potential of leaderless resistance for violence. While it has been argued that Tim- othy McVeigh did not conceive of himself as a lone wolf or a partici- pant in leaderless resistance, the fact is that what he and one or two co-conspirators did in Oklahoma City is basically what the advocates of leaderless resistance had been preaching to the most extreme mem- bers of the racist right. Some in the racist right consider Timothy McVeigh to be the appearance of yet another Phineas Priest.[47]

For the time being, the appeal of Christian Identity has ebbed. It has been estimated that at its high point in the 1980s the movement had 100,000 followers and sympathizers. Other experts have lowered that estimate to 50,000. Some scholars of Christian Identity suggest that its hardcore following consists of no more than a few thousand people. Neo-Nazi cults and white power paganism have also signifi- cantly challenged Christian Identity for adherents among youth in- clined to racism. In spite of these internal challenges within the racist community, defeats by the government, unrelenting negative expo- sure by the anti-cult movement and the widespread disapproval by the general population of the USA, Canada and Great Britain, Christian Identity is still out there. The Kingdom Identity Ministry of Harrison, Arkansas, has an active website as does Aryan Nations.[48] The pseudohistorical lore that provides the foundation for Christian Identity has entered the cultic milieu of the West where such ideas never fade away. Instead they mutate as Christian Identity did from British Israelism or are reborn somewhere else. British Israel organizations and websites also continue to exist, though the British Israel World Federation declined significantly from a membership of 5000 during the 1920s down to only 700 during the early 1990s. Offshots survive in Canada, Australia and the USA.[49]

Could Christian Identity someday topple the US government? It is hardly likely. Could it reverse its fortunes and start growing again? Yes, if social and economic conditions were right. Christian Identity became violent during the Reagan era, a time of economic dislocation for many people as well as renewed fears about the Cold War turning hot and disastrous. Ironically, a revival of Christian Identity would be more likely to occur if the evangelical right were to be discredited and collapse. Given the results of elections in the US during the autumn of 2008, that process might be underway. Right-wing evangelicals divert potential members away from joining Christian Identity. If that formidable rival lost its popular appeal, the more extreme ideology of Christian Identity would be a logical place for the extremists among the disenchanted to turn. Such a scenario would be very much aided by the recent election of Barack Obama as President of the United States and other liberal triumphs which have left the Christian Right humiliated and relatively impotent, at least for the time being. Meanwhile, the ulcer of war in Iraq and Afghanistan keep Americans and other Western nations divided and apprehensive as they reel from spikes in the price of oil and the continuing vague but very real threat of Islamic terrorism. What if some terrorist group detonated a nuclear device in an American city? Such events would prompt a national reassessment and some people would predictably blame these defeats and disasters on a sinful America abandoning its white, Anglo-Saxon and Christian heritage and obligations. Even prior to the presidential election of 2008, skinheads were caught plotting to assassinate Obama.[50] More plots are sure to follow. It would be just a small step to tack Christian Identity doctrines on to that response because for them too a member of the Mud People and a minion of Satan has been elected President. In a world where the future is always contingent upon unfolding events, anything is possible. And the cultic milieu is always there to give those events a pseudo-historical explanation.

CHAPTER 4

Mad Scientists, White Devils and the Nation of Islam: Racist Cosmogonies and Pseudohistory, Part II

> Between true science and erroneous doctrines,
> ignorance is in the middle.
> THOMAS HOBBES[1]

> False tales are, first of all, tales, and tales, like myths,
> are always persuasive.
> UMBERTO ECO[2]

On 18 February 1965, just three days before his assassination, Malcolm X appeared on WINS Radio in New York. He was participating in a live panel discussion and call-in radio show in which the topic was a critical look at the Nation of Islam. By that point in his life it was well known that Malcolm X had broken with Elijah Muhammad, the long-time leader of the Nation of Islam, and that he utterly rejected his teachings. His comments on the radio show reiterated that stance most clearly. He stated that, 'The religious ingredient in the Black Muslim movement was a fraud in the sense that it identified itself as an Islamic movement, as an Islamic [sic] – of being an Islamic nature. It was a fraud in that it had – it was diametrically opposed to Islam.' Malcolm X was neither the first nor the last to lay that accusation against the Nation of Islam. Most practising Muslims, scholars of Islam, and Wallace Muhammad, the son and successor of Elijah Muhammad, have made the same observation. Even if a cursory comparison of Islamic and Nation of Islam beliefs is made, it is hard to see how anyone could reach any other conclusion. True believers in the Nation of Islam, however, continue to insist their doctrines are genuinely Islamic. But as Malcolm X proceeded to point out during the radio show, some of the doctrines of the Nation of Islam were distinctly bizarre. Recalling his days as a faithful member of the Nation of Islam, he reminisced, 'We believed in Yacub. We believed in what Elijah Muhammad taught about an airplane in the sky. We believed in some of the most fantastic things that you could ever

135

imagine.'³ And he was not exaggerating. Of course, most extreme groups entertain some weird beliefs and doctrines in the eyes of observers in the mainstream of society. Such beliefs are often a logical consequence of a movement being extremist. What the doctrines of the Nation of Islam were and how they developed make for a fascinating story. They provide another case study of a pseudohistorical cosmogony being used to justify reprehensible prejudices. Ironically the beliefs of the Nation of Islam parallel and mirror those of the Christian Identity movement.

THE SETTING

> So long as the Negro is left in servitude, he can be kept in a state
> bordering on brutishness, but once he becomes free, there is no
> way to prevent him from learning enough to appreciate the extent
> of his afflictions and conceive a vague idea of the remedy.
> ALEXIS DE TOCQUEVILLE⁴

The Nation of Islam had its origin during 1930 in Detroit, the automobile capital of America. The Motor City was not a happy place that year. As in other northern industrial cities in the USA, the Great Depression was tightening its grip on the economy. Unemployment was increasing and with it came uncertainty, pessimism and fear. The mood of the people was one of wretched despair and conditions would continue to get worse. Particularly for Detroit it was a startling comedown. Prior to the advent of the Great Depression the city had shone as a bright star in the industrial firmament of the USA. The rise of the automotive industry had transformed Detroit over the previous decades from a pleasant medium-sized city into the fourth largest city in the USA with a population of over 1.25 million. Industrial growth brought wealth for the elite and extraordinarily high wages for the working class. High wages lured thousands of willing workers to Detroit and swelled its population. Potential workers left the farms and small towns of Michigan and its neighbouring states. European immigrants numbering in the hundreds of thousands took passage for the seemingly golden shores of the USA with their promise of prosperity. Among the industrial cities, Detroit was one of the favourite destinations.

Movement to industrial cities was not confined to white workers either. If whites flocked to the cities for higher wages and the excitement of living in a great urban centre, African-Americans from the South shared those reasons for moving but also had additional motivations unique to themselves. By 1900 the white supremacist regime of laws and culture collectively referred to as Jim Crow had come to dominate Southern states. Under the Jim Crow regime African-Americans experienced relentless and ruthless oppression. Segregation, poor schools, no opportunities for advancement, vigilantism, lynching and daily casual but systematic indignities plagued their existence. At the same time the news from the North indicated that things were different there, and much better. With the encouragement of African-American leaders in the North, blacks of the South began the exodus into the North known as the Great Migration. Prior to the Great Migration, over 90 per cent of African-Americans lived in the South. By the early 1930s millions had moved to Northern industrial cities seeking greater economic opportunities and the semblance of civil rights and equality. Initially the immigrants expected to find the North to be a land of milk and honey economically and a peaceable kingdom of racial relations. These expectations proved to be sadly mistaken for most of them. Racism was on the rise in white America from the last quarter of the nineteenth century into the 1930s aided and abetted by the pseudoscience of race and Social Darwinism. During this era Social Darwinism tainted assumptions about the biological and social consequence of race and its vile values oozed into Northern society to a significant degree. Furthermore, the massive influx of African-Americans into Northern industrial cities created social changes and disruptions that the white residents found profoundly disturbing. Xenophobic paranoia, burgeoning racism and fears about economic competition lead to a situation where the newly arrived African-Americans were increasingly unwelcome. Race riots and lynchings happened in the North that were every bit as horrific as the racist excesses in the South. While Northern states never instituted the *de jure* segregation of the South, *de facto* segregation denied African-Americans fair access to housing and public facilities. While the Northern practice of racial discrimination never came close to the systematic intensity of the Jim Crow South, it was a deeply depressing trend. This swelling of racism in the North, however, did not blunt the Great Migration. As the African-American population grew in the North, so did racial tensions and Detroit experienced more than its fair share of those tensions.[5]

Even during the relatively prosperous 1920s African-Americans moving to the Northern cities encountered painful problems as well as greater opportunities. Generally they were relegated to the least desirable and lowest paying jobs. Unions did not accept them for membership. Housing became a huge problem. The huge flood of African-Americans from the South led to them being herded into segregated neighbourhoods in the least pleasant parts of Northern cities. Whites living in established neighbourhoods did not want large numbers of blacks moving in and resisted integration with the newcomers by legal and illegal means, including violence. Savage race riots occurred across the North with those in East St Louis in 1917 and Chicago in 1919 being particularly deadly. Detroit experienced its own brand of racial violence in 1925 when outraged white homeowners gathered in a threatening manner around the newly purchased home of Ossian Sweet, an African-American physician and therefore a very unwelcome new neighbour. Gunfire from the Sweet house killed a man who was not part of the mob. Two high-profile trials followed in which the famous defence attorney Clarence Darrow successfully defended Sweet and the friends and family members who had helped him move in and stayed to help him defend his new home. While Sweet's trials showed that Northern justice was not totally stacked against African-Americans, as was the case in the Jim Crow South, it was a result that could only have provided minimal comfort to the vast majority of poor blacks. Unlike an educated professional like Dr Sweet, their choices were restricted to low paying jobs with unstable employment prospects and to overpriced and crowded slums for their residences.[6]

Such dire conditions in the Northern cities caused many African-Americans to gravitate to organizations that promised them self-improvement and a sense of identity, belonging and pride.[7] One important manifestation of this drive for self-help and self-esteem was created by Marcus Garvey (1887–1940), a Jamaican-born black nationalist. He came to the USA in 1916 and took up residence in New York City. What he saw there convinced him that the growing black populations in the cities of the North had the potential to create the wealth and the political unity needed to combat racism in America and European imperialism in Africa. In 1918 he incorporated his Universal Negro Improvement Association (UNIA) and published the newspaper *Negro World*. At its height the UNIA had as many as a million members in the USA, the Caribbean region and Africa. One of those members was Malcolm X's father, whose UNIA activities attracted the unfavourable attention of various white supremacist groups and in 1931 led to his murder by the Black Legion in Lansing, Michigan. Garvey founded various enterprises to increase black prosperity, but he proved to be a poor businessman. The FBI and the Justice Department closely monitored him and eventually charged him with mail fraud. He was convicted in 1923, imprisoned in 1925 and finally deported to Jamaica in 1927. From there he moved to London, where he died in 1940, having failed to revive the fortunes of the UNIA to their heights of the early 1920s. His UNIA possessed the distinction of being the largest secular organization in African-American history.

A contemporary religious movement for African-Americans was the Moorish Science Temple of America. Its founder was Noble Drew Ali, originally born Timothy Drew on 8 January 1886 in North Carolina. In 1913 he opened the Moorish Science Temple in Newark, New Jersey. Ten years later, in 1923, he moved his headquarters to Chicago and in 1928 changed the organization's name to the Moorish Science Temple of America (MSTA). Although Drew attracted nowhere near the number of followers that Garvey did, the MSTA managed to win over a fairly significant number of adherents considering its assumption of, what for that time, was a relatively unfamiliar and alien Islamic guise while rejecting Christianity and promoting some rather quirky doctrines. One source credits Noble Drew Ali with leading some 30,000 devotees by 1923 but another estimates that the MSTA only had about 15,000 to 20,000 members during the late 1920s.[8] The MSTA was an urban movement that established temples in various Northern and even some Southern cities. Like Garvey, Noble Drew Ali sought to provide African-Americans with a religious and racial identity that inspired pride.

Noble Drew Ali adopted the accoutrements of Islam for his Moorish Science Temple but his version of Islam was heterodox in the extreme while the depth of his knowledge of Islamic doctrines and history was questionable. One of his biggest deviations from Islam was his willingness to alter the text of the Quran and insert his own ideas or those of contemporary New Age writings, especially Levi H. Dowling's *Aquarian Gospel*. Besides adopting terminology and garb of seeming Islamic or Arabic provenance, such as the use of Arabic-sounding personal names, he borrowed other ideas and practices from Freemasonry and Theosophy. Interestingly, Drew did not advocate Afrocentrism or anything that could be construed as proto-Afrocentrism. He taught that the Islamic Moors of North Africa, which is the group he claimed to derive the Moorish Science Temple of America from, were actually Asiatic in origin.[9] In fact his goal was to persuade his followers to reject any associations with supposedly inferior African culture and racist Christianity and instead reveal their true origins in the culture of a respectable Islam and Asia. By managing this cultural and religious sleight of hand, Drew hoped to blunt and undermine some of the foundations of racism. He also added distinctly non-Islamic and heretical ideas about reincarnation to the doctrines of the MSTA.[10] In spite of or, perhaps, because of this esoteric mix of religious ideas, the MSTA appealed to thousands of African-Americans. The new converts were given new names that included 'El' or 'Bey' along with identity cards that proudly proclaimed the proselytes to be both faithful Muslims and citizens of the USA. Drew's followers invested these cards with a sort of talismanic power of protection and took to flashing them at bewildered white people on the streets of Chicago, including notably under-impressed policemen. Members of the MSTA also wore distinctive red fezzes which authorities in various cities came to equate as the headgear of chronic troublemakers.[11] The fervour of converts for the MSTA also manifested itself in the form of generous financial contributions which transformed the MSTA into a flourishing enterprise and one definitely worth fighting over.

Noble Drew Ali created a mystical persona for himself and his followers added to it. Tales of his origins claimed that he had learned his Islamic doctrines from ex-slaves of African Muslim origin or that he had actually studied Islam in Egypt or Arabia. Another legend claimed that the king of Morocco, the homeland of the Moors, had commissioned him to be an Islamic missionary to the African-Americans of the USA. Alternatively an unnamed president of the USA, sometimes identified as Theodore Roosevelt, had asked him to preach Islam to African-Americans, although the rationale for Roosevelt's request is not clear.[12] As will be shown later, the end of Drew's life suffers from the same ambiguities. Native-born, African-American Islamic organizations may have frightened whites with their rhetoric but their physical violence has been largely turned inward with people in leadership positions experiencing the highest casualty rates. The MSTA started the tradition of internal violence which the Nation of Islam has continued.

Lacking the necessary business expertise, Noble Drew Ali brought in various people to help him run the lucrative enterprises of the MSTA. Some of those associates eventually decided to take over the organization for themselves and a power struggle ensued. On 15 March 1929 one of Drew's rivals, Sheik Claude Greene, was shot and stabbed to death in Chicago. The police arrested Noble Drew Ali for the crime but he managed to obtain release on bail. At this point the narrative of events becomes conflicted and contradictory. One version claims that after his release he disappeared. Most accounts maintain that he died soon after leaving police custody. Some assert that supporters of Greene murdered him to avenge their leader. Others accuse the Chicago police of beating him so severely that he died of his injuries while awaiting trial. More prosaically, he supposedly succumbed to tuberculosis on 20 July 1929 and is buried either at the Burr Oaks cemetery or at the Lincoln cemetery in Chicago. The investigation of Sheik Greene's murder also revealed another unsavoury side of the leadership of the MSTA. Forty-three year old Drew turned out to be conducting concurrent sexual affairs with three female followers, two of them aged fourteen and sixteen while the third was in her twenties. At the same time other rumours claimed that Sheik Greene had been having an affair with Drew's third wife Pearl.[13] But in spite of the sordidness of Noble Drew Ali's demise as the leader of the MSTA, he managed to familiarize African-Americans with Islam, albeit a deeply heretical and flawed Islam, and so created a path for the Nation of Islam to follow.[14]

THE FOUNDERS: Wallace Fard and Elijah Muhammad

It is natural for the mind to believe and for the will to love; so that, for want of true objects, they must attach themselves to false.
BLAISE PASCAL[15]

The Nation of Islam (NOI) experienced many of the same problems as the Moorish Science Temple of America but it managed to survive and become a permanent feature among a segment of the African-American community. One place where the two organizations differed significantly was in the Nation of Islam's espousal of a virulent anti-white racism which it justified on the basis of a pseudohistorical cosmogony of human origins that is basically a mirror image of the Christian Identity movement's racist cosmogony.

The Nation of Islam originated in Depression-era Detroit. If the physician Ossian Sweet stands as the *cause célèbre* of the fight for racial justice in the bigoted Detroit of the Jazz Age, Elijah Poole, better known as Elijah Muhammad (1897–1975), exemplifies the more typical experience of the great majority of the African-Americans who moved to the industrial cities of the North during the Great Migration. Born in Sandersville, Georgia, into a sharecropping family, Elijah grew up poor and deprived of educational and economic opportunity. Both of his parents, William Poole and Mariah Hall, had white grandparents. In fact both of William Poole's grandfathers were white and the census of 1880 listed him as a mulatto. Besides sharecropping, William Poole also worked as a Baptist minister. Although ill-educated his son Elijah showed a marked interest in religion and religious knowledge, something that created a degree of resentment in the father.

As young Elijah grew up in Jim Crow Georgia he witnessed numerous racist incidents and even some lynchings. He also suffered from being relegated to dead-end, low-paying jobs and from underemployment along with many of his African-American neighbours. On 17 March 1919 he and his life long wife Clara Evans married. Within a few years, in 1923, 25-year-old Elijah gave up on the oppressions of the South and put his family on a train bound for Detroit in the hope of sharing in its burgeoning prosperity.[16] Upon arriving in Detroit the family settled in the community of Hamtramck, which had originally been a Polish neighbourhood. Initially Poole was attracted to Garveyism but the legal problems of Marcus Garvey and his movement soon led to disillusionment. He also experimented with Freemasonry and later the Moorish Science Temple of America, although it has been the official line of the Nation of Islam to deny any such connection. Even more demoralizing for Poole was his failure to secure a stable and decently paying job. He lacked the skills and education required for the better jobs but racial discrimination also held him back. The timing of his move to Detroit was not helpful either since it occurred during the final wave of the Great Migration. Arriving late, Poole and his family entered a job and housing market in which previously plentiful opportunities had long before been taken up by earlier arrivals. Falling into despair, Poole turned to alcohol as a counter-productive antidote. Eventually he managed to find a job in one of the least desirable parts of the Chevrolet Auto Plant, which he held for six years, but the coming of the Great Depression caused him to be laid off. His family was forced to accept public welfare, meagre as that was. The miserable condition of the Poole family mirrored the experiences of many African-Americans living in Detroit. The onset of the Great Depression during late 1929 and 1930 only served to exacerbate an already dire situation.[17]

Desperate people frequently turn to religion for solace but for someone in Elijah Poole's position it seemed that traditional Christianity had let him down badly. Other African-Americans shared his disillusionment and that created a spiritual vacuum, one that mysterious salesman Wallace Dodd Fard stepped in to fill. Fard's place in the history of the Nation of Islam is extremely conflicted. For faithful adherents of the Nation of Islam's doctrines, he was a messianic Allah come to earth to lead the lost-found African-Americans of the USA back to their homeland of Mecca and their rightful position of greatness and supremacy on the earth. Orthodox Muslims would consider Fard to be a detestable heretic who blasphemed when he claimed a form of godhead and continuous revelation beyond the Quran. African-American church leaders also called him a false prophet. The white police and municipal authorities of Detroit along with the FBI viewed him as a charlatan and confidence man who sought to cheat gullible, poor African-Americans of what little wealth that they possessed. Some scholars have even proposed the somewhat convoluted theory that Fard was actually some sort of Shiite or Ahmadiyya missionary operating incognito among African-Americans.

His strategy involved attracting disinterested blacks to the Nation of Islam's anti-white and racist doctrines while ultimately weaning them over to true Islam.[18] Obviously a consensus on Fard's true identity is highly unlikely when some people sincerely consider him to be an epiphany of Allah.

If anyone deserves the sobriquet of international man of mystery it is Wallace D. Fard. According to the testimony of committed members of the Nation of Islam, Fard declared, 'I am W. D. Fard and I came from the Holy City of Mecca. More about myself I will not tell you yet, for the time has not yet come. I am your brother. You have not seen me yet in my royal robes.'[19] He claimed to have been born in Mecca on 26 February 1887. His father was a black man named Alphonse from the tribe of Quraysh like the prophet Muhammad while his mother was a white woman, a Russian Jew from Azerbaijan named Baby Gee, who Alphonse civilized and married. The Fards had several children besides Wallace. Through some prophetic sense, Alphonse recognized Wallace as someone with a cosmic destiny. As he grew up, the young Wallace ignored that destiny and entered the greater world by studying at Oxford University in preparation for a career as a diplomat of the Kingdom of Hejaz which included Mecca. Later he travelled to the USA where he attended the University of Southern California in pursuit of a PhD. Along the way he came to speak sixteen languages. By 1930 he finally accepted his true destiny, which was to find and to save the kidnapped lost tribe of Shabazz and return them to their home of Mecca. The lost tribe of Shabazz consisted of scattered black people living among other African blacks under the racially oppressive conditions in the USA. The tribe of Shabazz, however, was Asiatic, not African, and some of its members were living in Detroit, which is where Fard travelled to begin his mission.[20]

As recently as 2003 it was written that, 'The question of Fard's identity is still not answered. The many mysteries surrounding this enigmatic figure are still at the heart of the enduring question: Who was the founder of the Nation of Islam.'[21] In fact quite a large amount of information about Fard has come to light over the years. None of it supports the Nation of Islam's official biography of Fard. The African-Americans who met Fard during his Detroit ministry generally viewed him as a white man of Arabic, Lebanese or other Middle Eastern background, some even serendipitously identified him as Pakistani. When the FBI and other law enforcement agencies began to investigate Fard they came up against a confused welter of seemingly contradictory information. Fard emigrated from New Zealand to Portland, Oregon during 1913. He was apparently born on 25 February 1891, making him four years younger than his disciples thought he was. His parents' names were Zared and Beatrice from Hawaii or New Zealand. Early accounts identified them as either of Hawaiian or of British and Polynesian ethnicity which would have accounted for Fard's somewhat ambiguous racial appearance. His place of birth was uncertain with some sources claiming he was born in Portland, Oregon, while others stated that it was New Zealand. From 1913 until his arrival in Detroit in 1930 Fard went through several failed marriages or intimate relationships, ran a restaurant, engaged in bootlegging, dealt drugs and spent three years in San Quentin prison from 1926 to 1929. Just prior to his arrival in Detroit he spent a bit of time in Chicago. This information comprises what is generally agreed upon as a thumbnail sketch of Fard's career among those who are not part of the Nation of Islam faithful.[22]

A big problem for anyone trying to determine the truth about Wallace D. Fard is that he used so many aliases. Figuratively he could have claimed with some honesty, 'My name is legion.' FBI records credit him with 58 aliases and there is good reason to believe that their list is not complete. His protégé Elijah Muhammad used aliases even more prodigiously. The FBI lists 127 for him. In Elijah (Poole) Muhammad's defence, unlike Fard, for a number of years he had rivals who were trying to kill him so he used many aliases for protection rather than for criminal purposes. In addition, a good portion of his aliases were the result of befuddled FBI agents trying to phonetically render Elijah Muhammad's mispronunciations of Muhammad and other Arabic names or copying his and his followers' misspellings. Fard also gave Elijah Muhammad several names. Fard's aliases were a different story. They were mostly variants of his real name of Wallace Dodd Fard and as such bear the earmarks of a criminal attempting to obscure or conceal his true identity. Among his aliases were Wallace Don Ford, Wally D. Ford and Wallace Farad. Other variants of his surname were Farrad, Ferrad, Farard and Farrow. Wallace was sometimes Arabicized as Wali, Wallay or Ali. After he adopted the surname of Muhammad, it, like Elijah Muhammad's name, appeared in records with a plethora of misspellings. Members of the Nation of Islam originally referred to him as One Mahadiah but later shifted almost exclusively to calling him Allah. Needless to say FBI investigators and later researchers have been left more than a little befuddled by all of these names.[23]

In 1963 the FBI investigated Fard's background in the hope of discovering something that would discredit Elijah Muhammad and the leadership of the Nation of Islam with the rank and file membership. While they discovered plenty of compromising and embarrassing information the FBI underestimated the capacity of true believers not to become confused by facts.[24] FBI probes into the labyrinth of Fard's career and his alter egos did manage conclusively to identify Wallace D. Fard and Wallace D. Ford as the same person and so connected Fard to Ford's criminal history. Using the records of the FBI investigations Karl Evanzz, a journalist and historian of Malcolm X's assassination, has constructed a convincing narrative of Fard's life that enhances rather than contradicts the existing sceptical accounts. Fard's parents, Zared Fard of East Indian and Pakistani lineage, married Beatrice, probably surnamed Dodd, a New Zealander of British ethnicity. Their son Wallace Fard was born on 25 February 1891 in New Zealand. In 1913 he entered the USA, probably illegally through Canada and took up residence in Portland, Oregon. Always a charmer, Fard married Pear Allen on 9 May 1914 and identified himself as white on the marriage licence. The couple had a child in 1915 but Fard found marriage and parenthood uncongenial. He asked Pearl for a divorce but she refused, so he simply abandoned wife and child and moved to Los Angeles, California, in 1916. Taking up work at a restaurant, Fard quickly rose to be manager and began living with one of the waitresses no earlier than late 1916 and lasting until early 1919. This woman discovered that in spite of his veneer of being an educated man he was functionally illiterate and she had to write most of his letters to his parents in New Zealand for him. After they broke up another woman, Hazel Barton, moved in with Fard and became his common-law wife later in 1919. Hazel, however, thought his name was Ford. On 1 September 1920 they had a son, Wallace Dodd Ford, Jr. After the birth of their boy Hazel discovered that her husband had aliases and had not been particularly honest with her. Deeply distressed by these revelations she moved out, taking their son. Her action left Fard despondent and he increased his use of drugs and alcohol.[25]

Late in 1920 Fard moved to San Francisco with his Chinese-American friend and partner, Edward Donaldson. At this point Fard disappears from the records but in his place arose a George Farr. Evanzz contends that Fard and Farr are the same person although FBI investigators failed to make that connection and the name of George Farr is not on their list of Fard's aliases. George Farr worked for a somewhat questionable Swami in the Theosophical Society and also became closely associated with the UNIA in San Francisco. Informants described Farr as Hindu in appearance with an educated demeanour, although he claimed to be a Negro. In the UNIA he used the Bible as a prophetic book and vehemently advocated anti-white sentiments, all of which anticipates Fard's ministry in Detroit. Farr also had a Chinese-American friend, who was probably Edward Donaldson, and they engaged in gambling and drug abuse.[26]

In 1922 Fard and Donaldson returned to Los Angeles while at the same time reports about Farr in San Francisco came to an end. Back in Los Angeles, under the name of Ford, Fard opened a restaurant although how he was able to finance such an enterprise is unclear. Once the restaurant began operation it served as a front for Fard and Donaldson's bootlegging and drug-dealing ventures. Early in 1926 undercover police arrested Fard and Donaldson on a series of violations of Prohibition and the drug laws. They were convicted on 14 May and together entered San Quentin prison on 12 June. Fard stated his race in prison documents as Hawaiian. Due to his good behaviour while incarcerated prison officials released him on 27 May 1929, not quite three years into his sentence.[27]

Soon after regaining his freedom Fard boarded a train for Chicago to work as a travelling salesman. Once he arrived there he began writing to Hazel Barton, using the name of W. D. Ford; their correspondence continued until his return to California in 1934. While in Chicago he joined the Moorish Science Temple of America and also attended the Ahmadiyya mosque in the South Side. He apparently rose rapidly in the ranks of the MSTA and on the death of Noble Drew Ali he claimed to be the reincarnation of the recently deceased leader. At least three others, however, made the same claim and an intense rivalry developed. Given the violent proclivities of the MSTA's internal struggles, Fard decided to get out of harm's way by fleeing to Detroit, another MSTA stronghold.[28]

Wallace Fard began working as a clothing peddler among the poor blacks of Detroit on 4 July 1930. His marketing strategy included claims that the clothing he sold was the same as that worn by the black people of Arabia and Asia, an obvious play on the teachings of the Moorish Science Temple of America. Fard combined clothes selling with proselytizing. While visiting the homes of his customers Fard began to dispense advice and proscriptions about diet and morals. Presenting himself as a mulatto, he claimed to have been born to royalty in Mecca on 26 February 1887. His African-American customers generally regarded him to be white of Arabic or Palestinian origin with an extraordinary level of sympathy for their problems. He began teaching them a religion that combined the old and the familiar with the new and the strange. This new religion originally called itself the Allah Temple of Islam but came to take the name of the Nation of Islam or the Lost-Found Nation of Islam. Its adherents have been frequently albeit incorrectly referred to as the Black Muslims, which they bitterly resent since according to their view all Muslims are by nature black. Many of the Nation of Islam's ideas about self-help derived from Garveyism while its Islamic trappings harken to the Moorish Science Temple of America and its earlier efforts to create identity and pride among alienated African-Americans. Initially Fard taught out of the Bible, a religious book that his intended flock knew well, but he used it to attack modern Christianity as racist. Gradually he introduced the Quran and Islamic beliefs as the true and original religion of black people. In the cosmogony that Fard presented blacks were the original people of God's creation, while whites were a later aberrant offshoot of the black race. White devilry brought evil and oppression to blacks, especially to the lost tribe of Shabazz, whose descendants were the downtrodden African-Americans living in America.[29]

For the poor African-American residents of Detroit, surrounded by an unsympathetic and frequently hostile white majority and struggling to survive the Great Depression, Fard's teachings offered an explanation of their desperate plight and hope for a way out of it. By the time he left Detroit in 1934, some 5,000 to 8,000 people had joined the Nation of Islam out of a population of African-Americans numbering about 120,000. The Nation of Islam absorbed the remnants of the Moorish Science Temple of America's membership in Detroit along with the many Christian African-Americans that it converted.[30] Like Marcus Garvey and Noble Drew Ali before him Fard offered his followers an identity and pride as the lost tribe of Shabazz along with the hope that he would lead them out of the racist wilderness of America and home to Mecca. This quest for a new identity involved Fard bestowing new names on his converts. These names were either Arabic or used the symbolic name of X which stood for the unknown names of the enslaved forebears of the modern African-Americans. Identity, however, came at a price – ten dollars to be exact.[31] For an employed African-American in Depression era Detroit, ten dollars was a substantial portion of a meagre week's take-home pay. For the unemployed on welfare it was a significant expenditure against the monthly support check. On Fard's end of the Nation of Islam's naming process, the cumulative revenues represented a princely sum for the prince from Mecca. If 5,000 converts paid the ten dollar fee, Fard would have taken in about half a million dollars over a three-year period. Given that he attracted additional donations from the newly converted faithful of the Nation of Islam, Fard and those he picked for his inner circle came to control significant financial resources. Much of this money went into schools and social services for members but it also caused some people to suspect Fard of being engaged in a scheme to fleece poor African-Americans of the pathetically little cash that they possessed. In fact the Detroit police would later claim that while in their custody

147

Fard confessed that the Nation of Islam was simply a racket to defraud gullible African-Americans of their savings. Given the rigorous interrogation techniques used by the police in large American cities during the pre-World War II era, it is entirely possible that the confession was coerced. Certainly true believers in the Nation of Islam vehemently reject that Fard ever said any such thing.[32]

Fard's success in attracting converts to the Nation of Islam soon necessitated that he move his meetings from private homes into rented meeting halls to accommodate the growing crowds. Word of Fard's ministry spread through the African-American community of Detroit and came to the attention of Elijah Poole and his family, who were told about it by relatives. In August 1931 Poole attended his first talk by Fard. It moved him deeply. According to one version of the two men's first encounter, as he moved through Fard's greeting line, Poole asked him, 'You are that one we read in the Bible that he would come in the last day under the name Jesus . . . You are that one?' Fard answered by whispering in Poole's ear, 'Yes, I am the One, but who knows that but yourself, and be quiet.'[33] Another account had Poole declare to Fard at their first meeting, 'I know who you are, you're God himself.' To which Fard responded, 'That's right, but don't tell it now. It is not yet time for me to be known.' Poole came to more of Fard's meetings and later asked him in private, 'Who are you and what is your name.' Fard replied, 'My name is Mahdi; I am God, I came to guide you into the right path that you may be successful and see the hereafter.'[34] Actually, there is strong evidence that it was actually a desperate Clara Poole who first introduced her alcohol-besotted husband to Fard by inviting the mysterious man to supper at their home. Such an uxorial pedigree for the conversion experience of the chief prophet of a strongly patriarchal movement like the Nation of Islam was simply a bad fit with the organizational mythos.[35]

Fard was apparently impressed with Poole's enthusiasm and devotion to the Nation of Islam and its leader. Within a few weeks of Poole's first attending Fard bestowed on him the name of Elijah Karriem and made him his Supreme Minister, which was the second highest position in the movement. It was an action that aroused the jealousy of those who had previously been closest to Fard. As long as Fard remained the leader of the Nation of Islam the rivalries between his subordinates remained simmering beneath the surface but, after his disappearance, it flared up into violence. Elijah Poole had good reasons for gravitating to the Nation of Islam. He had been drawn to religion almost from infancy but Christianity had disappointed him both in Georgia and Detroit. His personal experiences of poverty and oppression made him receptive to a religion that promised to uplift him and other African-Americans over their white oppressors. Also, for the marginally employed Poole, a place in the leadership of the Nation of Islam provided him with a wonderful economic opportunity.[36]

Fard and Poole proved to be a congenial team in their leadership of the Nation of Islam. Unfortunately Fard's teachings aroused growing opposition from African-American clergy and Detroit's city government. He taught converts to the Nation of Islam that they were citizens of Mecca, not the USA, and that they only owed allegiance to the flag of Islam. The Nation of Islam established its own schools, called the University of Islam, and its members removed their children from the public schools. Following a long-established pattern of the leaders of alternative religions Fard established a paramilitary force called the Fruit of Islam, although technically every adult male believer was part of it. All of these actions brought the Nation of Islam into direct conflict with the public school administration, the police and the leaders of the black churches.[37]

NATION OF ISLAM: Pseudohistorical doctrines

> Since whiteness is a mark of degeneracy in many animals near the pole, the negro has as much right to term his savage robbers albinoes and white devils, degenerated through the weakness of nature, as we have to deem him the emblem of evil, and a descendent of Ham, branded by his father's curse. 'I', might he say, 'I, the black, am the original man. I have taken the deepest draughts from the source of life, the Sun: on me, and on every thing around me, it has acted with the greatest energy and vivacity.' JOHANN GOTTFRIED VON HERDER[38]

The Nation of Islam espoused a group of doctrines that not only set them apart from their neighbours but were certain to arouse the animosity of many people, both white and black. At the same time, it is important to recognize that the Nation of Islam produced some extremely positive achievements among its members and the greater African-American community. Fard and Elijah Muhammad taught their followers to eat a healthy and abstemious diet and, in fact, members' health genuinely improved. They also imposed a rather puritanical code of behaviour on the members of the Nation of Islam which called upon them to refrain from drinking alcohol, smoking tobacco and, of course, using illegal drugs. Members were to avoid promiscuity, adultery, prostitution and gambling. Hard work, cleanliness, discipline and self-respect were demanded from anyone who joined. Erdmann Benyon, the sociologist to first study the Nation of

Islam during the late 1930s, observed that most members of the Nation of Islam had obtained jobs during the New Deal era and had come off welfare, something that he attributed to their lifestyle as members of the Nation of Islam. C. Eric Lincoln in 1961 made the same observation about the uplifting consequences of the Nation of Islam's moral code for its members. Since Benyon's study the Nation of Islam had converted numerous drug addicts, alcoholics and criminals to a life of purpose, stability and self-respect, the most notable example being Malcolm X.[39]

Critics charge the Nation of Islam with racism, advocating a heretical form of Islam and leading its members down a dead-end of bizarre and embarrassing beliefs that are antithetical to the true needs and interests of African-Americans. The cosmogony of the Nation of Islam is based on both a pseudo-prehistory and a pseudo-history that have no basis in science, archaeology, history or existing religious traditions. Basically Wallace D. Fard made it all up with the assistance of his messenger and protégé Elijah Muhammad. Of course, if one believes that Fard was Allah incarnate and that Elijah Muhammad was his anointed successor, prophet and messenger, there is no problem with the provenance of the Nation of Islam's beliefs. For everyone else these beliefs are, as Malcolm X said, 'some of the most fantastic things that you could ever imagine'.

The cosmogony of the Nation of Islam stretches 76 trillion years back into deep time to when an atom appears in the primordial void of chaos. From that atom appears the earth and then the first or original man evolves out of the atom. The original man was black and created other black men while assuming the name of God or Allah. These black humans were then organized into thirteen tribes that lived in Asia. They possessed advanced scientific knowledge which enabled them to create the earth's mountains and other physical features. The Nation of Islam also taught that the earth was not the only inhabited planet. Mars and other more distant planets had populations of intelligent humanoids.[40]

The Nation of Islam does not view God or Allah as an all-powerful and incomprehensible deity whose earthly presence is largely spiritual. They refer to this form of belief in God as 'spook' religion. Their view of Allah is considerably more corporeal. Instead of being immortal and eternal individually, Allah was a succession of black men who usually lived one or two hundred years although occasionally some reached a thousand years of age. For aeons these black Allahs chaired a committee of 23 other black scientists who wrote a future history of humans which the Allah interpreted. In the final analysis all black people were both gods and inherently good and they created a paradise on earth for most of the planet's existence. Unlike Christianity and orthodox Islam the Nation of Islam rejected the idea of heaven and hell in the afterlife. For them heaven and hell existed on earth, depending how people behaved, and at the present white people were making the earth a hell for blacks.[41]

The Nation of Islam does not attribute all evil to whites. Prior to the appearance of white people, some blacks made questionable decisions and outright mistakes or even committed terrible wrongs against their fellows. Around 66 trillion years ago a malcontent black scientist tried to destroy humanity by blowing up the earth. He managed to destroy one of the tribes while rending the earth and creating the moon in the process. Living conditions declined for a time but stabilized when the tribe of Shabazz assumed the rule of the twelve surviving tribes. To a large extent the paradise of the original black people was reestablished and things remained that way for further unimaginable ages. Decline and decay eventually reappeared. Fifty thousand years ago another black scientist persuaded the tribe of Shabazz to relocate to Africa. His goal was to make his people stronger due to their living in a harsher environment. It worked but environmental conditions transformed them into the Negroes of Africa with rougher features and a relative lack of culture. The original black race evolved in other ways as well; brown, red and yellow, but not white, peoples began to appear on the earth about 35,000 years ago. In India these brown peoples developed the Buddhist and Hindu religions, which were heresies of the original Islam. Then, about 16,000 years ago, red people in India misbehaved as such vile heretics that even the Hindu heretics found them to be intolerable. The Allah of that era banished the red Indians across the Bering Strait into the Americas and later sent the whites to punish them further for their sins. Still, in the Nation of Islam's racial schema black, brown, yellow and red people had a common, natural origin in the primordial original black man. Ultimately they were all Asiatic and by extension all black, a belief that belies any easy association between the Nation of Islam and Afrocentricism.[42]

Needless to say, the cosmogony of the Nation of Islam had no warrant in traditional Islamic cosmology. Traditional Islam bases its cosmogony on the Hebrew scriptures and the Old Testament of the Christian Bible, especially the accounts in the book of Genesis. The Nation of Islam's time frame of trillions of years and its somewhat spontaneous creation of the atom and then the original black man are not found in any Islamic traditions, nor are any of the other events such as the creation of the moon by the mad scientist's explosion.[43] Certainly their ideas about Allah being a succession of humans and their rejection of an afterlife in heaven or hell are beliefs that are deeply offensive to orthodox Islam. Instead some scholars have located the sources of the Nation of Islam's cosmogony in the popular culture and pseudoscience of the early decades of the twentieth century. It has been pointed out that the Nation of Islam's projection of history back into the deep time of 76 trillion years is an echo of Olaf Stapleton's science fiction novel *Last and First Men* which appeared in 1931 and presented a narrative of human history that spanned mind-boggling periods of time. Another source of such a conception of a cosmogony based on trillions of years could have been Theosophy and its incredibly ancient root-races. This connection is rendered even more plausible if Wallace D. Fard really did work for a Theosophist swami during the early 1920s under the alias of George Farr.[44] Certainly contemporary science fiction, fantasy and horror stories contributed to a milieu in which outlandish and unconventional reconstructions of prehistory and ancient history could be presented as possibilities or even plausibilities. H. P. Lovecraft produced numerous horror stories and novelettes that speculated about lost civilizations and shocking alien races from primordial epochs. H. G. Wells and other science fiction writers contributed to the popularization of the belief that other worlds might be inhabited by intelligent life.[45] One might argue that these products of popular culture were beyond the educational attainments of borderline illiterates such as Fard and Elijah Muhammad.[46] It is important to remember, however, that newspaper comics, radio dramatizations and casual conversations with more competent readers could provide a functional illiterate with access to the broad trends in popular culture. Orson Welles' radio dramatization of H. G. Wells' *War of the Worlds* in 1938 produced a mass hysteria among its listeners due to its realistic presentation. Theosophy, Freemasonry, the Moorish Science Temple and the early twentieth-century popular culture of science fiction and horror stories all formed the cultic milieu of the Nation of Islam.

The early twentieth century was also an era that placed great confidence in science as the means to solve humanity's problems. It is no wonder that the Nation of Islam's doctrines described the rulers of the original black people as scientists. Popular culture also programmed people to expect some scientists to make tragic errors as Dr Frankenstein did or simply go bad like Dr Jekyll. According to the Nation of Islam's teachings, in primeval times one mad black scientist almost annihilated humanity and instead created the moon but in near historic times a more sinister mad scientist appeared who transformed the primordial black paradise into a historic white hell. That man was Yacub, a youth with an extraordinarily large head and even greater intelligence. According to the legends of the Nation of Islam, he was born about 6,600 years ago near Mecca, the heartland of the black paradise. Unfortunately for humanity, Yacub, or Mr Yacub as he is frequently known, was a congenital and chronic malcontent who possessed the intelligence and education to do something about his discontents.[47]

Even as a child Yacub demonstrated his twisted nature by informing his uncle that he would create a race that would rule over the original black people. His plan was to breed the black genes out of humans. To accomplish that task he needed subjects for his eugenics experiments. So to attract such loyal and willing followers Yacub preached a form of Islam that promised luxury with little or no work. Large numbers flocked to the new movement and civil unrest followed. Authorities in Mecca filled the jails with Yacub and his followers but the movement still continued to grow. Finally the concerned king of Mecca held a meeting with Yacub and asked if they could reach some sort of understanding. Yacub said that they could, if the Meccans would allow him and his people to leave and to settle somewhere else while Mecca for a period of years supplied them with the goods and money to start a new civilization. The king accepted Yacub's offer and 60,000 malcontents, including Yacub, left Mecca for Pelan, more familiarly known as the Isle of Patmos. There Yacub began his breeding experiments on his heedless followers. His technique basically involved killing all black babies and breeding successive generations of brown babies to ever lighter colours of red, yellow and finally white. The process took 600 years and Yacub did not live to see it to fruition but his successors continued until their people were white. Elijah Muhammad and other Nation of Islam leaders have suggested that the biblical creation of Adam is actually a reflection of Yacub's creation of the white race.

Breeding out the black genes left the white humans weaker, less intelligent and inherently wicked. At the point that Yacub's people were all white they returned to Mecca. Within six months they had instigated so much trouble and tumult that they were driven into exile in West Asia or, as it is more commonly known, Europe. There the whites degenerated to the point of being hardly distinguishable from savage beasts. During his ministry among the African-Americans of Detroit, Fard described these whites as cavemen and disparagingly referred to them as 'cavics'. This situation persisted for 2,000 years until Allah sent Moses as a prophet to the degenerate whites with the goal of recivilizing them. While Moses was successful in reestablishing civilization among the whites, he failed to transform their innately wicked nature. Jesus and Muhammad would later make attempts to subdue the depraved spirit of the whites but to no avail. Instead they increasingly oppressed the black, brown, red and yellow races. An especially critical event took place in 1555 when John Hawkins began the kidnapping and enslavement of the tribe of Shabazz to the wilderness of America.[48] Four hundred years of hell on earth followed for the hapless tribe of Shabazz.[49]

Despite the bleak situation created by white domination of the earth in the modern era, Allah planned to undo the terrible damage that Yacub had caused. His plan entailed the destruction of the diabolical white race and the restoration of the downtrodden blacks to their true station as the natural rulers of the world. Initially the millennium of black revival should have started in 1914 but Allah decided to delay until the tribe of Shabazz reconverted to Islam. That is where Wallace D. Fard came into the picture in 1930. Initially acting as a missionary to the lost tribe of Shabazz, he eventually came to be revealed as Allah come to earth in human form. Besides teaching the lost, now found, members of the tribe of Shabazz about Islam, he also predicted the extermination of the whites, particularly those living in North America. Elijah Muhammad soon echoed Fard's prophecies and bears a large responsibility for promoting the deification of Fard as Allah.[50]

The means for bringing about the fall of America and the doom of the white race was the Mother Plane, which was linked to the biblical flying wheel of the prophet Ezekiel (Ezekiel 1:15–21). After his disappearance Fard would set about having this massive and awesome weapon built in Japan with plans provided by the black scientists of Mecca. It was a sort of giant flying saucer about a half-mile in width that could orbit above the earth without resupply for between six and twelve months. It also carried another 1,500 smaller planes equipped with powerful bombs. When the time was right the Mother Plane would rain down destruction on the white nations and leave the blacks once again in charge of the earth. When this event was to take place is unclear. Initially Fard and Elijah Muhammad taught that the appearance of the Mother Plane was imminent, sometime during the late 1930s.[51]

The Nation of Islam arose in a time of great international tension. The blight of the Great Depression had opened the way for the rise of totalitarian dictators like Hitler in Germany and Mussolini in Italy. Japan was also a highly militaristic and nationalistic state with imperial ambitions and its relations with the USA steadily worsened during the decade of the 1930s. Fard taught that the original blacks were Asiatics, which made the Japanese seemingly natural allies for the Nation of Islam against the white devils. Japan held the respect of many non-whites due to its victory over the whites of Russia in the Russo-Japanese War of 1905. Many took that victory as the beginning of the end of white oppression. Faced with an increasingly wary and hostile USA, some Japanese, in turn, courted African-Americans as potential allies. Colonel Satokata Takahashi came to the USA and set up a series of anti-white organizations or cults among African-Americans in various northern cities. The FBI and military intelligence agencies became concerned about his activities. At one point during the early 1930s Takahashi attempted to co-opt Fard's Nation of Islam but Fard balked at subordinating himself to Takahashi at that time. There is some intriguing evidence, however, that Fard eventually did come to work in one of Takahashi's groups during the mid-1940s – the Society for Development of Our Own in Gary, Indiana. Given these circumstances it becomes perfectly logical for Fard and Elijah Muhammad to credit the Japanese with the building of the Mother Plane.[52]

The eve of World War II was not an auspicious time for African-Americans to develop a high regard for Japan but several groups on the fringes of the African-American community, including the Nation of Islam, did just that. United States officials responded by placing these groups under surveillance. When open war finally came some African-Americans faced accusations of sedition which in some cases led to prison sentences. Certainly Elijah Muhammad's conviction and imprisonment for draft evasion should be seen in this context. He and his intimates appear to have expected the Mother Plane to attack at any time up until the middle of 1942.[53]

After his imprisonment for draft evasion Elijah Muhammad toned down his teachings and moved the judgement day of the white race into a more distant future, sometime during the years 1965 to 1970. Like the 1930s the early 1960s provided an imminently appropriate backdrop for Armageddon. The Cold War, especially events like the Cuban missile crisis; the dismantling of the European colonial empires, particularly France's defeats in Vietnam and Algeria; the Civil Rights movement in the USA, with its increasing violence and racial conflict; the increasingly onerous war in Vietnam and a general rise in social unrest all appeared to be harbingers of the predicted fall of America. Of course, the Nation of Islam had its own portentous, internal conflicts. Malcolm X, the real engine of the Nation of Islam's dramatic growth during the 1950s, had broken with Elijah Muhammad. Elijah Muhammad's son Wallace also challenged the un-Islamic teachings of his father and the Nation of Islam. All the while, the frail Elijah Muhammad's health declined amidst the growing knowledge among the faithful and the outside world of his harem of mistresses among the secretaries of the Nation of Islam headquarters in Chicago. Needless to say, his long-suffering wife Clara was extremely resentful. She was also threatening divorce, something that would have proved highly embarrassing to the leader of a puritanical religious movement. Faced with his own personal Armageddon and with no reason to believe that the Mother Plane was about to strike, Elijah Muhammad's predictions about the apocalyptic fall of America receded into an increasingly undefined future. Louis Farrakhan and his inner circle still continue to teach these aberrant and un-Islamic doctrines. In spite of the interlude of Wallace Muhammad's attempted genuine Islamization of the Nation of Islam, little has changed from the eras of Fard and Elijah Muhammad. The virulent anti-white racism and the pseudohistorical view of human origins and the broad course of human history all remain firmly entrenched in the Nation of Islam despite their lack of support from any established Islamic traditions, the historical record or the evidence of any scientific discoveries.[54]

FARD'S DEPARTURE AND ELIJAH'S WANDERINGS

But they carry themselves high, and as prudent men; and though they are fools, yet would seem to be teachers. HERMAS III, SIMILITUDE IX, V. 2005[55]

Rumours contributed to the troubles of Fard and the Nation of Islam in Detroit. Stories circulated about the bizarre and criminal secret rituals practiced by the prophet and his followers. Fard taught that he would lead his lost-found flock back to their original homeland of Mecca. On its own, this teaching was innocuous as well as being somewhat reminiscent of Moses, Garvey and Noble Drew Ali. Rumour, however, added the sinister proviso that believers had 'to sacrifice four Caucasian devils' before they could qualify for return to Mecca. America during the 1930s was fascinated and appalled by voodoo with its alleged sorcery and savage rituals of human sacrifice and enslavement. The authorities, the general public and even scholars quickly identified the Nation of Islam as a type of voodoo cult after the stories of human sacrifice accumulated. Ultimately these tales would crescendo into the ultimate rumour that Elijah Muhammad had sacrificed Fard for some obscure ritualistic reason. Needless to say, it was a rumour spread by Elijah Muhammad's rivals within the Nation of Islam.[56]

Unfortunately for Fard and the Nation of Islam, one episode of human sacrifice indisputably did occur and brought a firestorm down on them. On 20 November 1932 a follower of the Nation of Islam named Robert Harris, whose Muslim name was Robert Karriem, persuaded a boarder in his house named James Smith to serve as a human sacrifice. Harris set up an altar in the presence of twelve witnesses from the Nation of Islam along with his terrified wife and children. After getting his sacrificial offering to lie on the altar he killed Smith with multiple knife thrusts to the heart but not before Smith apparently thought better of his decision and tried to resist, which necessitated bludgeoning him.[57] Newspapers reported the incident and the next day the police arrested Harris with social workers coming forward to report that he had also threatened to sacrifice them. Others stepped up to claim that the Nation of Islam was engaged in other nefarious plots that included the planned assassination of Frank Murphy, mayor of Detroit and ironically a proven supporter of racial justice in the city. The police moved quickly and arrested Fard on 23 November. From that point onwards the campaign of Detroit authorities and African-American clergy to suppress the Nation of Islam intensified.[58]

While in police custody Fard denied knowing Robert Harris and teaching the requirement of the blood sacrifice of four whites. Harris was apparently a peripheral member of the Nation of Islam who suffered from mental instability. On the other hand there is evidence that Fard, in fact, had discussed the idea of blood sacrifice with the members of the Nation of Islam. Even if most of the stories told against the Nation of Islam were unfounded, the white officials of Detroit and the African-American clergy considered the influence wielded by the Nation of Islam to be intolerable.[59] However, many African-American Detroiters, but particularly Fard's followers, disapproved of the persecution of the Nation of Islam which they viewed as motivated by racism rather than any concern about the preservation of public safety or law and order. As a consequence the police dealt relatively cautiously with Fard lest they transformed him into a martyr. They finally decided that the best way to handle the situation was to order him to leave the city on 7 December 1932. Instead of leaving Fard simply attempted to assume a lower profile and tried to run the Nation of Islam through his lieutenant Elijah. Fard assumed the name of Wallace Fard Muhammad and bestowed the same potent surname on Elijah Poole, who was from that point known as Elijah Muhammad. Fard's goal was to enhance his personal divinity within the worldview of the Nation of Islam while at the same time solidifying Elijah Muhammad's position as his successor. He bestowed the title of Supreme Minister of the Nation of Islam on his loyal lieutenant. Eventually the Detroit police lost patience with Fard's dithering and arrested him for a second time on 25 May 1933. This time they turned up the pressure. Under interrogation Fard supposedly admitted that the Nation of Islam had been a moneymaking scheme from its start. He also agreed to leave Detroit for good but curiously he made the effort to negotiate an opportunity for a farewell with the faithful of his Nation of Islam. An emotional scene followed at which Fard promised to return and to lead his people out of 'hell'. His departure for Chicago left the Muslims of Detroit demoralized and divided.[60]

Elijah Muhammad inherited a bleak situation from Fard. Official harassment, aided by the African-American clergy, continued in Detroit. By the beginning of April 1934 the Michigan Board of Education was attempting to close down the University of Islam, which was really an elementary school for the children of the members of the Nation of Islam. Authorities attempted to arrest teachers at the University of Islam on the charge of depriving children of a proper public education. The instructors resisted and injuries occurred among the police and the teachers. Elijah Muhammad became the next target. On 17 April the police arrested him on the charges of contributing to the delinquency of a minor and voodooism. He remained in custody for ten days.[61] The hostility of the police and the educational bureaucracy, however, were not Elijah Muhammad's worst problems. Schism and internecine rivalries plagued the Nation of Islam and challenged his leadership of the movement, indeed threatened his very life. Splinter groups drew away members while disillusioned followers returned to the African-American churches or gravitated to Communism. Those who had been passed over when Fard so swiftly promoted Elijah Muhammad to be his second-in-command and successor worked against the new leader. The situation became so unpleasant that Elijah Muhammad began to escape periodically by visiting Temple Number Two in Chicago. During those visits he claimed to have met with Fard. At their last meeting, in June 1934, Fard gave Elijah Muhammad a list of 104 books to read (what specific books were on this list has never been revealed) and a Quran with an English translation.

The Chicago police had been periodically arresting Fard since his arrival and the final arrest in June and was what had prompted Fard to summon Elijah Muhammad. He again bestowed the leadership of the Nation of Islam on his second-in-command but this time gave him the title of Messenger of Allah. Although Elijah Muhammad implored Fard to stay, the prophet/messiah told him that he was no longer needed. When asked if he would ever come back, Fard instructed his lieutenant to study the Bible for the appropriate prophecy. With that cryptic farewell, according to Elijah Muhammad, Fard boarded an airplane and left the bemused Elijah Muhammad convinced more than ever that Fard was Allah incarnate. In fact Fard's disappearance followed the pattern of a Shi'ite doctrine known as *Ghaybah* or occultation.[62] *Ghaybah* consisted of a religious leader disappearing from human view, possibly even leaving the physical world, for a period of time and returning to bring redemption or a new age of good. The Quran claims that Jesus did not die on the cross, rather he disappeared and will return in the last days. The Twelfth Imam of the Shi'ites disappeared with the promise of a return as did Caliph Al-Hakim, according to the beliefs of the Druze. Fard would return to lead his lost-found people back to Mecca when the destruction of the wilderness of America and white domination commenced.[63]

For many years the rank and file of the Nation of Islam and law enforcement officials did not know what happened to Wallace D. Fard after his departure from Chicago. Ultimately FBI investigators pieced together information that revealed he had returned to Los Angeles. His meeting with Elijah Muhammad took place in June. During July 1934 he arrived at the home of the now-married Hazel Barton to visit her and their son. He was driving a 1929 Ford Model A and appeared to have plenty of money. The backseat of the car held numerous anti-white pamphlets. A shocked Hazel questioned Fard about these bizarre and odious materials but failed to get a convincing answer. A few days after his arrival he left again and said he was heading back to New Zealand. Coincidentally, Fard's old friend Edward Donaldson had obtained his release from San Quentin in July. Members of the Muhammad family have claimed to have been in contact with Fard over the years since 1934. Karl Evanzz postulates that Fard may have assumed the aliases of Emmanuel Pharr and John Walker, a man who worked in Gary, Indiana as the leader of the local branch of the Society for Development of Our Own during the mid-1940s. SDOO was a rival of the Nation of Islam founded in 1933 and based on MSTA beliefs. It was under the auspices of Satokata Takahashi, mentioned above, who had been working to create unrest among African-Americans during the 1930s and early 1940s. Fard and Takahashi had been in contact during the early 1930s when the Japanese agent showed some interest in coopting the Nation of Islam to his ends. It is possible that the two men developed a long-term relationship based on their efforts to uplift or exploit poor African-Americans, depending on one's point of view. Pharr ended up arrested on a rape charge in Gary. In 1973, according to charges by Hamas Abdul Khaalis, a disgruntled former NOI member and promoter of the Hanafi branch of Islam among African-Americans, Fard had died in Chicago in 1971, hence there was no occultation. He also accused Fard of a rape along with other crimes. Khaalis further asserted that top NOI leaders had known about it all along.[64]

If any of this information about Fard is true, it would seemingly destroy the Nation of Islam's fervently held belief that their founder was Allah incarnate. True believers in the Nation of Islam refused to believe any of it, some even declined opportunities to look at the evidence. They assert that because most of the negative information about Fard is based on FBI investigations, it is a tainted pack of lies. The trouble with that contention is that the accusations of Khaalis and others say basically the same things. Even Elijah Muhammad in his speeches and writings over the years added bits and pieces to Fard's biography that are consistent with what the investigations of the FBI and Karl Evanzz have revealed. It is also important to keep in mind that Khaalis, hardly a sympathetic figure himself, attracted the ire of the Nation of Islam with his accusations, which resulted in the slaughter of members of his family in a botched attempt to kill him. Furthermore, if Karl Evanzz's reconstruction of Fard's career is accurate, it paints the picture of a man whose ambiguous ethnicity allowed him to slip back and forth between white and black society with relative ease. Starting with his UNIA days in San Francisco, he appears to have learned that preaching an anti-white message to recent black migrants to American cities was an effective way to get into their wallets and make a comfortable living for himself. Of course, we could give Fard the benefit of the doubt and suggest that the racism he experienced as a person of uncertain ethnicity made him sympathetic to the plight of African-Americans, hence his motivation to preach anti-white politics and religions. Unfortunately, his penchant for taking up with white women, his criminal activities and his returning to white society during breaks from his missionary activities render that view of Fard rather implausible. Perhaps he was telling the Detroit police the truth when he confessed that his activities with the Nation of Islam were all just a racket?

After the final departure of Fard, Elijah Muhammad returned to Detroit but the turmoil surrounding the Nation of Islam there continued to intensify. Police harassment persisted but far worse was the negative reaction among Muslims to his announcement of his new title of Messenger of Allah. When one rival Muslim leader placed a $500 contract on his life in September 1934 Elijah Muhammad prudently relocated to Chicago which he made the new headquarters of the Nation of Islam,[65] but the move failed to bring Elijah Muhammad and the Nation of Islam any respite from official persecution and internal agitation. The Chicago authorities proved to be every bit as hostile to the Nation of Islam as those in Detroit. They were already ill disposed to the MSTA and were having trouble distinguishing between the two groups. Two high-profile confrontations with the legal system ended in mayhem and saddled the Nation of Islam with a reputation for violence and a rejection of lawful authority. Rosie Hassan, a member of the NOI, faced the charge of assaulting a white woman on a streetcar. Close to 60 fez-wearing members of the NOI showed up at the Women's Court to support Hassan on 25 March 1935. The decision, in fact, went their way and the charge against Hassan was dismissed. When the triumphant Muslims rose to exit the court in a precise military manner, they unfortunately tried to leave through the wrong door. Mingling with an unrelated group of women prisoners who had just entered the courtroom, exasperated bailiffs rushed to separate the two groups and a shoving match quickly degenerated into a riot. Unarmed Muslims threw punches and chairs while the guards responded by swinging their nightsticks and firing their pistols. Two Muslims and one policeman suffered gunshot wounds, the policeman's due to friendly fire. An elderly police captain, Joseph Palczynski, suffered a heart attack, the only fatality of the incident. Another 38 people were injured. A second confrontation took place during April when school officials brought a complaint against a Muslim parent for sending his child to the University of Islam in Chicago. Again Nation of Islam members packed the courtroom, again violence broke out between them and the nervous bailiffs, and once more gunfire ended the riot. More arrests and jailings followed. The University of Islam, however, remained open but the public reputation of the Nation of Islam was besmirched. Members continued to leave the fold while hostile authorities redoubled their vigilance.[66]

Even worse for Elijah Muhammad, rivals contested his leadership of the Nation of Islam in Chicago. Discontent mounted and a coup, which included Kalot Muhammad, Elijah's younger brother and the head of the Fruit of Islam, deprived him of his leadership of the NOI. Threats were made on his life as resentment mounted over his role as the Messenger of Allah. Some of the opposition pledged to fast and only 'eat a grain of rice a day until Elijah was dead'. As Elijah Muhammad put it, 'they [his enemies] began to seek my life. So Allah warned me to leave,' which he did in September 1935. Leaving his wife and children in Chicago Elijah Muhammad wandered for seven years, mostly in the East. During that time he preached the Nation of Islam, worked and experienced the generosity of sympathetic African-Americans. First he went to Milwaukee but left for Washington, DC, before the end of 1935. Using various assumed names he hoped to elude both his murderous rivals and hostile authorities. During 1939 he founded the Temple Number Four in Washington. Eventually the danger in Chicago abated and he returned in late July 1942 to his family and the leadership of the Nation of Islam there.[67]

Even before Elijah Muhammad returned to Chicago new problems had arisen for the Nation of Islam. Fard had identified the blacks of the Nation of Islam as Asiatic, which made them potentially sympathetic to Japan. During the 1930s the greater part of the population of the United States came to see Japan as a growing threat to their country and the attack on the naval base at Pearl Harbor on 7 December 1941 only sealed that judgment. In the tense and paranoid months that followed the entry of the United States into World War II the FBI investigated Japanese attempts to subvert the loyalty of African-Americans. Elijah Muhammad and the Nation of Islam came to their attention because they eschewed loyalty to the United States and refused to register for the draft. The FBI first arrested Elijah Muhammad for draft evasion in Washington on 8 May 1942 but released him on bond on 23 July.[68]

Elijah Muhammad returned to Chicago soon after where further surveillance and harassment by the FBI continued. On 28 September 1942 the FBI conducted raids on the Nation of Islam's Temple Number Two and the homes of prominent leaders, including Elijah Muhammad. The purported offences of the Muslims were sedition, conspiracy with Japanese agents and draft evasion. In fact the raids yielded no evidence of any collaboration between the Nation of Islam and Japan. Charges of draft evasion, however, were undeniable and the Roosevelt administration prosecuted Elijah Muhammad and other offenders vigorously during October and November. Much to his surprise and disgust authorities told Elijah Muhammad that an even bigger reason for removing him from public contact was that America did not need him preaching Nation of Islam doctrines to African-Americans during a time of war. After holding him in various jails Federal officials placed Elijah Muhammad in the Federal prison at Milan, Michigan, on 23 July 1943 where he remained until 24 August 1946. There is no evidence that prison authorities treated Elijah Muhammad or the other prisoners from the Nation of Islam differently or more harshly to other prisoners. Some members of the Nation of Islam have readily admitted to receiving decent treatment while in prison. For Elijah Muhammad there were problems. After his release he complained that the prison food, which did not adhere to the Nation of Islam's dietary rules, had permanently damaged his health. Mental evaluations and testing by the prison psychiatrist revealed that Elijah Muhammad had an IQ in the 70–79 range accompanied by paranoid and schizophrenic tendencies. These findings dovetailed nicely with the preconception of mainstream society that Elijah Muhammad and his associates were gullible dupes following the teachings of a bizarre cult of rather bogus provenance. That such preconceived notions influenced the psychiatrist's judgement is likely but to what degree is unclear.

What is clear is that Elijah Muhammad was no genius in an intellectual sense, for too many disillusioned renegades from the Nation of Islam, including Malcolm X, testified to the limited abilities of the Messenger of Allah. The FBI files credit Elijah Muhammad with variations of the aliases of Muck Muck and Muck Muhd, clearly phonetic renderings of his own mispronunciation of Muhammad. During the 1950s the Palestinian Arab Jamil Daib claimed to have taught Elijah Muhammad to pronounce Muhammad correctly. Later Gordon Hall, an expert on extremist organizations and a student of the Nation of Islam, put it most bluntly '[Elijah Muhammad's] an incoherent old man, he does not speak well, he doesn't make any sense in his public appearances.'[69]

However, if Elijah Muhammad reported to the psychiatrist that people were out to get him, he was hardly being paranoid. His rivals in Detroit and Chicago definitely wished him ill and he was a target of FBI investigations. Nor was he a schizophrenic because he claimed to talk directly with God, or at least his god. Elijah Muhammad believed that Fard was Allah and he most certainly had many conversations with Fard. Prison and the findings of the psychiatrist did nothing to end Elijah Muhammad's career as a religious leader. Instead, his time in prison made him a martyr in the eyes of the disgruntled and alienated segment of the African-American community that was attracted to or sympathetic to the Nation of Islam and similar movements. Elijah Muhammad emerged from prison with an enhanced standing among the faithful for his position as the Messenger of Allah but he had also learned caution. The era of confrontation with American society's laws and the engagement in violence in its courtrooms had passed. The Nation of Islam withdrew into separatism and promoted the establishment of an autonomous community that awaited the prophesied fall of America.[70]

AFTERMATH

> Turn to Allah and fear Him. Be steadfast in prayer and serve no other god besides Him. Do not split up your religion into sects, each exulting in its own beliefs. QURAN[71]

Elijah Muhammad and his followers strove to expand the membership of the Nation of Islam and the prosperity of its various business ventures. One of the new recruits was Malcolm Little, later much better known as Malcolm X, who joined in 1948 while in prison. An enthusiastic disciple, the talented and charismatic Malcolm X quickly rose to be *de facto* number two in the Nation of Islam. Many credit him with the bulk of the responsibility for the steady expansion of the membership of the Nation of Islam during the 1950s and early 1960s. His rise in the Nation of Islam was similar to Elijah Muhammad's in that it aroused the jealousy of those already around the Messenger of Allah, including members of the Muhammad family. Unlike Elijah Muhammad, the intelligent and inquiring Malcolm X eventually came to the conclusion that the Nation of Islam was not true Islam. By the early 1960s rumours of Elijah Muhammad's sexual dalliances and fathering children out of wedlock became virtually undeniable except by the truest of the true believers. From its genesis the Nation of Islam had preached an austere and puritanical code of morality, which was enforced with severity by Elijah Muhammad. That he walked on feet of clay profoundly disillusioned many of the faithful, especially Malcolm X. Meanwhile the growing influence and independence of Malcolm X finally triggered the jealousy of Elijah Muhammad as well of other members of the Muhammad family and leaders of the Nation of Islam. The two men parted ways over some intemperate remarks that Malcolm X had made concerning the assassination of John F. Kennedy but that was probably merely a pretext on the part of Elijah Muhammad. Tensions mounted as Malcolm X began to organize his own separatist movement and on 21 February 1965 assassins gunned down Malcolm X as he began to give a speech at a Harlem meeting hall. The gunmen almost certainly acted at the behest of Elijah Muhammad. Ironically Malcolm X's acclaimed *Autobiography* appeared soon after and immortalized him.[72]

Elijah Muhammad and the Nation of Islam survived the loss of Malcolm X. More importantly they survived the coming and going of the years 1965 and 1966, the long-predicted time of the Fall of America. Although the Nation of Islam's apocalypse failed to occur, like other millennialist religious movements before it, it adjusted and moved on to become a relatively stable religious denomination but with a somewhat eccentric theology and a more narrow audience than usual.[73] Aberrations from this trend did occur. During 1973 and 1974 a renegade group of four members from the San Francisco Temple Twenty-Six engaged in their own personal war against white America. Over a period of six months they murdered fifteen people and decapitated them while maiming twelve others, in the name of the Nation of Islam. They were captured, convicted and sentenced to life in prison for these so-called 'Zebra Killings'. Some officials have speculated that they might also be connected with another 80 unsolved murders in the San Francisco area that occurred about the same time. The 'Zebra Killings', however, were a macabre exception to the Nation of Islam's post-World War II policy of living at peace with white America while preaching a racist separatism.[74] Elijah Muhammad, chronically unhealthy, died on 25 February 1975, having spent over forty years as the leader of the Nation of Islam, most of them very well compensated materially. While he lived he had dampened down dissidence, which included his own son Wallace Muhammad, who along with Malcolm X harboured grave doubts about the authenticity of the Nation of Islam as an Islamic movement.

Wallace Muhammad succeeded his father as the leader of the Nation of Islam and from that position began its transformation into a genuinely Islamic body with the new name of the World Community of Islam. It eschewed the anti-white and separatist doctrines of the traditional Nation of Islam along with the rest of its heretical and bizarre beliefs and practices. This transformation, however, was controversial and threw the Nation of Islam into turmoil. For many members of the Nation of Islam the emphasis on black separatism and the religiously sanctioned racism directed against whites were important components of what had attracted them to the movement in the first place. Membership dwindled. Infighting developed as more and more traditionalists came to question the direction of Wallace Muhammad's leadership. Louis Farrakhan, a trusted lieutenant of Elijah Muhammad in the New York Temple, took the opportunity to challenge Wallace. Farrakhan had begun his career as a calypso singer before he began his rise in the Nation of Islam hierarchy through the mentorship of Malcolm X, who he turned on when the dispute with Elijah Muhammad occurred. After Elijah Muhammad's death he initially found himself frozen out of any influence by Wallace Muhammad and his supporters. Farrakhan even seriously contemplated returning to calypso singing when the growing opposition to Wallace supplied him with the opening that he needed. On 7 March 1978 he broke with Wallace Muhammad and on 19 March announced that he would begin the rebuilding of the traditional Nation of Islam. It was an effort that proved successful, far more so than Wallace Muhammad's effort truly to Islamicize the Nation of Islam. In the end Farrakhan's success proved the prescient C. Eric Lincoln, a pioneer scholar of the Nation of Islam, right. In 1961 he had observed:

The aegis of orthodox Islam means nothing in America's black ghettos. So long as the Movement [NOI] keeps its color identity with the rising 'black' peoples of Africa and Asia, it

165

could discard all its Islamic attributes – its name, its prayers to Allah, its citations from the Quran, everything – without risking in the smallest degree its appeal to the black masses.[75]

Critics and renegades from Farrakhan's Nation of Islam predict that his revival will ultimately fail and in the process will severely taint the reputation of all forms of Islam among African-Americans.[76] Until and if that time ever comes the preaching of a pseudohistorical cosmogony promoting racial separatism continues largely unabated.[77]

CHAPTER 5

Pseudohistoria Epidemica or Pseudohistorians in Collusion

> We see that the soul, in its passions, inclines rather to deceive itself, by
> creating a false and fantastical subject, even contrary to its own beliefs,
> than not to have something to work upon. MICHEL DE MONTAIGNE[1]

A shocking and rather pathetic event came to light on 26 March 1997.
Authorities discovered the bodies of 39 men and women in a large,
stylish house near San Diego – all participants in a mass suicide. Each
victim was found lying in a bed wearing a black shirt, sweat-pants
and new black Nike tennis shoes. A square purple cloth covered their
heads and upper bodies. Some of the men had undergone castration
at some point long before their deaths. The dead all belonged to the
Heaven's Gate cult and wore armbands proclaiming they were the
'Heaven's Gate Away Team'. Members of Heaven's Gate believed
that benevolent aliens, the Space Brothers, visited the earth millions
of years ago and began the process of human evolution. Their plan
was to return to the earth and gather up the most spiritually advanced
humans into their spaceships. There in the heavens they would be
transformed and become members of the Space Brothers' society. The
tricky part about this transformation was the spiritual methodology
behind it, which required players on the Away Team, the humans, to
abandon their physical bodies. In short, they needed to die – but they
would be better off for the experience. As for the rest of humanity,
the long-term outlook was not so good. The Space Brothers viewed
the spiritually degenerate remainder of humanity as weeds in their
earthly garden. Humanity would be annihilated to clear the garden
of weeds. Heaven's Gate taught that this ascension of the spiritual
humans and the accompanying alien apocalypse was imminent.

The event that triggered the group's mass suicide was the approach of the Hale-Bopp comet. Marshall Herff Applewaite, the
leader of Heaven's Gate, taught that the Space Brothers were travelling
in their flying saucers ahead of the comet. After the aliens picked up the
spirits of the faithful of Heaven's Gate the comet would crash into the
earth and devastate it. So in preparation for that event Applewaite

and his followers committed suicide, each dying with five dollars worth of quarters in their pockets. Apparently they thought the Space Brothers might need change for a five after being gone so long and travelling such vast distances. Alas, Heaven's Gate's end of days did not arrive. As far as we can tell the space ships didn't land, the Away Team didn't ascend and the Hale-Bopp comet blithely passed the earth without even the hint of a near miss. Most people would conclude that the adherents of Heaven's Gate died for nothing, but not so. They died for, and from, pseudohistory.

The theology of Heaven's Gate utilized two pseudohistorical themes: ancient astronauts and catastrophism. Their fatal beliefs were just an extreme example of the phenomenon of flying saucer religions that sprang out of the cultic milieu of pseudohistorical ideas about super-civilizations of the prehistoric era, cosmic disasters that changed the course of history and alien visits to the earth at various points in the past for good or ill purposes. Other UFO religions have tended to be quirky rather than deadly. The Raelian Movement is the largest with 45,000 members from 52 countries. Heaven's Gate, the Raelians and similar cults transformed pseudohistorical ideas into religious purposes and gave their members an identity and a meaning to their existence apart from the teachings of traditional religions.[2]

The pseudohistorians discussed in this chapter did their research and writing for more secular purposes and in most cases they would be appalled at how their ideas have been used by religious power-seekers and charlatans. Clearly some of these pseudohistorians were sincerely pursuing the truth about the past. Their motives were pure but their scholarly methods were flawed and their objectivity questionable. Others, however, discovered that fantastical ideas are far more marketable than solidly researched books about traditional history. Pyramids possess a perennial fascination for the reading public but pyramids built by visitors from another planet are simply irresistible to readers seeking light and supposedly factual books on mysterious and bizarre topics. The same observation applies to documentaries. Fanciful speculations are more fun to bounce around. They stimulate the imagination, give relief from the mundane and provide wonderful premises for films like *Stargate* and television series like *The X-Files*.

As for the authors of pseudohistorical books, if successful, they attract imitators. Their books enter the cultic milieu of pseudohistory where they influence and inspire other writers. The ideas get combined into new hypotheses about the past, reshuffled into other configurations, and even revert to earlier versions of some pseudohistorical interpretations of the past. Pseudohistory has its historiography and its genealogy of ideas. In this chapter a portion of that historiography will be traced through the careers and writings of Immanuel Velikovsky, Charles H. Hapgood, Erich von Däniken, Zecharia Sitchin and Graham Hancock.

IMMANUEL VELIKOVSKY: Catastrophism and revised chronology

> One generation passeth away, and another generation cometh: but the
> earth abideth for ever. ECCLESIASTES 1:4

Immanuel Velikovsky (1895–1979) produced some of the most influential pseudohistorical and pseudoscientific hypotheses to appear in the second half of the twentieth century. Although his ideas generated tremendous controversy they attracted a loyal and enduring following despite the audacious claims they put forth. Unlike many purveyors of pseudohistory and pseudoscience, Velikovsky's books were dense compilations of research and presented detailed and very specific hypotheses using the format and language of the scholarly world. He presented his ideas in three books that appeared in the 1950s: *Worlds in Collision* (1950), *Ages in Chaos* (1952) and *Earth in Upheaval* (1955). Each of these books presented different evidence for Velikovsky's hypotheses based respectively on astronomy, history and geology. Other books that followed elaborated on aspects of Velikovsky's hypotheses, particularly his contribution to pseudohistory, the radical revision of the synchronization of the standard chronology of ancient history.

Worlds in Collision, Velikovsky's first major book, appeared in 1950 and became an instant bestseller. The title promised high drama and the book delivered. Velikovsky claimed that Venus is a relatively new addition to the solar system's family of planets. Instead of being one of the original planets Venus had emerged from the planet Jupiter as a comet. Its orbit caused it to cross the orbits of other planets and so created the possibility of collisions or near misses. Two such near misses occurred around 1500 BC and again 55 years later. The first approach of Venus to the earth created worldwide catastrophes. Earthquakes, volcanic eruptions, massive tidal waves and hurricanes occurred all over the globe. The earth also passed through the tail of the comet that was Venus with odd effects. Specifically Velikovsky credited the earth's close encounter with Venus for causing the biblical Ten Plagues of Egypt and the parting of the Red Sea. Matter from the tail of the comet Venus consisted of hydrocarbons that rained on to the earth and created deposits of oil. Other items that fell to earth were the vermin described in the Bible and other ancient texts describing cataclysmic events. Other materials from the comet's tail combined to form the manna that helped to feed the Children of Israel as they wandered in the wilderness of Sinai. The comet's tail also formed the pillar of smoke and the pillar of fire that guided Moses and his people day and night through the desert.

While the earth and Venus almost colliding helped the Children of Israel to escape their Egyptian bondage, for the rest of the inhabitants of the earth the event was a colossal disaster. It was not a unique event either. Fifty-two years later Venus returned and again approached dangerously to the earth. Once again earthquakes, monstrous storms, huge tidal waves and volcanic eruptions plagued the earth indiscriminately killing plants, animals and humans. This second catastrophe coincided with Joshua's conquest of the land of Canaan for the Children of Israel. An earthquake caused by the near approach of Venus provided the force that shook down the walls of Jericho. More impressive, Venus and the earth came so close together that the rotation of the earth was slowed down and stopped temporarily. The angle of the earth's axis might even have been changed. In this way Venus's second approach to the earth contributed to the crushing victory of Joshua and the Israelites over the five kings of the Amorites at the battle of Gibeon. The Israelites had surprised the Amorite army which panicked and retreated through the descent of Beth-horon. There a hail of large stones fell from the sky on to the Amorites and killed more of them than the swords of Joshua's soldiers (Joshua 10:11). Velikovsky asserts that this phenomenon occurred because the earth had again passed through Venus's comet tail and that had led to showers of meteors striking the earth. To prolong the slaughter of the Amorites, Joshua commanded, 'Sun, stand thou still at Gibeon', which it did. Velikovsky explains this phenomenon as the result of an interaction between the earth's and Venus's gravity and electromagnetic fields which caused the earth's rotation to slow and finally stop. He also cites other ancient sources from around the world that purport to describe an event of a long day, a long morning, a long sunset or a long night depending on their location on the earth. These descriptions utilize sources from all over the world because the halting of the earth's rotation was a global event.

Later Venus closely approached Mars which resulted in Venus being pushed into its current planetary order around the sun, ending its career as a comet. Unfortunately for the earth that encounter dislodged Mars from its previously stable orbit into an irregular one that brought it dangerously close to the earth on several occasions. One such event took place during the reign of King Uzziah of Judah (reigned 783–742 BC). This near collision of the earth and Mars caused a great commotion within the earth, something that went far beyond a normal large earthquake. People in various parts of the world thought that the end was at hand. Another encounter coincided with King Sennacherib (reigned 504–681 BC) of Assyria's invasion of Judah around 688 BC. The biblical account at 2 Kings 18:31–19:37 tells how the Assyrians marched into Judah and threatened Jerusalem but 'it came to pass that night the angel of the Lord went out, and smote in the camp of the Assyrians an hundred four-score and five thousands and when they rose early in the morning, behold, they were all dead corpses' (19:35). Velikovsky attributes the destruction of Sennacherib's army to the earth and Mars almost colliding. Some sort of fire fell from the sky or an asphyxiating gas descended on certain places on the earth. According to Velikovsky the gases killed the Assyrians. When the cataclysm was over the length of the earth's orbit had been changed from 360 days to the present 365 days. Mars was propelled into its current orbit and the solar system returned to a period of stability, at least until Jupiter decides to spew out another giant comet like Venus again, or so Velikovsky hopes his readers would believe.

Ages in Chaos, Velikovsky's second book, appeared in 1952. Basically it argued that the chronologies of ancient Egypt and Greece were incorrect by about 500 years in comparison with the chronologies of ancient Israel and the rest of the ancient Middle East. If Velikovsky was right this error distorted ancient history up to the time of Alexander the Great, at which point Egypt and Greece's history are correctly synchronized with the rest of the ancient world. Although Ages in Chaos claimed to be the first volume of a two-volume work, in fact, it turned out to be the first of a five-volume work. Two of the four following volumes were published shortly before Velikovsky's death: Peoples of the Sea in 1977 and Ramses II and His Time in 1978. Two other volumes – The Assyrian Conquest and The Dark Age of Greece – have never been published but are available on the internet at the Velikovsky Archive.[3]

In Ages in Chaos Velikovsky presents his resynchronization of ancient history from the time of the biblical events of the Exodus through the reign of the infamous King Ahab of Israel and their relation to Egyptian history. The history of ancient Egypt is generally divided into a number of standard time periods:

Old Kingdom	c.2600–2130 BC
First Intermediate Period	2130–2040 BC
Middle Kingdom	2040–1640 BC

Second Intermediate Period or Hyksos Period	1640–1532 BC
New Kingdom	1550–1070 BC
Third Intermediate Period	1060–664 BC
Assyrian Conquest	664 BC
Persian Conquest	525 BC
Alexander the Great's Conquest	332 BC

Velikovsky claims that the Middle Kingdom did not end until 1300 BC. The barbarian Hyksos then ruled Egypt from a little after 1300 BC until about 1050 BC when the New Kingdom began, which is about 500 years later than the conventional chronology.

Scholars attempting to synchronize biblical history with events in the ancient world have tended to associate the Children of Israel with the Asiatic Hyksos who conquered and ruled northern Egypt during the Second Intermediate Period. The resurgence of native Egyptian rulers and the defeat of the Hyksos ushered in the New Kingdom era, Egypt's greatest age. For the Children of Israel the beginning of the New Kingdom resulted in enslavement and oppression for them as remnants of the hated Hyksos. This view of biblical history means that the events of the Exodus from Egypt took place during the reign of a pharaoh of the New Kingdom. Several pharaohs have been suggested as candidates for the pharaoh of the Exodus, including Ahmose, the founder of the eighteenth dynasty and Rameses II of the nineteenth dynasty. The date of the Exodus has been variously placed at approximately 1280, 1446 and before 1519 BC. Biblical scholars tend to favour the c. 1280 date and Rameses II but a strong argument can be made for the c. 1519 date, which would make Ahmose the pharaoh of the Exodus.[4]

Needless to say, Velikovsky's resynchronization of the Exodus with Egypt's history suggests a quite different sequence of events. He locates the Exodus to the time when the Middle Kingdom was collapsing just before the Hyksos invasion. Although *Ages in Chaos* does not discuss it, *Worlds in Collision* attribute the collapse of the Middle Kingdom and the triumph of the Hyksos to the devastations caused by Venus's first close approach to the earth. The Children of Israel escaped from Egypt and in the Sinai wilderness encountered the Amalekites, a nomadic people of supposed descent from Esau, the twin brother of the patriarch Jacob (Israel), the progenitor of the Children of Israel. Hostilities broke out between the two groups and the Children of Israel defeated the Amalekites.[5] Velikovsky identifies the Amalekites as the Hyksos on their way to conquer Egypt. Later the Egyptians managed to recover and to drive out the hated Hyksos and the era of the New Kingdom began with the eighteenth dynasty.

Conventional chronology dates this dynasty to *c.* 1580–1320 BC and it includes some of Egypt's better known pharaohs: Hatshepsut, Thutmose III, Akhenaton and Tutankhamun.

Velikovsky's revised chronology, however, places the eighteenth dynasty as roughly contemporary with the United Kingdom of Israel under Saul, David and Solomon and the Divided Kingdoms of Israel and Judah to the time of King Ahab. He goes on to identify the female pharaoh Hatshepsut as the biblical Queen of Sheba. The historical Hatshepsut sent a trading expedition to the mysterious land of Punt, which scholars usually identify as Eritrea on the Red Sea or Somalia. Velikovsky argues that Punt was actually Solomon's kingdom and that Hatshepsut made a visit to Israel that is unrecorded in the surviving Egyptian records but is preserved in the Bible as the Queen of Sheba's visit to Solomon. According to Velikovsky Hatshepsut's successor, Thutmose III (1458–1425 BC according to conventional chronology) intrigued to undermine Solomon's kingdom and bring about the split between Solomon's heir Rehoboam of Judah and Jeroboam of Israel that created the Divided Kingdoms. Conventional history depicts Thutmose defending and expanding Egypt's domination of Palestine and Lebanon by leading numerous military expeditions into the region. He decisively defeated the rival northern Mesopotamian kingdom of Mitanni at the battle of Megiddo and solidified Egyptian hegemony over the region. Velikovsky, due to the implications of his revised chronology, sees these same events in quite a different context. He identifies Thutmose III as the same person as the Libyan pharaoh Shishak (*c.* 931–910 BC) and the founder of the twenty-second dynasty according to conventional chronology. Shishak is also the pharaoh who the film *Raiders of the Lost Ark* credits somewhat dubiously with carrying off the Ark of the Covenant when he invaded Palestine and devastated both the kingdoms of Judah and Israel. King Rehoboam of Judah managed to save Jerusalem from complete devastation by paying Shishak a large tribute as part of his submission.[6] If Velikovsky's revised chronology were correct it would mean that the Divided Kingdoms of Israel and Judah were contemporary with Egypt's greatest era of imperial power rather than the declining and relatively weak Egypt of the Third Intermediate Period as most historians believe.

The eighteenth dynasty had its own troubles. Akhenaton (*c.* 1350–1336 BC), the heretical pharaoh, attempted to institute unpopular reforms of the Egyptian religion, all the while neglecting the defenses of the empire. Instability and unrest grew in the Egyptian domains of Palestine and Lebanon as is recorded in the archives of Ras Shamra and El-Amarna. Velikovsky argues that these documents actually refer to events contemporary with the reigns of notorious King Ahab of Israel (*c.* 874–*c.* 853 BC) and Shalmaneser III (858–824 BC) who is identified by Velikovsky as the King Burraburiash of the Amarna letters.

The conclusion of *Ages in Chaos* promised that a second volume would soon carry the revision of ancient chronology up to the time of Alexander the Great (reigned 336–323 BC). In fact readers had to wait over twenty years by which time the second volume had become four books. *Ramses II and His Time* (1978) contended that the nineteenth dynasty of Pharaohs was identical to the twenty-sixth Dynasty. If true, it would also mean that the traditional king-lists used by historians contain serious errors and duplications. According to Velikovsky Rameses I is the same person as Necho I, Seti I is also Psamtik I, and Rameses II (*c.* 1279–1213 BC) is also known as Necho II. Rameses II's great battle with the Hittite Empire at Kadesh in 1275 BC is actually the same event as Necho II's battle with the neo-Babylonian Empire of Nebuchadnezzar II at Carchemish in 605 BC. It is Velikovsky's judgement that there was no Hittite Empire. The Hittites were a non-existent ancient people concocted by historians and archaeologists who have been mislead by the errors of the traditional chronology. Their confusion has led them to misidentify neo-Babylonian remains as Hittite because of the huge error in the conventional chronology that went unrecognized prior to Velikovsky. *Peoples of the Sea* (1977) is chronologically the last volume in the *Ages in Chaos* series even though it was published before *Ramses II and His Time*. In this volume, Pharaoh Rameses III (reigned 1186–1155 BC) of the twentieth dynasty is identified as the same person as Nectanebo II (380–362 BC) of the thirtieth dynasty. Rameses III's great battle at the mouth of the Nile River with the mysterious Peoples of the Sea at the beginning of his reign is transformed into a battle with Greek mercenaries in the employ of the Persian Empire. The unpublished book *Dark Age of Greece* contends that there were no dark ages in Greek history. Instead of Mycenaean civilization falling in 1100 BC and ushering in the Dark Ages for over three hundred years, Velikovsky moves the fall of Mycenae to about 800–700 BC, the beginning of the Archaic Era when the *Iliad* and the *Odyssey* were composed and the Greeks began to establish colonies around the Mediterranean and the Black Seas. Clearly Velikovsky was not exaggerating when he said that his ideas, if proven correct, would force every history textbook to be rewritten. Conventional archaeologists and historians are still waiting for convincing evidence.

Earth in Upheaval (1955) marks Velikovsky's foray into geology. Critics have complained that all of the evidence for the ancient catastrophes discussed in *Worlds in Collision* came from ancient texts of questionable provenance containing vague descriptions and un-scientific observations. It was said that Velikovsky's interpretations of the ancient documents were without reasonable warrant. Velikovsky responded by writing a book that used nothing but scientific evidence and documents to provide evidence that vast catastrophic changes had occurred on the earth, some of them in relatively recent historic times of 3,000 and 500 years ago. According to Velikovsky mass ex-tinction occurred because of global catastrophes that precipitated gigantic hurricanes and tidal waves. Mountains such as the Alps and the Himalayas rose to their current heights in this historic period. The mysterious city of Tiahuanacu near Lake Titicaca in Bolivia had originally been situated near sea level but mountain-building activity had raised it up to 12,300 feet in altitude. The Sahara had once con-tained a great inland lake but a gigantic convulsion emptied the lake and created the present desert. The oval craters of the Carolina Bays were impact craters resulting from meteors. A comet passing near the earth created the meteor show. Velikovsky also suggested there were more comets in the past, as well as more seismic and volcanic activity, than in the present. Massive catastrophes and cataclysms occurred far back in time with the last outbreaks taking place about 1500 BC and during the years 776–687 BC. Velikovsky even linked the end of the ice age and mass extinctions to these catastrophes.

Although Velikovsky credited the earth's near collisions with comets as the cause of these catastrophes, he also believed in poleshifts, titanic slidings of the earth's crust and changes in the earth's axis. He credited these phenomena with starting and ending the ice ages. Close encounters with large comets only served to trigger or to aggravate poleshifts, crustal rotations and changes in the angle of the earth's axis. Velikovsky also claimed that the great global calamities of the past not only caused mass extinctions, but also released radiation that produced mutations essential to the emergence of new species. The sliding and rotation of the earth's crust, Velikovsky continued, gave rise with relative suddenness to great mountains. Geologists considered these theories outrageous and ridiculous. Velikovsky re-jected the theory of continental drift and plate tectonics which was just beginning to gain acceptance from the scientific community during the time when *Worlds in Collision* and *Earth in Upheaval* were being formulated, researched and written. Continental drift was assumed to take place slowly over the course of millions and millions of years, so it supported the concept of gradual change over time known as uniformitarianism supported by establishment science, making it anathema to Velikovsky who advocated catastrophism, the idea that sudden and violent changes were what shaped the natural world. It is ironic that Velikovsky rejected and even sneered at the theory of continental drift. Alfred Wegener, the scientist who formulated the theory of continental drift, suffered from years of professional ostracism and scepticism that were reminiscent of what Velikovsky went through, except that ultimately research for the most part vindicated Wegener. In the case of *Earth in Upheaval* Velikovsky was largely ignored by geologists and so did not provoke the same furore as *Worlds in Collision*.

Who was this Immanuel Velikovsky whose books challenged the theoretical and factual frameworks of the disciplines of astronomy, physics, history, geology and biology? He was born in 1895 at Vitebsk in the Russian Empire. His father Shimon Velikovsky and his mother Beila Gradensky were well-to-do and Jewish. They sent the young Immanuel to study at the Medvednikov Gymnasium in Moscow where he graduated in 1913. After a year of travel and study in Palestine and Europe he returned to Russia and entered the University of Moscow and graduated in 1921 with a medical degree. From 1921 to 1923 he lived in Berlin where he met Albert Einstein. In 1923 he married Elisheva Kramer. Moving to Palestine in 1924 he practised medicine, psychiatry and psychoanalysis there until 1939. During his residence in Palestine Velikovsky made various trips; one included a stop in Vienna for a period of study with Wilhelm Stekel, himself a student of Sigmund Freud.[7]

By 1939 the possibility of war in Europe was becoming more and more likely just as Velikovsky decided he needed access to a great library to continue his research. New York City seemed like a good place to go since it contained several great libraries and was far from the dangers of Europe. Velikovsky was working on a project concerning Freud and his heroes that would eventually be published as *Oedipus and Akhnaton: Myth and History* in 1960. The book theorized that the heretical pharaoh was the Oedipus of Greek mythology. It was also written in reaction to Freud's *Moses and Monotheism*.[8] This research on Akhenaton involved Velikovsky in the study of the Exodus of Moses and the Children of Israel as a historical event. In his search for Egyptian writings that mentioned the Exodus he read a printed and edited translation of the Ipuwer Papyrus, a lamentation about various calamities that were befalling Egypt, some of which seemed similar to the Ten Plagues of Egypt described in the Bible. The problem for Velikovsky was that the Exodus was generally dated around 1500 BC (that indefatigable scholar Archbishop James Ussher in 1654 quite precisely dated the Exodus to 1491 BC) or around *c*. 1280 BC. Neither of those dates matched the supposed date of the Ipuwer Papyrus. In 1939 scholars dated the Ipuwer Papyrus either to around 2130 BC during the Old Kingdom or around 1640 BC during the late Middle Kingdom. At best about 150 years separated the troubled times of Ipuwer's lamentation from the tumultuous events of the Exodus. Velikovsky believed that the Exodus occurred about 1450 BC so his solution to the problem of chronologically linking the biblical events with those of the Ipuwer Papyrus was to revise the chronology of Egyptian history almost 500 years forward.[9]

Velikokvsky was anxious to establish his priority in the discovery of the errors in the conventional chronology of ancient history and the cosmic catastrophes that mauled the earth during antiquity. So in 1942 he made an affidavit that briefly outlined his ideas.[10] He followed up with the publication of a pamphlet in 1945. It contained his basic ideas about revising the chronology of ancient history and was rather prosaically titled *Theses for the Reconstruction of Ancient History*. Velikovsky brought out another pamphlet about the same time titled *Cosmos without Gravitation*. In it he denied the existence of gravity and instead attributed its effects to electromagnetic forces.[11] Throughout the 1940s Velikovsky combed the library of Columbia University along with others for evidences from ancient writings, mythology and folklore as well as scientific works that supported his ideas about the revised chronology and cosmic catastrophes. It was a quest that would continue up to the time of his death as he laboured to amass overwhelming evidence for the later volumes in the *Ages in Chaos* series. Velikovsky's own testimony shows that his ideas about correcting ancient chronology, renegade planets and global catastrophes came first, by as early as the spring of 1945, then the research needed to prove them followed.[12] It is not a sequence of discovery that most scholars approve of. They generally expect theories and interpretations to proceed from research rather than the other way around. The way Velikovsky did his scholarship cast doubt on the entire enterprise.

Obviously Velikovsky's ideas about ancient history and the solar system were highly unconventional but he was determined to publish them. In the course of his efforts to find a publisher he also set in motion the beginnings of the acerbic controversy that would accompany the publication of *Worlds in Collision*. During 1942 Velikovsky began to seek support for his ideas from prominent academics. The Old Testament scholar Robert H. Pfeiffer of Harvard University showed interest in but not agreement with Velikovsky's ideas. He did express the hope that a university press or some other reputable publisher would agree to bring out Velikovsky's book. So Velikovsky submitted his manuscript to a university press in 1944 but after fourteen months of consideration, the press rejected it.[13]

Fatefully, in April 1946, Velikovsky sought out Harlow Shapley, the director of the Harvard observatory, to ask him about the atmospheres of Mars and Venus. He also asked Shapley to read his manuscript but Shapley said he was too busy to do it unless another reputable scholar recommended it to him. Shapley suggested that Velikovsky get Lynn Thorndike, the historian of science at Columbia University, to read his manuscript. If Thorndike was not able to read it, they agreed, at least according to Velikovsky, that a recommendation from Horace Kallen, a professor at the New School for Social Research, would be satisfactory for Shapley.[14] Kallen read the manuscript and recommended it but Shapley decided that he was still not interested in reading about such an implausible hypothesis.[15] The root of the problem with Shapley was that the forthright Velikovsky had given Shapley a copy of his recently published *Cosmos without Gravitation*, which denied the existence of gravity. That circumstance convinced Shapley that Velikovsky was a crank whose ideas were marginal and needed to be kept in the margins.[16] Velikovsky had unwittingly created the leader of the scientific Furies who would later relentlessly attack his ideas.

Velikovsky continued to seek a publisher. Eight more had turned him down when, at the suggestion of Horace Kallen, Velikovsky took his manuscript to John O'Neill, science editor of the New York *Herald Tribune*. O'Neill liked what he read and wrote favourably about it in his newspaper column on 11 August 1946. This recognition helped to give Velikovsky pull with other publishers. Although Appleton-Century turned down *Worlds in Collision* the editor advised Velikovsky to submit to Macmillan. Velikovsky met with James Putnam, an associate editor at Macmillan, and the two men hit it off immediately. They agreed on an option contract during May 1947 which became a regular contract in May 1948 after Velikovsky did more research and rewrites on the manuscript. By February 1949 Macmillan had prepared the galley proofs for *Worlds in Collision*.[17]

Other good things came Velikovsky's way. On 18 March 1949 the venerable Frederick Lewis Allen, editor of *Harper's Magazine*, wrote to him to inquire about a prepublication serialization of portions of *Worlds in Collision*. Allen and James Putnam were friends and Putnam had told him about Velikovsky's forthcoming book. Allen's offer was a tremendous coup for Velikovsky in terms of potential publicity for his book, and was sure to boost sales. Ultimately in January 1950 *Harpers* published an article titled 'The Day the Sun Stood Still' by Eric Larrabee that summarized *Worlds in Collision*. Even though Velikovsky proved difficult to work with, the experience converted Larrabee into a long-time supporter of Velikovsky but the article also tipped off Harlow Shapley and like-minded scientists about the impending publication of *Worlds in Collision*. Additional publicity followed through two articles by John Lear that appeared in *Collier's Magazine* in the 25 February and 25 March issues titled 'The Heavens Burst' and 'World on Fire' and another in the *Reader's Digest* for March 1950 by Fulton Oursler titled 'Why the Sun Stood Still'.[18] The scientists only became more irate.

Soon after Larrabee's article appeared in *Harper's*, on 18 January 1950, Harlow Shapley wrote a letter to the editors of Macmillan asking if a rumour that Macmillan had decided not to publish *Worlds in Collision* was true and stating his relief if it was. When James Putnam informed him that the rumour was false, Shapley informed Putnam that a colleague, Celia Payne-Gaposchkin, was preparing a rebuttal of Velikovsky and asked for a copy of the proofs 'so that it will be Dr V. who is discussed and not Larrabee'. Shapley also clearly expressed his opinion that Velikovsky's ideas were demented. Over the weeks that followed the scientists exerted continuous and escalating pressure on Macmillan to pull the book. Meanwhile, on 10 March, Macmillan launched *Worlds in Collision* and released it a few weeks later. In between Gaposchkin's rebuttal appears in the 14 March issue of the news magazine *The Reporter* with the title 'Nonsense, Dr Velikovsky'. Her criticism did nothing to blunt sales and *Worlds in Collision* became an instant bestseller. Velikovsky's joy was blunted, however, when his supporter Gordon Atwater, the chair of the astronomy department at the American Museum of Natural History and the curator of the Hayden Observatory, was abruptly fired.[19]

The scientists brought further pressure on Macmillan by threatening a boycott of its textbooks and by pulling or not submitting their own books to Macmillan. A worried textbook division at Macmillan sought relief from company president George Brett. By the end of May he decided to drop *Worlds in Collision* despite its impressive sales. Brett arranged to turn the book over to Doubleday, a publisher without a vulnerable textbook division. Brett informed Velikovsky in a polite but take-it-or-leave-it manner and Doubleday became his new publisher. Soon after Brett fired the man who signed *Worlds in Collision*, James Putnam.[20]

What the scientists really wanted was for Velikovsky's book to be pulled completely so that it was no longer available to purchase and to read. In that effort they failed. Sales of *Worlds in Collision* remained brisk as controversy has never hurt a book's sales and efforts at suppression only arouse the curiosity of the reading public. Meanwhile favourable and hostile reviews of the book appeared in the press along with articles for and against and accompanying rebuttals and rejoinders during 1950–53. The publication of *Ages in Chaos* kept the controversy going and brought concerned archaeologists and historians into the fray.

The attempts of scientists and other scholars to debunk Velikovsky failed to strike a knockout blow. Velikovsky and his supporters always managed to produce a seemingly plausible comeback. Several curious circumstances developed during the first phase of the so-called Velikovsky affair. First, the frantic attacks of the scientists and the boycott of Macmillan proved to be counter-productive in that they aroused sympathy for Velikovsky among people who did not agree with his hypotheses but did not want to see anyone persecuted and censored for their ideas. Second, events in the controversy progressed in such a way that it became presumed that the scientists and other scholars bore the burden of proving Velikovsky wrong. In fact, given that he was making a number of rather extraordinary claims, by all rights the burden of proof lay on Velikovsky and his followers to prove his ideas scientifically and historically to the reasonable satisfaction of scholars in those disciplines. Third, the scientists failed to recognize that Velikovsky's writings were about topics of science and history but they were not really scientific or historical scholarship in a conventional sense. Velikovsky's claims about planetary motion, electromagnetic forces versus gravitation and the chemical composition and temperatures of Jupiter and Venus were vague and non-specific. As such they provided the highly intelligent and rhetorically clever Velikovsky with lots of room for manoeuvre when confronted by a scientific rebuttal. Fourth, the scientists' behaviour played into popular and unfavourable stereotypes about scientists and experts that were prominent in the early 1950s and persist as a fluctuating grassroots anti-intellectualism that is chronic in most societies. The scientists opposing Velikovsky came across to the public as arrogant in an era when a popular science fiction movie like *The Thing* (1950) could portray the scientist character as an overbearing fool who almost gets everyone killed by the hostile alien. It was not an uncommon way of portraying scientists in the popular culture of that era.[21] Fifth, Velikovsky and his supporters did a highly effective job of conflating and thereby obfuscating the concepts of what is possible and what is probable, a common rhetorical device of pseudohistorians and pseudoscientists as well as trial lawyers.

The scientists attempted to refute Velikovsky in rushed articles that relied as much on readers simply accepting or acquiescing to the superior expertise of the scientist rather then the logical argument and convincing evidence they deployed. The academic experts seem to have been genuinely taken by surprise when many people simply did not take their word for it that Velikovsky was wrong. Adding to the credibility problem of the scientists, their early rebuttals were done by people such as Celia Payne-Gaposchkin, who had not read *Worlds in Collision* before attempting to refute it. Other scholars even proudly announced that they had not read the book and had no intention of ever reading it. Supporters of Velikovsky used this to undermine the scholars' claims of intellectual objectivity and purity. Such criticisms by Velikovskians are not completely fair. At the beginning of the controversy, Larrabee's article was the only source for Velikovsky's ideas. Shapley did ask Putnam to provide galley proofs of *Worlds in Collision* for Payne-Gaposchkin to use in preparing her article. This apparently was not done. Still the overall impression was that the scientists had behaved badly and performed poorly.[22]

After 1953 the Velikovsky controversy faded dramatically with only modest and brief flare-ups with the publication of *Earth in Upheaval* in 1955 and *Oedipus and Akhnaton* in 1960. A second phase of the controversy ignited in 1962 with the publication of a letter by scientists V. Bargmann of Princeton University and Lloyd Motz of Columbia University to the prominent magazine *Science*.[23] Bargmann and Motz pointed out that Velikovsky had predicted in 1953 that Jupiter emitted radio signals and in 1950 that Venus had a high surface temperature. At the time no one had observed radio signals coming from Jupiter and it was widely assumed that Venus's surface temperature would be cold or only modestly warmer than the earth's. By 1961 scientists had detected radio signals emanating from Jupiter and had measured the surface temperature of Venus to be 600 degrees Kelvin. So Bargmann and Motz concluded their letter, 'Although we disagree with Velikovsky's theories, we feel impelled to make this statement to establish Velikovsky's priority on prediction of these two points and to urge in view of these prognostications, that his other conclusions be objectively reexamined.'[24] Once again Velikovsky's opponents denounced the letter and his ideas while Velikovsky and his supporters decried his critics.

During this second phase of the Velikovsky controversy the focus of the debate shifted from his ideas to how established science operated to advance and establish the truth or sometimes to retard knowledge along with a discussion about how and if establishment scientists had mistreated Velikovsky and so betrayed the ideals of science. Scholars sympathetic to Velikovsky devoted the entire September 1963 issue of *American Behavioral Scientist* to a discussion of Velikovsky's ideas along with the shabby treatment they received. The entire issue was reprinted as a book, *The Velikovsky Affair*, in

1966. Besides the issues raised by Bargmann and Motz, Velikovsky and his supporters picked out other ideas from his writings, the so-called 'advanced claims', that they thought had been proved correct by subsequent scientific discoveries. Opponents of Velikovsky angrily disagreed. As in the first phase of the controversy they at times engaged in less than honourable behaviour. Pressure was placed on individuals not to do anything or say anything that might be construed as support for Velikovsky or, if they did, to retract it. Various publications did not allow Velikovsky to answer or rebut criticisms of him that they had published. These actions only encouraged others to rally around Velikovsky as an underdog and he became the darling of students during the 1960s who wanted to rebel against authority but were not inclined to leftist causes. As a result journals devoted to Velikovskian ideas sprang up and invitations to lecture on various college campuses began to arrive. Velikovsky's isolation had ended and his ideas acquired something of a cult following.

The widespread acceptance of Velikovsky's ideas reached an extent that it prompted the Cornell University astronomer Carl Sagan and other members of the American Association for the Advancement of Science (AAAS) to do something about it. As part of the AAAS conference at San Francisco in 1974 they organized a symposium on Velikovsky's ideas for 25 February. Sagan and other scholars gave papers criticizing Velikovsky's hypotheses while Velikovsky and another sympathetic scholar defended them. Observers and reporters at the meeting credited the scientists with winning the debate although Velikovsky and his supporters indignantly disagreed. The plan to publish all the papers from the session collapsed over a dispute with Velikovsky, who could be prickly, demanding and uncompromising, as Larrabee and the editors of *Collier's Magazine* had discovered when they attempted to publish summaries of his hypotheses that pleased him. Ultimately in 1976 the papers of the anti-Velikovsky scientists were published with an additional paper by the astronomer David Morrison as *Scientists Confront Velikovsky*.[25] The cornerstone of the collection was Carl Sagan's paper, 'An Analysis of *Worlds in Collision*', which identified ten primary ideas of Velikovsky's that were wrong. Sagan's paper was really an essay of debunking aimed at the general public rather than a research paper discussing scientific results related to the truth or falsity of Velikovsky's ideas. Unfortunately Sagan made a number of minor errors that Velikovsky and his supporters exploited to the full in an effort to undermine Sagan's credibility. Even scholars who disagreed with Velikovsky found Sagan's paper to be weak and plagued by small but irritating errors, a condition he never corrected in later publications using the same basic material.[26] The incensed Velikovskians retorted to *Scientists Confront Velikovsky* with two collections of their own essays: *Velikovsky and Establishment Science* in 1977 and the confrontationally titled *Scientists Confront Scientists Who Confront Velikovsky* in 1978.[27] Among Velikovskians the AAAS symposium of 1974 cemented a halo on Velikovsky and his work that lasted largely untarnished until after his death in 1979. For years after the symposium diehard Velikovskians continued to complain bitterly about the ill-mannered and unfair treatment he received at San Francisco.[28]

Was Velikovsky treated poorly and unfairly by some of his opponents? The answer is clearly yes. On the other hand, he was also extraordinarily well treated by many people, both friends and foes. Certainly he was also rather lucky in his endeavours. Few aspiring authors manage to secure the services of major publishing houses like Macmillan and Doubleday. Given the outlandish nature of his ideas about science and ancient history, his success might seem even more astounding until one realizes that wild and crazy ideas make for significantly more profitable publishing ventures than well-done works on mainstream topics. Some of the credit for Velikovsky's success is attributable to his dogged determination and his urbane European manners. Still he also had to have luck. He was lucky that James Putnam was the first person at Macmillan to talk with him. He was lucky that Putnam happened to know Frederick Lewis Allen at *Harper's*. He was lucky that Harlow Shapley and his fellow scientists decided to attempt the censorship and suppression of *Worlds in Collision*. As Isaac Asimov, scientist and author of many books on popular science and science fiction, wrote in 1977, 'To paraphrase Fouché, it was worse than immoral, it was a blunder.'[29] He was lucky that Bargmann and Motz wrote their letter to *Science* and reignited the controversy over *Worlds in Collision*. In this case there was a bit more than luck involved. Velikovsky had known Motz since the beginning of 1950 and had met frequently with him in the years that followed. By 1954 they were close enough that Velikovsky mentioned in a letter to Albert Einstein that Motz had edited the astronomy material in the manuscript of *Earth in Upheaval*. Bargmann and Velikovsky became acquainted in 1953 through their mutual friendship with Einstein. Motz and Bargmann may not have agreed with all of Velikovsky's ideas but they were apparently good enough friends to give him an assist. Certainly their letter revived the controversy and resulted in Velikovsky becoming something of a celebrity.[30]

As a result of these circumstances fair-minded people rushed to Velikovsky's defence and for a time a good number became converts to his ideas. All the while Velikovsky sold a lot of books. One of these converts was Leroy Ellenberger, for some years deeply committed to Velikovskian ideas but now a determined critic. Ellenberger has complained that various scientists who opposed Velikovsky simply took a stance of pronouncing *ex cathedra* that he was wrong and left it at that. People like Ellenberger would not have become enamoured with Velikovskianism if scientists had taken the time to provide detailed point by point refutations in language that non-specialists could understand. If they had performed this basic task, he says, 'I would never have gotten as involved with Velikovsky as I later did.'[31]

Ellenberger was not a unique case and several journals devoted to Velikovskian studies sprang up at various times from the mid-1960s to the 1990s. The first of these was *Pensée*, founded by students in Oregon. It appeared briefly during 1966 and was revived from 1972 to 1975 when ten issues were published. British Velikovskians launched their own journal in 1974, the *SIS Review* of the Society for Interdisciplinary Studies (SIS). It changed its named to *Chronology and Catastrophism Review* in 1986 and is still being published. When *Pensée* died, its place in the USA was taken by *Kronos: A Journal of Interdisciplinary Synthesis* which appeared from 1975 to 1988. It was associated with the Kronos Press which was published Velikovskian books. *Aeon: A Journal of Myth, Science, and Ancient History* took over from *Kronos* in 1988 and was published until 2004. Another periodical, *The Velikovskian: A Journal of Myth, History, and Science*, first appeared in 1993 and was associated with Ivy Press Books, a Velikovskian publisher. It is unclear whether this journal has remained active after 2004. Despite claims to the contrary Velikovsky and his ideas received plenty of favourable attention along with all the fair and unfair criticism. Most scholars would be overjoyed to experience half of his success.

Unfortunately for Velikovsky, his ideas ultimately had little or no impact on the disciplines of astronomy, biology, geology, archaeology and history. The great scientific ogre that Velikovsky attacked through his revival of the long-discredited idea of catastrophism was the intellectually popular mainstream concept of uniformitarianism, which contends that most fundamental changes in nature take place over very long periods of time. In this view the building of mountains, the rise and decline of ice ages, the evolution of new species and the creation of the solar system are plodding things requiring eons to run their course. The English scientist Charles Lyell (1797–1875) promoted uniformitarian ideas in geology, and Charles Darwin (1809–1882) adapted them to underpin his theory of biological evolution. Lyell's work eloquently rejected the age-old concept of Catastrophism, which claimed that most changes in nature occur suddenly as a result of great and universal calamities. Chiefly through the cosmic drama of the biblical account of Noah's universal flood Christianity had programmed people to think in terms of catastrophism. Other cultures throughout the world held to similar legends of universal floods or other great catastrophes like the supposed sinking of Atlantis. Because of Lyell's influence on the inner workings of science and Darwin's powerful appeal to the popular mind uniformitarianism had risen to a dominant position in scientific thinking by the time *Worlds in Collision* appeared in 1950.[32]

Worlds in Collision sought to restore catastrophism as the prime cause of change in nature, specifically in the form of Venus as a comet repeatedly devastating the earth before settling into its current stable orbit as a planet. Velikovsky claimed that his Venus-as-comet idea proceeded out of the extensive research he did in the Columbia University library during the 1940s. Others have pointed out, however, that Velikovsky was not all that original. William Whiston (1667–1752), an English theologian, historian and scientist, wrote *A New Theory of the Earth* in 1696 that attributed the biblical deluge of Noah to a close encounter with a comet. The great pseudohistorian of Atlantis, Ignatius Donnelly (1831–1901), also claimed the earth had experienced a catastrophic encounter with a comet in prehistoric times in his book *Ragnarok: The Age of Fire and Gravel* (1883). Velikovsky mentions both men's books briefly in footnotes in *Worlds in Collision* that take a rather dismissive view of their ideas. Martin Gardner, a specialist in debunking pseudoscience, in his classic *Fads and Fallacies in the Name of Science* (1957) maintained that both Whiston and Donnelly's ideas played an important role in the formation of Velikovsky's hypotheses.[33] Even closer at hand, Velikovsky had the classic science fiction novel *When Worlds Collide* (1932) by Philip Wylie and Edwin Baumer, which told of the destruction of the earth when it collides with a rogue planet. *When Worlds Collide* is considered to be the first science fiction novel to postulate the destruction of the earth by a cosmic collision, although Jules Verne and H. G. Wells both wrote novels involving collisions or close encounters with comets. In 1951, the year after the publication of *Worlds in Collision*, Hollywood brought out a film version of *When Worlds Collide*. Was Velikovsky part of some sort of cosmic collision Zeitgeist?

Another little remarked upon influence on Velikovsky's scientific and historical ideas was his deep commitment to Zionism. From late 1947 to the middle of 1952 Velikovsky wrote a weekly political column for the *New York Post* using the name 'Observer'. The columns took Zionist positions when appropriate, which is not surprising considering the many years that Velikovsky lived in Palestine.[34] Velikovsky was no Jewish fundamentalist but the study of the biblical setting of the Exodus, the conquest of Canaan and the United and Divided Monarchy formed the starting point of his research. In spite of his branching out to legends of ancient catastrophes from throughout the world the biblical setting continued to remain the primary focus of his books. Zionist beliefs also united Velikovsky with his friend, patron and defender, the philosopher Horace Kallen of Columbia University.[35]

The same Zionist connection applies to Velikovsky's relationship with Albert Einstein. They had known each other in Germany during the 1920s where they both worked on the foundation of Hebrew University. Velikovsky renewed his acquaintance with Einstein when he moved to New York City in 1939 and their correspondence continued until Einstein's death on 18 April 1955. By 1946 Velikovsky was clearly hoping to get Einstein's prestigious endorsement for his hypotheses. Unfortunately for him, while Einstein was willing to accept the role of catastophism in the natural world and human history, he consistently rejected Velikovsky's ideas about Venus originally being a comet and the attempt to reject the existence of gravity and to substitute electromagnetic forces. Much to Velikovsky's dismay, Einstein was impressed by Charles H. Hapgood's hypotheses about pole shifts and crustal displacement being the source of catastophic change. While Velikovsky vehemently protested I. Bernard Cohen's characterization of Einstein as an opponent of Velikovsky's hypotheses, it is hard to read the two men's correspondence and conclude he was a supporter. Instead Einstein saw Velikovsky's work as containing some interesting ideas mixed with some he considered to be nonsensical. He did deplore the shabby and rude treatment that some academics inflicted on Velikovsky but that by no means meant that he endorsed Velikovsky's ideas.[36]

Many scientists wrote against Velikovsky but the quality of their refutations was surprisingly poor. Even Carl Sagan remarked during the AAAS's Velikovsky symposium in 1974 on the unsatisfactory nature of the scientific writings about Velikovsky but himself proceeded to deliver an error-plagued and sometimes ill-thought-out debunking. Henry H. Bauer has shown that a thorough and critical dissection and debunking of Velikovsky's science is entirely possible. Unfortunately the effort is a tedious and time-consuming exercise in research and writing. It makes for tedious reading as well.[37] The basic problem for Velikovsky and his ideas about electromagnetic forces replacing gravity, Venus as a comet, catastrophic mountain-building and rapid extinction and evolution of species as a result of catastrophes is that new developments in science since the mid-1950s, such as plate tectonics, have made his hypotheses less likely rather than more likely to be correct. That is not the sign of a successful theory or even of a hypothesis.

Historically and archaeologically, Velikovsky's books are also based on a house of cards in terms of evidence, however seemingly voluminous that evidence might appear. Velikovsky claimed that ancient writings, particularly those from Egypt, could be linked to the biblical accounts of the Ten Plagues, the Exodus, the conquest of Canaan by Joshua and events during the Divided Monarchy to prove that the earth had experienced global catastrophes. To make everything fit together properly Velikovsky asserted that about 500 years had to be removed from the traditional histories of Egypt and early Greece. This radical resynchronizing of ancient chronology made King Solomon and Pharaoh Hatshepsut as well as Rameses II and Nebuchadnezzar of Babylon contemporaries. It also eliminated the Dark Age of Greece and the Hittite Empire while moving the beginning of the Iron Age back five centuries. If Velikovsky was correct historians would have had to rewrite much of ancient history.

What most ancient historians understand, while other non-specialists do not, is that the conventional chronology of ancient history is quite tentative and subject to revision if new evidence is discovered. At the time Velikovsky researched and wrote his books the conventional ancient chronology could not be confirmed by any scientific means. Scholars had established a chronology from existing historical documents and inscriptions. Classical Greek and Roman history possess an unbroken chain of historical evidence that makes for a reliable and firm chronology. The Greeks kept lists of Olympiads and the Romans had lists of the terms of consuls and reigns of emperors unbroken for hundreds of years. These could easily be linked to the system of BC and AD dating that long prevailed in the Christian West. Egyptian history could be linked to this firm chronology through the list of pharaohs compiled by the hellenized Egyptian scholar Manetho (fl. c. 280–260 BC).

This type of chronology is called an absolute chronology because it assigns real dates to events, persons and artefacts. The other form of chronology is called relative chronology. It assigns an order to events, persons or artefacts based on circumstances but which cannot be linked to the absolute chronology. Other ancient civilizations left historical documents and archaeological remains that allow scholars to know that kings, cities and events existed or took place in a certain relative chronological order. What they lack is a conventional king-list like Manetho's that can be linked to the existing absolute chronology. In relative chronology scholars know the order of events for an ancient culture but are not sure how those events correlate and synchronize to other ancient cultures and the absolute chronology. What they do is sift through archaeological remains looking for links to the known absolute chronology, usually through a connection to something dateable from ancient Egypt. Historians and archaeologists have worked together on this effort for centuries. Prior to the late nineteenth and twentieth centuries they also attempted to link the biblical narrative to an absolute chronology of ancient history. Both Archbishop James Ussher and Sir Isaac Newton compiled chronologies, as have many others, and none of them completely agree with each other. Keep in mind that modern historians and archaeologists continue to argue and to debate over the details of the absolute chronology of the ancient world before the classical era of the Greeks and Romans. Their disagreements, however, are usually concerned with differences of a year or two, perhaps up to fifty years. Disagreements involving differences of over a hundred years are rare and almost always involve the very earliest eras of ancient history. What Velikovsky proposed by eliminating 500 years of Egyptian and Greek history would completely destroy a longstanding and reasonably well-documented consensus about the absolute chronology of the ancient world of the eastern Mediterranean. Most scholars considered Velikovsky's claims to be almost unimaginably audacious.

Just as Velikovsky was finishing *Worlds in Collision* several new scientific methods of dating ancient materials came into use.[38] One was radiocarbon dating, which was developed after World War II by Williard F. Libby of the University of Chicago and his associates. Radiocarbon dating measures the decay of radioactive Carbon 14 in organic material to determine how old it is. Although radiocarbon dating is based on certain assumptions that cannot be directly tested it has been checked against ancient woods of a known age and found to be reasonably accurate. Reasonably accurate in radiocarbon terms, however, means that a date of anywhere from plus or minus 50 to 300 years will be assigned to an ancient artefact. Contamination by organic material from earlier or later times can produce inaccurate results and occasionally unexplained anomalous results occur. At present radiocarbon dating provides an accepted and reasonably reliable scientific method for dating the absolute age of artefacts. When Velikovsky's early books appeared in the 1950s radiocarbon dating was extremely expensive, required a fairly large sample to be used for destructive testing, and was still in the process of being calibrated through artefacts of known age. Radiocarbon dating had the potential to prove Velikovsky's revised chronology definitively right or wrong. The problem for Velikovsky was that after some initially promising radiocarbon datings, subsequent datings based on more accurate techniques and better equipment supported the conventional chronology.

Dendrochronology is a scientific technique that uses the study of tree-rings to date wood artefacts and also to study ancient climate and environment. Andrew Ellicot Douglass pioneered tree-ring research in the southwestern United States and slowly but surely sequences of tree-rings going further and further back in time accumulated. Currently the two oldest sequences go back 9,000 years and 10,000 years respectively. Dendrochronology provides a system of absolute dating that can be used as an independent check on radiocarbon dates. Where applicable the available tree-ring evidence has supported the conventional chronology of ancient history rather than Velikovsky's revised chronology. The climatological and environmental information provided by dendrochronology also does not reveal any signs of the global catastrophes that Velikovsky claims occurred in *Worlds in Collision* and *Earth in Upheaval*.

Scientists have also discovered that the glaciers of Greenland and Antarctica preserve information about environmental changes that can date back hundreds of thousands of years. Each year adds a new layer of ice to the polar glaciers and those layers contain information about the atmosphere and climate of the earth. To study such information, scientists bore into the glaciers and remove cores of sample ice hundreds of feet long and going back hundreds of thousands of years at the lower levels. These ice cores contain airborne ash, dust and pollen from ancient forests and grasslands or the eruptions of volcanoes such as Krakatoa in 1883, Tambora in 1815 and other earlier volcanic events. Unfortunately for Velikovsky the ice cores show no evidence of dust and ash from the worldwide cataclysms that he describes in his books.[39]

Historians and archaeologists never took Velikovsky's ideas very seriously from their first appearance in 1950. His use of historical evidence was fatally defective even without the testimony of the new scientific techniques of dating. The revised chronology cannot be reconciled with large amounts of available archaeological evidence. Because archaeologists study the past by examining the remnants of human societies they dig into the sites of ancient abandoned cities. When humans occupy the same location for long periods of time layers of remains build up, known as strata. An ancient city might be destroyed in a war or an earthquake but it would later be rebuilt. The destroyed city would be one layer or stratum, the rebuilt city would eventually become another stratum. Other destructions and rebuildings would follow one after another over the course of time and other strata would be added. The layers or strata are obviously laid down in chronological order with the oldest on the bottom and the most recent on the top. The study of these layers is known as archaeological stratigraphy.

Another aspect of archaeological stratigraphy is that artefacts from one culture can be found in the archaeological remains of another society. The foreign artefacts almost certainly got to the other society through trade. Their presence helps to document that trade occurred but they can also be used to approximately date a site of unknown age by means of a foreign artefact of known age. One would expect that artefacts both native and foreign found in the same layer would be approximately the same age. Of course, exceptions can occur if people from a later period of time dig down into the older strata, perhaps to bury someone or to lay a foundation. Archaeologists are trained to recognize such occurrences when they are excavating a site. Velikovsky's revised chronology necessitates that some higher and presumably more recent strata are actually older than strata that are lower in the archaeological site. Strata would have to have been flip-flopped if Velikovsky's revised chronology is correct and that is just not physically possible.[40]

Scholars also object to the way Velikovsky interpreted and used ancient documents. Velikovsky assumed they could be taken as literal descriptions of historical events that took place instead of being metaphorical or allegorical tales, engaging in the discredited practice of euhemerism in the study of mythology. Ancient people identified the planets with certain gods, the names of the planets Jupiter, Mars and Venus being prime examples of this phenomenon. So if a myth describes Mars or Venus as engaged in a war or a battle, Velikovsky assumes that it is a euhemeristic description by some ancient witness of the calamitous events associated with the close encounters between the earth and the planets Mars or Venus. Such a use of ancient myths is much too literal and simplistic for most scholars of myth and folklore. Velikovsky compounds the problem by claiming that ancient myths from all over the world were describing the same apocalyptic events and therefore dated from the same time or at least referred to events that occurred at the same time. When the biblical narrative describes Joshua commanding the sun to stand still, Velikovsky looked for other ancient accounts of an extraordinarily long day or (on the other side of the world, as in Mayan or Chinese myth), the description of an extraordinarily long night. Scholars do not find that this sort of evidence adequate to support Velikovsky's hypotheses. First, they are not tales of actual events. Second, most of

the disaster accounts from around the world are not roughly con-
temporaneous and so could not describe the same phenomenon even
if they were accounts of literal events.[41]

Close study has also reveals that Velikovsky's use of ancient
sources could frequently be inaccurate, sloppy or tendentiously selective. A devastating revelation of the deficiencies of Velikovsky's
scholarship was delivered by Abraham Sachs, a historian of mathe-
matics who could read cuneiform texts. Sachs participated in a panel
discussion with Velikovsky on 15 March 1965 at Brown University.
Whereas Velikovsky managed to appear to have bested his scientist
opponents in the panel discussion by means of clever rhetoric, he
could not rebut Sachs's devastating presentation. Sachs began by
pointing out that cuneiform studies were constantly improving and
to rely on books that are 40, 50 or 80 years old as Velikovsky had
done was to rely upon obsolete and sometimes erroneous scholarship. After that he presented a sampling of Velikovsky's bigger errors
in the use of cuneiform scholarship. Sachs pointed out that an Assyrian king-list that Velikovsky was unaware of completely supports
the conventional chronology's dating of the Amarna Letters. Furthermore, the cuneiform characters used in the Amarna Letters were
those of the fourteenth century BC, not the ninth century BC as Velikovsky claimed they should be dated. Next Sachs delivered a point by
point refutation of Velikovsky's evidence for redating the Ras Shamra
tablets from the fourteenth to the ninth century BC. From there he
showed that Velikovsky's claims that Babylonian astronomy originally
did not include Venus among the planets is based on the use of a translation of an ancient text in which the cuneiform character for 'star'
had been mistranslated as 'planet'. Other errors, however, stemmed
from Velikovsky selectively or inaccurately conveying the contents of
some documents to his readers. Sachs concluded by suggesting that
Velikovsky really ought to learn to read cuneiform if he planned on
using cuneiform texts for evidence in the future. Velikovsky promised
the audience that he would prove Sachs wrong the next day with a
point by point refutation. Nothing happened next day and Velikovsky studiously ignored that the encounter with Sachs had ever
occurred for the rest of his life.[42]

What Sachs started, Bob Forrest finished. Forrest, a mathe-
matician, spent several years compiling a seven-volume work titled
Velikovsky's Sources that he had privately printed. He felt that Velikovsky cited his sources selectively and inaccurately so that only
material that supported his ideas was presented and material from
the same documents that undermined his hypotheses was ignored or
suppressed. To prove his point, Forrest compared Velikovsky's writings

with the sections of the documents he cited in his footnotes. What Forrest found is that time after time Velikovsky ignored contrary evidence; cited evidence selectively and tendentiously or presented evidence that was insufficient, inadequate or irrelevant to prove his claims. Forrest's seven-volume work is rather rare but he also produced a brief and more convenient version *A Guide to Velikovsky's Sources* in 1987.[43] Sachs and Forrest have both shown conclusively that Velikovsky was a poor historian in terms of his technical skills, tendentious citations and biased analysis.

Was Velikovsky influential? If by influence we mean that he possessed a significant following, the answer is obviously yes. If we mean that his books sold many copies, the answer is also yes. While the number and enthusiasm of Velikovsky's supporters has dwindled since his death they still persist as organized groups. His books are now largely out of print although still available new in Hebrew editions. A brisk demand exists for Velikovsky titles on the second-hand book market, so he is not forgotten by readers and collectors. Still, if by influence we mean did Velikovsky change the theoretical foundations of astronomy, physics or geology or the accepted chronology of ancient history, the answer is no. Velikovskians claim that he began the rise of neo-catastrophism in science but genuine neo-catastrophists generally feel that Velikovsky's influence was negative and held them back because of the disrepute and suspicion that the Velikovsky controversy inflicted on any catastrophist hypotheses, no matter how well researched and formulated.[44] The premature claims by Bargmann and Motz along with other Velikovskians in the early 1960s and after that Velikovsky's 'advance claims' have been proved correct by advances in scientific research have since withered. Further research has basically added no evidence that Velikovsky's hypotheses are at all correct and has produced much evidence that his ideas are almost certainly wrong. Neo-catastrophism is now an important aspect of the earth sciences and astronomy but it has been compromised and merged with uniformitarianism through the concept of punctuated equilibrium. Punctuated equilibrium combines uniformitarianism and catastrophism. Most of the time the gradual processes of geological and biological change proceed but occasionally, very occasionally, a great catastrophe wreaks massive and rapid change on the natural world. The most famous catastrophic event on record is the apparent extinction of the dinosaurs as the result of a comet or asteroid striking the earth some 65 million years ago.[45] As for Venus once having been a comet and terrorizing the earth around 1500 BC or Mars doing the same about 700 years later, no evidence of even moderate credibility has emerged.

Some have seen the Velikovskian hypotheses about catastrophes and biblical events and their naturalistic explanations as a perfect combination with Creationist ideas about the past. That has not proven to be the case. Creationists find Velikovsky's giving other ancient texts an authority and authenticity equal to the Bible to be repugnant and suspicious. Some seem to think that he was an adherent of evolutionary theory and denied the universal flood described in Genesis.[46] Some of the Creationists' criticisms of Velikovsky betray a lack of understanding or familiarity with his ideas. It may be that the real problem lies in the fact that Velikovsky never took the step from secular and scientific to religious explanation for his hypotheses by identifying the God of Jews and Christians as the force behind the catastrophes and the seeming miraculous events associated with them.

If Velikovsky failed to revolutionize science and history with his hypotheses or attract the support of Creationists, he and his books did do one thing: they provided a roadmap and encouragement for other pseudohistorians and pseudoscientists to walk the path of catastrophism – many have done just that. Velikovsky's books have entered the cultic milieu of catastrophic pseudohistory. His obvious success stands as a beacon for others even if his hypotheses are not followed or imitated. One of those people was Charles H. Hapgood, who advocated his own form of catastrophism and also managed to make his own enduring addition to the cultic milieu of pseudohistory: the Piri Reis map as a mysterious artefact of the past.

CHARLES H. HAPGOOD: Crustal displacement and Ice Age civilizations

> False facts are highly injurious to the progress of science, for they often endure long; but false views, if supported by some evidence, do little harm, for everyone takes a salutary pleasure in proving their falseness. CHARLES DARWIN[47]

Charles H. Hapgood (1904–1982) was a college professor whose first book, *Earth's Shifting Crust* (1958), followed on the heels of Immanuel Velikovsky's *Worlds in Collision*, *Ages in Chaos*, and *Earth in Upheaval*. Although their ideas share broad similarities, it is much more accurate to say that they worked in parallel rather than to suggest that Velikovsky directly influenced Hapgood. In fact Velikovsky was aware of Hapgood's hypotheses when he was finishing *Earth in Upheaval* and he clearly did not think too much of them, although his friend Albert Einstein did.[48] Still Velikovsky and his books promoted catastrophism and rejected uniformitarianism as explanations of changes in the earth and so smoothed the way for Hapgood and other advocates of pseudohistorical and pseudoscientific hypotheses to follow.

Hapgood graduated from Harvard with an AB in history and literature in 1929 and an MA in medieval and modern history in 1931. Although he started a PhD specializing in the history of the French Revolution, the Great Depression prevented him from finishing it. During the remainder of the 1930s he worked as a teacher or in programmes related to the New Deal. When World War II began Hapgood worked in intelligence for the Office of Strategic Services, for the Red Cross and as a liaison officer between the White House and the Secretary of War. After the war ended he took up teaching at Springfield College in Massachusetts, moving to Keene State College in New Hampshire in 1956 and finally to New England College in 1966. He retired in 1967.

Earth's Shifting Crust presented the hypothesis that the earth's thin but hard outer crust slides around its soft and semi-fluid inner core. This condition has resulted in the north and south poles shifting their geographical locations a number of times in the past although it is really the crust that is moving around. The sliding of the earth's crust took place over periods of time lasting about 5,000 years after which the poles would remain stationary for approximately 20,000 to 30,000 years. According to Hapgood the shifts in the earth's crust caused the expansions and retreats of the glaciers of the Ice Ages. Temperate lands would drift into polar regions while polar regions moved into more temperate latitudes. Glaciers formed and grew in one place while in other places glaciers melted. The shifts in the earth's crust moved unevenly so that crustal material would pile up in some places, thereby forming mountains. In other regions the crust would stretch out to form plains and plateaus. Hapgood believed that crustal shifts occurred when polar ice accumulated sufficiently to create an unbalanced distribution of weight while the planet rotated. At that point the earth's crust would begin to move until it stabilized at a new location.[49]

Hapgood's second book *Maps of the Ancient Sea Kings: Evidence of Advanced Civilization in the Ice Age* appeared in 1966. A revised edition came out in 1979. This study focused on the Piri Reis map of 1513, a manuscript map depicting the east coast of South America and part of Africa. Piri was an admiral (*reis*) of the Ottoman Turkish Empire and the nephew of another great Ottoman admiral, Kemal Reis. He was an avid cartographer and drafted many maps including a world map based on both ancient and contemporary maps. Only some sections of the world map have survived, one of which is known as the Piri Reis map. Piri Reis stated that he used a captured chart of Christopher Columbus' to draft his map. It is a beautiful example of Renaissance era cartography, but most historians of cartography do not consider the Piri Reis map to be exceptional in its geographical accuracy or the precision of its measurements.

Hapgood, however, claimed the Piri Reis map was exceptional. He believed that it depicted a portion of the coastline of Antarctica as it would have appeared before being covered by the southern polar ice cap. The problem was that Antarctica was not visited by European explorers until 1819, which meant that prior to that date nobody knew what its ice-covered geography looked like, let alone what it looked like ice-free. Hapgood studied other sixteenth-century maps depicting a suppositional antarctic continent. Eventually he came to the conclusion that these maps contained accurate representations of Antarctica's geography. But how could anyone have this information if European ships did not land on Antarctica for another 400 years? Hapgood's answer was to postulate the existence of an advanced civilization during the Ice Age,[50] a civilization that had reached a level of scientific and technological knowledge equivalent to that of late eighteenth-century Europe. Those unknown ancients could determine longitude, construct grid maps and could sail their ships all over the world. They mounted expeditions that explored the coastline of Antarctica around 4000 BC before it became covered by glaciers as the result of an earlier pole shift. Hapgood claimed that the maps of these ancient sea kings were passed down or copied through the centuries. The ancient Greeks, Carthaginians and Romans had access to this knowledge. Some of it came into the possession of the Greeks of the Byzantine Empire from whom first marauding Crusaders and later conquering Ottoman Turks acquired it. Piri Reis used some of this ancient knowledge to draw his own mysterious map, particularly that section of Antarctica's coastline.

In 1970 Hapgood brought out his third book *The Path of the Pole*, which was basically a revision of *Earth's Shifting Crust*. The major difference between the two books is that Hapgood abandoned the idea that accumulated polar ice destabilized the earth and triggered crustal shifts relocating the north and south poles. Instead he fell back on the hypothesis that somehow an undiscovered force within the earth's core caused crustal shifts. Otherwise he retained his original hypothesis of pole shifts largely intact.

Hapgood's ideas about pole shifts and the Piri Reis map depicting Antarctica were not original to him.[51] Hugh Auchincloss Brown (1875–1975) first conceived the idea that the weight of polar ice caused the earth to become unbalanced and disrupted how it rotated.

Brown was an electrical engineer and graduate of Columbia University. He claimed that the weight of polar ice caused pole shifts to occur suddenly and with great devastation about every 6,000 years. Being a true believer in his own hypothesis, Brown feared that a natural disaster of global proportions was approaching. He advocated using nuclear bombs to melt Antarctica's ice cap to prevent the impending pole shift from occurring. What sort of havoc that plan would have inflicted on the world's climate, let alone a bunch of innocent penguins, cannot be calculated but it is probably a very good thing that Brown and General Curtis Lemay, the man who organized the Strategic Command of the US Air Force into a formidable nuclear strike force, never got together. Brown worked hard to find people with the authority to carry out his rather drastic proposal. He wrote to or visited members of the Congress or the media in an effort to secure their support. Someone at the *New York Times* actually listened and on 1 September 1948 they published an editorial that discussed Brown's predictions of doom as something to worry about. *Time Magazine* followed the lead of the *New York Times* and published a small news item concerning Brown's hypothesis. About that time Brown privately published his ideas about polar ice and crustal shifts as *Popular Awakening Concerning the Impending Flood*. Nor was Brown even the originator of the idea of pole shift. In 1923 A. E. Eddington suggested that the sliding of the earth's crust caused gradual pole shifts. After Brown the electrical engineer Karl Pauly published an article in *Scientific Monthly* in 1952 that advocated a hypothesis that crustal sliding caused pole shifts, which is what really caused the Ice Age.[52]

Hapgood and his students at Springfield College heard about Brown's ideas. When one of the students started asking Hapgood questions about Brown's ideas in 1949, he decided it would be a good project for him and his students to investigate. Having his students research some mystery or unsolved problem was a technique that Hapgood employed throughout his career. In the course of the research project Hapgood contacted Brown, who proved to be quite helpful. Given the state of knowledge about geology immediately after World War II Hapgood and his students concluded that Brown was correct. At the time the theory of continental drift and plate tectonics had not established itself as scientific orthodoxy so Brown's hypothesis explained a fair amount of the available geological evidence. Hapgood became an advocate of pole shifts and crustal sliding. From that point he began to correspond with other scientists about his ideas, including Albert Einstein. Einstein was intrigued but rejected the notion that the weight of polar ice caused the instability of the earth's crust. Still he agreed to write a foreword to *Earth's Shifting Crust*.[53] Other scientific notables, with some caution, also chose to endorse Hapgood's hypothesis including Kirtley F. Mather, a retired professor in Harvard's geology department and a former president of the American Association for the Advancement of Science. He wrote the foreword for the British, Spanish and Italian editions of *Earth's Shifting Crust*. Like Einstein, Mather found Hapgood's book fascinating but he too rejected the weight of the ice caps being the cause of pole shifts. On the other hand, Yves Rocard, a professor of physics at the University of Paris, wrote a preface for the French edition that actually accepted Hapgood's hypothesis that the weight of the ice caps was the mechanism that caused the pole shifts. Hapgood even managed to get Velikovsky's old nemesis Harlow Shapley of the Harvard observatory interested in his ideas in a positive way. Eventually the continuing accumulation of new scientific knowledge made it more and more improbable that the ice caps were responsible for pole shifts, which caused Hapgood to abandon that aspect of his hypothesis when he published the *Earth's Shifting Crust*'s second edition *The Path of the Pole* in 1970.[54] In fact the growing evidence supporting continental drift and plate tectonics had also made his entire theory of pole shifts implausible. Hapgood, however, was unwilling to disown his first book entirely, especially since his second, *The Maps of the Ancient Sea Kings*, also depended on that hypothesis but, unlike most purveyors of pseudohistory and pseudoscience, he showed a refreshing willingness to admit it when it became clear that a hypothesis could not be correct. Just how far Hapgood's open-mindedness actually went is unclear. He was preparing a third edition of *The Path of the Pole* when an automobile struck and killed him in 1982. The new edition has never been published but a letter from Hapgood to Rand Flem-Ath on 12 October 1982 shows that he maintained a firm belief in the occurrence of pole shifts and the possibility of Ice Age civilizations just weeks before his death.[55]

The idea that Piri Reis's map charted part of the coastline of an ice-free Antarctica did not originate with Hapgood; rather it started with Captain Arlington H. Mallery (d. 1968), a retired civil and structural engineer for the Long Island Railroad and the United States Army as well as an amateur archaeologist. The Piri Reis map first came to the attention of cartographers and historians when it was rediscovered in the Turkish archives in 1929 where it had rested undisturbed for centuries. Ottoman Sultan Suleiman I had ordered the execution of Piri Reis due to his failure to dislodge the Portuguese from the Persian Gulf. The Ottoman authorities also seized Piri Reis's papers and put them in the state archives where they were promptly forgotten. Initial scholarly interest centred on the early date of the map's portrayal of the newly discovered Americas and what it showed about diffusion of the geographical knowledge gained as a result of the voyages of Columbus. After a while interest in the map faded, until 1953 when Arlington H. Mallery suggested that the coastline shown at the bottom of the map was an accurate representation of the ice-free coastline of Queen Maud Land in Antarctica. He concluded that Piri Reis must have drawn his map using information from very ancient maps produced by an unknown advanced civilization at a time when Antarctica was ice free. Mallery, however, is best known for advocating the hypothesis that Celts and Vikings had come to North America in pre-Columbian times. They then proceeded to set up iron smelting furnaces and other settlements, some of which Mallery identified and excavated in Ohio and Virginia.[56]

It was Mallery's ideas about the Piri Reis map depicting Antarctica that caught the attention of Charles H. Hapgood. Mallery had broadcast his conclusions about the Piri Reis map during a radio panel discussion on 26 August 1956 sponsored by Georgetown University. A transcript came into Hapgood's hands and he found Mallery's ideas intriguing. As he had done earlier with Brown's hypothesis of poleshifts, Hapgood, now a professor at Keene State College, presented the Mallery hypothesis to his classes and they began to investigate it as a group. Hapgood concluded that Mallery was right and published his findings as *Maps of the Ancient Sea Kings: Evidence of Advanced Civilization in the Ice Age* in 1966. He even dedicated the book to Mallery and managed to get John K. Wright, a former president of the American Geographical Society, to write a foreword.[57] It was a seemingly impressive book of cartographic detective work and history.

Hapgood and Mallery's ideas about the Piri Reis map and its depiction of the coastline of Antarctica dissolve under critical scrutiny. One of Hapgood's claims was that the map was an azimuthal equidistant projection based on the centre of the map being located at or near Cairo, Egypt. That suggestion appears to be true and it explains the apparent distortions of the shape of South America on the map.[58] But when Hapgood and Mallery go on to identify parts of the map as the coastline of Antarctica, they have gone beyond any credible interpretation of the map. One problem is that Hapgood and a German named Paul Kahle who wrote about the Piri Reis map during the 1930s both attempted to match every geographical feature portrayed on the Piri Reis map with an existing one. In doing so they ignored the fact that sixteenth-century mapmakers often added speculative geographical features in the absence of any certain knowledge of the actual geography. Both Hapgood and Kahle also only compared the Piri Reis map with a modern map instead of also comparing it to other early sixteenth-century maps. Such a broader comparison would have helped them to avoid a number of misidentifications of places on the Piri Reis map. Furthermore, it did not help that Hapgood and Kahle often ignored the original Turkish labellings on the map. They also misidentified some of the rivers and said that the mountains shown on the Piri Reis map were the Andes. In fact they were merely notional mountains that medieval cartographers placed in the empty interiors of unexplored lands.[59]

Arlington Mallery and Hapgood also brought in the depictions of *Terra Australis*, or the southern land, that appear on many sixteenth- and seventeenth-century maps, to support their hypothesis, even though Antarctica was not explored until 1820. One important element of geographical history that both Mallery and Hapgood failed to take into account was the persistent belief in the existence of a great southern continent that had existed in one form or another from ancient times until the last quarter of the eighteenth century. It was believed that symmetry required that there should be roughly the same amount of land in the southern hemisphere as there was in the northern. European explorers scoured the South Pacific looking for it until Captain James Cook's second voyage of 1772–5 systematically proved that no great southern land existed.[60] As a result cartographers from the beginning of the sixteenth century onwards placed lands in the southern oceans and Antarctic region on the basis of pure speculation. One cartographer, a Frenchman named Oronce Fine or Finaeus, produced a map in 1531 which included an Antarctic land that Mallery, Hapgood and others claim looks very similar to an ice-free Antarctica. To make this claim they had to ignore or alter crucial aspects of Fine's map. First, his Antarctic land is about nine times larger than the real Antarctica. Second, to get a good fit for comparison of the two Antarcticas, Hapgood had to rotate the Fine map by some 20 degrees of longitude, move the South Pole a thousand miles and ignore the existence of the 900-mile Palmer Peninsula. Many sixteenth-century maps featured a *Terra Australis*, including the maps of the great Gerard Mercator. It is important to remember that Mercator also included a landmass at the North Pole where no land exists. Fine's is the only one of these *Terra Australis* that bears a resemblance of sorts to the real Antarctica. It has been that suggested that his depiction may be evidence for an undocumented exploration of Antarctica during the early sixteenth century. But David C. Jolly has pointed out that if such knowledge of Antarctica was circulating, it would have appeared on more than just Fine's map. He argues that a more plausible explanation is that Fine's speculative depiction of *Terra Australis* just happened coincidentally to look more like the real Antarctica than any of his contemporaries' speculation.[61]

Mallery and Hapgood argue that the Piri Reis map was crafted based on knowledge surviving from very ancient times going back anywhere from 10,000 to 6000 BC, well before the beginning of recorded history. Other pseudohistorians like Erich von Däniken and Rand and Rose Flem-Ath have accepted the existence of such ancient knowledge, although they have used it to formulate different interpretations and hypotheses. Mainstream scholars contend that it is impossible for such ancient knowledge to have been preserved and passed down through hundreds of generations without accumulating massive numbers of errors, particularly if the knowledge, such as pyramid-building, was not actually used for centuries or even millennia.[62]

Another problem with Hapgood's analysis of the Piri Reis map is that he has to cut 2,000 miles out of the eastern coast of South America if he identifies the southernmost coastline on the map as Antarctica. That raises the question, what happened to that part of South America? If the southernmost land on the map was indeed Antarctica, the Piri Reis map inexplicably shows South America and Antarctica to be joined together. What happened to the Straits of Magellan? Both of these circumstances are particularly vexing if the map is as extraordinarily accurate as Hapgood and others have claimed. It has been pointed out that a simpler explanation is that the entire southern coastline appearing on the map is only South America and not Antarctica. The missing 2,000 miles of South America reappear and there is no problem of a missing Straits of Magellan.[63]

Hapgood also assumed that an Antarctica without an ice cap would be the same as the Antarctica that is currently covered by ice and above sea level. The weight of the massive polar ice cap has depressed the elevation of Antarctica by several hundred feet. Without the weight of the ice it would buoy up and parts of Antarctica that are submerged would rise high above the sea. At the same time, if the ice cap melted and caused the sea level to rise, outlying parts of Antarctica would disappear under the water. Recent studies of ice cores from Antarctica also show that it has been covered by ice for at least 100,000 years, which is not at all compatible with hypothesis about an advanced ice age civilization exploring an ice-free Antarctica around 10,000 BC.[64] There is evidence that Hapgood recognized that continuing scientific research was rendering his original hypotheses untenable. Just as he abandoned the idea that the weight of the ice caps caused the pole shifts, Hapgood attempted to incorporate the new findings into hypotheses or to alter his hypotheses to accommodate new hypotheses.[65] Others less critical and discriminating than Hapgood, and sometimes perhaps less scrupulous, have used his *Maps of the Ancient Sea Kings* to help prove all sorts of versions of a pseudohistorical past. His ideas continue to intrigue and to attract new supporters and to draw renewed debunking from the experts. It is a cycle that shows no sign of ending, for Hapgood's interpretation of the Piri Reis map has entered the cultic milieu of pseudohistory as the works of von Däniken, Hancock and the Flem-Aths amply show.[66]

ERICH VON DÄNIKEN AND ZECHARIA SITCHIN: ancient astronauts

Doth any man doubt that if there were taken out of men's minds vain opinions, flattering hopes, false valuations, imaginations as one would, and the like, but it would leave the minds of a number of men poor shrunken things, full of melancholy and indisposition, and unpleasing to themselves? SIR FRANCIS BACON[67]

Erich von Däniken (1935–) is probably the most famous advocate of the existence of ancient astronauts who visited the earth thousands of years ago, brought civilization to humanity and even mated with primitive humans to produce truly modern, intelligent beings – us. In making this argument he managed to combine Ufology, the belief that extraterrestrials were visiting the earth in spaceships or flying saucers, and pseudohistory. Modern interest in Unidentified Flying Objects or UFOs began in 1947 with the supposed sighting of flying saucers near Mount Rainer, Washington, on 24 June 1947 and the alleged crash of an alien spaceship near Roswell, New Mexico, about the same time.

The study of UFOs quickly became known as Ufology. This quite specific beginning makes Ufology a relatively recent phenomenon despite the complementary idea that ancient astronauts had visited the earth thousands or even tens of thousands of years earlier. It should also be pointed out that while modern Ufology began in 1947, the sighting of unexplained aerial phenomena has been occurring throughout recorded history, the difference being that these unexplained objects in the sky were not considered to be flying saucers or spacecraft from other worlds. Prior to the end of the nineteenth century and the appearance of H. G. Wells's *War of the Worlds* in 1898, people did not possess the necessary worldview to consider UFOs to be alien spaceships. Instead they were manifestations of the gods, angels, demons and other supernatural phenomena; weird natural phenomena or early secret flying machines such as those imagined by Jules Verne in his *Robur the Conqueror* (1886) and *Master of the World* (1904).

Although some writers on Ufology touched on the possibility that ancient astronauts had visited the earth during prehistory and much of recorded history, the mainstream of Ufologists rejected or ignored the hypothesis of ancient astronauts as unscientific and sensationalistic. They feared it would bring the serious study of UFOs into disrepute. The amazing and unanticipated popularity of Erich von Däniken's books and his hypotheses about ancient astronauts changed that situation.[68] By no means the first person to write about ancient astronauts, von Däniken earned his literary fame through a combination of good timing and an emerging popular hunger for his ideas, which struck a resonant chord with the reading public. His first book *Chariots of the Gods* (1968) became a bestseller and was followed by others. Traditional religion was at a low ebb during the 1960s which has led some people to suggest that von Däniken's ancient astronaut's hypothesis provided disillusioned people with a sort of new religion. It was better suited to the spirit of the times particularly because it was based on scientific and historical evidence. In fact von Däniken's evidence was largely pseudosicentific or pseudo-historical when it was not just plain wrong.[69] That bit of negativity, however, did not deter the rise of UFO or ancient alien cults – Scientology being the most successful and Heaven's Gate being the most tragic. Most people read von Däniken because they enjoy quirky and off-beat explanations of odd artefacts and events from ancient times since they are so much more fun than conventional archaeology and history. The books are written in a conversational style that makes for light and enjoyable reading if one is moderately interested in the subject and willing to suspend disbelief, at least temporarily.

Whatever the reason for his popularity, von Däniken has been able to write and sell 29 books on the topic of ancient astronauts, although critics point out the later books are reshufflings and rewrites of *Chariots of the Gods*. That criticism is a bit extreme but some of von Däniken's books are repetitive of or derivative from his earlier books. He has been translated into 32 languages, but only fifteen of his books have been translated into English.[70] During the 1970s he even experienced a wave of popularity in India due to some of his books being translated into Bengali.[71] Von Däniken has been the subject of documentaries – the 1978 'The Case of the Ancient Astronauts' by *Nova* was an effective debunking of his ideas and fabrication of evidence.

A few years after that his popularity sank and he had a difficult time finding a publisher for his new books. His tenth and temporarily last book to appear in English was *The Gods and Their Grand Design* in 1982. Although he managed to publish eleven more books in German between 1983 and 1994, it was not until *The Eyes of the Sphinx* in 1996 that he managed to have another book translated into English.[72]

It is not a coincidence that the revival of von Däniken fortunes coincided with the rise to international popularity of the television series *The X-Files*, which debuted on 10 September 1993. Although the series utilized all sorts of paranormal phenomenon in its plots, the great story arc dealt with a terrible conspiracy involving alien visitations both in the ancient past and in the present including the manipulation of human evolution. The appearance of the film *Stargate* in 1994 also helped. The film begins with the discovery of a strange alien artefact in some Egyptian ruins. It proves to be a fantastic piece of advanced technology that allows for instantaneous travel between distant star systems. Travelling through the Stargate, the intrepid earthlings find other humans. They also discover that some rather nasty parasitic aliens inspired the mythology of the gods of ancient Egypt. While the film was only moderately successful it inspired the *Stargate SG1* television series that first aired on 27 July 1997 with new seasons continuing through 2007. A spin-off series, *Stargate Atlantis*, premiered on 16 July 2004 and continues to be popular. *Stargate: The Ark of Truth* is another film based on the television series that was released directly to DVD in 2008. The *X-Files* and *Stargate* phenomenon provided a dramatization of von Däniken's hypotheses about the human past and popularized them further.

Buoyed by the renewal of interest in his books, the enterprising von Däniken wrote more. He also opened a theme park based on his ideas at Interlaken, Switzerland – Mystery Park – on 23 May 2003. An entry ticket cost $38.[73] However, apparently people visiting Switzerland had better things to do with their time and money than to visit a place devoted to ancient astronauts because Mystery Park closed in 2006. Now a grandfather in his mid-seventies, von Däniken continues to write, his last book being *Falsch Informiert* (False Information) in 2007, but things have quieted down for him once again. Whether von Däniken's writing has another life remains to be seen.

Who is Erich von Däniken? He was born at Zofingen, Switzerland, in 1935. Although his parents were committed Roman Catholics and sent their son to the Catholic boarding school of St Michel at Fribourg, Von Däniken turned out to be something of a non-conformist as well as a disinterested student. Behaviour problems and poor grades inevitably followed. It was not just Catholic school that disagreed with von Däniken, neither did the Boy Scouts. A local magistrate investigated him for stealing from the Scouts' local treasury. So in 1954 von Däniken left St Michel's to work as a waiter and bartender at a hotel in Berne.

Although von Däniken was a poor student in a formal setting he took an avid interest in archaeology. He saved the money that he earned to visit ancient sites. In 1960 he married Elisebeth, who remains his wife, and they worked together in hotels and restaurants throughout Switzerland. Unfortunately von Däniken seemed to have trouble distinguishing between his money and other people's. Charges and convictions for fraud and petty theft resulted in his being fined and spending time in prison. He also continued to travel and during a trip to Mexico saw the Palenque Stone that he claims depicts an ancient astronaut. He also began to write his first book. By 1966 he started to submit it to publishing houses.[74] Twenty-two rejections followed. During the summer of 1967 the forlorn von Däniken approached Thomas von Randow, the science editor for the weekly *Die Zeit*, to see if they would publish his manuscript as a serialization. Von Randow gave the manuscript a quick look and decided that it was not appropriate for *Die Zeit*. He told von Däniken that it needed to be published as a book. Von Däniken asked for advice on finding a publisher and von Randow offered to call Edwin Barth von Wehrenalp, the head of Econ Publishing, a press that had already turned down von Däniken's manuscript. Von Randow made the telephone call and recommended that von Wehrenalp meet with von Däniken. Von Wehrenalp asked the aspiring author to come over and they reached an agreement on publication after lunch.[75] On the basis of such happenstances are bestsellers born.

Econ brought out von Däniken's *Chariots of the Gods* in March 1968 with a somewhat cautious initial print-run of 6,000 copies. It was said that the manuscript had been extensively rewritten by Wilhelm Roggersdorf, a screenwriter with a feel for the tastes of the popular reading public. Originally von Däniken titled his book *Erinnerungen an die Zukunft* (Memories of the Future).[76] That title reflects more accurately what von Däniken was attempting to do when he first wrote the book. Basically he argued that travel into outer space was the destiny of humanity. The fact that alien astronauts had visited the earth in the past, had biologically improved humans, taught them the foundations of technological civilization and then departed is what makes it imperative that the peoples of the earth should strive to return to the stars. The reading public ignored his arguments for space travel; instead it was the ancient astronauts who captured the public's imagination. In 1968 people were already sold on space exploration.

Contrary to Econ Publishing's expectations sales of *Erinnerungen an die Zukunft* took off and by December it was the bestselling book in West Germany. It was translated into English as *Chariots of the Gods*, appearing in Britain in 1969 and the US in 1970. The book proved to be extremely popular in the English-speaking market with millions of copies selling over time. Translations into other languages appeared as did television documentaries and even a theatrical film. The public and the publishers wanted more *Chariots* and von Däniken gave it to them, in 29 books and counting over 40 years. His second book *Gods from Outer Space* appeared in German in 1968 and in English in 1970 with a preface by Roggensdorf that neglected to mention his role as a reviser. Von Däniken's foreword to *Gods* concluded with the curious statement, 'I should like to thank everyone who helped me to write this new book. I wrote it during my imprisonment on remand in the Remand Prison of the canton of Graubünden in Chur.' Interpol had arrested von Däniken for failure to pay a business tax during 1968 but further investigations disclosed that he had accumulated a personal debt of about £350,000 ($750,000). The courts found him guilty and sentenced him to three and a half years in prison along with a fine. Fortunately for von Däniken his books earned substantial royalties which allowed him to pay off his fines and debts. He did not serve his full sentence and later made an unsuccessful attempt to get his conviction nullified. While some people viewed von Däniken's troubles as a logical consequence of his dishonesty and lack of integrity, traits that cast doubt on the factual and analytical reliability of his books, others drew different conclusions. Von Däniken's hypotheses replaced God, his angels and their miracles with ancient astronauts and their advanced technology. German churches and their members found such ideas deeply offensive especially since they attracted an enthusiastic following of readers. They vigorously attacked von Däniken in the media. As a result others concluded that von Däniken's legal troubles may have been based on trumped-up charges instigated by the Christian clergy. Like Velikovsky, von Däniken was able to assume the martyr's mantle despite his long history of financial misdeeds.[77]

Just what did von Däniken claim about ancient astronauts in his books and what was his evidence? Basically he asserts that highly advanced extraterrestrials visited the earth between 40,000 and 10,000 years ago with some sporadic visits in the years that followed. The aliens came to earth seeking some raw material that was important to them, probably radioactive substances for use as an energy source. They established bases and dug mines. In addition, they encountered primitive humans and put them to work. The ancient astronauts concluded that humans needed improvement in terms of intelligence. So they performed genetic experiments with the humans and even interbred with them. One result was that aliens, also known as angels, mated with human women and produced a race of giants known as the Nephilim. Meanwhile the genetic breeding experiments produced a better human. According to von Däniken Noah's flood was really an attempt by the ancient astronauts to exterminate the inferior humans and give Shem, Ham and Japheth a fresh start with an earth cleansed of animalistic humans. But the ancient astronauts were not necessarily benevolent toward the improved humans either. Von Däniken claimed the destruction of Sodom and Gomorrah resulted from a nuclear blast unleashed by irate aliens. He further claimed that the ancient Indian epic the *Mahabharata* is actually an account of a war of the ancient aliens using nuclear weapons and flying machines. Van Däniken identified the great trident-shaped earthworks at Pisco Bay in Peru as a directional signal for an alien airfield. The actual airfield is supposedly located nearby in the desert plain containing the enigmatic Nasca lines. Alien castaways also built the monumental statues known as *moai* on Easter Island. The Palenque tablet depicts an ancient astronaut in his spaceship, not a pre-Columbian Maya king ascending from the world of the living to the afterlife. All of these contentions can be found in *Chariots of the Gods* and *Gods from Outer Space* along with other books by von Däniken published during the 1970s. His more recent books focus on ancient Egypt and Greece, with the Pyramids and the Sphinx being alien artefacts and the Greek myths garbled tales of the adventures and conflicts of alien astronauts. Von Däniken even manages to give Atlantis an ancient astronaut-related explanation.[78]

Needless to say von Däniken and his books have attracted many debunkers. The idea of alien visitors mating with humans and actually producing a viable offspring is biochemically absurd. A praying mantis and a sperm whale would have a genetically better chance of producing a child than a human and an extraterrestrial even though the *Star Trek* series has programmed viewers to accept that interspecies dating is both possible and really sort of fun. The biblical account of the annihilation of Sodom and Gomorrah is not consistent with an atomic blast, contrary to von Däniken's assertions. His identifying the battles in the *Mahabharata* as ancient alien wars using atomic weapons stretches the credulity of any reader familiar with the epic. Similarly the idea that the Nasca lines are remnants of runways on an ancient alien airfield simply does not ring true. As others have asked, why would sophisticated spaceships need a runway when they land and take off vertically? Another problem is that the Nasca lines look nothing like an airfield runway. They are either abstract figures or effigies of animals. Nor is the ground on the Nasca plain suitable for being used as a runway. It is too soft.[79]

Furthermore, von Däniken's claim that the human inhabitants of Easter Island were incapable of constructing the giant *moai* has been conclusively shown to be wrong. One particularly devastating rebuttal came from the celebrated Thor Heyerdahl of *Kon Tiki* fame, who possessed significant first-hand knowledge of the archaeology of Easter Island and with other scholars has published on that subject. Unfortunately, as he points out, von Däniken 'totally ignored these findings and publications and concocted sheer nonsense to satisfy and entertain his space-hungry readers . . . There is not the slightest base of fact in what von Däniken writes concerning the origins of the giant statues on Easter Island.' He also asks a very pertinent question of von Däniken. Given that the material used to build spaceships would have to be extremely durable, why have no artefacts belonging to ancient astronauts ever been found at any of the many locations of alien bases identified by von Däniken? As for moving the giant statues from their quarry to the ceremonial site, archaeologists have a very clear idea how it was done using Stone Age technology. No extraterrestrial technology is required to get the job done.[80]

It is interesting that Heyerdahl refuted von Däniken so vehemently. Heyerdahl himself occupies a position that bestrides history and pseudohistory. While his archaeological work on Easter Island was first-class in its day, his ideas about ancient transoceanic contacts and Polynesians originating in the Americas are controversial and even viewed as pseudohistorical by most mainstream scholars. Pseudohistorians tend to close ranks against mainstream scholars even when their individual hypotheses significantly contradict each other. Clearly Heyerdahl does not see himself as part of that company. Rather than classifying him as a pseudohistorian it would be more fair and accurate to call him a careful scholar who sincerely holds some highly speculative hypotheses that are widely viewed as wrong. In contrast von Däniken is at best not a careful scholar and at worst, as many regard him, a cynical charlatan.

While much of the evidence that von Däniken presents will be suspect to an intelligent and critical reader without any prompting from debunkers, some of his evidence can cause people to stop and ponder if there is perhaps something to what he writes. The crown jewel of that type of evidence is the Piri Reis map, first used by von Däniken in *Chariots of the Gods*. Citing Mallery and Hapgood for support, von Däniken claims that the Piri Reis map is 'absolutely accurate' and that the coastlines of North and South America along with Antarctica are 'precisely delineated'. He goes on to suggest that the Piri Reis map is so accurate because it was based on aerial photography done from a spaceship flying above Cairo and attributes that idea to Hapgood. Von Däniken stubbornly ignores that missing 2,000 miles of South American coastline and the Straits of Magellan that do not appear on the Piri Reis map. In fact Hapgood did not claim that the Piri Reis map was all that accurate. Its particular accuracy only appears after Hapgood manipulates some errors that crept into the map by the time Piri Reis drafted it. Nor did Hapgood remotely suggest that the map was based on photographs taken from space by ancient astronauts. Clearly von Däniken is not a careful researcher because he erred in stating that the rediscovery of the Piri Reis map occurred during the early eighteenth century rather than 1929, as Hapgood and other works about the map correctly state. When von Däniken returned to discussing the Piri Reis map in his 1998 book *Odyssey of the Gods*, he managed to correct the date of the rediscovery to 1929. Otherwise he continued to insist on how accurate the map was, particularly the coastline of Antarctica. What he adds is the suggestion that the garbled outline of Cuba on the Piri Reis map may be some echo of Atlantis which would have existed when the original ancient source maps used by Piri Reis were first drafted.[81] Hapgood's *Maps of the Ancient Sea Kings* possesses a superficial credibility with its panoply of maps, charts, tables and footnotes that requires technological expertise and time to debunk. That is why it has become a favoured text among other pseudohistorians including von Däniken. In the final analysis its hypothesis is wrong and von Däniken even managed to misstate it in his books. What von Däniken's use of *Maps of the Ancient Sea Kings* shows is how firmly the ideas of Mallery and Hapgood have become part of the great chain of badly flawed and inaccurate scholarship that forms the cultic milieu of pseudohistory.

Where else did von Däniken get his ideas? Despite his claims to the contrary he is hardly original. *Chariots of the Gods* combines the idea of UFOs with the idea that an ancient super-civilization existed to produce ancient astronauts. Although *Maps of the Ancient Sea Kings* contains the idea of an advanced civilization in the Ice Age, in fact the idea of ancient aliens pre-dated Hapgood. The first book to suggest the existence of ancient astronauts appeared a few years after the beginning of modern Ufology. Desmond Leslie and George Adamski brought out *The Flying Saucers have Landed* in 1953 and it proved very popular. George Adamski (1891–1965) claimed to have met a Venusian in the California desert in November 1962 and wrote an account of the experience. His narrative was combined with a manuscript about alien visits to the earth throughout history written by Desmond Leslie, an occultist from Ireland. Although the book's primary concern was contemporary occurrences of UFOs and extraterrestrial visits, Leslie's research laid out the basic ancient sources used ever since by writers on ancient astronauts.[82] Another early author to mention ancient astronauts was Donald E. Keyhoe (1897–1988), who served as a major in the Marine Corps during World War II. Developing an interest in the flying saucer phenomenon in 1949, he published *Flying Saucers are Real* in 1950, which sold half a million copies in paperback. Other books followed, such as *Flying Saucers from Other Space* (1953), which was turned into the science fiction film *Earth vs. the Flying Saucers* (1956). Keyhoe thought he had sold the film rights for his book to be made into a documentary and when he found out the true nature of the film he tried to get his name removed from the credits. It was not until *Flying Saucers: Top Secret* appeared in 1960 that Keyhoe touched on the topic of ancient astronauts.[83]

It is doubtful that von Däniken knew about or read Leslie or Keyhoe's books but it seems quite certain that he knew about the books of the French authors Louis Pauwels, Jacques Bergier and Robert Charroux. Pauwels and Bergier wrote *Le Matin des Magiciens* in 1960; the English translation *The Morning of the Magicians* appeared in 1960. It is a rambling book that speculates about the existence of secret knowledge of the alchemists; mutant super-humans living in the present as the next stage of evolution; occult connections with Nazism and atomic energy and extrasensory perceptions as well as other similar topics. The authors also discuss the existence of ancient super-civilizations (pp. 70–71) and ancient astronauts (pp. 215–17).[84] Of more significance, many of von Däniken's evidences for ancient astronauts were discussed by Bergier and Pauwels such as the electrical battery in the Baghdad museum (p. 71), Easter Island and its giant statues (pp. 113–14), the Nasca lines as airfield markings (pp. 116–17), Arlington Mallery and the Piri Reis map as a product of observations from a spaceship (p. 120), the destruction of Sodom and Gomorrah by an atomic bomb (p. 216) and the ruins of Baalbek as a port for spaceships (p. 217). The same observation applies to Robert Charroux's *One Hundred Thousand Years of Man's Unknown History*, published in France in 1963 as *Histoire inconnue des hommes depuis cent mille ans*. Charroux's book maintained that a super-civilization existed in the past and that knowledge of its existence has been suppressed and kept secret. Furthermore, that great civilization and humanity itself were the products of a migration from another planet: Venus. Like Pauwels and Bergier, Charroux discussed evidences that would later appear in von Däniken's books: the Piri Reis map (pp. 16–18), the Gate of the Sun at Tiahuanacu (pp. 18–19 and 41–4), and extraterrestrials visiting the earth (pp. 99–126), including the Baalbek spaceport and the atomic wars supposedly described in the *Mahabharata*.[85] Von Däniken, however, gave little or no recognition to the books of Pauwels, Bergier and Charroux. He would almost certainly have known about them as they were extremely popular for many years in France and were translated into German in 1966 and 1970.[86] Also, since von Däniken was Swiss, a French book would not have been inaccessible to him.

Chariots of the Gods' immense international popularity soon brought its similarities of content with the French books to the attention of Charroux and his publishers. Accusations of plagiarism and threats of lawsuits followed which resulted in Charroux's book being added to the bibliography of later printings of *Chariots of the Gods*, although unfortunately not properly alphabetized. In *Gods from Outer Space* von Däniken mentioned that Pauwels, Bergier and Charroux were working on similar questions about the past. He just failed to include the fact that they had been working on those questions quite some time before him. Roggersdorf, his virtual ghost writer, wrote the preface to *Gods from Outer Space* in which he admitted that von Däniken was not the first to write about ancient astronauts 'but his questions were more impartial, more direct, and more audacious'. And he remained silent about who actually was first.[87] Von Däniken did give Charles Hapgood credit for the ideas he derived from *Maps of the Ancient Sea Kings* even though he probably first learned about the Piri Reis map from Bergier, Pauwels and Charroux. He even met Hapgood during a trip to the United States. At that time Hapgood informed him that Albert Einstein 'was in complete sympathy with the idea of prehistoric visits by extraterrestrial intelligences'.[88] Just as Erich von Däniken tapped into the existing cultic milieu about ancient astronauts to create *Chariots of the Gods* and the books that followed, others found inspiration from him or merely copied his ideas and tried to cash in on his amazing success. Most experienced minimal success but not all. One of the more successful writers to follow von Däniken's lead was Zecharia Sitchin.

Zecharia Sitchin was born at Baku, Azerbaijan in 1922, in the early years of the Soviet Union. He grew up in Palestine. While at school there he learned Hebrew along with other languages. History and archaeology also fascinated him, particularly the era of the Old Testament and ancient Mesopotamia. He also developed an interest in the mysterious beings known as the Nephilim described in Genesis 6:4:

> There were giants [Nephilim] in the earth in those days; and also after that, when the sons of God came in unto the daughters of men, and they bare children to them, the same became mighty men which were of old, men of renown.

Because Sitchin knew Hebrew, he considered the traditional translation of Nephilim as giants to be erroneous since it literally meant 'fallen ones'. Needless to say, others had noted the same problem of translation in the many years of biblical scholarship prior to Sitchin. The scholarly consensus was that the Nephilim were fallen angels.[89] Sitchin's curiosity was aroused and he continued to study the Nephilim, the Bible and ancient history for 40 years while he earned a degree in economic history from the University of London and worked as a journalist and editor in Israel. He now lives in New York.

The first fruit of Sitchin's researches appeared in 1976 as *The Twelfth Planet*. In this book he put forward some extraordinary claims. The title *The Twelfth Planet* refers to his claim that ancient Mesopotamian astronomers believed there were twelve planets. Most modern people think there are nine planets although Pluto's demotion to a planetoid has confused the issue. Who knows what a latter day Sitchin working 6,000 years in the future will make of that? Be that as it may, Sitchin asserts that the ancient Mesopotamians arrived at twelve planets by this count: the Sun, Mercury, Venus, Earth, the Moon, Mars, Jupiter, Saturn, Uranus, Neptune, Pluto and Marduk (or Nibiru). Normally the Sun and the Moon are not counted as planets but Sitchin says that the Babylonians and their predecessors the Akkadians and the Sumerians classified them as planets. That leaves the question, what is Marduk? Sitchin claims it is a wandering planet that joined the solar system late. It entered on an elongated comet-like orbit that takes 3,600 years to complete. At its nearest approach – or perigee – to the Sun, Marduk passes through the asteroid belt between Mars and Jupiter. Despite spending most of its time in the depths of space far from the warming rays of the Sun or any other star Marduk is a planet full of living things. Its composition causes the planet to emit heat and a thick and humid atmosphere prevents the heat from escaping too rapidly and leaving Marduk a frozen wasteland. Marduk also possesses plenty of water. Sitchin does not address the question of where Marduk gets its natural light but apparently it is not a problem.

Prior to the arrival of Marduk the solar system contained a planet that Sitchin calls Tiamat which orbited between Mars and Jupiter but not Earth. What happened to change things was the Sun's gravity capturing Marduk as it passed near the solar system. The wandering planet entered the solar system and during one of its orbits Marduk and Tiamat passed too near to each other. Tiamat split into two halves. One half became Earth and entered into its present orbit. During this encounter biological material from Marduk was pulled to Earth and started life on that previously dead world. This transfer meant that life on Marduk and Earth shared a closely related biochemistry; Earth's process of evolution was just many years behind Marduk's. On a later orbit Marduk again passed close to the remaining half of Tiamat, which disintegrated and became the asteroids.

Over time an advanced civilization developed on Marduk that was capable of space travel and faster-than-light travel. These humanoids from Marduk are extremely long lived by earth standards since one of their years is equal to 3,600 earth years. They have observed the earth and can see that it is a water world full of life just like Marduk. So 450,000 years ago the first Nephilim or Anunnaki visited the earth. They used water landings for their first spacecraft. They needed to settle at a location with access to plenty of water and petroleum, so they established their first base in Mesopotamia. The Nephilim initially came looking for gold, which was an important raw material in their technology. Mines were established in southern Africa but the work was dangerous and hard. Rank and file Nephilim became disgruntled and mutinied. The leaders decided to create a slave race by genetically engineering the existing primitive *Homo erectus*. The result of this process was modern humans, *Homo sapiens*. This momentous event took place 300,000 years ago and, although the new species was initially a sterile hybrid, eventually the improved humans developed the ability to procreate and multiply. The problem was that their sexual unions became indiscriminate. Modern humans sometimes mated with *Homo erectus* and produced regressive offspring. Some Nephilim married human women and produced hybrid children, inferior to the Nephilim but superior to the modern humans. Some of the Nephilim, led by Enlil, became concerned and angry about the interbreeding. Enlil tried to destroy the modern humans with disease and famine but his efforts were thwarted by another Nephilim leader, Enki, who consistently befriends humanity.

The great crisis came 13,000 years ago when the long Ice Age ended. Antarctic glaciers began to melt and on this orbit of Marduk the wandering planet would pass dangerously close to the earth. Marduk's gravity would cause massive glaciers to slide into the sea and create massive tidal waves – a worldwide deluge. The Nephilim knew that the catastrophe was approaching and could take refuge in space. Enlil hoped that the deluge would destroy degenerate humanity and refused to let the Nephilim warn them. Ever contrary, Enki disobeyed Enlil and warned the humans. Noah built a sort of submarine as his

Ark. Total desolation followed the deluge, including all the Nephilim bases. The massive rebuilding required much labour and Enlil realized that the Nephilim needed humans to get the work done. To aid the human population's recovery, the Nephilim helped them to domesticate plants and animals and so started the agricultural phase of human history.

In the books *The Stairway to Heaven* (1980) and *The Wars of Gods and Men* (1985) Sitchin describes how the deluge rendered Mesopotamia uninhabitable for a long time. So the Nephilim relocated to the Sinai Peninsula where they built a new space-port with its mission control centre at Jerusalem and a landing site at Baalbek in Lebanon. They also built the complex of the three great pyramids and the Sphinx at Giza to serve as a beacon for incoming spaceships. The Nephilim taught humans more skills and the Neolithic era commenced about 7400 BC. In 2750 BC the great civilization of Sumer arose in Mesopotamia with the assistance of the Nephilim. Sumer is the mother civilization of humanity and aspects of its culture spread to Egypt and the Indus Valley. Unfortunately rivalries and conflicts flared up among the Nephilim and between the human kings. The biblical patriarch Abraham was born at Nippur in Mesopotamia just before the conflicts came to a tragic climax. Wars raged throughout the Middle East from Egypt to Mesopotamia. A human army threatened the space-port of the Nephilim on the Sinai Peninsula. To prevent the humans taking over the space-port high-ranking Nephilim used nuclear weapons to destroy the space-port and the rebellious cities of Canaan. Winds blew the radioactive fallout to Sumer, killing the human population and devastating the land. The great civilization came to an abrupt end.

Other books by Sitchin discuss the Nephilim's role in the construction of Stonehenge and the civilization of the ancient Americas. *The End of Days: Armageddon and the Prophecy of the Return* (2007) discusses the impending return of the Nephilim as early as 2012, the year of the ominous Maya prophecy of doom. This book has inspired an internet hoax which claimed that the FBI and the district attorney of New York City had arrested Sitchin for plotting to overthrow the US government. Apparently the government had not been taking the threat of the Nephilim's return seriously enough, so Sitchin and his followers hatched a plot to take over the government and do the job properly.[90]

Sitchin's view of ancient history combines von Däniken's ancient astronauts with Velikovsky's ideas about wandering planets and catastrophism. Like both men he studies ancient texts of myths and religion and interprets them as literal accounts of past events. He is yet another euhemerist. In his research he is a kindred spirit of Velikovsky. Both men deploy large numbers of ancient writings and make detailed use of them. Sitchin's greater documentation of his hypothesis can be thought of as a sort of von Däniken hypothesis after an injection of evidential steroids. It is much more voluminous and detailed. Unfortunately, unlike Velikovsky, Sitchin does not provide footnotes, which makes it difficult to check his sources. Another strength of Sitchin's is his command of ancient Hebrew and it is said that he reads Sumerian and cuneiform. He does not, however, delve into the biological and astrophysical implications of the cosmology and narrative that he presents.

Sitchin's books also contain fatal or at least potentially fatal weaknesses. When critics have checked Sitchin's references, they have found that he frequently quotes out of context or truncates his quotes in a way that distorts evidence in order to prove his contentions. Evidence is presented selectively and contradictory evidence is ignored. That is not the way that history or any other empirical discipline is supposed to be approached. Sitchin's assignment of meanings to ancient words is tendentious and frequently strained. He states that the Sumerian term for the Nephilim, which is DIN-GIR, means 'pure ones of the blazing rockets' although the literal translation would actually be 'sharp-edged object'. It has been suggested that a more common-sense and contextual interpretation of DIN-GIR referred to a god in a totemic sense. At a factual level, it has also been pointed out that Sitchin's twelfth planet is not borne out by the ancient sources, which only mention the existence of five planets. Finally there is that pesky problem of physical remains. Heyerdahl's question to von Däniken of why no physical remains of highly durable space ships have ever been found applies equally well to Sitchin's Nephilim.[91] Despite the superficial appearance of a higher level of scholarship and a better education than von Däniken, Sitchin is not the greatly scholarly hope of pseudohistory that some of his adherents claim him to be. Meanwhile Graham Hancock has become the new torchbearer for alternative interpretations of prehistory and ancient history.

GRAHAM HANCOCK AND COMPANY: Ancient Ice Age civilizations

Secrets are in vain sought within the pyramids, or concealed wisdom from the obelisks. JOHANN GOTTFRIED VON HERDER (1874)[92]

Graham Hancock was born in Scotland in 1950. During his early childhood he lived in India where his father worked as a surgeon. His school and university years were spent at Durham where he earned a degree with first-class honours in sociology. After graduation he pursued a career in journalism and wrote for *The Times*, the *Independent* and the *Guardian*, along with other newspapers. From 1981 to 1983 he worked as the East African correspondent of the *Economist*.

In 1981 Hancock began to publish books, starting with *Journey Through Pakistan*. His experiences with Africa and the problem of poverty led to other books: *Under Ethiopian Skies* (1983), *Ethiopia: The Challenge of Hunger* (1984), AIDS: *The Deadly Epidemic* (1986), *Lords of Poverty* (1989) and *African Ark* (1990). All of these were nicely done travel books or investigations of social issues but they were not bestsellers. Hancock put his Ethiopian experience to another use when he brought out *The Sign and the Seal: The Quest for the Lost Ark of the Covenant* in 1992. Various traditions and lore associated Ethiopia with the Ark of the Covenant while the film *Raiders of the Lost Ark* (1981) once more associated the Ark of the Covenant with adventure and mystery in the mind of the public. Hancock melded these elements together into a book that the *Guardian* proclaimed was 'a new genre, an intellectual whodunit by an do-it-yourself sleuth'.[93] *The Sign and the Seal* hit the bestseller list and still remains in print. It is considered by many to be a possible if not necessarily plausible speculation on the history of the Ark of the Covenant. In his later books Hancock would mix history with pseudohistorical speculations in far greater degrees of implausibility, which captured the imaginations of many readers but not the approval of professional scholars. Scholarly approval, however, was a minor consideration when weighed against handsome royalty cheques and fame. He had discovered a formula for producing bestsellers and, with a reputation for successful sales, would use that formula again and again.[94]

Hancock's second foray into pseudohistory appeared in 1995 and was titled *Finger-Prints of the Gods*.[95] In it Hancock argued that there was evidence that an advanced civilization had existed about 15,000 to 10,000 BC. This mysterious culture possessed scientific and technological knowledge equal or superior to modern civilization. A terrible global catastrophe wiped out the super-civilization and almost rendered humanity extinct. Survivors managed to preserve mere vestiges of the knowledge of that wonderful society that are recorded as the so-called myths of the culture-givers: Viracocha, Quetzalcoatl, Thoth, Osiris and Prometheus. The global catastrophe stemmed from a sudden displacement of the earth's crust that moved temperate regions into frigid areas and arctic lands into tropical locations. The distribution of the earth's climatic regions changed radically.

Crustal displacement triggered earthquakes, tidal waves, myriad volcanic eruptions and the rapid raising of new mountains. It is possible that a secondary catastrophe or an aftershock followed the first event. The entire experience was also preserved in the myths of universal floods and other catastrophes from around the world. If this account sounds like a reiteration and expansion of the ideas of Charles H. Hapgood, that's because it is. Hancock begins *Finger-Prints* with chapters on Hapgood's hypotheses. Velikovsky is brought into the discussion to a lesser degree. *Finger-Prints* goes further than Hapgood by specifically identifying Antarctica as the homeland of the lost super-civilization. As Hancock generously pointed out, he solidified his idea about the location of the lost super-civilization when a pair of latter-day Atlantologists, Rand and Rose Flem-Ath, contacted him about their theory that Antarctica was Atlantis. Like Hancock they were supporters and adapters of Hapgood's ideas about the Piri Reis map, advanced Ice Age civilizations, crustal displacement and global catastrophism. Unlike Hancock they had been in correspondence with Hapgood about his hypothesis and their hypothesis for some time prior to his death. Their book *When the Sky Fell: In Search of Atlantis* appeared in 1995, the same year as *Finger-Prints*.

Hancock published more books presenting evidence and speculations about the lost civilization and the global catastrophe that destroyed it. In 1996 Hancock and Robert Bauval, another advocate of prehistoric advanced civilization, co-authored *The Message of the Sphinx: A Quest for the Hidden Legacy of Mankind*, which purported to reveal awesome secrets about the Sphinx and the lost history of humanity.[96] Two years later, in 1998, Hancock brought out *The Mars Mystery: The Secret Connection Between Earth and the Red Planet*. This time he advanced the claim that Mars had once been home to an advanced civilization whose monumental architecture mirrored the supposed celestial map contained in the layout of the pyramid complex at Giza. The same year he and his wife, the photographer Santha Faiia, published *Heaven's Mirror: Quest for the Lost Civilization*. In this book his text and her pictures attempt to present various ancient sites as the remnants of an advanced Ice Age civilization. Its quest ranges from the Central America of the Olmecs, Mayas and Aztecs to the Egypt of the pyramids to Cambodia, Easter Island, the mysterious ruins off the island of Yonaguni near Taiwan, the Nasca lines and Tiahuanacu in the high Andes. *Underworld: The Mysterious Origins of Civilization* came out in 2002 and included additional discussion of the alleged underwater ruins at Yonaguni. Hancock also looked at other evidence of an ancient civilization that had been submerged during the catastrophic end of the last Ice Age. Channel 4 in Britain gave Hancock exposure by allowing him to write and produce two documentaries: 'Underworld: Flooded Kingdoms of the Ice Age' and 'Quest for the Lost Civilization', which they aired and were distributed as videos.

By 2005 Hancock was moving in a somewhat different direction with *Talisman: Sacred Cities, Secret Faith*, again co-authored with Robert Bauval. They claim to see traces of a secret religion in the architecture and monuments of various cities throughout history going back to Luxor in Egypt and proceeding through Alexandria, Rome, Paris, London and New York, among others. It is evidence of a vast conspiracy by a gnostic organization that has been guiding human destiny for thousands of years. In the same year Hancock also published *Supernatural: Meetings with the Ancient Teachers of Mankind*, which attempts to connect the beginnings of human civilization some 25,000 years ago with the cave art that appeared at that time. Apparently Hancock is not yet interested in seeking evidence of the really ancient super-civilizations that preceded the Ice Age civilization of 10,500 BC and were destroyed by older catastrophes generated by earlier crustal displacements and pole shifts.

Rand Flem-Ath has also continued to write. In 2000 he brought out *The Atlantis Blueprint: Unlocking the Ancient Mysteries of a Long-Lost Civilization* with co-author Colin Wilson, another writer specializing in occult and highly speculative reconstructions of ancient history. This book basically takes the ideas of *When the Sky Fell* and expands them. Meanwhile others have worked in parallel with Hancock and proposed their own theories of civilizations going back much further in time that 3000 BC. Michael Cremo and Richard L. Thompson in *Forbidden Archaeology: The Hidden History of the Human Race* (1993, revised 1996 and 1998) claim to have found evidence of modern humans going back many millions of years. They assert that a powerful conspiracy has worked to suppress this evidence of humanity's tremendous antiquity. Cremo and Thompson's goal is to link a scientific hypothesis about the lost history of the human race with the alleged myths of Hinduism. These myths tell the story of humanity's existence on the earth for millions of years. That existence, according to Cremo, might even be linked to ancient astronauts! Although Cremo and Thompson present a different hypothesis about prehistory, they provide aid and comfort to other pseudohistorians and so help to continue that peculiar circle of supposed scholars.[97]

Critics and debunkers have been quick to point out that both Hancock and the Flem-Aths have basically recycled the already debunked and discredited ideas of Charles H. Hapgood and to a lesser extent

Immanuel Velikovsky and others writing on similar topics. Hancock and the Flem-Aths engage in the usual flawed methodologies of pseudohistorians.[98] They pick and choose from the relevant evidence while distorting the theories accepted by historians and scientists. In arguing for Hapgood's hypothesis of crustal displacement, Hancock and the Flem-Aths either ignore or seem unaware that since the 1960s considerable research has accumulated to solidify the broad acceptance among geologists of continental drift/plate tectonics as the dominant theory. They focus on anomalies rather than on the main body of existing evidence. They make no attempt to integrate the Piri Reis and the Oronteus Finaeus maps into the context of early sixteenth-century cartography. The same observation applies to archaeological evidence like the Pyramids and the ruins of Tiahuanacu, which they date as far older than radiocarbon dating and the surrounding archaeological context would support. Both Hancock and the Flem-Aths continue to use an euhemeristic approach to myths by assuming they are accounts of literal events rather than allegorical or tropological stories. They also make claims that solid science can back their claims about such things as the extreme age of the Sphinx. Although they have located one geologist, Robert Schoch, who supports them, other geologists have not been persuaded that Schoch's science is correct. Schoch is not too worried, though, since he has launched his own career as a pseudohistorical and pseudoscientific writer with several books with mainstream publishers to his name.[99] In common with many pseudohistorians Hancock and the Flem-Aths employ the rhetorical device of initially discussing an idea as speculative while later treating it as a proven fact. Erich von Däniken has made considerable use of this technique. Pseudohistorians, including Hancock, often use a legal rather than a empirical or scientific approach to argumentation. Lawyers argue to win cases, arriving at the objective truth is a secondary goal. They only present evidence that supports their case and ignore evidence that casts doubt on it. For scholars finding the truth, or at least the closest possible approximation to it, is paramount. They look at all the evidence to determine what happened. Pseudohistorians and pseudoscientists generally argue in the style of lawyers. It is an approach that professional scholars consider to be both ineffectual for advancing knowledge and contemptible because the professional scholars know the crucial information and evidence that has been left out or ignored by the pseudohistorians. Lay readers expecting a good faith attempt to find the truth from the author of a book are often blithely unaware that their trust has been abused. Debunkers arise to reveal the deception but the new pseudohistorians always manage to appear several steps ahead of them.

CONCLUSION

This chapter has looked at pseudohistorical hypotheses about global catastrophes in ancient times, advanced Ice Age civilizations and ancient astronauts, along with the authors who advocate these ideas. When Immanuel Velikovsky and Charles H. Hapgood formulated their ideas the state of scientific and historical knowledge was such that they had a marginally plausible possibility of being right. It was similar to the situation of Ignatius Donnelly when he wrote *Atlantis: the Antediluvian World*. Its historical and scientific evidence was vaguely plausible at the time of publication but advances in science quickly rendered it untenable and obsolete. Continuing advances in science, history and archaeology since 1960 have provided new evidence that has also rendered Velikovsky and Hapgood's hypotheses about catastrophism or ancient super-civilizations implausible. That does not mean that their ideas are dead letters consigned to oblivion. Instead, their ideas and their books, along with Donnelly's, have entered the cultic milieu where they can be recycled by other pseudohistorical writers who cite them as respected and authoritative sources of knowledge. The Native American activist Vine Deloria, Jr, was a great fan of Velikovsky's. He incorporated Velikovskian ideas into his own books and tried to get Velikovsky and Barry Fell, the author of the implausible pseudohistory *America BC* together. Charles Hapgood acknowledged the help of Mrs Ruth Verrill in both *Earth's Shifting Crust* and *The Path of the Pole*. A. Hyatt Verrill and Ruth Verrill co-authored a number of popular books about the pre-Columbian Americas that sometimes incorporated dubious hypotheses about contacts between the Eastern Hemisphere and the Americas.[100] The Hapgood-Verrill connection is another example of pseudohistorical cross-fertilization. Von Däniken, Sitchin, Hancock and the Flem-Aths have all borrowed from Velikovsky or Hapgood or both of them. These more recent writers, however, have produced pseudohistories that have never been grounded on good historical, archaeological and scientific evidence but that has not hurt their credibility.

In popular culture many people cannot distinguish good evidence from bad, or logical and empirical argumentation from seemingly impressive but ultimately empty rhetoric. Sadly, formal education has slighted the development of critical thinking. It is a difficult, time-consuming, under-appreciated and even dangerous thing for educators to teach. So many don't and many can't. That leaves the way open for pseudohistorians and pseudoscientists to sell books and develop followings among the gullible, the ill-informed and those who simply want to believe something regardless of compelling evidence to the contrary. While most pseudohistorians and pseudo-scientists do not hold academic positions at colleges and universities, some do, such as Charles H. Hapgood, albeit on the periphery of higher education. The next chapter, however, will look at an academic with an enviable academic familial background, impeccable educational credentials and a previously respectable although not outstanding record of scholarship. This academic completely changed the focus of his research and took up outrageous interpretations of historical evidence and thanks to postmodernist obfuscation, political correctness and the raging culture wars of the 1980s and '90s made it pay in terms of notoriety and some decent royalties.

CHAPTER 6

Professors Gone Wild: The *Black Athena* Controversy

> We were glad to have seen the land [Egypt] which was the mother of civilization – which taught Greece her letters, and through Greece Rome, and through Rome the world . . . MARK TWAIN[1]

IN THE BEGINNING

Academic books in the humanities very rarely sell many copies or generate much interest from the educated reading public. That situation is not surprising since most topics of academic research are so esoteric and detailed as to be bewildering, if not boring, to the non-specialist. Occasionally, however, a scholarly book will grab attention outside of academe and bask in a certain degree of fame. Generally for this to occur the book needs to strike a chord or a nerve with the public. In the case of Martin Bernal, and his two-volume *Black Athena*, he managed to strike both a chord and a nerve in popular culture's view of ancient history.

The year 1987 witnessed the publication of one of the most controversial works of historical scholarship to appear in the second half of the twentieth century. Its full title was *Black Athena: The Afroasiatic Roots of Classical Civilizations*, volume 1: *The Fabrication of Ancient Greece 1785–1985*. Martin Bernal, a professor at Cornell University, was its author. He followed it with a second volume in 1991: *The Archaeological and Documentary Evidence*. Initially Bernal envisioned that *Black Athena* would be a three-volume work, but by 1991 he had revised his plan and stated that ultimately it would consist of four volumes. The third and fourth volumes would deal with the linguistic and mythological evidence for his theories of ancient history. Meanwhile the first two volumes generated many book reviews, both pro and con; sessions at conferences; public debates; online debates; several collections of essays, both critical and apologetic; books attacking and defending Bernal's conclusions and numerous websites of variable quality. Since the *Black Athena* controversy began in the late 1980s it has boiled intensely at times and at least continued to simmer ever since. What Bernal wrote was a deliberate assault on the established view of the history of the Bronze Age in the eastern Mediterranean. As he put it, 'the political purpose of *Black Athena* is, of course, to lessen European cultural arrogance'.[2]

Bernal puts forward two interpretations of the structure of ancient history and its historiography in *Black Athena*. First, he asserts that the Greek culture of the Bronze Age arose as a result of colonization by Egyptians and Phoenicians. This Near Eastern influence over the culture of the Greeks also did not end with the Bronze Age. The Greek civilization of the Archaic, Classical and Hellenistic eras continued to derive significant aspects of its science, religion and philosophy from the cultures of Egypt and Phoenicia. Second, Bernal claims that from the time of Herodotus and Classical Greece through the eighteenth century it was commonly accepted that ancient Greek civilization had its origins in the civilizations of Egypt and Phoenicia. He labels this view of early Greek history as the Ancient Model.

Bernal realizes that his contention that Egypt and Phoenicia exercised massive influence over early Greek civilization is at odds with the general view of ancient history held by historians and classicists since the middle of the nineteenth century. For decades the dominant view of early Greek history was that an Indo-European invasion from the north destroyed the Mycenean civilization of Bronze Age Greece. A 'dark age' ensued which was followed by a recovery in the Archaic era and then the wonderful flowering of the Classical era of Athenian democracy; Herodotus' and Thucydides' histories; the philosophy of Socrates, Plato and Aristotle; Greek drama and comedy and all the other things that modern Western society commonly associates with the Greeks. In this version of ancient history the Greeks developed their culture on their own with very little borrowing from other cultures, the alphabetical writing of the Phoenicians being an important exception but also an exceptional borrowing. Bernal labels this version of ancient history as the Aryan Model.

According to Bernal, but contrary to scholarly claims, the Aryan Model is not the product of empirical research, improved methodologies and the discoveries of new evidence, especially of an archaeological nature. Instead, growing racism in the late eighteenth century followed by growing anti-Semitism in the second half of the nineteenth century produced the Aryan Model. First came the Broad Aryan Model of ancient history, which denied any Egyptian influence on Greek. Next came the Extreme Aryan Model, which also rejected all Phoenician influences on Greece except the alphabet.

Bernal's first volume of *Black Athena* traces the history of the historiography of ancient Greek history during the Bronze Age. According to Bernal, what he calls the Ancient Model, the recognition of Greece's cultural indebtedness to the Egyptians and the Phoenicians, was commonly accepted during the Classical and Hellenistic periods. Later during the Medieval, Renaissance and Enlightenment eras, people interested in ancient history regarded Egypt with great respect as one of the foundations of Classical Greek civilization and hence Western Civilization. Things, however, began to change in the eighteenth century and Europeans began to view Egypt in a more negative light. Orthodox Christians grew more hostile to the alleged religion and philosophy of ancient Egypt when it appeared to pose a threat to Christianity. Isaac Newton and like-minded scholars considered the pantheistic aspects of Egyptian religion to be particularly objectionable. Bernal asserts that a growing racism, spurred on by colonialism and the Atlantic slave trade, contributed to the devaluation of Egypt since it was an African civilization. Europeans started to value the maintenance of racial purity as the essential condition for any culture or civilization to be successful and to move forward. The development of historical linguistics also hurt ancient Egypt's standing in late eighteenth-century European culture. When scholars developed the concept of an Indo-European or Indo-Aryan family of languages, it directed the quest for the origins of Western civilization away from Egypt and towards India, the India of the Vedic Age and the Aryan Invasions (c. 1500–500 BC). These white invaders from the north conquered India and set up robust kingdoms of intrepid warriors. They were part of the movements of other hardy barbaric peoples like the Achaeans of Indo-European origin, who were thought to have invaded Greece somewhat earlier around 1750 BC. Furthermore, Bernal contends that the Hellenomaniacs of the early nineteenth century began to cast doubts on the whiteness of the ancient Egyptians. As a result the racist scholars of that era began to reject Egypt as a highly sophisticated culture and as the supposed cradle of civilization.

These external developments, according to Bernal, led to the fall of the Ancient Model of Bronze Age Greek history. Among the great culprits in the demise of the Ancient Model are German scholar Karl Otfried Müller and his fellow professors at the first modern university, the University of Göttingen. They used source criticism to discredit the Ancient Model and to bring about the rise of the Aryan Model including its spread to England. Bernal also includes among this motley crew of villainous Eurocentric racists Johann Gottfried von Herder, Immanuel Kant, Bartold Niebuhr and George Grote. By 1860 Egypt had been dethroned from its place of eminence in the Ancient Model. The fall of Phoenicia as an important influence on Greece soon followed. In this case French scholars such as Jules

Michelet led the assault. For Michelet the sin of the Phoenicians was being too similar to the English, but the ultimate objection for most European scholars of at least a nominally Christian background was that the Phoenicians were really just another type of ancient Jew. By 1885 anti-Semitic scholars had managed to limit the Phoenicians' contributions to Greek civilization to the introduction of the alphabet and the Extreme Aryan Model of ancient history was born. This Extreme Aryan Model persisted through the very anti-Semitic decades of the 1920s and '30s. After World War II and the Holocaust resulted in the discrediting of anti-Semitism, Jewish scholars such as Cyrus Gordon and Michael Astour argued successfully for once again crediting the Phoenicians with significant influence on the culture of Bronze Age Greece. Bernal labels this new view as the Broad Aryan Model, which he says held sway over the interpretation of ancient history well into the 1980s.

Anyone with even a superficial familiarity with the *Black Athena* controversy knows that Bernal blames racism and anti-Semitism for creating the distorted Aryan Model in its various forms. Such charges are scattered profusely throughout the two published volumes. His actual argument, however, is more complex than that duo-causal explanation of the genesis of the Aryan Model. Bernal actually identifies four forces that brought about the destruction of the Ancient Model: Christian reaction, the concept of progress, the growth of racism and romantic Hellenism. The Christian reaction consisted of a growing enmity toward Egyptian religion and philosophy that was seen as threatening to traditional Christianity. Egyptian hermeticism was seen as contributing to pantheistic beliefs. Even Sir Isaac Newton, a crypto-Arian and proto-deist, came to consider Egyptian religion and philosophy, especially its polytheism, as a threat to Christianity.

The concept of progress also worked to discredit Egypt. Advocates of progress asserted that healthy and enlightened civilizations were engaged in a continual process of changing and evolving into better and better societies. Ancient Egypt had the reputation of being a stable and unchanging culture. Prior to the rise of the cult of progress Egypt's stability was considered a positive trait. Afterwards it became a liability. Enlightenment thinkers viewed Egypt as a civilization that had entered a cultural dead end.

Racism also hurt Egypt's status as a fount of European civilization. As people came to value racially pure societies, that is, racially pure white societies, Egypt with its racially mixed population saw its favoured position deteriorate. Its close geographical position to black Africa did not help, as anything associated with Negroes was increasingly devalued and denigrated. Blacks came to be viewed as inferior savages incapable of civilization. In Bernal's reconstruction European racism became more vicious and more pervasive as the eighteenth and nineteenth centuries progressed. It dominated the worldview of Western civilization.

Bernal also makes the claim that romantic Hellenism contributed to the decline of Europeans' respect for the civilization of ancient Egypt. Romantics valued the concept of nation and nationhood. Eighteenth-century German intellectuals, such as Johann Gottfried von Herder, began a quest to rediscover their German roots and recover an authentic German culture. His effort was a reaction against France's cultural domination of the German lands during the Enlightenment and the Revolutionary eras. Romantics also admired small, virtuous and homogeneous (pure) societies, and the ancient Greeks were thought to live in those sorts of communities. Hence the Greeks became objects of admiration among German and British intellectuals. On the other hand, large heterogeneous kingdoms and empires, such as Egypt, were seen as tyrannical and stifling of the human spirit.[3]

Jacques Berlinerblau, a generally sympathetic critic and commentator on Bernal's work, takes Bernal's explanation for the fall of the Ancient Model and the rise of the Aryan Model to an even more complex level. He rejects as simplistic those people who reduce Bernal's argument to explaining the shift in historical interpretations merely on the basis of racism and anti-Semitism.[4] Berlinerblau identifies some fourteen variables that helped to bring about the decline of the Ancient Model. These historical conditions obviously include racism, anti-Semitism, the concept of progress, romanticism and Christian reaction. Berlinerblau points out that there were other significant variables that influenced the shifts in European scholarly thinking during the eighteenth and nineteenth centuries. These additional variables included Eurocentrism, imperialism, Philhellenism, positivism, nationalism, the Industrial Revolution, the French Revolution, Northernism, climatic determinism and childhood(!).[5] The problem for Berlinerblau is that as he delineates these many additional historical attitudes and phenomena, it also becomes clear just how tightly connected they are to each other and how virtually inseparable they are. Philhellenism and Northernism are offshoots of romanticism. Eurocentrism, nationalism and imperialism are also interrelated phenomena which can be allied with and bolstered by racism and romanticism. When Berlinerblau cites 'childhood' as a variable, he is making reference to romanticism's fascination with the concept of childhood, that is, the origin and formative stage of individuals and cultures. Romantics viewed ancient Greece as the childhood of Western civilization.[6] Obviously Berlinerblau's fourteen variables are hardly discrete entities and in many cases are subsets or consequences that arise out of Bernal's fundamental emphasis on race and anti-Semitism. Berlinerblau states, 'I hope the preceding discussion forever inters the odd notion, cherished by journalists, culture warriors, and even a few serious scholars, that *Black Athena* explains the paradigm shift in terms of "racism and anti-Semitism".'[7] While Berlinerblau is right, to a certain degree, to point out these additional variables, he tends to ignore the fact that Bernal's own rhetorical presentations in his books and essays promotes and encourages that very focus on racism and anti-Semitism.

Bernal asserts that these external forces caused the shift in Western historical thinking from the Ancient Model to the Aryan Model. He denies that internal reasons within scholarship such as the discovery of new evidence and the development of new techniques had anything to do with the rise of the Aryan Model. For example, he claims that Champollion's decipherment of Egyptian hieroglyphics did not bring about a significant change in Western society's view of ancient Egypt. Developments in the field of historical linguistics or philology and the classification of languages into families, such as Indo-European languages, had no impact other than where alleged racism and Eurocentrism tainted the interpretations of that scholarship. Archaeological discoveries did not have any appreciable impact on scholarship. The development of the techniques of higher criticism of ancient texts did not have a genuine internal impact. According to Bernal, European scholars did not adopt the Aryan Model because new evidence or new techniques had made it the more plausible theory. Rather they were influenced by prevailing social attitudes of increasing racism, anti-Semitism, Eurocentrism, romanticism and the rest.

Bernal suggests that the tainted and inaccurate Aryan Model of ancient history should be replaced by what he calls the Revised Ancient Model. This view of ancient history argues that Phoenicia and Egypt exerted a very significant influence on the cultural development of the Aegean region through a moderate diffusionism. These influences were carried there by conquest, by Egyptian or Phoenician colonies and by trade. Bernal claims that the aboriginal Aegean population of the Pelasgians was related linguistically to the Hittites. The Pelasgians came under Egyptian and Phoenician influence during the fourth millennium BC. Around 2500 BC Indo-European invaders entered the lands of the Pelasgians and settled there. Other invasions followed. During the early second millennium BC Pharaoh

Sesostris led a conquering expedition through Asia Minor and the Aegean basin that even resulted in a permanent garrison at fabled Colchis in the Caucasus Mountains. This infusion of black Egyptians into Colchis is the reason why, according to Bernal, the ancient Greeks referred to the Colchians as black people. Yet another invasion brought the Hyksos conquerors of Egypt into the Aegean region where they established colonies between 1750 and 1570 BC. Bernal describes the Hyksos as a military juggernaut that began an odyssey of conquest as a group of Semitic nomads but along the way picked up and added various groups of Indo-European speakers to create a multi-ethnic army and society. After their conquest of Egypt some groups of Hyksos took to the sea and conquered Minoan Crete, where they were absorbed, while others entered the Aegean basin, where they became the Mycenaeans and apparently took up the Greek language. This Hyksos invasion of the Aegean definitely introduced Egyptian and Phoenician culture into Greece and thereby created the foundations of Bronze Age Greek culture. The contributions of the Hyksos invaders to the Greeks included the introduction of the alphabet, which they acquired through their Phoenician contacts. Alternatively Bernal suggests that Phoenician traders brought the alphabet to Mycenaean Greece during the period 1470–1200 BC, which he calls the era of Pax Aegyptica. These dates are considerably earlier than the great majority of ancient historians are willing to accept. Most of them believe that the Phoenician alphabet arrived in the Aegean during the early eighth century, before about 740 BC, the date of the earliest example of a Greek alphabet.

Another innovation of Bernal's is his rejection of the so-called Dark Ages of Greece (1000–800 BC) brought on by the Doric invaders from the north. In the Aryan Model the Doric invaders were Greek-speakers and racially pure, albeit barbarians. They smashed the Mycenaean civilization and when a more cultured and settled society reemerged from the ruins in the eighth century it was a local product with few cultural roots in Egypt or Phoenicia except the alphabet. Bernal rejects this version of ancient history. He asserts that there was no Dark Age in Greece and therefore no sharp break with the Bronze Age civilization of the Mycenaeans. As a consequence Archaic and Classical Greek civilization were permeated by Egyptian and Phoenician influences on religion, philosophy, science and material culture. Egypt was Greece's Athena, the bringer of knowledge and culture. As Jacques Berlinerblau puts it:

> Now, when Martin Bernal says that to accept the Revised Ancient Model is 'to rethink the fundamental bases of "Western

Civilization"' [emphasis in original], we must take him literally and figuratively. Figuratively, he is saying that the Western intellectual tradition, whose origins are placed in Classical Greece, owes a debt to the achievements of the Afroasiatic East. Yet the literal dimensions of this claim are even more jarring. From the very moment of its conception, Greek culture and language were inextricably bound with those of Semitic and African civilizations. Bernal's Revised Ancient Model, then, contends that the delicate flower which we refer to as Classical Greece is a hybrid from its seed to its petals.[8]

Bernal claims to have plenty of evidence for his radical revisions of ancient history. *Black Athena 2* was simply the archaeological and documentary evidence while *Black Athena 3* supplied the linguistic evidence. The as-yet-unpublished fourth volume is supposed to present evidence from religion and mythology. But since *Black Athena 2* was published in 1991 and *Black Athena 3* in 2006, interested potential readers may be waiting a long time for the promised fourth tome which, in fact, appears to have been abandoned.[9]

In fact Bernal has shown some of his evidentiary cards in his preliminary presentations of his Revised Ancient Model in volumes one and two of *Black Athena*. Various etymologies of words and place-names were presented which he claims prove massive Egyptian and Phoenician influences on the Bronze Age Aegean. He draws parallels between Egyptian and Greek religion, which he claims clearly show significant Egyptian influences on Greece. One such claim is that the Greek goddess Athena derived from the Egyptian goddess Nēit (Neith or Neg) and possibly from a Semitic goddess Anât (Anat or Anath). The Greeks of the Classical Era recognized a parallel between Neith and Athena. Both goddesses were closely associated with domestic arts and weaving along with fertility, while both also had some connection to warfare. The difficulty for Bernal is that most scholars do not find his etymological argument for the name of Athena evolving out of Neith at all convincing. Furthermore, while Neith is an ancient goddess, she was long a local deity of the city of Säis in the Nile delta, and only rose to national prominence with the establishment of the Säite or twenty-sixth dynasty of Psamtek I (664–610 BC). Psamtek allowed Greek traders to settle at Naucratis near Säis in 620 BC, which is an alternative way for Greeks to have learned about Neith, unfortunately occurring too late to be of any support for Bernal's theories.[10] Anat is a Canaanite war-goddess but, while there are some parallels between Anat and Athena, it is hard to imagine the benevolent Athena being a Greek evolution of the unrelentingly malevolent Anat. This particular piece of evidence also combines Bernal's use of linguistics and mythology to support his theories.

Bernal strenuously argues that ancient myths and ancient writers should be taken at their word, that is, literally. His contention is that myths contain considerable truth about the actual historical events of the past. Therefore, when myths record that Cadmus the Phoenician founded Thebes in Greece, that means Thebes was one of Bernal's postulated Phoenician colonies. When Danaus flees from Libya to avoid being killed by his twin brother Aegyptus, he sails to Greece and takes over Argos from its native king Gelanor. Is this story an echo of ancient Egyptian conquests of Greece? Martin Bernal would say yes. The same technique is applied to ancient writers from Herodotus to Plato to Diodorus Siculus. When they make statements about conquests, invasions and cultural borrowings, Bernal asks his readers to take them seriously and at their literal word. As Berliner-blau describes the situation, 'Professional scholars of antiquity, as we have seen, place far less trust in ancient texts than does Martin Bernal. Conversely, Martin Bernal places far more trust in ancients than he does in professional scholars of antiquity.'[11] Needless to say, many Classicists, linguists, Egyptologists, archaeologists and intellectual historians have found much to disagree with in Bernal's methodologies and his evidence.[12] Numerous reviews and articles, along with an entire book of essays, have attacked and demolished virtually every aspect of Bernal's arguments in terms of methodological flaws, bad or insufficient evidence, or just plain errors of fact. Contrary to Bernal's own prediction the academic community did not ignore him. In fact, it gave him a fair hearing and came away largely unconvinced.

THE RECEPTION OF BLACK ATHENA

> It is too easy to be original by doing the opposite of what everyone else is doing . . . People try to be original and have a personality on the cheap. ANTONIO GRAMSCI[13]

Black Athena is a work that has aroused a passionate response from its readers, both positive and negative. In the judgement of one well-known scholar, 'Martin Bernal's massive and ambitious work is grandiose in the best sense', but that same scholar, Gerda Lerner, goes on to say that 'the book is badly organized, tediously repetitious, and overloaded with technical details'.[14] Apparently Molly Myerowitz Levine read a different book (which in a way she did, since she was commenting on the newly published Black Athena 1, whereas Lerner was referring to both *Black Athena 1 and 2*). Levine describes a weekend spent devouring *Black Athena 1* including reading it in bed and in the bathtub. For her the experience was 'that rarest of intellectual phenomena, the academic page-turner . . . Bernal's ideas were interesting.'[15] Many others, such as Michael Poliakoff, did not agree.[16] John R. Lenz found *Black Athena 2* to be 'extremely heavy going and problematic'.[17] Emily Vermeule came to an even more severe conclusion. saying 'confusion is the cost of reading it', while John Baines characterized it as a 'strange mixture of the conventional and the bizarre'.[18] The eminent intellectual historian Paul O. Kristeller, in a review of both volumes of *Black Athena*, devastatingly concluded 'that Bernal's work is full of gross errors due to political prejudices and fashions and cannot be trusted in any of its assertions or statements unless it is confirmed by other, more reliable sources and authorities'. He also ventured an observation that would become increasingly common as the *Black Athena* controversy unfolded, 'this work . . . has not received the sharp criticism which it deserves, obviously for political reasons'.[19]

In fact Bernal and *Black Athena* received plenty of criticism. Dozens of reviews, review articles and critical essays were written. According to Jacques Berlinerblau, author of a book-length study of the *Black Athena* controversy, negative scholarly reviews of *Black Athena* outnumbered 'positive or moderate ones by a margin of seven to three'. Berlinerblau recognizes that some might conclude that such numbers are an eloquent testimony as to just how badly the scholarly consensus was running against Bernal and his revisionist interpretations. Instead he renders the judgement that, 'What is significant . . . is that the majority of Bernal's defenders have emanated from the radical tier of the academic world.'[20] Actually, what seems even more significant, if one continues to believe in the existence of scholarly expertise and authority, is that most of Bernal's positive reviews were written by people who are not scholars of the classics, Egyptology, ancient Near Eastern studies, archaeology or European intellectual history. As radicals they found Bernal's arguments to be politically congenial and they were not equipped or particularly interested in critically evaluating the evidence he presented. An observation of this nature raises the issues of authority, credentials and evidence – all aspects of the scholarly enterprise that Bernal seeks to ignore, minimize or reject.

The fact that Bernal and *Black Athena* prompted a controversy was almost inevitable, given its publication in 1986/7 and 1991. The decade of the 1980s and well into the 1990s was an era that witnessed acrimonious debates over political correctness that escalated into the culture wars.²¹ Although the intensity of the culture wars in academe has diminished, skirmishes still occur and the conflict could easily reignite. Bernal's books and ideas in the form of the *Black Athena* controversy became a battleground of the culture wars. If Bernal's goal was to gain notoriety he could not have chosen a more opportune time to publish. *Black Athena* quickly became well known and widely read among all sorts of academics and even entered the popular market. By 1999 the American sales of *Black Athena* had reached 70,000 copies, and there were also substantial international sales in English and in translation.²² Sales figures of this size are extremely rare for an academic title and almost miraculous for a book that is as arcane in its details and as opaque in its prose as *Black Athena* can be. Obviously Bernal's ideas happened to be introduced at the right time and the right place to garner such attention. Some observers and participants in the *Black Athena* controversy have also pointed out that Bernal actively courted attention from the press and media, more so than was considered normal or even possibly seemly for academic celebrities.²³ The process of academic debate that evolved into the *Black Athena* controversy may not have been all that spontaneous.

The *Black Athena* controversy is a vast phenomenon involving a stream of hundreds of reviews, journal articles, essays, videos, collections of essays, journal debates and discussions, letters to editors, newspaper and magazine reports and books or parts of books. Four whole books deal with *Black Athena* and its controversy. The first two were published in 1996 and were highly critical of Bernal's ideas: *Black Athena Revisited*, edited by Mary R. Lefkowitz and Guy MacLean Rogers (University of North Carolina Press), and *Not Out of Africa: How Afrocentrism Became an Excuse to Teach Myth as History* by Mary Lefkowitz (HarperCollins). In 1999 Jacques Berlinerblau brought out *Heresy in the University: The Black Athena Controversy and the Responsibilities of American Intellectuals* (Rutgers University Press), which claims to be a critique of all sides of the controversy. Although attacked by radicals for being too critical of Bernal, it is likely that most readers would actually consider Berlinerblau to be sympathetic, perhaps even unduly so, to Bernal. That is the *Rashomon* nature of the *Black Athena* controversy. In 2001 Bernal brought out *Black Athena Writes Back: Martin Bernal Responds to His Critics*, edited by David Chioni Moore (Duke University Press), largely a collection of previously published essays and review articles in which Bernal defends his ideas. The intention of *Black Athena Writes Back* is to serve as a sort of counter-*Black Athena Revisited*, from which Bernal bitterly complains that he was unfairly excluded as a contributor. Meanwhile those interested in the next instalment of the saga saw the publication of the long antici-pated third volume of the saga of *Black Athena* in 2006. Plans for a promised fourth volume appear to have been abandoned but Bernal has mentioned that he will write another related book, *Moses and Muses*, which is supposed to be a condensation of the arguments of *Black Athena*. Molefi Asante and Karenga have also stated that they are working on a collection of pro-Bernal essays with the title of *Truly Out of Africa* while another promised but as yet unpublished pro-Bernal work is to be called *Just Out of Africa*.[24] Since these books were first mentioned as forthcoming in 1996, it might not be a good idea for eager readers to hold their breath in anticipation of their publication. With or without them much ink has already been spilled debating and arguing about *Black Athena*.

Because the *Black Athena* controversy and the criticisms of Bernal's ideas are so detailed and technical the remainder of this chapter will focus on several topics where the issues are relevant to or possibly comprise a sort of borderland between history and pseudo-history. One topic is the controversy over the title *Black Athena* itself. Another section will look at Bernal's concept of 'competitive plausi-bility' and its viability. A third topic is Bernal's use of the concepts of race and racism. Out of this discussion will proceed a fourth section describing Bernal's relations with Afrocentric scholars and their uses of *Black Athena*. The fifth and final section will investigate the orig-inality of Bernal's ideas about Egyptian and Near Eastern influences on Greece within the historiography of the late twentieth century.

CONTROVERSY OVER THE TITLE

What's in a name? That which we call a rose
By any other name would smell as sweet.
ROMEO AND JULIET, II, ii, 43–4

During an interview conducted in 1993 Martin Bernal remarked, 'with the exception of *of*, I have been criticized for every word in my title, *Black Athena: The Afroasiatic Roots of Classical Civilization*'. In par-ticular the choice of *Black Athena* was considered to be distinctly problematic or contentious by many critics. But in the pugnaciously subversive style that those familiar with the *Black Athena* controversy have come to know and love, or in some cases, know and loathe, Bernal went on to say, 'I am particularly ashamed of the last two [words]. I should never have left *Classical* unmarked; and *Civilization* implied both Eurocentricism and progressivism – the implication that

Afroasiatic 'cultures' had only the teleological function of leading to European civilization.'[25] In this way Bernal flaunts his politically correct radicalism while disingenuously ignoring the other criticisms of his title. His comment additionally ignored the disputed sub-title of volume one: *The Fabrication of Ancient Greece 1785–1985*. Many commentators have complained that Bernal's use of 'fabrication' strongly implied the existence of a conspiracy among many scholars of the ancient Mediterranean world.

Bernal's use of 'Athena' in his title underscores his contention that the culture of ancient Greece was deeply rooted in Egypt and Phoenicia. Athena was the Greek goddess closely associated with wisdom and artisanal skills; in other words, she was a bringer of culture. Furthermore, Bernal argues that the Greeks derived their concept of Athena from a similar Egyptian goddess, Nēit. In fact, as discussed above, he claims the name Athena has its etymological roots in the Egyptian word meaning 'house of the goddess Neith'.[26] Linguists, however, have remained unconvinced by his continued defence of his etymology.[27]

Far more contentious and misleading is Bernal's use of the word 'Black' in his title. Margaret Washington, writing in a forum on *Black Athena* published by the *Journal of Women's History* in 1993, commented that she had initially started to read *Black Athena* but stopped when she soon discovered that it had nothing to do with gender and little to do with black history.[28] Washington's assumption that the use of 'Athena' in the title implied that gender issues would be prominent in *Black Athena* is perhaps unique but readily understandable. Her reaction that *Black Athena* 'did not have a direct bearing on black history' is one that is shared by many. In 2003 I had an African-American student who wanted to do an independent study on *Black Athena* and its controversy. He was interested in what the book had to say about black history. Since I was also interested in studying Bernal's writings in detail, I agreed. Like Washington, we quickly discovered that *Black Athena* had little to say about the history of black people in the ancient world. Apart from occasional and gratuitous sidebar remarks about 'black' pharaohs and the like, there is little about black people in *Black Athena*.

Not surprisingly, criticism of the use of 'black' in the title *Black Athena* arose from the start. Scholars such as Frank Snowden objected to the conflation of Egyptians with the peoples of Ethiopia or even West and Central Africa. Bernal replied by accusing Snowden of being too precise in his definition of 'black' as negro.[29] This aspect of the title controversy is simply an episode in the long-running debate over the blackness of the ancient Egyptians that will be discussed elsewhere.[30]

But Bernal also raised another issue behind the problematic titling of his book. As he described it, 'I must admit that I did originally suggest it [Black Athena] a possible title, but on thinking it through I wanted to change it. However, my publisher insisted on retaining it, arguing: "Blacks no longer sell. Women no longer sell. But black women still sell."'[31] In other words, Bernal initially suggested the title, later thought better of it and wanted to make a change, but his publisher insisted on keeping Black Athena as a marketing ploy. From a marketing point of view the publisher was absolutely right. From the point of view of scholarly integrity, that decision appears considerably more questionable. A year later, in 1990, Bernal would admit that repeating his publisher's remarks on marketing the book was a 'cheap shot'.[32] Frank Snowden suggested that the title should have been 'Egyptian Athena' but Bernal, ever the stealth Afrocentrist, riposted with the alternative of 'African Athena'.[33] Numerous people have commented that by using the title Black Athena Bernal is clearly indicating that he considers ancient Egyptian society to have been black, although he tends to back off that contention when pressed.[34] As early as 1989 David Gress went further and suggested that Bernal chose Black Athena for his title to pander to an audience of Afrocentric extremists:

> I consider it harmful for Bernal to title his work Black Athena, since he well knows how this will be read by the audience for which he is writing, namely as an argument that Greek culture was black culture. The black activists who have seized Bernal's book could not care less about the serious ethnographic, linguistic, and anthropological questions that Bernal's argument raises . . . They will use Black Athena the same way they used the claim that Beethoven was black: as a truncheon in their battle against the place of European thought and history in the academic curriculum. [35]

And later he adds this concluding assessment, 'Black Athena is pernicious because it serves a political purpose hostile to the culture of scholarship. Its very title is deceptive.'[36] Other participants in the Black Athena controversy reached conclusions similar to Gress.

Some critics have found Bernal's attempt to shift the blame for the use of Black Athena as a title onto his publisher to be problematic at more than one level. Anyone famil ar with academic publishing knows that many books have titles that promise far more than the books actually deliver. Titles often lack a modicum of precision while others border on deceptive. Authors also know that they are sometimes not the creators or the final arbiters of the titles of their own books as publishers will weigh in with their own concerns. The boundary between good practice and bad is very fuzzy and also quite broad. The question for students of the *Black Athena* controversy is whether Bernal crossed that wide and fuzzy line. Radical scholars would mostly answer, no. Afrocentrics would emphatically answer, hell no! Traditionalists, however, are far more critical of Bernal's action. In response to Bernal's blaming the title on the publisher's business decision, Muhly remarked, 'I find this cynical attitude towards publishing books entirely unprofessional.' Muhly also pointed out that Bernal had for some years been teaching a course at Cornell University which he titled 'Black Athena'. Bernal has never called the course anything else, like 'African Athena', for example. Under this circumstance, Muhly rhetorically asked, 'Is it [the title *Black Athena*] not then one that he [Bernal] himself favors, rather than one forced on him by his publisher?'[37] When Bernal responded to Muhly's overall critique, he ignored that question by glossing over it with a nod to taking seriously Frank Snowden's qualms about the blackness of the ancient Egyptians and admitting that blaming his publisher was a 'cheap shot'. In a way Bernal did finally tell everyone where he stood a few years later during his 1993 interview with *Social Text*. When he discussed his regrets over his choice of words for the title, neither 'Black' nor 'Athena' were among them.[38] Meanwhile the disputed title phenomenally fulfilled the publisher's (and Bernal's?) intention and helped to generate publicity and sales far, far beyond the norm for even highly successful academic books.[39]

COMPETITIVE PLAUSIBILITY?

> If history is going to be scientific, if the record of human action is going to be set down with that accuracy and faithfulness of detail which will allow its use as a measuring rod and guidepost for the future of nations, there must be set some standards of ethics in research and interpretation. W.E.B. DUBOIS[40]

In the course of constructing the arguments that form the text of the two volumes of *Black Athena*, Bernal introduced a concept that he calls 'competitive plausibility'. Scholars of the ancient world know that it is a field of study fraught with uncertainty due in large part to the paucity of evidence. Some ancient scripts remain undeciphered. No written records exist for whole cultures, while only enigmatic remains survive for others. Archaeological remains can be spotty and reflect only certain aspects of a culture. Linguistic evidence can be slim and uncertain, while dating artifacts, where no radiocarbon dating is possible, can be problematic. As a result many aspects of knowledge about antiquity are speculative or educated guesses. Under these circumstances scientific certainty is impossible, which leads Bernal to argue that 'all one can hope to find is more or less plausibility'.[41] Therefore the theory which appears to be the most plausible of the several competing theories should be the one that wins the greatest acceptance from other scholars. It is not necessary to prove the other theories wrong by some legal or scientific standard; a scholar only has to show that a new theory, for example Bernal's Revised Ancient Model, is the more plausible explanation of the available evidence. That is competitive plausibility. To this competitive plausibility, Bernal adds a rejection of what he calls 'archaeological positivism', the idea that archaeology is an objective, scientific discipline. He also condemns archaeologists' use of 'argument from silence', by which he means that they use an absence or relative scarcity of certain types of artefacts to help formulate their theories.[42]

From the appearance of the first volume of *Black Athena* in 1986, Bernal's ideas about the Bronze Age of the eastern Mediterranean have prompted criticism. A standard dictum of debunking in scholarship is that extraordinary claims require extraordinary proofs. Bernal, however, rejects that dictum saying, 'I do not think that even "extraordinary" schemes should require *proof* for them to be accepted as working hypotheses.' Because the surviving historical evidence from the ancient world is so uncertain and incomplete Bernal contents that it is unreasonable and impractical to demand that new theories of the past present 'scientific' evidence of an unequivocal nature. Instead, 'all that new challenges need is competitive plausibility: they must simply be less implausible than the scheme they replace'.[43] At a theoretical level almost all scholars would agree that theories and interpretations come and go. Theories and interpretations are always contingent. What makes them contingent, however, is the weight of the evidence. Bernal likes to place his *Black Athena* in the context of it creating a paradigm shift of the type described by Thomas Kuhn in his classic *The Structure of Scientific Revolutions* (1962 and 1970). Kuhn described how various scientific theories come into general acceptance but over time evidence begins to accumulate that contradicts the accepted theory. Ultimately a critical mass of dissonant evidence is reached and a new theory or paradigm based on that evidence swiftly replaces the other theory. Bernal sees his Revised Ancient Model as the new paradigm of ancient history.

Bernal's critics reject his claims to greater 'competitive plausibility' on several levels. One is that Bernal himself tends to argue from silence or the lack of evidence at crucial points. He criticizes archaeologists for an approach which says we have no archaeological evidence for this possibility therefore it did not happen or we have little archaeological evidence for this phenomenon therefore it was insignificant or highly exceptional. Critics, in turn, object to Bernal postulating that something might have occurred even though no positive evidence exists to prove it. An example of this approach is Bernal's claim for an Egyptian colonization of Boeotia in the Bronze Age. Emily Vermeule vehemently disagrees with his suggestion that colonization took place, saying: 'The complete lack of archaeological evidence for Egyptians having been in Boeotia does not disturb Bernal, because he is dealing only in "competitive plausibility" and is not deterred by the absence of archaeological artifacts.'[44] Another recurrent criticism is that Bernal mines the evidence selectively and uncritically to support his theories. Critics see this methodology, or absence of methodology in the traditional academic sense, as an abandonment of real objective scholarship. And Bernal and his supporters would readily agree. They reject the contention that objective scholarship exists and instead embrace relativism. Gerda Lerner and others have found Bernal's 'competitive plausibility' to be quite congenial.[45] Jacques Berlinerblau is a bit more cautious, calling the concept 'one of *Black Athena*'s most timely contributions to the study of the ancient world'.[46] But is it?

Martin Bernal's worldview of scholarship presents a rather authoritarian picture of complacent certainty about knowledge. *Black Athena* argues that its Revised Ancient Model of the history of the Bronze Age is a radical break from the existing modern historiography. Furthermore, it argues that modern historiography is deeply mired in subjective racist and anti-Semitic assumptions. Are Bernal's interpretations all that original and is his view of scholarship all that radical? The fact is, scholar after scholar has pointed out that it has been long recognized in the academic world that Egyptian and Near Eastern influence had a significant impact during the Bronze Age era of Greece and later. Chester Starr advocated such an interpretation years before Bernal. Less flamboyantly marketed and far more painstakingly researched than Bernal, the scholarship of Walter Burkert, Emily Vermeule and others has reinforced Starr's conclusions while rendering many of Bernal's most outrageous claims implausible in the competition of scholarship.[47] Furthermore, it is hard to imagine that any scholar, particularly a historian, would argue that any interpretation can become a fully proven and permanent fact.

Revisionism abounds in every sub-field of history. Competing interpretations of the English Reformation, the historical demography of the pre-Columbian Americas, the American Civil War, the New Deal and the Cold War, to name just a few, vary so greatly that at times a bewildered reader might wonder if rival historians are actually discussing the same event. Bernal attributes the uncertainty or 'competitive plausibility' of ancient historiography to the relative scarcity of evidence. It is obvious, however, that even far more well-documented events and time periods are subject to radically different interpretations. New evidence and new scholarly methodologies can force shifts in historical interpretation along with changing social worldviews and ideologies. Every generation rewrites history because knowledge is contingent and uncertain. As Berlinerblau points out, 'This state of affairs is well known to most historians. So much so, that they rarely feel obliged to address the matter in their own articles and monographs.'[48] Bernal, however, obviously feels obliged to confront it.

More traditional scholars have found Bernal's concept or, at least, his application of 'competitive plausibility' to be lacking in scholarly rigour. While Berlinerblau strives to lionize Bernal as a heroic academic heretic whose challenges keep other scholars honest, he also admits that Bernal 'does not give any indication of how to apply competitive plausibility to distinguish between plausible and implausible ideas'.[49] A recurring criticism of Bernal is that he does not distinguish between an interpretation that is possible, albeit highly improbable, and one that is both possible and probable. As Guy MacLean Rogers puts it, 'what may have happened in the past is not the same thing as what probably happened, as best we can reconstruct it, based on careful, thorough, contextualized evaluation of *all* the evidence'.[50] Reading the debate over *Black Athena* the trend tends to be that radical scholars welcome Bernal because they like his ideas and theories but spend little or no time discussing his evidence. Traditional scholars find his ideas either uncongenial, unoriginal, exaggerated or biased and cite empirically based reasons for reaching their conclusions.[51] As one reviewer quipped, they find Bernal's interpretations neither competitive nor plausible.

BERNAL AND RACE

There would be no reason to impugn history, or to withhold agreement, if those who ought to have had the highest standards had had regard for truth and trustworthiness. Since, however, disagreement among historians is such that some not only disagree with others but even contradict themselves, either from zeal or anger or error, we must make some generalizations as to the nature of all peoples

or at least of the better known, so that we can test the truth of
histories by just standards and make correct decisions about
individual instances. JEAN BODIN[52]

Issues of race and ethnicity permeate large parts of both volumes
of *Black Athena*. Bernal rails against the racism and anti-Semitism
of two centuries' worth of European scholarship and how it has
twisted the interpretation of the past. Everyone agrees that racism
and anti-Semitism are evil and that they existed and continue to
exist, although to a lesser degree. Racism and imperialism both had
their high tide during the late nineteenth and early twentieth centuries as political, social, cultural and scientific conditions in the West
combined to provide them with powerful support and the mirage of
justification. Many people, however, disagree with Bernal's contention that racist and anti-Semitic ideology, combined with related
concepts of progress and romanticism, were the primary driving
forces in historical scholarship at that time and later.[53] Others accuse Bernal of simply taking the racialized scholarship of the
nineteenth and twentieth centuries and flipping it on its head. As a
result Bernal's own scholarship, as is the case with his Afrocentrist
allies, is just as racialized as nineteenth-century scholarship and ultimately just as Eurocentric in its focus. Many scholars disagree with
Bernal's injection of anachronistic racial and ethnic concepts into
his interpretation of the Bronze Age. Some go on to suggest that
Bernal's relentless use of race goes beyond ideology and is a politically correct rhetorical weapon for silencing or muting criticism
from timid academics, the simple equation of this strategy being:
if you disagree with Martin Bernal, you must be a racist like all
those earlier scholars. Finally, some critics see Bernal as cynically
using the race issue to pander to Afrocentric scholars and thus gain
their support.

When the second volume of *Black Athena* appeared in 1991,
Bernal wrote 'there has been a general acceptance of my historio-
graphical scheme and of my contention that most of the men who
established the Aryan model were – to put it bluntly – racists and
anti-Semites'.[54] At that time Bernal's statement was true to a significant degree. And in spite of considerable well-documented
dissent by other scholars during the intervening years, as thought-
ful a scholar as Jacques Berlinerblau continued in 1999 to accept
Bernal's basic assertions about the racist and anti-Semitic distortions of classical scholarship.[55] Traditionalists, however, contend
that such widespread support for Bernal's thesis of racist scholarship is based on shaky foundations. First, radical scholars assume

somewhat ahistorically that racist and anti-Semitic concerns dominated in the past in much the same way as they do today. In fact many knowledgeable people would assume or contend that conditions of prejudice in the past were actually worse than in the present. Hence Bernal's argument that classical scholarship of the nineteenth and twentieth centuries was badly tainted by racist and anti-Semitic prejudices is only what radicals and others would have expected. Second, many of the people who found the first volume of *Black Athena's* parade of racist and anti-Semitic scholarship convincing knew little about classical historiography and the intellectual history of the years 1785–1985. They accepted Bernal's authority on faith.

Experts in intellectual history and classical historiography, in fact, found much to criticize in Bernal's *Black Athena*. In his generally irenic concluding comments on *Black Athena 1* at the American Philological Association meeting in 1989, the well-known historian of Hellenism in Victorian Britain Frank M. Turner stated: 'Professor Bernal discerns larger ideological sweeps that escape my discernment and, I believe, that of many intellectual historians.'[56] Later John Ray, in a review of *Black Athena 2* published in 1991, found Bernal's characterization of the racist, anti-Semitic nature of classical scholarship to be too one-sided, 'These motives exist, to be sure, and each age has its own defective vision, but Bernal is sometimes reminiscent of La Rochefoucauld, who argued from the fact that all human actions have an element of self-interest to the conclusion that they contained nothing else.'[57]

More devastating were the criticisms of Bernal's scholarly methodology (or lack thereof), the superficiality or selectivity of his presentation of classical historiography, and factual errors. Frank M. Turner led the way by objecting to Bernal's inaccurate characterization of German scholar Barthold Niebuhr. He called upon Bernal to read Niebuhr's writings more closely, rather than relying on secondary sources, before drawing such sweeping conclusions. Bernal replied by conceding most of Turner's corrections, but also played to the crowd at the American Philological Association session by asking, 'I would be interested to know how many people in the audience have actually read Niebuhr's *Roman History* in its entirety? I would be surprised if there were more than one or two.'[58] And his guess was probably right. On the other hand, how many people in the room were proposing a radical revision of the interpretation of the intellectual history of Classical scholarship, besides Bernal? Doing intellectual history properly requires the historian to read the appropriate texts, which in Bernal's case would be Niebuhr.

The publication of *Black Athena Revisited* in 1996 supplied a collection of essays that raised serious questions about the accuracy, methodology and even-handedness of Bernal's reconstruction of Classical historiography, including his misrepresentations of the ideas of George Grote, Immanual Kant and Johann Gottfried von Herder.[59] Even more devastating was the appearance of the essay 'Martin Bernal and His Critics' by Suzanne Marchand and Anthony Grafton in 1997. As they put it quite starkly, 'Bernal simply has not done enough work to deserve respect or attention as a historian of European thought about the ancient world. The ability to make noises entitles no one to a hearing, and up to now Bernal has made noise, not historical argument.'[60] They go on to provide a detailed critique of how Bernal has violated the basic rules for doing intellectual history. At the same time they also criticize Bernal's critics for simply nitpicking errors rather than providing a counter-narrative and interpretation.[61] Though generally extraordinarily quick to respond to his critics, Bernal has never directly replied to Marchand and Grafton. In the end, one must wonder how Bernal could characterize Johann Gottfried von Herder, for example, as one of the providers of 'a firm basis for the chauvinism and racism of the following two centuries'.[62] In fact, Herder was someone who knew that race was a meaningless way to classify humans, as demonstrated when he wrote:

> The black colour of the negro has nothing in it more wonderful than the white, brown, yellow, or reddish, of other nations. Neither the blood, the brain, nor the seminal fluid of the negro is black, but the reticular membrane beneath the cuticle, which is common to all, and even in us, at least in some parts, and under certain circumstances, is more or less coloured.[63]

Would that Bernal had followed Herder's example.

Many scholars are uncomfortable with Bernal's application of modern racial and ethnic concepts to the ancient world. One argument is that race is a pseudoscientific concept that has no validity in modern biological terms, all humans are one species and any physical differences between groups are inconsequential. Bernal agrees heartily with that viewpoint, as would any educated person. But he goes on to state that he is concerned with the concept of race as a sociological construct.[64] People think different races exist and that there are important innate differences between these races. These prejudices are not true in a biological sense but many people continue to believe they are. Bernal argues that circumstance makes race an important phenomenon that

241

is worth studying. When the racial attitudes of Western nations from 1750 to 2000 are being studied, Bernal is right. When the peoples of the ancient Mediterranean during the Bronze Age are the objects of study, it is anachronistic to impose modern racial attitudes upon them. Scholar after scholar has criticized Bernal's use of the concept of race as inappropriate and inaccurate. He is actually acting as a mirror image of the racist scholars of the nineteenth and early twentieth centuries that he so abhors. In effect, Bernal's critics are saying that Bernal has met the enemy and he is him.[65]

Bernal has a political reason for anachronistically injecting modern prejudices about race onto the Bronze Age Mediterranean. First, he argues that Egypt is a significant fount of Greek civilization and hence of the Western civilization that followed. Next, he asserts that Egypt was a black or partly black culture with stronger cultural affinities to African civilizations further down the Nile than to the Near East of Asia. Put the two together and black people stand at the origins of Western civilization with the result that white racist beliefs in black inferiority are refuted historically.[66] Bernal has stated that this is his goal quite clearly on a number of occasions but his comments to critics in an issue of the *Journal of Mediterranean Archaeology* in 1990 convey his sentiments quite succinctly:

> What many African-Americans object to is the fact that they are told constantly, directly or by implication, that people like them are incapable of philosophy, science, or cultural creativity in important spheres. Thus, they are angered at this refusal to recognize their similarities to the Ancient Egyptians. It is for this reason that I have stressed the 'Blackness' of some Ancient Egyptians and the African nature of the culture as a whole.[67]

Even a commentator as sympathetic as Jacques Berlinerblau has pointed out that Bernal's comments on the race of the Egyptians in *Black Athena* are actually highly ambiguous.[68] For example, as early as 1989, Bernal states, 'In the text of my book [*BA1*], I make no claim that the Egyptians are black.'[69] To paraphrase a little from an earlier quote from Bernal, he does, in fact, 'directly or by implication' give the impression that Egypt was a black civilization, as his very title so clearly states.

This issue of the ethnicity of the Egyptians is just one example of Bernal's use of vague and tentative language to provide a convenient fallback position when the critical reaction becomes too intense. Other participants in the *Black Athena* controversy have noted this rhetorical strategy and commented unfavourably on it. As Ann

Michelini observed, 'Bernal continually protects himself with ambiguous language' and 'gives himself too many permissions'. Gerda Lerner somewhat apprehensively noticed the same thing, 'The book is strewn with the author's disavowals of the implications of his work, yet he does not define its limits and boundaries sharply enough to avoid the grossest kind of misuse of it.'[70] Although Bernal would plead that he only does this because he does not believe that he has all the answers, at other times he asserts the same theories in a very self-assured manner. And he even excuses his ambiguous language with the comment 'but I am no worse in this regard than most conventional scholars'.[71] Even Berlinerblau finds Bernal's rhetorical tactics somewhat off-putting, 'Nor am I sympathetic to the author's tendency to advocate completely contradictory positions. A certain opportunism characterizes *Black Athena*.'[72] Bernal's apparent rhetorical use of the blackness of ancient Egyptian civilization appears to be one example of such opportunism. As we know, however, the blackness or the whiteness of the ancient Egyptians has long been a battleground for pseudohistorical ideas.[73] Of course, what is a little anachronism when your purpose is 'to lessen European cultural arrogance' and attract the support of Afrocentrists?

BERNAL AND THE AFROCENTRISTS

Untruth naturally afflicts historical information. There are various reasons that make this unavoidable. One of them is partisanship for opinions and schools. IBN KHALDUN[74]

No one involved in the *Black Athena* controversy objects to the general goal of lessening or eliminating racism. Many critics of Bernal, however, not only seriously question whether *Black Athena*'s racializing of the Bronze Age is historically accurate or appropriate in terms of anachronism, but also go on to accuse Bernal of hypocrisy and cynical manipulation.[75] They suggest that Bernal may have deliberately set out to appeal to a constituency of extreme Afrocentric scholars in order to generate publicity and book sales. Afrocentricism originated as an intellectual movement that sought to correct the traditional Western conceit, labelled Eurocentricism, that assumes that European and white history and culture form the paramount aspect of world history. Originally Afrocentrists simply tried to show that African peoples, particularly blacks, had also played an important part in world history. An extreme Afrocentricism, however, arose later and has gone well beyond the necessary and reasonable correction and amplification of the narrative of world history to give black people their due. Extremists have created a fantasy realm in which all knowledge and goodness flows out of Africa while Europe and by extension white America comprise a society of cultural thieves, cruel oppressive barbarians and basically inferior and defective humans. Extreme Afrocentricism is the mirror image of Eurocentricism and it is this type of Afrocentricism that is referred to in this chapter.[76]

Certainly Bernal's publisher followed the tactic of catering to an Afrocentric and feminist audience when it came to titling *Black Athena*, if Bernal is to be believed.[77] Scholar after scholar has criticized Bernal for aiding and abetting the myths and fantasies of the extreme Afrocentrists. They argue that, at best, feel-good mythmaking will only lead to disillusionment and disappointment when the Afrocentrically schooled student is confronted by the history learned, not just by the supposedly Eurocentric majority in the USA, but by the rest of the world as well. Such a view of *Black Athena*'s negative relationship with Afrocentricism is not held solely by the allegedly traditionalist and conservative contributors to *Black Athena Revisited* either. Even Molly Myerowitz Levine, an early and ardent supporter of Bernal, came to see *Black Athena*'s bolstering of extreme Afrocentrist positions as educationally and socially dangerous. Furthermore, Bernal's approach to scholarship at least indirectly promotes a relativism that is so extreme as to be corrosive of all knowledge or a cynicism about scholarship that is equally corrosive. Facts would cease to exist, all learning would become opinion, and all opinions would be equally valid.

Just as disturbing is the use to which some people have put *Black Athena*. A good example of this phenomenon is the extreme Afrocentrist Leonard Jeffries, a professor at the City University of New York. Jeffries apparently approves of Bernal's message since he sows copies of *Black Athena* around New York City like Cadmus sowed dragon's teeth around Thebes. He has given copies of the book to ex-mayor Ed Koch and a sitting mayor, David Dinkins. What Martin Bernal thinks of Jeffries is once again unclear. During an interview in 1992 Bernal kept his distance from Jeffries and contrasted the 'racialism' of Jeffries' Afrocentrism with the moderate Molefi Asante and Ivan van Sertima. All the while, he never repudiated Jeffries. A year later, in another interview, Bernal expressed his appreciation at how most Afrocentrists have supported his work. He then described with a certain pride how Jeffries placed that copy of *Black Athena* on Mayor Dinkins's desk. He identifies Jeffries as 'a symbol of radical Afrocentrism and "Black Racism"' but his placing of 'Black Racism' in quotes indicates his doubts about the charge.[78] One wonders how Bernal would react to Stanley Crouch's assessment that 'City College buffoon Leonard Jeffries made a bad joke of higher learning as head of a black studies department for over twenty years'.[79] He might call Crouch a racist for such an opinion, but if he did, he would be caught in yet another Bernalian contradiction. According to Bernal, racism is 'a term that should be restricted to whites'.[80] Crouch, however, is African-American. White participants in the *Black Athena* controversy are not similarly immune to the charge of racism.

Many of those who disagree with Bernal complain of his extravagant use of the phenomenon of racism as an explanatory device for assessing the positions of scholars of the past and the present. As Frank Yurco has pointed out, many historical interpretations of ancient history that Bernal has labelled as racist were anchored in the best evidence available at the time. As new evidence became available scholars altered their interpretations to accommodate it. They did not ignore evidence of an ancient Nubian civilization due to a racist defence of the Aryan Model of the Bronze Age, rather for many years they simply lacked it. Conditions in the Sudan had been too unstable for archaeologists to do much exploration there.[81] Bernal, however, does not limit his accusations of racism to the dead scholars of the nineteenth century. His identifications of racists can be both incredibly general and intimately personal at the same time, as in this depiction of the respected twentieth-century Egyptologist Alan Gardiner, his beloved maternal grandfather, 'He [Gardiner] was a racist like all his generation.'[82] Such a sweeping generalization staggers its readers with its audacity. It also shows that, despite all his years of studying China, none of the virtues of venerating one's ancestors rubbed off on Bernal. Those who disagree with Bernal in the *Black Athena* controversy suffer from insinuations or even accusations that their dissent is racially motivated. Jasper Griffin has characterized 'some features of Bernal's scholarly style . . . [as] determinedly polemical, with constant implication that those who disagree, past and present, are motivated by racism: a catchall charge that seems to fit every defendant. He is also quick to hint of conspiracies where none exist.'[83] It has also been suggested by the generally supportive Molly Myerowitz Levine that 'the fact that Bernal put racism at the forefront of the scholarly equation may inhibit many who differ with him from speaking out, lest they, too, be labeled racist'.[84]

Bernal is not the only scholar to make white racism a central ingredient in the rise of the Aryan model as well as the primary motivator of the Classics and ancient history establishment's resistance to *Black Athena*'s criticism. Reviewing *Black Athena Revisited*,

Molefi Asante seemed to scoff at the idea that most white scholars are not racists. As he put it, 'Nothing seems to bring out the circling of the wagons of Europe more than the questioning of European culture [sic] superiority.'[85] African-American historian Cheryl Johnson-Odim in 1993 cited an anecdote about a white male colleague who was quite bewildered to learn that someone with ideas like Bernal's was white. It is apparently an easy mistake to make, however, since shortly after *The Journal of Blacks in Higher Education* listed Bernal as the seventeenth most frequently cited African-American scholar of 1993. Johnson-Odim cited her colleague's reaction to demonstrate how completely political the *Black Athena* controversy had become. She remarks: 'While much of the debate over Bernal's 'Revised Ancient Model' thesis has railed over the "political" uses to which Afrocentric scholars may put *Black Athena*, there is little discussion over the "political" scholarship of the nineteenth and twentieth centuries which his thesis debunks or of other political implications of the work.'[86] This comment could cause one to question how closely Johnson-Odim was following the *Black Athena* controversy. Prior to the publication of *Black Athena 2* Bernal's interpretation of nineteenth- and twentieth-century classical scholarship as heavily motivated by racism and anti-Semitism was assumed by many people to be accurate. In his preface to *Black Athena 2* Bernal spends much time talking about his surprise at the widespread positive reaction to *Black Athena 1*.[87] That moment, in retrospect, probably marked the zenith of Bernal's and *Black Athena*'s scholarly reputation. Afterwards, unfavourable reviews and commentary began to accumulate.

Some even hinted that Bernal might not be free of racial bias himself. As Gerda Lerner commented in 1993, 'Whether Athena was "black" or "white" is significant only in the context of racist thought.' Later, in 1996, Jasper Griffin expressed concern at Bernal's choice of the phrase 'white scholarship'. As Griffin sees it, 'the phrase is a chilling one, more reminiscent than its author can have intended of such familiar notions as "Jewish science." We had hoped for a scholarship that would be colorblind.'[88] Scholars critical of Bernal also find his acceptance of extreme Afrocentrist scholarship, albeit frequently muted, perplexing and infuriating. In the first volume of *Black Athena* Bernal told how after eight years of research he came across the writings of Afrocentrists, like George G. M. James, author of *Stolen Legacy* (1954), which claims that the Greeks literally stole their philosophy from the black scholars of ancient Egypt. As Bernal described his initial reaction, 'After making this contact, I found myself very torn. On the one hand, my training made me recoil at the lack of so many of the outward trappings of scholarship; on the other hand, I found that my intellectual position was far closer to black literature than it was to the orthodox ancient history.'[89] Frank Snowden, an African-American scholar in the traditional mould, criticized Bernal for following the ideas of James about black Egyptians and stolen legacies. Bernal quickly denied the charge: 'At no point do I say or even suggest that I accept James' claim that Aristotle "stole" his ideas from the library at Alexandria. My admiration for James comes from his achievement – made in extraordinarily difficult circumstances – in perceiving the racist biases in classical scholarship.'[90] Michael Poliakoff, however, has pointed out that Bernal's disavowal of James is questionable since in *Black Athena 1* when he writes about Aristotle's position as the tutor of Alexander the Great, there is a sidebar comment buried in a footnote, 'G.G.M. James . . . claims that this position gave him [Aristotle] access to Egyptian libraries, which in turn could explain the almost incredible quantity and range of Aristotle's writings.'[91] When this material is combined with other respectful comments about James's work in general and his comments on the stolen legacy in his review of Mary Lefkowitz's *Not Out of Africa*, it is no wonder that Poliakoff asks and others might also ask, 'What does Bernal really think?'[92]

Bernal's comment about James working 'in extraordinarily difficult circumstances' introduces another of his themes, that Afrocentrists are the preservers of the Ancient Model. While other scholars have gone astray, they kept the faith. Of course, Bernal is perfectly willing to concede that Afrocentrists 'make many mistakes in detail'. But, according to Bernal, their mistakes do not matter; as adherents of the Ancient Model, the Afrocentists' basic interpretation is correct while mainstream scholarship corrupted by the Ayran Model is wrong. Earlier Bernal defended Afrocentric scholarship, commenting: 'That Afrocentrists should make so many mistakes is understandable. Theirs is a sense of being embattled in a hostile world and possessing an absolute truth that makes for less concern about factual detail.'[93] Apparently when scholarship becomes political, and for Bernal all scholarship is ultimately political, facts are not important. He goes on to lament the conditions under which Afrocentrist scholars laboured and which explain and excuse any of the manifest shortcomings in their work. 'More important, however, are the extraordinary material difficulties confronted in acquiring training in the requisite languages, in finding time and space to carry on research, money to buy books, or access to libraries, let alone finding publishers who can provide academic checks and competent proofreaders.'[94] He goes on to chide Mary Lefkowitz for elitism, considering her privileged place in academe with an abundance of resources. Being a professor at Cornell University, Bernal enjoys the same access to first-class support for his scholarship and he is quick to admit it. What he seems to be oblivious to is that the great majority of professors in the USA of all ethnicities, the great majority being white, do not enjoy the same availability of resources that he does. They labour under conditions that are the same or only marginally better than the Afrocentrists, yet many of these same professors produce solid scholarship, some of which is as good as the best published in the elite colleges and universities. Furthermore, as Lefkowitz has noted, 'The inadequacy of libraries and facilities still does not explain why G.G.M. James was able to conclude that the Greeks stole their philosophy from the books that are cited in the bibliographical notes at the end of each section of his book.'[95] In the end she shows James's *Stolen Legacy* to be a book that tries to look scholarly but which is ultimately a pseudohistory that is disingenuous and extremely tendentious in its conclusions. Mario Liverani, an Italian scholar, agrees with Lefkowitz and considers Bernal and the Afrocentrists to be far more biased and guilty of falsification than any of the allegedly racist scholars who, Bernal claims, created the Aryan Model of ancient history. Liverani's solution is for scholars 'to work without prejudices and hidden agendas'. It is difficult to see how Bernal could accept that suggestion since he considers all scholarship to be intrinsically political and hopelessly mired in the self-interested values of the society around it.[96]

Not all Afrocentrists welcomed Martin Bernal and *Black Athena* with open arms. There are a variety of reasons for this hostility. First, they do not find him to be original. Black writers and scholars have been saying the same thing since at least 1829 when David Walker published his *Appeal*. Second, they disagree emphatically with Bernal's characterization of Egypt as a mixed-race culture, albeit one with a large number of black people in its population, some of whom established dynasties of pharaohs at frequent intervals. For this group of Afrocentrists Bernal's depiction of the ancient Egyptians as a mixed-race people is unacceptable; instead the ancient Egyptians were solely black. To them Martin Bernal is no hero, rather he seems to be perpetuating the theft of yet another black legacy, that of a black and African Egypt in ancient times.[97]

In spite of such snubs many Afrocentrists have embraced Bernal and *Black Athena*. Bernal has appeared on the Afrocentrist side of panel discussions and has spoken to audiences sympathetic to those ideas. Even if Bernal is not original in his ideas, as Jacques Berlinerblau has described, the fact 'that a white Ivy League professor would seem to endorse these ideas did much to bring previously peripheral claims of Afrocentrists into the epicenter of American intellectual debate'.[98] As mentioned earlier, Leonard Jeffries seems to treat *Black Athena* as a sort of talisman for the cause of extreme Afrocentrism. And that is the problem as opponents of Bernal see it: *Black Athena* has become the tool of the dubious racial theories of Afrocentric extremists. Guy McLean Rogers felt that by 1996 the situation was serious enough for him to conclude the collection of essays comprising *Black Athena Revisited* with this challenge to Bernal: 'The editors of this volume call upon Bernal to reject publicly, explicitly, and unambiguously any theories of history which conflate race and culture. Not to do so would be a signal that he supports a view of the past which has in fact been one of the causes of racism and anti-Semitism in the modern world.' While Bernal has replied in detail to many of the essays in *Black Athena Revisited* he has never responded to this concern of Rogers's.[99]

Is the *Black Athena* controversy winding down? That would appear to be the case. *Black Athena Writes Back: Martin Bernal Responds to His Critics* appeared in 2001. Although it was largely a reply to *Black Athena Revisited*, the flames of the controversy did not flare up anew. Nor did the publication of *Black Athena 3* in 2006 reignite the controversy. Linguistic scholars had been highly critical of Bernal's ideas concerning ancient languages and what they revealed about cultural exchanges in the first and second volumes of *Black Athena*. The appearance of the third volume, which focuses on linguistic evidence, has not changed their opinions.[100] The promised fourth volume of evidence from religion and mythology appears to have been abandoned, but would it have mattered anyway? Another volume of essays defending Bernal, *Debating Black Athena*, announced in 2001 has so far failed to appear. It would appear that interest has waned, although the publication in 2008 of Mary Lefkowitz's memoir *History Lesson: A Race Odyssey* could well change that. Although much of her book is concerned with the troubles she experienced when she criticized the teaching of the pseudohistory promoted by Afrocentric extremists at Wellesley College, she also discusses Martin Bernal and *Black Athena* extensively and critically. *History Lesson* has been reviewed favourably for the most part but it is too early to say if that trend will continue or if Martin Bernal and his allies will gird themselves for battle once more.

RESULTS OF THE CONTROVERSY

> We cannot restore old policies
> Or follow an antique drum. T. S. ELIOT[101]

With all the discussion, debate and rancour that came out of the *Black Athena* controversy, what were the results? Did Bernal convince people that his Revised Ancient Model was the most competitively plausible interpretation of the Bronze Age Mediterranean's history? So far the answer is no. Besides the numerous factual refutations of Bernal's research, it has been pointed out that his broad argument for Egyptian and Levantine influences on Greece is an approach that his contemporaries and predecessors in the study of ancient history had been following for some time.[102] Even the Afrocentric aspects of Bernal's interpretations are hardly original to him. Early suggestions that *Black Athena* represented a paradigm shift of Kuhnian proportions have proved to be mistaken.[103] Others do give Bernal credit for shaking the fields of ancient history and Classics out of a sort of complacency by forcing them to examine long-unexamined assumptions about their disciplines. The public attention focused on the *Black Athena* controversy has revived interest in the Classics and ancient history at many universities. Suddenly these supposedly stodgy disciplines have been shown to be relevant to the life and thought of people living in the present, whether they are inside or outside higher education.[104]

At the same time Bernal and *Black Athena* have suffered a series of seemingly irrefutable confutations by experts in the various subfields of ancient studies. At an early stage of the *Black Athena* controversy in 1991 Michael Poliakoff made the damning assessment that 'The sum of a series of weak or unprovable arguments does not often add up to one strong one, and *Black Athena's* readers will need to ask just how many real props are left for Bernal's ambitious synthesis.'[105] Gerda Lerner echoed Poliakoff in 1993, pointing out that 'Bernal based his argument on evidence from linguistics, historical chronology, archaeology, myths, religion, and art history, and he was promptly found wanting to a greater or lesser degree in each of these fields by the appropriate specialists.'[106] The pinnacle of unfavourable criticism of Bernal came in 1996 with the publication of *Black Athena Revisited*. Most of its twenty essays present strong indictments of the quality of Bernal's scholarship in which, as John Coleman put it, 'The lack of scholarly method, of "disciplinary rigour," is everywhere apparent.' Mario Liverani was equally harsh, 'Hardly a single chapter (or even page) of *Black Athena* escapes the

blame of ignoring correct methodology, adopting old-fashioned explanations, and omitting relevant data and literature.' Linguistic
scholars Jay H. Jasanoff and Alan Nussbaum went so far as to classify Bernal's work with the pseudo-linguistic and pseudohistorical
writings of Barry Fell.[107] Generally most reviewers of *Black Athena
Revisited* viewed it as definitely discrediting *Black Athena* as a work
of scholarship. In the judgement of Jasper Griffin, 'From the stand-
point of scholarly inquiry and academic discussion as we know it,
there can, I think, be no doubt that all the positive assertions of his
[Bernal's] two large volumes have been refuted.' John Ray concluded
his review of *Black Athena Revisited* saying, 'So Bernal's book is
dead.'[108] Bernal and *Black Athena*, however, might well have replied
that the reports of their deaths were very much exaggerated.

BLACK ATHENA AND THE PROBLEM OF AUTHORITY

> But the mortallest enemy unto Knowledge, and that which hath done
> the greatest execution upon truth, hath been a peremptory adhesion
> unto Authority, and more especially, the establishing of our belief
> upon the dictates of Antiquity. SIR THOMAS BROWNE[109]

Jasper Griffin, even as he positively reviewed *Black Athena Revisited*'s demolition of Bernal, recognized that, 'an ordinary scholarly
book, receiving such crushing criticisms on so many fronts, would
be annihilated. It can be predicted with confidence that such will not,
in North America, be the fate of *Black Athena*.'[110] Susan Marchand
and Anthony Grafton would the next year in 1997 express wonder at
how much positive forbearance that classicists had shown Bernal.

> These paeans [to Bernal], which often provide little more than
> comic distraction in the course of Bernal's evisceration by a
> specialist in yet another field, puzzle us. For intellectual history
> does have a few modest standards – standards not identical
> with, but certainly related to, those that obtain in the older and
> better established field of classical scholarship. And Bernal's
> work violates every one of these, so egregiously and often so
> implausibly, that it seems extraordinary to find it cited with
> respect by scholars who would not welcome – or forgive – a
> similar approach to the study of the ancient world.[111]

Meanwhile Bernal was not sleeping. He wrote letters protesting the
one-sided nature of the essays in *Black Athena Revisited* and the editors' refusal to let him contribute to the volume. Eventually in 2001

he produced *Black Athena Writes Back*, which used about half of its over 500 pages to attack the arguments of *Black Athena Revisited*. Even earlier, in 1999, Jacques Berlinerblau dismissed the traditionalist scholars' claims to victory over Bernal as an 'optical illusion' based on their ignoring his substantial support from radical scholars.[112] That is most certainly true, but it is odd that Bernal's defenders have not rushed into print to support him.

Berlinerblau has described Bernal as a 'heretic' in the world of higher education. By 'heretic', Berlinerblau means that Bernal agitates from within the academic establishment but as a disciplinary outsider who challenges scholarly orthodoxies in academic fields that are not his speciality. Furthermore, Berlinerblau sees nothing dishonourable in Bernal's heresy. In fact he advocates that all academic disciplines need one or two heretics like Bernal to keep the creative and imaginative aspects of the scholarly enterprise alive.[113]

Berlinerblau's discussion of Bernal's heresy brings up the subject of epistimology, or the aspect of it concerned with the problem of establishing authority in the evaluation of scholarship. Bernal has argued that consciously or unconsciously scholars are very much affected by intellectual, political and cultural influences around them when they are forming their interpretations and conclusions. Scholars such as Berlinerblau and Cheryl Johnson-Odim agreed with Bernal's assessment although Berlinerblau refers to it as a 'rather bland sociological truism'. Other scholars, such as Frank M. Turner at the very beginning of the *Black Athena* controversy, contend that Bernal has taken the idea of subjective scholarship too far because it seems that *Black Athena* 'suggests that all knowledge – or what we regard as scholarly knowledge – is merely ideology'. Much of the training and ethos of scholarship concerns the effort to achieve as much objectivity as possible in the pursuit of the best approximation of the truth possible. As Turner notes, the level of professionalism among scholars has never been higher. Nonetheless Bernal views the whole enterprise of scholarship as a pretty hopeless morass of subjectivity and relativism which has been heavily influenced by racist and anti-Semitic prejudices, *except* his own work.[114]

Such a view of scholarship is corrosive of concepts of authority, objectivity and factual evidence. For Bernal, Berlinerblau and other radical scholars, everything is relative. That relativism explains why even though many highly trained experts have refuted all of the most important claims of *Black Athena* and piled up lists of errors of greater or lesser significance, yet the book retains a high level of respect. The situation leaves many scholars mystified. Trained to believe that sloppiness and factual errors will fatally undermine a scholar's reputation for reliability and that blatant subjectivity will throw suspicion on a scholar's conclusions, they find Bernal's survival and success flying in the face of their scholarly values. Some critics react in anger and strike back. Others try to find a middle ground that reconciles realism and relativism in scholarship. Another approach is to defend traditional scholarship as basically objective and the most effective way to advance knowledge. If one accepts the values and the standards of traditional scholarship it is possible to distinguish between sound scholarship and the extremist scholarship that degenerates into pseudohistory.[115] But, as Mary Lefkowitz has pointed out, the post-modernist climate of contemporary academics provides a protective environment for Bernal and his radical and Afrocentric allies. Their epistemological attitudes place some serious impediments in the way of a scholarly repudiation of *Black Athena*.

> First, there is the deconstructive notion that all historical writing is fiction, and that therefore any history is potentially true, or at least as persuasive as any other. Then there is the lively notion that anything is possible: *si potest esse, est*. And most important, there is the deep and lasting resentment of centuries of European supremacy by the peoples of the African diaspora.[116]

Martin Bernal has tapped into all three of these pathologies of modern scholarship in his researching, writing, and marketing of *Black Athena*.

What is it that motivated Bernal? If we take him at his word, his political goal was 'to lessen European cultural arrogance'.[117] One would have thought that World Wars I and II, the Great Depression, Fascism, Stalinism and the Holocaust had already accomplished that goal quite effectively. Bernal has also steadfastly maintained that he believes that his Revised Ancient Model is the most competitively plausible interpretation of ancient history. His background also programmed him for academic heresy and radicalism. His father was John Desmond Bernal, a respected scientist, who was also a committed communist and political activist. Early on Martin Bernal exhibited the same political engagement, which manifested itself in opposition to the Vietnam War and sympathy for the Maoist cause in the People's Republic of China. Then in 1975, as he describes it, Bernal suffered a midlife crisis. After becoming more conscious of his Jewish roots, Bernal began to study Hebrew. In the course of that study he began to discern patterns and anomalies in ancient histories and languages. Reading the works of Cyrus Gordon and

Michael Astour further persuaded him that he was on to something important. That something became *Black Athena*, his yet unfinished *magnum opus*.[118]

Others read Bernal's midlife crisis a bit differently. Guy McLean Rogers sees Bernal's personal crisis as an identity crisis. Bernal's subsequent scholarly production basically imposed that identity crisis on to the history of the Bronze Age Mediterranean. Such a view serves to explain Bernal's extraordinary pugnaciousness in the defence of his ideas, his manic marketing of *Black Athena* to the media and the public and his manifest desire for attention by everyone and anyone. For Bernal it was not a case of how he would be remembered, it was enough that he be remembered. Fame and notoriety became conflated. Needless to say Bernal reacted with derision to Rogers's psychoanalysis.[119]

Rogers, however, is not a lone voice crying in the wilderness. It is clear that Bernal likes all the attention that his *Black Athena* has generated, which goes a long way to explain those provocative actions of his that seemed designed to goad his critics into frenzied rage. If someone sat out deliberately to manufacture an academic controversy, no more effective course of action or set of rhetorical strategies could have been devised than those employed by Martin Bernal.

A survey of the *Black Athena* controversy reveals a ball of confusion apparently seeking to discredit traditional scholarship and replace it with a radical, politicized relativism. Its triumph would be the nadir of objective and empirical knowledge. But would it not be amusing if Bernal's true purpose was exactly the opposite? What if he actually wanted to strengthen traditional scholarship and to discredit radical scholarship? Perhaps Bernal is engaged in an immensely elaborate practical joke similar to the one pulled by Alan Sokal on the post-modernist editors of *Social Texts*.[120] Post-modernists continually push the idea that all knowledge and perception is simply a social construct, that there is no objective reality. The implication is that all ideas are equal, neither better or worse, good or bad. Post-modernists would argue that history is a fiction, a created story, and that so too are the endeavours of science. There are no objective truths or facts. Such a view is anathema to the scientific enterprise and post-modernists have long lamented their inability to find a scientist with a post-modernist worldview. Then, out of the blue, Sokal submitted a manuscript to *Social Texts* that subjected the study of physics to a post-modern deconstruction. The over-eager editors pounced on the opportunity and promptly published his piece. Unfortunately for them, Sokal's article was a hoax, a mishmash of jargon that he had concocted. As soon as it was published he announced what he had done, to the immense embarrassment of the editors of *Social Texts*. Sokal's point was to demonstrate the intellectual bankruptcy of the post-modernism of the radical scholars. What if the perpetration of a similar hoax has been Martin Bernal's plan all along, only his joke was far more elaborate than Sokal's? We can imagine a sort of deathbed confession at which Bernal reveals that he did not really believe any of what he had written in *Black Athena*. And then with his last breath, he says,

> 'Beauty is truth, truth beauty,' – that is all
> Ye know on earth, and all ye need to know.

But at this point, we too have entered the twilight zone of history and it is time to pull back from the abyss of fantasy.

References

INTRODUCTION

1 Geoffrey Barraclough, *History in the Changing World* (Oxford, 1956), pp. 24–5.
2 Abraham Lincoln, *Speeches and Writings 1859–1865*, ed. Don E. Fehrenbacher (New York, 1989), p. 415.
3 Robert Silverberg, *Mound Builders of Ancient America: The Archaeology of a Myth* (Greenwich, CT, 1968).
4 *Coast to Coast* AM website at www.coasttocoastam.com (accessed 14 October 2008). For the list of past guests click on 'Show Info' and then click on 'Guests'. Bell's show broadcast the idea that Comet Hale-Bopp was being followed by an alien spaceship which led some people to accuse him of provoking the suicide of the Heaven's Gate cultists. In 1998 the Council on Integrity in Media gave Bell the Snuffed Candle award for his encouraging of credulity and promotion of pseudoscience to the general public. See 'Art Bell' at http://en.wikipedia.org/wiki/Art_Bell.
5 Jane MacLaren Walsh, 'Legend of the Crystal Skulls: The Truth Behind Indiana Jones' Latest Quest', *Archaeology*, LXI/3 (May/June 2008), pp. 36–41. Brian Haughton, 'The Crystal Skull of Doom', in *Hidden History: Lost Civilizations, Secret Knowledge, and Ancient Mysteries* (New York, 2008), pp. 171–5, points out the problems with the provenance of the Mitchell-Hedges Skull and shows that other crystal skulls are of nineteenth-century manufacture. Also see Time-Life Books, *Feats and Wisdom of the Ancients* (Alexandria, VA, 1990), pp. 73–4 and esp. Chris Morton and C. L. Thomas, *The Mystery of the Crystal Skull*, 2nd edn [1997] (London, 2002) for good examples of sensationalism regarding crystal skulls. Both the History Channel and the Science Fiction Channel presented documentaries on the crystal skulls in anticipation of the appearance of *Indiana Jones and the Kingdom of the Crystal Skull*, titled respectively 'Indiana Jones and the Ultimate Quest' and 'Mystery of the Crystal Skulls'. They cover a lot of the same ground and provide good background for the movie. Unfortunately, although both discuss the research of Jane MacLaren Walsh, neither do any debunking and they present the ideas of professional scholars and pseudohistorians as equally valid. For a case study of this phenomenon see Christopher Hale, 'The Atlantean Box', in *Archaeological Fantasies: How Pseudoarchaeology Misrepresents the Past and Misleads the*

Public, ed. Garrett Fagan (London, 2006), pp. 235–58.

6 The *Bloodline* website is at www.bloodline-themovie.com, accessed 15 October 2008.

7 See the articles for 'Michael Baigent', 'Dan Brown', 'The Da Vinci Code', 'The Holy Blood and the Holy Grail', 'Richard Leigh' and 'Henry Lincoln' at http://en.wikipedia.org and Michael Baigent, Richard Leigh and Henry Lincoln, *Holy Blood, Holy Grail* (New York, 1982).

8 Graham Philips, *The End of Eden: The Comet that Changed Civilization* (Santa Fe, NM, 2007) and Joel Levy, *The Atlas of Atlantis and Other Lost Civilizations: Discover the History and Wisdom of Atlantis, Lemuria, Mu, and Other Ancient Civilizations* (London, 2007).

9 See the American Historical Association statement on Holocaust denial at www.historians.org/perspectives/issues/1991/9112/9112RES. CFM, accessed 15 October 2008.

10 The following paragraphs on David Irving and Holocaust denial are based on Deborah E. Lipstadt, *Denying the Holocaust: The Growing Assault on Truth and Memory* (New York, 1993) and *History on Trial: My Day in Court with David Irving* (New York, 2005); Richard J. Evans, *Lying about Hitler: History, Holocaust, and the David Irving Trial* (New York, 2001); D. D. Guttenplan, *The Holocaust on Trial* (New York, 2001); Michael Shermer, *Denying the Holocaust: Who Says the Holocaust Never Happened and Why Do They Say It* (Berkeley, CA, 2000) and the Wikipedia articles on 'Deborah Lipstadt' and 'David Irving'.

11 Christopher Hale, *Himmler's Crusade: The Nazi Expedition to Find the Origins of the Aryan Race* (Hoboken, NJ, 2003); Heather Pringle, *The Master Plan: Himmler's Scholars and the Holocaust* (New York, 2006); Trevor Ravenscroft, *The Spear of Destiny* (New York, 1973) and *The Cup of Destiny: The Quest for the Holy Grail* [1982] (York Beach, ME, 1997).

12 Samathi Ramaswamy, *The Lost Land of Lemuria: Fabulous Geographies, Catastrophic Histories* (Berkeley, CA, 2004).

13 Paul K. Conkin and Roland N. Stromberg, *The Heritage and Challenge of History* (New York, 1971), p. 131.

14 Colin Campbell, 'The Cult, the Cultic Milieu and Secularization', in *A Sociological Yearbook of Religion in Britain 5*, ed. Michael Hill (London, 1972), pp. 119–36.

15 Kendrick Frazier, 'The Path Ahead: Opportunities, Challenges, and an Expanded View', *Skeptical Inquirer*, XI (Fall 1986), pp. 2–4.

16 For a good discussion of this phenomenon see John Grant, *Discarded Science* (Wisley, Surrey, 2006).

17 Jason Colavito, *The Cult of Alien Gods: H. P. Lovecraft and Extraterrestrial Pop Culture* (Amherst, NY, 2005).

18 G. E. Daniel, *Myth or Legend* (New York, 1968), pp. 14–15.

19 Zecharia Sitchin, *The Twelfth Planet* (New York, 1978), esp. ch. 7, 'The Epic of Creation', pp. 204–35. Modern astronomers have abandoned the theory that asteroids are the remnants of planets that had catastrophically broken up or exploded. The current scientific consensus is that asteroids are materials that never managed to coalesce into a planet due to interference from Jupiter's gravitational field. See the Wikipedia articles 'Asteroids', 'Asteroid Belt' and 'Planetesimals'.

20 Garrett G. Fagan, 'Diagnosing Pseudoarchaeology', in *Archaeological Fantasies*, pp. 23–46.

21　Miguel de Cervantes, *Don Quixote* [1605–15] (Chicago, IL, 1952), p. 23.
22　Mark Twain, *The Innocents Abroad* [1869] (New York, 1984), p. 248.

CHAPTER 1: ATLANTIS: MOTHER OF PSEUDOHISTORY

The title of this chapter is a play on *Atlantis: Mother of Empires*, the title of Robert B. Stacy-Judd's classic of Atlantology, which first appeared in 1939, reprinted by Adventures Unlimited Press in 1999.

1　Benjamin Jowett, trans. and ed., *The Dialogues of Plato*, 4 vols (Oxford, 1953), III, p. 703.
2　Lewis Spence, *The Problem of Atlantis*, 2nd edn (London, 1925), pp. 231–2.
3　James Bramwell, *Lost Atlantis* (New York, 1938), p. 137.
4　This section describing the setting and the eruption of Bronze-Age Thera is based on the following sources: Rodney Castleden, *Atlantis Destroyed* (London, 1998), pp. 97 and 114–33; J. V. Luce, *The End of Atlantis* (St Albans, Herts, 1970), pp. 45–85 and Walter L. Friedrich, *Fire in the Sea: The Santorini Volcano: Natural History and the Legend of Atlantis* (Cambridge, 2000), who reconstructs the eruption of Thera somewhat differently from Castleden.
5　A. G. Galanopoulos and Edward Bacon, *Atlantis: The Truth behind the Legend* (Indianapolis, IN, 1969), pp. 193–9. Also see the comments of Richard Ellis, *Imagining Atlantis* (New York, 1998), pp. 165–7.
6　L. Sprague de Camp, *Lost Continents: The Atlantis Theme in History, Science, and Literature* [1954] (New York, 1970), pp. 237–8.
7　Eberhard Zangger, *The Flood from Heaven: Deciphering the Atlantis Legend* (New York, 1992) for Troy and Peter James, *The Sunken Kingdom: The Atlantis Mystery Solved* (London, 1995) for Sipylus.
8　E. M. Whitshaw, *Atlantis in Andalucia* (London, 1928) reprinted as *Atlantis in Spain* and Edwin Björkman, *The Search for Atlantis* (New York, 1927), pp. 73–119. Also see the comments of Ellis, *Imagining Atlantis*, p. 36.
9　Jowett, *Plato*, III, p. 781.
10　Sprague de Camp, *Lost Continents*, pp. 314–18, has compiled a list of Atlantis theories and their authors to 1954. Many more books and articles have been written in the following fifty years although most are enhanced or recycled versions of the older theories.
11　Plato, *Timaeus* in *The Dialogues of Plato*, trans. Benjamin Jowett in *Great Books of the Western World* (Chicago, IL, 1952), p. 446 column A.
12　Ibid.
13　Ibid.
14　Plato, *Critias*, in *The Dialogues of Plato*, p. 482A.
15　Ibid., pp. 484A&B.
16　Ibid., pp. 481B and 482A.
17　Ibid., pp. 485A&B.
18　Bramwell, *Lost Atlantis*, p. 137.
19　Plato, *Timaeus*, pp. 444A&B.
20　Andrew Collins, *Gateway to Atlantis: The Search for the Source of a Lost Civilization* (New York, 2000), p. 68.
21　Plutarch, 'Solon', in *The Rise and Fall of Athens: Nine Greek Lives* (London, 1960), p. 76.

22 P.B.S. Andrews, 'Larger than Africa or Asia?', *Greece & Rome*, XIV (1967), pp. 78–9. Andrews' article supports the theory that volcanic Thera was the model for Plato's Atlantis story.

23 Plato, *Timaeus and Critias*, trans. Desmond Lee (London, 1971), pp. 22–3 and Daniel A. Dombrowski, 'Atlantis and Plato's Philosophy', *Apeiron*, XV (1981), pp. 125–6.

24 Lee in Plato, *Timaeus and Critias*, p. 23.

25 Jowett, *Plato*, III, 702.

26 Strabo, *Geography* (Cambridge, MA, 1924), vol. III, iii, 6.

27 Collins, *Gateway to Atlantis*, p. 99.

28 Alan Cameron, 'Crantor and Posidonius in Atlantis', *Classical Quarterly*, III/1 (1983), pp. 81–5.

29 Plutarch, 'Solon', pp. 75–6.

30 Sprague de Camp, *Lost Continents*, pp. 18–19.

31 Lee Eldridge Huddleston, *Origins of the American Indians: European Concepts, 1492–1729*, (Austin, TX, 1967) and Ronald H. Fritze, *Legend and Lore of the Americas before 1492: An Encyclopedia of Visitors, Explorers, and Immigrants* (Santa Barbara, CA, 1993).

32 Huddleston, *Origins of the American Indians*, p. 25.

33 Agustín de Zárate, *The Discovery and Conquest of Peru* (Baltimore, MD, 1968), pp. 21–4.

34 Pedro Sarmiento de Gamboa, *History of the Incas*, ed. Clements Markham (London, 1907), pp. 15–27.

35 Huddleston, *Origins of the American Indians*, p. 112.

36 José de Acosta, *Natural and Moral History of the Indies* (Durham, NC, 2002), pp. 67–8.

37 Acosta, *Natural and Moral History*, pp. 43–4, 67–8, 98 and Huddleston, *Origins of the American Indians*, pp. 51, 56, 80.

38 Huddleston, *Origins of the American Indians*, pp. 60–76.

39 William van Wyck, *The Sinister Shepherd: A Translation of Girolomo Fracastoro's 'Syphilidis Sive De Morbo Gallico Libri Tres'* (New York, 1992), pp. 68–9 and Paul Jordan, *The Atlantis Syndrome* (Stroud, Gloucestershire, 2001), pp. 52–3.

40 Sprague de Camp, *Lost Continents*, pp. 28–9.

41 Michel de Montaigne, 'Of Cannibals', *Essays* in *Great Books of the Western World* (Chicago, IL, 1952), pp. 92A&B.

42 Richard Hakluyt, *Principall Navigations, Voyages, Traffiques, and Discoveries of the English Nation*, 8 vols (London, n.d.), I, 48.

43 Huddleston, *Origins of the American Indians*, p. 65.

44 Antoine Febre d'Olivet (1767–1825) was a French writer on the Bible and Hebrew whose books influenced various occultists. He used the Atlantis in America theory in his writings and based his belief on Bacon's *New Atlantis*. See Antonello Gerbi, *The Dispute of the New World: The History of a Polemic, 1750–1900* (Pittsburgh, PA, 1973), p. 339.

45 Sprague de Camp, *Lost Continents*, p. 29; Huddleston, *Origins of the American Indians*, p. 65 and John Josselyn, *An Account of Two Voyages* (Boston, MA, 1865), pp. 167 and 169.

46 Huddleston, *Origins of the American Indians*, pp. 19, 106–7.

47 Ibid., pp. 89–90 and Gerbi, *Dispute of the New World*, pp. 235n, 398–9, 400, 447n, 457n, 568, 615. Sprague de Camp credits Georges-Louis Leclerc, Comte de Buffon (1707–1788) with holding the Atlantis in America theory (see *Lost Continents*, p. 29) and probably based his opinion on James Bramwell's *Lost Atlantis* (see p. 29). Buffon did not

hold the Atlantis in America theory because it would have undermined his argument that the Americas were relatively young continents. An academic adversary of Buffon's, Gian Rinaldo Carli (1720–1795), however, used the Atlantis in America theory in his *American Letters* (1777). See Gerbi, *Dispute of the New World*, pp. 3–34, esp. pp. 14–15 for Buffon and pp. 233–9 for Carli and also Henry Steele Commanger and Elmo Giordanetti, *Was America a Mistake?: An Eighteenth-Century Controversy* (New York, 1967), pp. 49–74.

48 Bramwell, *Lost Atlantis*, p. 109.

49 Jordan, *Atlantis Syndrome*, pp. 53–4 and 201–4 and Scott McLemee, 'Athanasius Kircher, Dude of Wonders', first published in the 28 May 2002 issue of the *Chronicle of Higher Education* and available at http://chronicle.com/free/2002/05/2002052804n.htm (accessed 23 Novemeber 2008).

50 David King, *Finding Atlantis: A True Story of Genius, Madness, and an Extraordinary Quest for a Lost World* (New York, 2005) is a modern biography of Rudbeck.

51 Ignatius Donnelly, *Atlantis: The Antediluvian World* (New York, 1976), p. 3.

52 Martin Ridge, *Ignatius Donnelly: Portrait of a Politician* (Chicago, IL, 1962), p. 197. Subsequent details of Donnelly's life and career are based on Ridge's fine biography along with the excellent essay 'The Wild Jackass of the Prairie: The Heroism of Ignatius Donnelly', in Roger G. Kennedy, *Rediscovering America* (Boston, MA, 1990).

53 Recently a group of geophysicists has theorized that a comet did explode over North America about 13,000 years ago. The explosion wiped out the larger mammals and human inhabitants of North America while triggering the cold phase of the Younger-Dryas period. Comet debris is credited with the mysterious depressions known as the Carolina Bays. While this research is tentative and its conclusions are controversial, it is eerily similar to what Donnelly proposed in *Ragnarok*. See Rex Dalton, 'Archaeology Blast in the Past', *Nature*, CDXLVII (16 May 2007), pp. 256–7 and Robin McKie, 'Diamonds Tell Tales of Comet that Killed Off the Cavemen', *Observer* (20 May 2007), available at http://observer.guardian.co.uk/print/0,,329882682-119093,00.html, accessed 14 October 2008.

54 Ignatius Donnelly, *Caesar's Column: A Story of the Twentieth Century*, ed. Nicholas Ruddick (Middletown, CT, 2003) is a modern scholarly edition with an excellent introduction that places the novel in the context of Donnelly's career and late Gilded Age America.

55 Samuel Schoenbaum, *Shakespeare's Lives* (Oxford, 1991), pp. 404–8.

56 Ridge, *Ignatius Donnelly*, pp. 201–2.

57 Sprague de Camp, *Lost Continents*, pp. 47–54 and Sumathi Ramaswamy, *The Lost Land of Lemuria: Fabulous Geographies, Catastrophic Histories* (Berkeley, CA, 2004), pp. 19–52.

58 Leonard Alberstadt, 'Alexander Winchell's Preadamites – A Case for Dismissal from Vanderbilt University', *Earth Science History*, XIII/2 (1994), pp. 97–112.

59 E. F. Bleiler, 'Ignatius Donnelly and Atlantis', in Donnelly, *Atlantis*, pp. xi–xvi.

60 Donnelly, *Atlantis*, pp. 1–2.

61 Ridge, *Ignatius Donnelly*, p. 198.

62 Charles Portis, *Masters of Atlantis* [1985] (Woodstock, NY, 2000), p. 124. This novel is a satire of the excesses of the occult movement.

Lamar Jimmerson is the protagonist of the story and is the leader of the Gnomon Society, a Theosophical or Rosicrusian-like organization. Fanny Jimmerson is his long-suffering wife. The quote is a statement of Fanny Jimmerson to Lamar Jimmerson.

63 My account of H. P. Blavatsky, Henry Steele Olcott and the origins of the Theosophical Society is largely based on Peter Washington, *Madame Blavatsky's Baboon: A History of the Mystics, Mediums, and Misfits Who Brought Spiritualism to America* (New York, 1995), pp. 26–46; Bruce F. Campbell, *Ancient Wisdom Revived: A History of the Theosophical Movement* (Berkeley, CA, 1980), pp. 1–29; Rosemary Ellen Gulley, 'Blavatsky, Madame Helena Petrovna' and 'Theosophy' in *Harper's Encyclopedia of Mystical & Paranormal Experience* (New York, 1991). For a recent summary of the history of Theosophy see James A. Santucci, 'The Theosophical Society', in *Controversial New Religions*, ed. James R. Lewis and Jesper Aagaard Petersen (Oxford, 2005), pp. 259–94.

64 Washington, *Madame Blavatsky's Baboon*, p. 78.

65 Campbell, *Ancient Wisdom Revived*, pp. 32–5.

66 H. P. Blavatsky, *Isis Unveiled*, 2 vols (Wheaton, IL, 1972), I, pp. 413, 529, 545, 591–5.

67 Washington, *Madame Blavatsky's Baboon*, chs 3–8 and Campbell, *Ancient Wisdom Revived*, ch. 4.

68 Washington, *Madame Blavatsky's Baboon*, pp. 78–84 and Campbell, *Ancient Wisdom Revived*, pp. 87–95.

69 Quoted in Washington, *Madame Blavatsky's Baboon*, p. 83. Hodgson's report is available online at http://blavatskyarchives.com/sprrpcontents.htm, accessed 14 October 2008.

70 Vernon Harrison, *H. P. Blavatsky and the SPR: An Examination of the Hodgson Report of 1885* (Pasadena, CA, 1997). The monograph contains Harrison's original article in the *Journal of the Society for Psychical Research* and additional material. It is available online at www.theosociety.org/pasadena/hpb-spr/hpbspr-h.htm.

71 Campbell, *Ancient Wisdom Revived*, pp. 40–48 and Washington, *Madame Blavatsky's Baboon*, pp. 92–3.

72 Sprague de Camp, *Lost Continents*, pp. 54–70 and Stephen Williams, *Fantastic Archaeology: The Wild Side of North American Prehistory* (Philadelphia, PA, 1991), pp. 140–45 for the contributions of Blavatsky's ideas to the pseudohistory of Atlantis.

73 H. P. Blavatsky, *The Secret Doctrine: The Synthesis of Science, Religion, and Philosophy*, 2 vols (London, 1888), II, pp. 86–108.

74 Ibid., pp. 109–30.

75 Ibid., pp. 131–85.

76 Ibid., pp. 191–250.

77 W. Scott-Elliot, *The Story of Atlantis & The Lost Lemuria* (London, 1925).

78 Washington, *Madama Blavatsky's Baboon*, pp. 152–7.

79 Gary Lachman, *Rudolf Steiner: An Introduction to His Life and Work* (New York, 2007), pp. 194–8, 214–33.

80 Lachman, *Rudolf Steiner*, p. 146 and Rudolf Steiner, *Atlantis: The Fate of the Lost Land and Its Secret Knowledge: Selections from the Work of Rudolf Steiner* (Forest Row, East Sussex, 2001) for a sampling of Steiner's views of Atlantis.

81 Frances A. Yates, *The Rosicrucian Enlightenment* (London, 1972) for a

scholarly overview of the history of Rosicrucianism.

82 For an example of current Rosicrucian views about Atlantis see 'Atlantis', *Rosicrucian Digest*, LXXXIV/3 (2006), a theme issue focusing on Atlantis. It includes excerpts from Plato, Sir Francis Bacon, H. P. Blavatsky, Ignatius Donnell and Jules Verne and some contemporary writings by Rosicrucians.

83 Edgar Evans Cayce, *Edgar Cayce on Atlantis* (New York, 1968), pp. 26–7.

84 Wendy Stein, *Atlantis Opposing Views* (San Diego, CA, 1989), pp. 46–57, provides a clear and concise summary of Cayce's concepts about the history of Atlantis and is the foundation for this paragraph and those that follow.

85 Rosemary Ellen Gulley, 'Edgar Cayce', in *Harper Encyclopedia of Mystical and Paranormal Experience* (New York, 1991), p. 84.

86 Geoffrey Ashe, *Atlantis: Lost Lands, Ancient Wisdom* (New York, 1992), pp. 12–13, 88–9 and Sprague de Camp, *Lost Continents*, pp. 71–2.

87 Some sources list Knight's place of birth as Dexter, New Mexico, which is near Roswell.

88 Gail M. Harley, 'From Atlantis to America: JZ Knight Encounters Ramtha', in *Controversial New Religions*, ed. James R. Lewis and Jesper Aagaard Petersen (Oxford, 2005), pp. 319–30 and 'J. Z. Knight (b. 1946)' in *Harper's Encyclopedia of Mystical and Paranormal Experience*, ed. Rosemary Ellen Guley (New York, 1991). See also the entries on JZ Knight at www.answers.com/topic/JZ.Knight; http://en.wikipedia.org.wiki/JZ_Knight; and http://the-psychic-detective.com/JZ.Knight.htm..

89 Jowett, *Plato*, III, p. 787.

90 Plato, *Timaeus*, p. 446A.

91 Voltaire, *The Philosophy of History* in *The Works of Voltaire: Romances and Philosophy* (New York, 1927), p. 372.

92 L. Sprague de Camp and Willy Ley, *Lands Beyond* [1953] (New York, 1993), p. 9.

93 In 2003 Sarmast published the first edition of his *Discovery of Atlantis: The Startling Case for the Island of Cyprus* with Origin Press. According to Sarmast's website, www.discoveryofatlantis.com (accessed 14 October 2008), the book became a bestseller and started 'a global media frenzy'. The History Channel and Science Fiction Channel documentaries followed along with an expanded edition of the book, *Discovery of Atlantis: The Startling Case for the Island of Cyprus* (Tallahassee, FL, 2006). Sarmarst founded First Source Enterprises in 2004 to promote exploration of the eastern Mediterranean.

94 Sprague de Camp, *Lost Continents*, pp. 276–7.

95 H. P. Lovecraft, *The Thing on the Doorstep and Other Weird Stories*, ed. S.T. Joshi (New York, 2001) and *The Call of Cthulhu and Other Weird Stories*, ed. S.T. Joshi (New York, 1999). Besides the texts of the three stories, these editions include excellent explanatory notes.

96 H. P. Lovecraft, *Selected Letters 1925–1929*, ed. August Derleth and Donald Wandrei (Sauk City, WI, 1968), p. 253.

97 Ibid., p. 268.

98 L. Sprague de Camp, *Dark Valley Destiny: The Life of Robert E. Howard* (New York, 1983), pp. 85, 195–6, 223–4; 'Robert E. Howard's Library', an appendix in Don Herron, ed., *The Dark Barbarian: The Writings of Robert E. Howard, A Critical Anthology* (Westport, CT,

1984), pp. 183–200. Not all of Howard's library has been preserved and some of his reading could have been borrowed from friends or libraries.

99 Sprague de Camp, *Dark Valley Destiny*, pp. 195–6, 223–5 and Lauric Guillaud, 'Barbarism and Decadence', *The Barbaric Triumph: A Critical Anthology on the Writings of Robert E. Howard*, ed. Dan Herron (Rockville, MD, 2004), pp. 81, 83–4.

100 Scott Connors, 'Twilight of the Gods: Howard and the *Völkstumbewe-gung*', in *The Barbaric Triumph*, pp. 97–9. Connor quotes Howard's letter to Preece on p. 98. The complete letter can be found in Robert E. Howard, *Selected Letters 1923–1930*, ed. Glenn Lord with Rusty Burke and S. T. Joshi (West Warwick, RI, 1989), p. 20. Robert M. Price, an-other Howard scholar, definitely feels that Howard had some difficulty distinguishing between history and fiction, see his 'Introduction' to Howard, *Selected Letters 1931–1936*, p. v.

101 Clive Cussler, *Atlantis Found* (New York, 1999), pp. [vii] and 533–4. Cussler's novels *Treasure* (1988) and *Serpent* (1999) also use plots based on fringe archaeology and pseudohistory.

102 Luanne Hudson, 'East is East and West is West? A Regional Comparison of Cult Belief Patterns', in *Cult Archaeology and Creationism*, ed. Francis B. Harrold and Ramond A. Eve (Iowa City, IA, 1987), pp. 49–67, but esp. p. 57.

103 Thomas Hobbes, *Leviathan* [1651] (Chicago, IL, 1952), p. 56.

104 Jordan, *Atlantis Syndrome*, pp. 183 and 279–80; Sprague de Camp, *Lands Beyond*, pp. 21–2; Christopher Hale, *Himmler's Crusade: The Nazi Expedition to Find the Origins of the Aryan Race* (Hoboken, NJ, 2003), pp. 30–31, 86, 119–20; Heather Pringle, *The Master Plan: Himmler's Scholars and the Holocaust* (New York, 2006), pp. 59–61, 149, 179.

CHAPTER 2: WHO'S ON FIRST? THE PSEUDOHISTORY OF THE DISCOVERY AND SETTLEMENT OF ANCIENT AMERICA

1 Gonzalo Fernández de Oviedo, *The General and Natural History of the Indies: Part I* [1535], in *Oviedo on Columbus*, ed. Jesus Carrillo, *Repertorium Columbianum IX* (Turnhout, 2000), p. 44.

2 Nicholas Noyes, 'Prefatory Poem', in Cotton Mather, *Magnalia Christi Americana* [1702] (Cambridge, MA, 1977).

3 The Kennewick Man controversy generated a number of books by par-ticipants and outside observers. Unfortunately the rush to publish the first book about the Kennewick man controversy resulted in most of them appearing before the final legal resolution of the court case. Aftershocks of the controversy continue as the supporters of the Native Americans and the scientists continue to introduce conflicting legisla-tion in the United States Congress. Reading the various books is a sort of Rashomon experience as there are as many versions of the story of the Kennewick controversy as there are books with differing and con-flicting heroes and villains. The relevant books are J. M. Adovasio, *The First Americans: In Pursuit of Archaeology's Greatest Mystery* (New York, 2002), pp. 243–54, 291–2; Jeff Benedict, *No Bone Unturned: The Adventures of a Top Smithsonian Forensic Scientist and the Legal Battle for America's Oldest Skeleton* (New York, 2003), pp. 95–281; James C. Chatters, *Ancient Encounters: Kennewick Man and the First Americans*

(New York, 2001), Elaine Dewar, *Bones: Discovering the First Americans* (New York, 2001), pp. 28–31, 102–9, 122–225, 417–47, 497–518, 545–52; Roger Downey, *Riddle of the Bones: Politics, Science, Race, and the Story of Kennewick Man* (New York, 2000); David Hurst Thomas, *Skull Wars: Kennewick Man, Archaeology, and the Battle for Native American Identity* (New York, 2000), pp. xvii–xxv, xxxiv–xxxix, 112–19, 226–43, 267, 275. The Benedict and Chatters books are by or about scientists involved in the controversy. Adovasio is sympathetic to the scientists' position. Downey is definitely pro-Native American and very anti-James Chatters, but lacks depth. Thomas's book provides a fascinating history of American anthropology marred by an excess of political correctness. Dewar wavers between sympathy to the Native American and the scientific positions and while she supplies much wonderful information and insights about the study of both North and South American prehistory, she concludes on a note of ambivalence.

Many websites discuss the Kennewick Man controversy but the three most useful and authoritative are the Kennewick Man Virtual Interpretive Center (www.tri-cityherald.com/kman/) established by the *Tri-City Herald*, the newspaper of the Kennewick area. It includes an archive of news stories from the *Tri-City Herald*, a detailed timeline, the texts of legal documents relating to the controversy, photos, and biographical sketches of the participants. The Friends of America's Past is a group opposed to the repatriation and reburial of very ancient human remains without a tribal affiliation that is demonstrable in a scholarly and legal sense. Its website (www.friendsofpast.org) includes a 'Kennewick Man Case' section, with a useful chronology and the texts of news stories, comments, press releases and court documents. The Burke Museum of Natural History and Culture at the University of Washington is currently the court-ordered repository for the remains of Kennewick Man. Its website (www.washington.edu/burkemuseum/kman) has a section 'Kennewick Man on Trial' which provides a chronology and background to the controversy. The National Park Service/US Department of the Interior website has a 'Kennewick Man' section (www.nps.gov/history/archaeology/Kennewick) that contains many of the documents concerning government studies of the Kennewick Man remains (websites accessed 15 October 2008).

4   'Skull Found on Shore of Columbia River', *Tri-City Herald* (Monday 29 July 1996) and 'Skull Likely Early White Settler', *Tri-City Herald* (Tuesday 30 July 1996) and Chatters, *Ancient Encounters*, pp. 20–21.

5   Thomas, *Skull Wars* and Dewar, *Bones* both contain considerable detail about these issues.

6   Chatters, *Ancient Encounters*, p. 35.

7   Dewar, *Bones* includes a good account of the politics of the US Army Corps of Engineers' clean up of the nuclear sites and the need for Native American cooperation.

8   Chatters, *Ancient Encounters*, pp. 50–54.

9   Downey, *Riddle of the Bones*, pp. 119–20; Dewar, *Bones*, pp. 103, 107; Chatters, *Ancient Encounters*, pp. 93, 104, 106, 111, 116; Adovasio, *First Americans*, p. 245; Thomas, *Skull Wars*, p. 118. The Asatru Folk Assembly maintains a website at www.runestone.org and there is another website that deals specifically with 'Kennewick Man and Asatru' at www.irminsul.org/arc/199704a.html. There is a useful

Wikipedia article at http://en.wikipedia.org/wiki/Asatru_Folk_Assembly. (Websites accessed 15 October 2008.)

10 The Kennewick Man Virtual Interpretive Center and the Friends of America's Past websites both provide information about the latest legislative efforts (see note 3 above).

11 Jose de Acosta, *Natural and Moral History of the Indies*, ed. Jane Mangan (Durham, NC, 2002), bk. 1, ch. 24, p. 71.

12 David J. Meltzer, *Search for the First Americans* (Washington, DC, 2003) is a good if somewhat dated overview of the state of academic knowledge about the peopling of the Americas. His chapter 'A History of the Controversy' provides the origins of the Clovis First Theory while 'North American Paleoindians' gives a concise description of Clovis culture and artefacts. J. M. Adovasio with Jake Page, *The First Americans: In Pursuit of Archaeology's Greatest Mystery* (New York, 2002) provides a complementary account in 'Goodbye Glacial Man; Hello, Clovis' and 'Timing is Everything'. For an interesting account of the history of North American archaeology that suffers from lapses of political correctness see Thomas, *Skull Wars*.

13 Meltzer, 'Find the Traces' and 'Who Were the First Americans?', in *Search*, has a good discussion of these matters. Adovasio and Page, *First Americans* has a good brief discussion of Thomas Dillehay's work at Monte Verde in ch. 8, 'Another Angle of View'. Thomas Dillehay, *The Settlement of the Americas: A New Prehistory* (New York, 2000) provides a detailed look at the findings from the archaeological site at Monte Verde, Chile, along with an overview of the state of the archaeology of the human settlement of South America. Elaine Dewar in *Bones* provides an outsider's look at the Kennewick Man controversy and the fluid state of knowledge about the peopling of the Americas.

14 Jon M. Erlandson, 'Anatomically Modern Humans Maritime Voyaging, and the Pleistocene Colonization of the Americas', in *The First Americans: The Pleistocene Colonization of the New World*, ed. Nina Jablonski (Berkeley, CA, 2002), pp. 59–92.

15 Dennis Stanford and Bruce Bradley, 'Ocean Trails and Prairie Paths? Thoughts about Clovis Origins', in *The First Americans*, ed. Jablonski, pp. 255–71. Chatters, *Ancient Encounters*, pp. 239–64, provides a good summary of the state of archaeological theories about the settling of North America. Adovasio and Page, *First Americans*, pp. 272–85, provides a more critical assessment of the same theories.

16 Discussions of the controversial Pedra Furada archaeological site and its dating and other aspects of South American archaeology can be found in Dewar, *Bones*, pp. 362–68 and chs 12 and 17. Adovasio and Page, *First Americans,* pp. 204–7 and Dillehay, *Settlement of the Americas*, pp. 187–96, provide sceptical views of the extremely old dates for Pedra Furada. Dillehay dismisses the idea of trans-oceanic contacts between South America and Africa or Australasia in his section 'Settlement of the Americas before 12,500 BC', in the entry 'First Settlement of the Americas', in Brian M. Fagan, ed., *The Companion to Archaeology* (New York, 1996).

17 Mark Twain, *The Innocents Abroad* [1869] (New York, 1984), p. 52.

18 Von Humboldt is quoted in Samuel Eliot Morison, *The European Discovery of America: The Northern Voyages, AD 500–1600* (New York, 1971), p. 81.

19 Nigel Davies, *Voyagers to the New World* (New York, 1979); Eugene R.

Fingerhut, *Explorers of Pre-Columbian America? The Diffusion-Inter-ventionist Controversy* (Claremont, CA, 1994) and *Who First Discovered America? A Critique of Pre-Columbian Voyages* (Claremont, CA, 1984); Ronald H. Fritze, *Legend and Lore of the Americas before 1492: An Encyclopedia of Visitors, Explorers, and Emigrants* (Santa Barbara, CA, 1993); Robert Wauchope, *Lost Tribes and Sunken Continents: Myth and Method in the Study of American Indians* (Chicago, IL, 1962) and Stephen Williams, *Fantastic Archaeology: The Wild Side of North American Prehistory* (Philadelphia, PA, 1991) are all debunking studies of pre-Columbian discovery theories by mainstream scholars. For a brief survey see Ronald Fritze, 'Goodbye Columbus: The Pseudohistory of Who Discovered America', *Skeptic* II/4 (1994), pp. 88–97, reprinted in Michael Shermer, *The Skeptic Encyclopedia of Pseudoscience*, 2 vols (Santa Barbara, CA, 2002), vol. II, pp. 567–79. For some examples of books that give credence to sundry theories of pre-Columbian contacts between the Old World and the Americas see Charles M. Boland, *They All Discovered America* (Garden City, NY, 1961); Donald Y. Gilmore and Linda S. McElroy, eds, *Across Before Columbus: Evidence for Transoceanic Contact with the Americas prior to 1492* (Edgecomb, ME, 1998); Cyrus Gordon, *Before Columbus: Links Between the Old World and Ancient America* (New York, 1971) and *Riddles in History* (New York, 1974); Patrick Huyghe, *Columbus Was Last* (New York, 1992); Frederick Pohl, *Atlantic Crossings Before Columbus* (New York, 1961) and Gunnar Thompson, *American Discovery: The Real Story* (Seattle, WA, 1992).

20 See the introductions to John L. Sorenson and Martin H. Raish, *Pre-Columbian Contacts with the Americas across the Oceans: An Anno-tated Bibliography*, 1st and 2nd edns, 2 vols (Provo, UT, 1990 and 1996).

21 Samuel Eliot Morison, *Admiral of the Ocean Sea: A Life of Christopher Columbus* (New York, 1942) is the classic biography of Columbus and the winner of a Pulitzer Prize. The book discusses Columbus' personal problems in chs 35, 41, 48 and 49. See also the more recent biography by Felipe Fernández-Armesto, *Columbus* (Oxford, 1991), esp. ch. 7 and pp. 177–86. For the legal battle of Columbus's heir see Otto Schoenrich, *The Legacy of Columbus: The Historical Litigation Involving His Discoveries, His Will, His Family, and His Descendants* (Los Angeles, CA, 1949).

22 Morison, *Admiral of the Ocean Sea*, pp. 61–3.

23 Garcilaso de la Vega, *Royal Commentaries of the Incas and General History of Peru*, 2 vols (Austin, TX, 1966), I, pp. 12–14.

24 Carrillo, *Oviedo on Columbus*, pp. 44–5, gives a translation of the Unknown Pilot story extracted from Oviedo's *General and Natural History of the Indies*. Thomas Herbert, *A Relation of Some Yeares Travaile Begunne Annon 1626 into Afrique and the Greater Asia, Especially the Territories of the Persian Monarchy . . .* [1634] (New York, 1971), p. 223. In the second edition of his book, titled *Some Yeares Travels into Africa and Asia the Great Especially Describing the Famous Empires of Persia and Industani . . .* (London, 1638), p. 361, Herbert takes a more sceptical approach and calls the Unknown Pilot story 'a Spanish lye, invented merely to derogate from his [Columbus'] worth, and that an Italian should not master so much glory'. For a modern analysis of the Unknown Pilot story see Paolo Emilio Taviani, 'Columbus's Secret', in Christopher Columbus, *The Journal: An*

Account of the First Voyage and Discovery of the Indies, with an introduction and notes by Paolo Taviani and Consuelo Varela (Rome, 1990), part 2, pp. 109–25.

25 Ferdinand Columbus, *Life of the Admiral Christopher Columbus by His Son Ferdinand* (New Brunswick, NJ, 1959), pp. 228–34. For a more recent translation see Ferdinand Columbus, *Historie Concerning the Life and Deeds of the Admiral Don Christopher Columbus*, ed. Paolo Emilio Taviani and Ilaria Luzzana Caraci, trans. Luciano F. Farina, vol. IV, pts 1 and 2 of the *Nuova Raccolta Colombiana* (Rome, 1998), pt 1, pp. 48–9.

26 Morison, *Admiral of the Ocean Sea*, pp. 61–3.

27 John Larner, 'The Certainty of Columbus', *History*, LXXIII/237 (February 1988), pp. 3–23.

28 Lee Eldridge Huddleston, *Origins of the American Indians: European Concepts, 1492–1729* (Austin, TX, 1976), pp. 16–33. For Oviedo's use of the Hesperides theory see Carillo, *Oviedo on Columbus*, pp. 17–18, 41, 45, 59, 86–7. Ferdinand Columbus rebutted Oviedo in his *Historie Concerning the Life and Deeds of the Admiral Don Christopher Columbus*, pt 1, pp. 50–59.

29 Frederick W. Lucas, *The Annals of the Voyages of the Brothers Nicolo and Antonio Zeno in the North Atlantic* (London, 1898) proved conclusively that the Zeno narrative was a hoax. That conclusion has not proved much of a deterrent as various writers have continued to accept the narrative as true, e.g., William H. Hobbs, 'The Fourteenth-Century Discovery of America by Antonio Zeno', *Scientific Monthly*, LXXII (January 1951), pp. 24–31; Frederick J. Pohl, *Prince Henry Sinclair: His Expedition to the New World in 1398* (London, 1974) and Andrew Sinclair, *The Sword and the Grail: Of the Grail and the Templars and the True Discovery of America* (New York, 1992) which along with Dan Brown's *Da Vinci Code* has inspired a flood of Templars in pre-Columbian America books.

30 John Fiske, *The Discovery of America*, 3 vols (Boston, MA, 1902), III, p. 323 and Morison, *Northern Voyages*, pp. 81–2.

31 Gwyn A. Williams, *Madoc: Making of a Myth* (London, 1979) is the best scholarly treatment of the Madoc story.

32 Zella Armstrong, *Who Discovered America? The Amazing Story of Madoc* (Chattanooga, TN, 1950) is a good source for this version of the Madoc story, in particular, see pp. 39–103.

33 Williams, *Madoc*, pp. 35–47 and David Powel, *The History of Cambria, now called Wales: A Part of the Most Famous Yland of Brytaine . . .* [1584], pp. 227–9. Although Dee used the Madoc myth to justify English claims to North America, he actually put more emphasis on transatlantic voyages by King Arthur and his knights, see Peter French, *John Dee: The World of an Elizabethan Magus* [1972] (New York, 1989), pp. 197–9.

34 Williams, *Madoc*, pp. 49–52.

35 Sir Thomas Herbert, *A Relation of Some Yeares Travaile*, pp. 217–24 and the same author's *Some Yeares Travels into Africa and Asia the Great*, pp. 355–62.

36 Williams, *Madoc*, pp. 69–72, 141–83, 199–203 and his 'John Evans' Strange Journey: Part I. The Welsh Indians', *American Historical Review*, LIV/2 (January 1949), pp. 277–95 and 'John Evans' Strange Journey: Part II. Following the Trail', *American Historical Review*,

LIV/3, April 1949), pp. 508–29.

37 Williams, *Madoc*, pp. 204–6 and John D. Fair, 'Hatchett Chandler and the Quest for Native Tradition at Fort Morgan', *Alabama Review*, XL (July 1987), pp 163–198, esp. pp. 172–5, 187–8. During a visit to Fort Morgan at Mobile Bay in 1989 I asked a park ranger about the location of the DAR's Madoc plaque. She told me that it has been swept away by a storm. Since then I have learned that the plaque is actually kept in storage at Fort Morgan. The plaque, a legacy of Hatchett Chandler's regime at Fort Morgan, has been a source of embarrassment for park officials.

38 David Ingram, *The Relation of David Ingram* [1589] (Ann Arbor, MI, 1966), p. 560, and Raynor Urwin, *The Defeat of John Hawkins* (New York, 1960), pp. 293–312.

39 'Welsh Indians' in F. W. Hodge, *Handbook of Indians North of Mexico*, 2 vols (Washington, DC, 1910).

40 Bernard De Voto, *The Course of Empire* (Boston, MA, 1952), p. 72.

41 Stephen Williams, *Fantastic Archaeology*, pp. 103–206. For detailed demolitions of the hoax of the Kensington Runestone see Theodore Blegen, *The Kensington Rune Stone: New Light on an Old Riddle* (St Paul, MN, 1968) and Erik Wahlgren, *The Kensington Stone: A Mystery Solved* (Madison, WI, 1958). The classic defender of the authenticity of the Kensington Runestone was Hjalmar R. Holland whose most accessible book is *Norse Discoveries and Explorations in America, 982–1362: Leif Erikson to Kensington Stone* [1940] (New York, 1968). Books supporting the Kensington Runestone continue to appear, e.g., Duane R. Lund, *Europeans in North America before Columbus* (Cambridge, MN, n.d.) and Michael Zalar, *The Kensington Runestone FAQ Book* (St Paul, MN, 2006). These are among the books for sale at the gift shop of the museum housing the Runestone in Alexandria, Minnesota.

42 Anne Stine Ingstad and Helge Ingstad, *The Norse Discovery of America*, 2 vols (Oslo and Oxford, 1985); Birgitta Linderoth Wallace, 'The L'Anse aux Meadow Site', in Gwyn Jones, *The Norse Atlantic Saga: Being the Norse Voyages of Discovery and Settlement to Iceland, Greenland, and North America* (Oxford, 1986), pp. 285–304 and the essays by Birgitta Linderoth Wallace, Gisli Sigurdsson, Patricia D. Sutherland and Peter Schledermann in *Vikings: The North Atlantic Saga*, ed. William W. Fitzhugh and Elisabeth I. War (Washington, DC, 2000).

43 The various theories claiming that ancient Egyptians visited the Americas are discussed in Robert Wauchope's *Lost Tribes and Sunken Continents* and Nigel Davies' *Voyagers to the New World*. Thor Heyerdahl attempted to show that such contact was possible by building facsimiles of ancient reed ships and sailing them across the Atlantic Ocean, a feat chronicled in his *The Ra Expeditions* (Garden City, NY, 1971). Rafique Ali Jairazbhoy's books *Ancient Egyptians and Chinese in America* (Totowa, NJ, 1974) and *Rameses III: Father of Ancient America* (London, 1992) are detailed attempts to prove that ancient Egyptians discovered and settled the Americas.

44 Michael Bradley, *The Black Discovery of America: Amazing Evidence of Daring Voyages by Ancient West African Mariners* (Toronto, 1981) and Ivan Van Sertima, *They Came Before Columbus* (New York, 1976) discuss these theories.

45 James Bailey, *The God–Kings and the Titans: The New World Ascendancy in Ancient Times* (New York, 1973) pp. 45, 275 and Constance

Irvin, *Fair Gods and Stone Faces* (New York, 1963), pp. 124–8.

46 Van Sertima, *They Came Before Columbus*, pp. 123–79.

47 Leo Wiener, *Africa and the Discovery of America*, 3 vols (Philadelphia, PA, 1919–22).

48 The plants commonly cited as evidence of pre-Columbian contacts between Africa and the Americas, among other places, are cotton and corn. Herbert G. Baker, *Plants and Civilization*, 2nd edn (Belmont, CA, 1970) is an excellent global history of domesticated plants that supplies reliable information on the origin and distribution of various plants. The most authoritative history of corn is Paul C. Mangelsdorf, *Corn: Its Origin, Evolution, and Improvement* (Cambridge, MA, 1974).

49 Alexander von Wuthenau, *Unexpected Faces in Ancient America: The Historical Testimony of the Pre-Columbian Artist* (New York, 1975), pp. 59–82, 135–204.

50 D. T. Niane, ed., *Africa from the Twelfth to the Sixteenth Century* (Berkeley, CA, 1984), pp. 146–56, 664–6.

51 Van Sertima, *They Came Before Columbus*, pp. 37–49.

52 Wauchope, *Lost Tribes and Sunken Continents*, pp. 7–27 and Davies, *Voyagers to the New World*, pp. 158–65.

53 Harold S. Gladwin, *Men Out of Asia* (New York, 1947), esp. pp. 187–292 and Stephen Williams, *Fantastic Archaeology*, pp. 224–39. The widow of Campbell Grant, Gladwin's illustrator and a friend of Gladwin's, rejected Stephen Williams' theory about *Men Out of Asia* being a practical joke when she was informed about it (pers. comm.).

54 Barry Fell's books on ancient contacts between the Americas and the Old World consist of *America BC: Ancient Settlers in the New World*, revd edn [1976] (New York, 1989), *Saga America* (New York, 1980) and *Bronze Age America* (Boston, MA, 1982).

55 Fell is critically discussed by Davies, *Voyagers to the New World*, pp. 152–6 and Williams, *Fantastic Archaeology*, pp. 264–73. Devastating critiques of Fell's scholarship by professional historians and archaeologists are too numerous to list here. The following are a sampling. Noted British archaeologist Glyn Daniel gave a bad review to Fell's *America BC* and to Van Sertima's *They Came Before Columbus* in the *New York Times Book Review* (13 March 1977), pp. 12–13. The Smithsonian Institution received so many inquiries about the factual reliability of *America BC* that two of its scholars, I. Goddard and W. Fitzhugh, wrote up a critique to serve as a handout. It was then published in some archaeological magazines: 'Barry Fell Reexamined', *Biblical Archaeologist*, XLI (1978), pp. 85–8 and 'A Statement Concerning *America BC*', *Man in the Northeast*, XVII (1979), pp. 1966–72. The Davenport Tablets, which Fell accepts as genuine, are conclusively shown to be a hoax by Marshall B. McKusick in *The Davenport Conspiracy* (Iowa City, IA, 1970), published in a revised edition as *The Davenport Conspiracy Revisited* (Ames, IA, 1991).

56 Voltaire, *The Philosophy of History* in *The Works of Voltaire: Romances and Philosophy* (New York, 1927), p. 387.

57 Thomas Jefferson, *Notes on the State of Virginia* (New York, 1984), p. 226.

58 See above, pp. 30–31.

59 Huddleston, *Origins of the American Indians*, pp. 16–17, 20–21, 26.

60 Antonio Galvão, *The Discoveries of the World*, ed. C.R.D. Bethune (London, 1862), p. 34.

61 Huddleston, *Origins of the American Indians*, pp. 16–17, 20–21, 23, 26, 28–9, 65–9, 80–81.

62 Huddleston, *Origins of the American Indians*, 124–5, 136.

63 Marc Lescarbot, *The History of New France*, 8 vols [1609] (Toronto, 1907, 1911 and 1914), I, pp. 43–4; Dan Vogel, *Indian Origins and the Book of Mormon* (n.p., 1986), pp. 121–2 and Huddleston, *Origins of the American Indians*, pp. 37–8, 113.

64 Williams, *Fantastic Archaeology*, p. 214; Davies, *Voyagers to the New World*, p. 148; Huddleston, *Origins of the American Indians*, pp. 106–7.

65 Frank Moore Cross, 'The Phoenician Inscription from Brazil: A Nineteenth-Century Forgery', *Orientalia*, XXXVII (1968), pp. 437–60 and Michael F. Doran, 'Phoenician Contact with America?', *Anthropological Journal of Canada*, XII/2 (1974), pp. 16–24.

66 Cross, 'Phoenician Inscription'; Cyrus H. Gordon, 'The Authenticity of the Phoenician Text from Parahyba', *Orientalia*, XXXVII (1968), pp. 75–80; 'Reply to Professor Cross', *Orientalia*, XXXVII (1968), pp. 461–3; *Before Columbus*, pp. 120–27 and *Riddles in History* (New York, 1974), pp. 71–92.

67 Thomas Crawford Johnston, *Did the Phoenicians Discover America?* (London, 1913).

68 Huddleston, *Origins of the American Indians*, pp. 33–43.

69 Allen H. Godbey, *The Lost Tribes a Myth: Suggestions Towards Rewriting Hebrew History* [1930] (New York, 1974), ch. 1, 'The Lost Tribes Theory', and Tudor Parfitt, *The Lost Tribes of Israel: The History of a Myth* (London, 2002), chs 1–5.

70 Vogel, *Indian Origins and the Book of Mormon*; Wauchope, *Lost Tribes & Sunken Continents*, pp. 50–68; Williams, *Fantastic Archaeology*, pp. 158–67; Thomas Stuart Ferguson, *One Fold and One Shepherd* (Salt Lake City, UT, 1962); Milton R. Hunter and Thomas Stuart Ferguson, *Ancient America and the Book of Mormon* (Oakland, CA, 1950) and John L. Sorenson, *An Ancient American Setting for the Book of Mormon* (Salt Lake City, UT, 1985).

71 Wauchope, *Lost Tribes & Sunken Continents*, pp. 54–6.

72 Huddleston, *Origins of the American Indians*, pp. 33–5 and Geoffrey Eatough, *Selections from Peter Martyr, Repertorium Columbianum* V (Turnhout, 1998), pp. 45, 59.

73 Huddleston, *Origins of the American Indians*, pp. 35–40, 93–4 and Diego Durán, *The History of the Indies of New Spain* (Norman, OK, 1994), pp. 3–11.

74 Acosta, *Natural and Moral History of the Indies*, bk. 1, ch. 23, p. 70.

75 George Weiner, 'America's Jewish Braves', *Mankind*, IV/9 (October 1974), pp. 56–64; David S. Katz, *Philo-Semitism and the Readmission of the Jews to England, 1603–1655* (Oxford, 1982), pp. 127–57 and Parfitt, *Lost Tribes of Israel*, pp. 77–90.

76 Vogel, *Indian Origins and the Book of Mormon*, pp. 41–4; Parfitt, *Lost Tribes of Israel*, pp. 95–103 and James Adair, *Adair's History of the American Indians*, ed. Samuel Cole Williams (New York, 1930).

77 Gordon, *Before Columbus*, pp. 175–87 and Marshall B. McKusick, 'Canaanites in America: A New Scripture in Stone', *Biblical Archaeologist*, XLII (1979), pp. 137–40.

78 Huddleston, *Origins of the American Indians*, pp. 107, 112 and Thomas Morton, *New England Canaan; or New Canaan, Containing An Abstract in Three Books* [1637] (New York, 1947).

79   Williams, *Fantastic Archaeology*, pp. 40–42 and Samuel F. Haven,
     Archaeology of the United States (New York, 1973), pp. 36–7.
80   Wauchope, *Lost Tribes & Sunken Continents*, p. 91.
81   Robert Heine-Geldern, 'Traces of Indian and Southeast Asiatic Hindu-
     Buddhist Influences in Mesoamerica', *Proceedings of the 35th Interna-
     tional Congress of Americanists* (1962), pp. 47–54; Robert Heine-Geldern
     and Gordon Ekholm, 'Significant Parallels in the Symbolic Arts of
     Southeast Asia and Middle America', *The Civilization of Ancient
     America*, ed. Sol Tax (Chicago, IL, 1951), pp. 299–309 and Robert
     Heine-Geldern, 'The Problem of Transpacific Influences in Mesoamer-
     ica', in *Handbook of Middle American Indians*, ed. Robert Wauchope,
     vol. IV: *Archaeological Frontiers and External Connections*, ed. Gordon
     F. Ekholm and Gordon R. Willey (Austin, TX, 1966), pp. 277–95. The
     next article in the volume, by Philip Phillips, 'The Role of Transpacific
     Contacts in the Development of New World Pre-Columbian Civiliza-
     tions', pp. 296–315, rejects such Hindu influences. Also see Davies,
     Voyagers to the New World, pp. 108–13 and Wauchope, *Lost Tribes &
     Sunken Continents*, pp. 93–5.
82   Antonio Galvão, *The Discoveries of the World*, pp. 19–22.
83   Huddleston, *Origins of the American Indians*, pp. 73–5.
84   Acosta, *Natural and Moral History of the Indies*, pp. 63–4, 71–2.
85   For a brief summary of the Bering land-bridge/Strait theory see the
     entry 'Bering Land Bridge/Strait Theory', in Ronald H. Fritze, *Legend
     and Lore of the Americas before 1492: An Encyclopedia of Visitors,
     Explorers, and Immigrants* (Santa Barbara, CA, 1993), pp. 29–32.
86   Polybius, *The Rise of the Roman Empire*, trans. Ian Scott-Kilvert
     (Harmondsworth, 1979), p. 432.
87   Louise Levathes, *When China Ruled the Seas: The Treasure Fleet of the
     Dragon Throne, 1405–1433* (New York, 1994) and Edward R. Dreyer,
     *Zheng He: China and the Oceans in the early Ming Dynasty, 1405–
     1433* (New York, 2007). For a contemporary account of Zheng He's
     voyages see Ma Huan, *Ying-Yai Sheng-Lan: 'The Overall History of
     the Ocean's Shores' [1433]* translated and introduced by J.V.G Mills
     (London, 1970). For brief accounts of the Zheng He voyages see Robert
     Finlay, 'The Treasure-Ships of Zheng He: Chinese Maritime Imperial-
     ism in the Age of Discovery', *Terrae Incognitae*, XXIII (1991), pp. 1–12
     and Ronald H. Fritze, 'Voyages of Cheng Ho (or Zheng Ho) (1405–
     1433)', in *Travel Legend and Lore: An Encyclopedia* (Santa Barbara,
     CA, 1998), pp. 63–6. Robert Finlay, 'China, the West, and World History
     in Joseph Needham's *Science and Civilization in China*', *Journal of
     World History*, XI/2 (2000), pp. 265–303, de-emphasizes the significance
     that Joseph Needham places on the Zheng He voyages.
88   Robert Finley, 'How Not to (Re)Write World History: Gavin Menzies
     and the Chinese Discovery of America', *Journal of World History*, XV
     (June 2004); David Buisseret, 'Review of Gavin Menzies, *1421*', *Terrae
     Incognitae*, XXXVI (2004), pp. 118; P. J. Rivers, *'1421' Voyages: Fact and
     Fantasy* (Ipoh, Malaysia, 2004); Geoff Wade, 'Popular History and
     Bunkum', at www.maritimeasia.ws/topic/1421bunkum.htmp; Bill
     Itartz, 'Gavin's Fantasy Land, 1421: The Year China . . .' on the website
     The Hall of Ma'at at www.hallofmaat.com/modules.php?name=
     Articles&file=ariticle&sid=91.; J. R. Masson, 'Comment on Gavin
     Menzies, 1421: The Year China Discovered the World', on the Society
     for the History of Discoveries website at www.sochistdisc.org/2006_

articles/masson_article.htm; numerous articles debunking Menzies and *1421* can be found at the website *The '1421' Myth Exposed* at www.1421exposed.com; Mark Newbrook, 'Zheng He in the Americas and Other Unlikely Tales of Explorations and Discovery' (September 2004) on the website of the Committee for Skeptical Inquiry at http://csicop.org/sb/2004-09/tales.html; Ken Ringle, 'A Fast Boat from China: If Zheng Beat Columbus, an Army of Skeptics Remains', *Washington Post* (12 January 2004), p.c01, available at www.friends-partners.org/piper-mail/fpspace/2004-January/010843.html. The Australian Broadcasting Corporation's show *Four Corners* with reporter Quentin McDermott interviewed the prominent historian of exploration Felipe Fernandez-Armesto for their showing discussing Gavin Menzies and his book *1421*. During the course of his interview Fernández-Armesto vehemently questioned Menzies's sanity and honesty and raised the possibility that *1421* was written as a joke. His interview can be accessed at www.abc.net.au/4corners/content/2006/s1701728.htm. (Websites accessed 16 October 2008.)

89   Gavin Menzies, *1421: The Year China Discovered America* (New York, 2002), pp. 3–12.

90   Two interviews with Gavin Menzies are available in transcript on the Internet. One with Veronica Pedrosa on the CNN show *Talk Asia* was aired on 28 August 2004. It is available at http://edition.cnn.com/2004/world/asiapcf/09/13talkasia.menzies.script/index.html. A second interview took place on the Australian Broadcasting Corporation's show *Four Corners* with reporter Quentin McDermott. Other people besides Menzies were interviewed for the show. It aired on 31 July 2006 and can be accessed at www.abc.net.au/4corners/content/2006/s1702333.htm. These two interviews provided information about the genesis of *1421* that is not found in the book's introduction or contradict its account. (Websites accessed 16 October 2008.)

91   Veronica Pedrosa's *Talk Asia* interview with Gavin Menzies at Block B.

92   Quentin McDermott's *Four Corners* interview.

93   Ibid. and Veronica Pedrosa's *Talk Asia* interview with Gavin Menzies in Block B.

94   Quentin McDermott's *Four Corners* interview.

CHAPTER 3: MUDPEOPLE, SATAN'S SPAWN AND CHRISTIAN IDENTITY: RACIST COSMOGONIES AND PSEUDOHISTORY, PART I

1   John Milton, *Paradise Lost*, book II, ll. 565–6.

2   Alexis de Tocqueville, *Democracy in America* [1835–40] (New York, 2004), p. 486.

3   James Corcoran, *Bitter Harvest: Gordon Kahl and the Posse Comitatus: Murder in the Heartland* (New York, 1990) provides a detailed account of the Gordon Kahl incident including his adherence to the beliefs of Christian Identity.

4   The twelve sons of Jacob in their Biblical order of birth were Reuben, Simeon, Levi, Judah, Dan, Naphtali, Gad, Asher, Issachar, Zebulon, Joseph and Benjamin.

5   Genesis 48:19.

6   The classic study of the lore of the Ten Lost Tribes from an evangelical point of view is Allen H. Godbey, *The Lost Tribes A Myth – Suggestions*

Towards Rewriting Hebrew History [1930] (New York, 1974). More recent is Tudor Parfitt, *The Lost Tribes of Israel: The History of a Myth* (London, 2002).

7 Also see 1 Chronicles 5:26.

8 Isaiah 11:11, Jeremiah 31:8 and Ezekiel 37:19–29.

9 Flavius Josephus, *Antiquities of the Jews*, book 9, ch. XIV, sec. 1 and book 11, ch. V, sec. 2.

10 Gershom Scholem, *Sabbatai Sevi: The Mystical Messiah 1626–1676* [originally published in Hebrew in 1957] (Princeton, NJ, 1973).

11 Richard H. Popkin, 'The Rise and Fall of the Jewish Indian Theory', in *Menasseh ben Israel and his World*, ed. Henry Méchoulan and Richard H. Popkin (Leiden, 1989), pp. 63–82 and Parfitt, *The Lost Tribes of Israel*, chs 2, 4 and 5.

12 'Richard Brothers' in *Oxford Dictionary of National Biography*, ed. H.C.G. Matthew and Brian Harrison (Oxford, 2004); Frank Felsenstein, *Anti-Semitic Stereotypes: A Paradigm of Otherness in English Popular Culture, 1660–1830* (Baltimore, MD, 1995), pp. 95–8; and Michael Barkun, *Religion and the Racist Right: The Origins of the Christian Identity Movement* (Chapel Hill, NC, 1994), p. 6.

13 Barkun, *Religion*, pp. 6–9.

14 Ibid., p. 9.

15 Ibid., pp. 9–11 and Edward Hine, *Forty-Seven Identifications of the British Nation with the Lost Ten Tribes of Israel* (London, 1874), pp. 97–102. Not that all British Israelists accepted Hine and the anti-Germanism of the Anglo-Israel Association. The Canadian W. H. Poole took an approach similar to John Wilson's, see e.g., Poole's *Anglo-Israel or the Saxon Race Proved to be the Lost Tribes of Israel in Nine Lectures* (Toronto, 1889), pp. 140–41.

16 Joseph Wild, *The Lost Ten Tribes* [1879] (Boston, MA, 1919), pp. iii–iv, 9, 73–83, 87–9; Barkun, *Religion*, pp. 17–18 and 'Joseph Wild', in *Appleton's Cyclopedia of American Biography*, ed. James Grant Wilson and John Fiske, 7 vols (New York, 1887–1900).

17 *National Cyclopedia of American Biography*, vol. XI, pp. 237–8; 'James Totten', in *Appleton's Cyclopedia of American Biography* and Barkun, *Religion*, pp. 18–22.

18 Wild, *Lost Ten Tribes*, p. 25 and passim.

19 See the catalogue in the back of Wild, *Lost Ten Tribes*.

20 Barkun, *Religion*, pp. 21–7.

21 Ibid., pp. 29–45.

22 Ibid., pp. 60–70, 207–8, 221–2.

23 Blaise Pascal, *Pensées* [1670] (Chicago, IL, 1952), p. 272, no. 560.

24 Richard Popkin, 'The Pre-Adamite Theory in the Renaissance', in *Philosophy and Humanism: Renaissance Essays in Honor of Paul Oskar Kristeller*, ed. Edward P. Mahoney (New York, 1976), p. 53.

25 Lee Eldridge Huddleston, *Origins of the American Indians: European Concepts, 1492–1729* (Austin, TX, 1967), esp. pp. 9–10, 138–41.

26 Huddleston, *Origins*, pp. 138–41; Popkin, 'Pre-Adamite Theory in the Renaissance,' pp. 64–9; Richard Popkin, 'The Philosophical Bases of Modern Racism', in *Philosophy and the Civilizing Arts: Essays Presented to Herbert S. Schneider*, ed. Craig Walton and John P. Anton (Athens, OH, 1974), pp. 140–44 and *Isaac La Peyrère (1596–1676): His Life, Work, and Influence* (Leiden, 1987) an exhaustive study of La Peyrère's pre-Adamite theories and their later influences.

27 David N. Livingstone, 'The Preadamite Theory and the Marriage of Science and Religion', *Transactions of the American Philosophical Society*, LXXXII/3 (1992) is an excellent overview of harmonizing theory and the role of pre-Adamism. Also see Leonard Alberstadt, 'Alexander Winchell's Preadamites – A Case for Dismissal from Vanderbilt University', *Earth Sciences History*, XIII/2 (1994), pp. 97–112.

28 Stephen R. Haynes, *Noah's Curse: The Biblical Justification of American Slavery* (New York, 2002) studies the orthodox position of anti-black Southerners.

29 A good selection of these arguments can be found in the writings of D. G. Phillips, A. Hoyle Lester and Charles Carroll collected in *The Biblical and Scientific Defense of Slavery: Religion and 'The Negro Problem'*, ed. John David Smith which of volume six, part II of the series *Anti-Black Thought, 1863–1925*, 11 vols (New York, 1993), the introduction on pp. xxv–xxix places these anti-black writings using the concept of pre-Adamic races in their historical context.

30 George M. Frederickson, *The Black Image in the White Mind: The Debate on Afro-American Character and Destiny, 1817–1914* (New York, 1971), pp. 87–8.

31 Livingstone, 'Preadamite Theory', pp. 40–52 and Alberstadt, 'Alexander Winchell's Preadamites'.

32 Barkun, *Religion*, pp. 162–7. Mrs Sydney Bristowe's *Sargon the Magnificent* remains in print and a yahoo.com search will show that it remains very much discussed among by people associated with British Israelite or Christian Identity beliefs.

33 Wesley Swift, *Testimony of Tradition and the Origin of Races* (Harrison, AR, n.d. but based on a sermon preached during February 1962), p. 20; *Michael Prince of Space* (Harrison, AR, n.d. but based on a sermon preached on 1 April 1962 [Given the date, a sceptical reader might wonder if Swift was joking]), and Barkun, *Religion*, pp. 183, 248.

34 Barkun, *Religion*, pp. 121–2 and 145.

35 Livingstone, 'Preadamite Theory', p. 9.

36 Barkun, *Religion*, pp. 160–62.

37 Charles Lee Mange [Dan Gayman], *The Two Seeds of Genesis 3:15* [1978] (n.p., 1998).

38 Barkun, *Religion*, pp. 150–1, 155, 162–8, 170–1 and 177–85.

39 Voltaire, 'Fanaticism', in *The Philosophical Dictionary*, ed. and trans. Theodore Besterman (New York, 1988), pp. 201–2.

40 Barkun, *Religion*, pp. 77–8; Jonathan Kirsch, *A History of the End of the World: How the Most Controversial Book in the Bible Changed the Course of Western Civilization* (New York, 2006), pp. 10–11, 321; 'Rapture', at http://en.wikipedia.org/wiki/rapture and 'The Rapture: Hoax or Hope?' at www.religioustolerance.org/rapture.htm (websites accessed 16 October 2008).

41 Jeffrey Kaplan, 'Zionist Occupation Government', in *Encyclopedia of White Power: A Sourcebook on the Radical Racist Right*, ed. Jeffrey Kaplan (Walton Creek, CA, 2000).

42 Barkun, *Religion*, pp. 70, 75–6, 84, 104–12 and chs 10 and 11; Jeffrey Kaplan, *Radical Religion in America: Millenarian Movements from the Far Right to the Children of Noah* (Syracuse, NY, 1997), pp. xvi–xvii and 'Aryan Nations' and 'Covenant, Sword, and Arm of the Lord', in *Encyclopedia of White Power*.

43 Kaplan, *Radical Religion*, p. 65.

44 Ibid., p. 34.
45 Barkun, *Religion*, pp. 228–33; Kaplan, 'The Order', in *Encyclopedia of White Power* and *Radical Religion*, pp. 61 and 64.
46 Kaplan, 'Phineas Priesthood', in *Encyclopedia of White Power* and *Radical Religion*, p. 65.
47 Kaplan, 'Leaderless Resistance', in *Encyclopedia of White Power* and *Radical Religion*, pp. 167–8. Kaplan de-emphasizes Christian Identity's potential for violence.
48 The website for Kingdom Identity Ministry is www.kingidentity.com/ and the Aryan Nations website address is www.aryan-nations.org/ index.html (websites accessed 16 October 2008).
49 Barkun, *Religion*, p. 15; Matthias Gardell, 'White Racist Religions in the United States: From Christian Identity to Wolf Age Pagans', in *Controversial New Religions*, ed. James R. Lewis and Jesper Aagaard Petersen (Oxford, 2005), pp. 387–422, and the website for the British Israel World Federation at www.britishisrael.co.uk/. This webpage is for the UK organization but it lists contact information for British Israel groups in the USA, Canada, New Zealand, Australia and South Africa.
50 'Federal Agents Foil Skinhead Plot to Kill Obama', CBS News, 28 October 2008, at http://cbs5.com/campaign08/obama.assasination. plot.2.849858.html.

CHAPTER 4: MAD SCIENTISTS, WHITE DEVILS AND THE NATION OF ISLAM: RACIST COSMOGONIES AND PSEUDOHISTORY, PART II

1 Thomas Hobbes, *Leviathan* [1651] (Chicago, IL, 1952), p. 56.
2 Umberto Eco, 'The Force of Falsity', in *Serendipities: Language & Lunacy* (New York, 1998), p. 19.
3 Malcolm X, *February 1965: The Final Speeches* (New York, 1992), pp. 208–9. His references are to Yacub, or Mr Yacub, the mad scientist who created white people from black people and to the Mother Ship, the great airplane that would attack and destroy the United States.
4 Alexis de Tocqueville, *Democracy in America* [1835–40] (New York, 2004), p. 410.
5 Arna Bontemps and Jack Conroy, *They Seek a City* (Garden City, NY, 1945) and *Anyplace but Here* (New York, 1966): the first history of the Great Migration and a retitled and greatly expanded second edition. Milton C. Sernett, *Bound for the Promised Land: African American Religion and the Great Migration* (Durham, NC, 1997) focuses on the religious consequences of the Great Migration.
6 Kevin Boyle, *Arc of Justice: A Saga of Race, Civil Rights, and Murder in the Jazz Age* (New York, 2004) and Phyllis Vine, *One Man's Castle: Clarence Darrow in Defense of the American Dream* (New York, 2004) tell the story of Ossian Sweet and race relations in Detroit during the mid-1920s.
7 E. U. Essien-Udom, *Black Nationalism: A Search for Identity in America* (Chicago, IL, 1962), p. 83. Essien-Udom's analysis of the attraction of the Nation of Islam for African-Americans was anticipated by Arthur Huff Fauset, *Black Gods of the Metropolis: Negro Religious Cults in the Urban North* (Philadelphia, PA, 1944), pp. 76–95. Fauset's study focused on Philadelphia and the second, third and fourth decades of the twentieth century. He missed the Nation of Islam, which was a rela-

tively small organization in Detroit, Chicago and Washington, DC, at that time, with its leader Elijah Muhammad in federal prison for draft resistance. Fauset did discuss the Moorish Science Temple of America. Also see Erdmann Doane Benyon, 'The Voodoo Cult Among Negro Migrants in Detroit', *American Journal of Sociology*, XLIII (May 1938), pp. 898–9.

8 Philip Jenkins, *Mystics and Messiahs: Cults and New Religions in American History* (New York, 2000), p. 107 and Richard Brent Turner, *Islam in the African-American Experience*, 2nd edn (Bloomington, IN, 2003), pp. 90–93.

9 Essien-Udom, *Black Nationalism*, pp. 33–5; Fauset, *Black Gods of the Metropolis*, pp. 42–4; Jenkins, *Mystics and Messiahs*, pp. 106–9 and Turner, *Islam*, pp. 90–93. Also see Algernon Austin, *Achieving Blackness: Race, Black Nationalism, and Afrocentrism in the Twentieth Century* (New York, 2006), ch. 2, 'Asiatic Identity in the Nation of Islam', makes this point about the Nation of Islam's lack of an Afrocentric focus and briefly mentions the Moorish Science Temple of America in the same context, see p. 45.

10 Turner, *Islam*, pp. 94 and 96–7.

11 Fauset, *Black Gods of the Metropolis*, pp. 42–3 and Karl Evanzz, *The Messenger: The Rise and Fall of Elijah Muhummad* (New York, 1999), p. 65.

12 Essien-Udom, *Black Nationalism*, p. 34; Evanzz, *The Messenger*, pp. 62–3; and Turner, *Islam*, pp. 90–93.

13 Essien-Udom, *Black Nationalism*, pp. 35, 43; Jenkins, *Mystics and Messiahs*, p. 107 and Turner, *Islam*, pp. 99–100.

14 Turner, *Islam*, pp. 107–8.

15 Blaise Pascal, *Pensées* [1670] (Chicago, IL, 1952), vol. 33, p. 186, no. 81.

16 Claude Andrew Clegg III, *An Original Man: The Life and Times of Elijah Muhammad* (New York, 1997), pp. 5–13.

17 Clegg, *Original Man*, pp. 15–17 and Turner, *Islam*, pp. 154–5.

18 Jenkins, *Mystics and Messiahs*, p. 111 and Turner, *Islam*, p. 164.

19 Turner, *Islam*, p. 148.

20 Clegg, *Original Man*, pp. 60–62; Evanzz, *Messenger*, pp. 398–9; Jenkins, *Mystics and Messiahs*, pp. 108–9 and Turner, *Islam*, pp. 148–51 and 160–1. Karl Evanzz searched for and found no record of Fard having attended the University of Southern California.

21 Turner, *Islam*, p. 148.

22 Clegg, *Original Man*, p. 20; Turner, *Islam*, p. 165 and Vibert L. White, Jr, *Inside the Nation of Islam: A Historical and Personal Testimony by a Black Muslim* (Gainesville, FL, 2001), p. 30. Vibert is a professor of African-American studies at the University of Illinois in Springfield. He is also an apostate from the Nation of Islam and gives full faith and credit to reports of Fard's past as a criminal and a scam artist.

23 Evanzz, *Messenger*, pp. 444–5.

24 Ibid., p. 398.

25 Ibid., pp. 400–2.

26 Ibid., pp. 402–4.

27 Ibid., pp. 405–6.

28 Ession-Udom, *Black Nationalism*, p. 45 and Evanzz, *Messenger*, p. 407. Ession-Udom accurately reported Fard's close connection to the MSTA at the early stage of scholarly inquiry into the rather secretive Nation of Islam, something most other writers ignored until Evanzz.

29 Clegg, *Original Man*, pp. 20–22; Jenkins, *Mystics and Messiahs*, pp. 108–9 and Turner, *Islam*, pp. 148–51.

30 Clegg, *Original Man*, p. 36.

31 Benyon, 'Voodoo Cult', p. 901.

32 Clegg, *Original Man*, pp. 33–4.

33 Ibid., pp. 21–2.

34 Turner, *Islam in the African American Experience*, p. 151 and Clegg, *Original Man*, pp. 20–22.

35 Evanzz, *Messenger*, pp. 71–4.

36 Clegg, *Original Man*, pp. 23–4 and Turner, *Islam*, p. 151.

37 Benyon, 'Voodoo Cult', p. 902; Clegg, *Original Man*, p. 36 and Turner, *Islam*, pp. 166–7.

38 Johann Gottfried von Herder, *Outlines of a Philosophy of the History of Man*, trans. T. Churchill [1784] (New York, 1966), p. 146.

39 Benyon, 'Voodoo Cult', pp. 905–6 and Lincoln, *Black Muslims in America*, pp. 80–83, 115.

40 Clegg, *Original Man*, pp. 41–4; Mattias Gardell, *In the Name of Elijah Muhammad: Louis Farrakhan and the Nation of Islam* (Durham, NC, 1996), pp. 144–5 and Prince-A-Cuba, 'Black Gods of the Inner City', *Gnosis* (Fall 1992), pp. 56–63, passim.

41 Clegg, *Original Man*, pp. 41–4; Gardell, *In the Name of Elijah Muhammad*, pp. 144–5 and Elijah Muhammad, *Message to the Black Man in America* [1965] (Atlanta, GA, 1997), pp. 108–9.

42 Austin, *Achieving Blackness*, pp. 42–4; Clegg, *Original Man*, pp. 44–8 and Gardell, *In the Name of Elijah Muhammad*, pp. 145–6.

43 For studies of traditional Islam's view of creation and human origins see Husâm Eldîn al-Alousî, *The Problem of Creation in Islamic Thought* (Baghdad, 1965); Majid Ali Khan, *Islam on Origin and Evolution of Life* (Lahore, 1978) and Thomas J. O'Shaughnessy, *Creation and the Teachings of the Qurān* (Rome, 1985). Nowhere does anything remotely resembling the Nation of Islam cosmogony appear in the various scriptures although some strains of Islamic thought do allow for a natural theology capable of reconciling modern science to orthodox doctrines.

44 Evanzz, *Messenger*, pp. 402–4 and Jenkins, *Mystics and Messiahs*, pp. 110–11.

45 Clegg, *Original Man*, pp. 42–3 and Jenkins, *Mystics and Messiahs*, pp. 139–41.

46 Fard's literacy could have improved from its state prior to 1920 when his girlfriend had to write his letters for him. He did spent three years in Saint Quentin and as a model prisoner may have used his forced leisure to improve his education.

47 Clegg, *Original Man*, p. 49; Gardell, *In the Name of Elijah Muhammad*, p. 147 and Elijah Muhammad, *Message,* pp. 110–11.

48 Sir John Hawkins' first slaving voyage actually took place in 1562, not 1555 as stated by Elijah Muhammad.

49 Clegg, *Original Man*, pp. 49–58; Gardell, *In the Name of Elijah Muhammad*, pp. 147–8, 152–3; Elijah Muhammad, *Message*, pp. 111–22 and 133–4.

50 Ernest Allen, Jr, 'Religious Heterodoxy and Nationalist Tradition: The Continuing Evolution of the Nation of Islam', *Black Scholar*, XXVI/3–4 (1996), pp. 10–11; Clegg, *Original Man*, pp. 58–63 and Gardell, *In the Name of Elijah Muhammad*, pp. 155–7 and 161.

51 Clegg, *Original Man*, pp. 64–7; Evanzz, *Messenger*, p. 415; Gardell, *In the Name of Elijah Muhammad*, pp. 158–65.

52 Ernest Allen, Jr, 'When Japan was 'Champion of the Darker Races': Satokata Takahashi and the Flowering of Black Messianic Nationalism', *Black Scholar* XXIV/1 (1994), p. 25.

53 Allen, 'When Japan was "Champion of the Darker Races"' and Ernest Allen, Jr, 'Waiting for Tojo: The Pro–Japan Vigil of Black Missourians, 1932–1943', *Gateway Heritage*, XVI (Fall 1995), pp. 38–55.

54 Evanzz, *Messenger*, chs 12–14 and Gardell, *In the Name of Elijah Muhammad*, pp. 158–65.

55 *The Lost Books of the Bible and The Forgotten Books of Eden* (New York, 1926 and 1927), p. 261.

56 C. Eric Lincoln, *The Black Muslims in America* (Boston, MA, 1961), pp. 181–2.

57 Evanzz, *Messenger*, pp. 83–6.

58 Boyle, *Arc of Justice*, pp. 138–40 and 341–2; Clegg, *Original Man*, pp. 30–2; Jenkins, *Mystics and Messiahs*, pp. 111–12 and Turner, *Islam*, pp. 166–7.

59 Benyon, 'Voodoo Cult', pp. 903–4; Clegg, *Original Man*, pp. 30–32 and Martha F. Lee, *The Nation of Islam: An American Millenarian Movement* (Syracuse, NY, 1996), pp. 24–5.

60 Clegg, *Original Man*, pp. 33–4 and Jenkins, *Mystics and Messiahs*, pp. 111–12.

61 Benyon, 'Voodoo Cult', p. 903.

62 Jenkins, *Mystics and Messiahs*, p. 111.

63 Clegg, *Original Man*, pp. 35–6.

64 Evanzz, *Messenger*, pp. 105–6, 380–2, 407–9, 412.

65 Clegg, *Original Man*, pp. 36–7.

66 Ibid., pp. 36–7 and Essien-Udom, *Black Nationalism*, pp. 64–6.

67 Clegg, *Original Man*, pp. 40 and 77–87 and Lee, *Nation of Islam*, p. 25.

68 Clegg, *Original Man*, pp. 82–7.

69 Ibid., pp. 122–3; Evanzz, *Messenger*, p. 444 and Malcolm X, *Final Speeches*, p. 188.

70 Clegg, *Original Man*, pp. 84–98 and Essien-Udom, *Black Nationalism*, pp. 66–8.

71 'The Greeks', Sura 30, verses 29–31, *The Koran*, trans. N. J. Dawood (Harmondsworth, 1959), p. 189.

72 Clegg, *Original Man*, chs 6 and 8 and Malcolm X, *Autobiography*, chs 12–16 and 19 .

73 Lee, *Nation of Islam* is a study of this shift in the millenarianism of the Nation of Islam.

74 White, *Inside the Nation of Islam*, p. 28.

75 Lincoln, *Black Muslims in America*, p. 210.

76 Both Evanzz, *Messenger* and White, *Inside the Nation of Islam* are strongly critical of Farrakhan and they are not alone.

77 Gardell, *In the Name of Elijah Muhammad* contains numerous citations from Farrakhan and other contemporary Nation of Islam officials that promote belief in the racist Yacub myth and the Mother Plane. In fact Farrakhan has claimed that Elijah Muhammad did not die but instead was taken up into the Mother Plane, presumably joining his old teacher Fard. If so it is another occultation unless it can be better classified as an alien abduction. Farrakhan reported that in 1985 he encountered the Mother Plane during a trip to Mexico when he climbed

to the top of an Aztec temple. The voice of Elijah Muhammad spoke to him out of the Mother Ship. See Gardell, *In the Name of Elijah Muhammad*, pp. 131–4.

CHAPTER 5: PSEUDOHISTORIA EPIDEMICA OR PSEUDOHISTORIANS IN COLLUSION

1 Michel de Montaigne, 'That the Soul Discharges Her Passions upon False Objects, Where the True are Wanting', in *Essays* (Chicago, IL, 1952), vol. XXV, p. 10.
2 Tim Callahan, 'A New Mythology: Ancient Astronauts, Lost Civilizations, and the New Age Paradigm', *Skeptic*, XIII/4 (2008), pp. 32–41.
3 The Velikovsky Archive is at www.varchive.org (accessed 20 October 2008).
4 K. A. Kitchen, 'The Exodus', *The Anchor Bible Dictionary*, ed. David Noel Freedman, 6 vols (New York, 1992); Werner Keller, *The Bible as History* (New York, 1964), pp. 100–7 and Ian Wilson, *The Bible is History* (Washington, DC, 1999), pp. 44–53.
5 Exodus 17:8–13.
6 1 Kings 14:21–8 and 2 Chronicles 12:1–12.
7 Velikovsky's autobiography *Days and Years,* chs 'My Years in Berlin' and 'Home Ancestral', at www.varchive.org.
8 Immanuel Velikovsky, *Stargazers and Gravediggers: Memoirs to Worlds in Collision* (New York, 1983), pp. 27–31.
9 Velikovsky, *Stargazers and Gravediggers*, pp. 32–7.
10 'Collected Essays' and the file 'Affidavit (1942)' at www.varchive.org.
11 Immanuel Velikovsky, *Earth in Upheaval* (Garden City, NY, 1955), pp. 274–7. Both *Theses for the Reconstruction of Ancient History* and *Cosmos without Gravitation* are available in the 'Collected Essays' section under their own titles at www.varchive.org.
12 Velikovsky, *Earth in Upheaval*, pp. 274–7 and *Stargazers and Gravediggers*, p. 38.
13 Velikovsky, *Stargazers and Gravediggers*, pp. 45–6.
14 Ibid., pp. 47–9.
15 Ibid., pp. 50–7.
16 Ibid., pp. 96–7 and Henry H. Bauer, *Beyond Velikovsky: The History of a Public Controversy* (Urbana, IL, 1984), p. 233. Bauer only speculates that Shapley had seen a copy of *Cosmos without Gravitation* but Shapley states emphatically in a letter to Ted Thackrey that Velikovsky had sent him a copy. This letter is printed in *Stargazers and Gravediggers* and has a notation from Shapley to Thackrey, 'Not for publication, HS'.
17 Velikovsky, *Stargazers and Gravediggers*, pp. 61–7.
18 Ibid., pp. 68–75.
19 Ibid., pp. 81–116 and Bauer, *Beyond Velikovsky*, pp. 3–7.
20 Velikovsky, *Stargazers and Gravediggers*, pp. 131–42 and Bauer, *Beyond Velikovsky*, pp. 11–26.
21 Peter Biskind, *Seeing is Believing: How Hollywood Taught Us to Stop Worrying and Love the Fifties* (New York, 1983), pp. 126–36.
22 Bauer, *Beyond Velikovsky*, pp. 27–40.
23 'On the Recent Discoveries Concerning Jupiter and Venus', *Science*, CXXXVIII (1962), p. 1350, reprinted in *The Velikovsky Affair: Scientism vs. Science*, ed. Alfred de Grazia (New Hyde Park, NY, 1966), pp. 247–9.

24 Bargmann and Motz in Grazia, *Velikovsky Affair*, p. 249.

25 Donald Goldsmith, ed., *Scientists Confront Velikovsky* (Ithaca, NY, 1977).

26 Carl Sagan, 'An Analysis of *Worlds in Collision*', in Goldsmith, *Scientists Confront Velikovsky*, pp. 41–104; Bauer, *Beyond Velikovsky*, pp. 76–8, 223–6, 235–6, 307; David Morrison, 'Velikovsky at Fifty: Cultures in Collision on the Fringes of Science', *Skeptic* IX/I (2001), pp. 66–9.

27 Lewis M. Greenberg, ed., *Velikovsky and Establishment Science* (Glassboro, NJ, 1977) and Lewis M. Greenberg, ed., *Scientists Confront Scientists Who Confront Velikovsky* (Glassboro, NJ, 1978).

28 Morrison, 'Velikovsky at Fifty', p. 69 and John Kettler, 'The Martyrdom of Immanuel Velikovsky', in *Forbidden History: Extraterrestrial Intervention and the Suppressed Origins of Civilization* (Rochester, VT, 2005), pp. 59–60.

29 Isaac Asimov, 'Forward', in *Scientists Confront Velikovsky*, p. 14.

30 'Before the Forum', in *Before the Day Breaks*, an unpublished autobiographical manuscript available at www.varchive.org and letter from Velikovsky to Einstein, 16 June 1954, at www.varchive.org/cor/einstein/540616ve.htm.

31 Leroy Ellenberger, 'A Lesson From Velikovsky', p. 2 at http://abob.libs.uga.edu/bobk/vlesson.html.

32 Peter J. Bowler, *The Norton History of the Environmental Sciences* (New York, 1992), pp. 237–45, 425–7.

33 Velikovsky, *Worlds in Collision*, pp. 39–42n and 330n; Velikovsky, *Stargazers and Gravediggers*, p. 42; and Martin Gardner, *Fads and Fallacies in the Name of Science* (New York, 1957), pp. 33–7.

34 'The Observer Articles', in 'Collected Essays' at www.varchive.org.

35 James Gilbert, *Redeeming Culture: American Religion in an Age of Science* (Chicago, IL, 1997), pp. 174–8.

36 A search of the Archival Database of the Einstein Archives Online (www.alberteinstein.info) using the term 'Velikovsky' produced 27 items from 1 June 1939 to 12 March 1955. Four of the items date from after Einstein's death. The Velikovsky Archives (www.varchive.org) under 'Correspondence' provide the text for fifteen letters between Velikovsky and Einstein. That correspondence is placed in a narrative context in Velikovsky's unpublished autobiography *Before the Day Breaks* which tells the story of his discussions with Einstein, also available at the Velikovsky Archive, see esp. the chapters 'July 21, 1954' and 'In Einstein's Study' for the discussions of Charles H. Hapgood's ideas. Also see the letters: Einstein to Velikovsky, 8 July 1946; Velikovsky to Einstein, 26 August 1952; Velikovsky to Einstein, 16 June 1954; Einstein to Velikovsky, 17 March 1955 and Velikovsky to I. Bernard Cohen, 18 July 1955. Hapgood's ideas are discussed in the next section of this chapter.

37 Sagan, 'An Analysis of *Worlds in Collision*', pp. 45, 92–3 and Bauer, *Beyond Velikovsky*, ch. 7, 'Velikovsky's Physical Science', which strives so hard to be fair in its conclusions that Bauer almost undermines his proof that Velikovsky is a pseudoscientist, see pp. 132–4.

38 For brief but authoritative summaries of the archaeological topics discussed in the following paragraphs see the entries for 'Dendrochronology', 'Radiocarbon Dating' and 'Stratigraphy' in *The Oxford Companion to Archaeology*, ed. Brian M. Fagan (New York, 1996).

39 Morrison, 'Velikovsky at Fifty', p. 73.

40   William H. Stiebing, Jr, *Ancient Astronauts and Cosmic Collisions and Other Popular Theories About Man's Past* (Buffalo, NY, 1984), pp. 75–80; 'A Criticism of the Revised Chronology', *Pensée*, III/3 (1973), pp. 10–12 and 'Rejoinder to Velikovsky', *Pensée*, IV/5 (1974), pp. 24–6.

41   Stiebing, *Ancient Astronauts*, pp. 62–7.

42   'Address of Abraham Sachs at Brown Univ. 3/15/65', transcript prepared by Leroy Ellenberger at http://abob.libs.uga.edu/bobk/vsachs.html, accessed 23 November 2008.

43   Bob Forrest, *Velikovsky's Sources*, 7 vols (Manchester, privately printed, 1981–3) and Bob Forrest, *A Guide to Velikovsky's Sources* (Santa Barbara, CA, 1987). The fact that Stonehenge Viewpoint published Forrest's smaller work is something of an anomaly since that press generally dealt with books of alternative history, archaeology and science, in other words, pseudohistory and pseudoscience.

44   Morrison, 'Velikovsky at Fifty', pp. 70–72.

45   Trevor Palmer, *Perilous Planet Earth: Catastrophes and Catastrophism through the Ages* (Cambridge, 2003), pp. 133–60, 215–51.

46   William D. Stansfield, 'Creationism, Catastrophism, and Velikovsky', *Skeptical Inquirer*, XXXII (January/February 2008), pp. 48–50.

47   Charles Darwin, *The Descent of Man* (Chicago, IL, 1952), vol. XLIX, p. 590.

48   Velikovsky's unpublished autobiography *Before the Day Breaks*, chs 'July 21, 1954' and 'In Einstein's Study', available at www.varchive.org.

49   Hapgood's ideas form the premise of Clive Cussler and Paul Kemprecos, *Polar Shift* (New York, 2005).

50   The polar regions remain largely unexplored and therefore mysterious, so providing wonderful settings for realistic science fiction stories and novels. Edgar Rice Burroughs placed the location of the entrance to his hollow-earth world of Pellucidar at the North Pole when he wrote *Tarzan at the Earth's Core* (published 1929). H. P. Lovecraft speculated about immensely old civilizations buried under the glaciers of Antarctica in his novel *At the Mountains of Madness*, written in 1931 but not published until 1936. The 1935 film version of H. Rider Haggard's novel *She* by RKO Pictures set the location of the mysterious realm of the ancient Queen Ayesha in the Arctic rather than Africa. Robert Perry is supposed to be the first person to have reached the North Pole, allegedly in 1909, but that claim has been disputed. It may be that science fiction provided the inspiration for pseudoscience (and pseudohistory!) just as it has provided the inspiration for many future scientists.

51   For a useful although sometimes credulous account of the various hypotheses of pole shift and the people associated with them, see John White, *Pole Shift: Predictions and Prophecies of the Ultimate Disaster* (New York, 1980).

52   Ken Kasten, 'Mystery Under the Ice: Antarctica's Many Secrets Remain Tightly Held', *Atlantis Rising*, LXVIII (March/April 2008), pp. 22–3; Palmer, *Perilous Planet Earth*, p. 114 and Charles H. Hapgood, *The Path of the Pole* (Philadelphia, PA, 1970), pp. xix, 21, 71–2.

53   Charles H. Hapgood and James H. Campbell, *The Earth's Shifting Crust: A Key to Some Basic Problems of Earth Science* (New York, 1958), pp. 1–2. The foreword is reprinted in *Path of the Pole*. A search of the Archival Database of the Einstein Archives Online (www.albert-einstein.info) using the term 'Hapgood' produced 45 items from 15 November to 9 March 1955. Three items date from after Einstein's

death, of which one is the foreword to Hapgood's book.

54 Hapgood, *Path of the Pole*, pp. xi–xv, xviii–xix, 325–6, 346–7 and Palmer, *Perilous Planet Earth*, pp. 114–15.

55 Colin Wilson and Rand Flem-Ath, *The Atlantis Blueprint: Unlocking the Ancient Mysteries of a Long-Lost Civilization* (New York, 2000), pp. 328–30, a partial transcription of the letter from Hapgood to Rand Flem-Ath.

56 Arlington H. Mallery, *Lost America: The Story of Iron Age Civilization Prior to Columbus* (Washington, DC, 1951); Arlington Mallery and Mary Roberts Harrison, *The Rediscovery of Lost America* (New York, 1979), an extensive revision by Harrison of *Lost America* based on Mallery's notes or entirely researched and written by Harrison. See pp. 199–207, particularly pp. 205–6 concerning Mallery and the Piri Reis map. Gregory McIntosh, *The Piri Reis Map of 1513* (Athens, GA, 2000), pp. 53–8.

57 Charles H. Hapgood, *Maps of the Ancient Sea Kings: Evidence of Advanced Civilization in the Ice Age* (Philadelphia, PA, 1966) with a revised edition (New York, 1979), p. [x], [xii] and 2–3. This and subsequent references are to the revised edition published in 1979.

58 Hapgood, *Maps of the Ancient Sea-Kings*, pp. 42–7.

59 McIntosh, *Piri Reis Map*, pp. 2 and 40–2 and Peter James and Nick Thorpe, *Ancient Mysteries* (New York, 1999), p. 73.

60 Miriam Estensen, *Discovery: The Quest for the Great South Land* (New York, 1998) and David Fausett, *Writing the New World: Imaginary Voyages and Utopias of the Great Southern Land* (Syracuse, NY, 1993).

61 James Enterline, 'The Southern Continent and the False Strait of Magellan', *Imago Mundi*, XXVI (1972), pp. 48–58; McIntosh, *Piri Reis Map*, pp. 56, 63–5; David C. Jolly, 'Was Antarctica Mapped by the Ancients?', *Skeptical Inquirer*, XI (Fall 1986), p. 38 and James and Thorpe, *Ancient Mysteries*, p. 74.

62 McIntosh, *Piri Reis*, p. 63 and James and Thorpe, *Ancient Mysteries*, pp. 60–76 discuss the scientific and historical fallacies. Garrett G. Fagan, 'Diagnosing Pseudoarchaeology' and Katherine Reece, 'Memoirs of a True Believer', in Garrett G. Fagan, ed., *Archaeological Fantasies: How Pseudoarchaeology Misrepresents the Past and Misleads the Public* (London, 2006) both discuss the works of von Däniken, Hapgood, Hancock and the Flem-Aths as pseudohistory and pseudoscience. So does Palmer: *Perilous Planet Earth*, chs 12, 27 and 28 detail the problems with the theories of Hapgood, Hancock and the Flem-Aths. Jason Colavito, *The Cult of Alien Gods: H. P. Lovecraft and Extraterrestrial Pop Culture* (Amherst, NY, 2005) demonstrates the place of Hapgood and Hancock in the pseudohistorical theory that ancient astronauts visited and colonized the earth.

63 James and Thorpe, *Ancient Mysteries*, pp. 71–2.

64 Ibid., pp. 73–5.

65 Ibid., pp. 75–6.

66 Time-Life Books, *Feats and Wisdom of the Ancients* (Alexandria, VA, 1990), pp. 126–7, provides an uncritical and credulous account of Hapgood's ideas about the Piri Reis map. The books of McIntosh and James and Thorpe are recent debunkings of Hapgood's hypotheses as is John Grant's brief account in *Discarded Science* (Wisley, Surrey, 2006), pp. 204–5.

67 Sir Francis Bacon, 'Of Truth', in *Essays* (Roslyn, NY, 1942), p. 4.

68 'Introduction', in James R. Lewis, ed., UFOs *and Popular Culture: An Encyclopedia of Contemporary Myths* (Santa Barbara, CA, 2000), pp. xxxii–xxxviii; this volume also contains a chronology of UFO sightings from 1837 to 1998. Also see Curtis Peeples, *Watch the Skies: A Chronicle of the Flying Saucer Myth* (Washington, DC, 1994); Benson Salor, Charles A. Zeigler and Charles B. Moore, UFO *Crash at Roswell: The Genesis of a Modern Myth* (Washington, DC, 1997); Robert Sheaffer, *The* UFO *Verdict: Examining the Evidence* (Amherst, NY, 1986); Toby Smith, *Little Grey Men: Roswell and the Rise of a Popular Culture* (Albuquerque, NM, 2000). For another point of view see Alan Baker, *Destination Earth: A History of Alleged Alien Presence* (London, 1998).

69 See www.rotten.com/library/bio/mad-science/erich-von-daniken (accessed 21 October 2008).

70 See www.daniken.com/e/bibliography.shml (accessed 21 October 2008).

71 See www.evdaniken.com/e/aboutevd.htm (accessed 21 October 2008).

72 See www.world-mysteries.com/pex_3.htm (accessed 21 October 2008).

73 See http://en.wikipedia.org/wiki/erich_von_daniken and www.rotten.com/library/bio/mad-science/erich-von-daniken (accessed 21 October 2008).

74 See www.channel4.com/history/microsites/R/real_lives/daniken.html, accessed 23 November 2008.

75 Ibid., and Erich von Däniken, *Chariots of the Gods: Unsolved Mysteries of the Past* (New York, 1999), pp. vii–viii. This edition includes a foreword by von Däniken written in June 1995 that tells the story of his dealings with von Randow and von Wehrenalp. The copyright page also contains a statement that declares 'This is a work of fiction . . .'. Erich, was ist los?

76 Ronald Story, *The Space-Gods Revealed: A Close Look at the Theories of Erich von Däniken* (New York, 1976), pp. 1–2, Story's account is based on articles from *Der Spiegel*, XII/1969 (17 March 1969), p. 184 and XII/1973 (19 March 1973), p. 145; another reference to Roggersdorf's ghostwriting can be found in 'Anatomy of a World Best-Seller: Erich von Däniken's Message from the Unknown', *Encounter*, XLI/2 (1973), p. 10 and von Däniken, *Chariots* (1969), p. viii.

77 Von Däniken's legal problems are discussed in these sources: Story, *Space-Gods Revealed*, pp. 2–6, which cites the newspaper article 'Auch ein Erfelgsauter muss sich aus Gesagz halten', *Tages-Azeiger* (4 February 1971); 'Anatomy of a World Best-Seller: Erich von Däniken's Message from the Unknown', *Encounter*, XLI/2 (1973), p. 16; 'Playboy Interview: Erich von Däniken', *Playboy*, XXI (August 1974), pp. 51–2 and 'The Real Erich von Däniken'.

78 *The Eyes of the Sphinx: The Newest Evidence of Extraterrestrial Contact in Ancient Egypt* (New York, 1996) and *Odyssey of the Gods: The Alien History of Ancient Greece* (London, 2002).

79 Detailed debunkings of von Däniken's evidence can be found in William H. Stiebing, Jr, *Ancient Astronauts*, ch. 4, 'The Search for Ancient Astronauts'; Kenneth L. Feder, 'Ancient Astronauts', in *The Skeptic Encyclopedia of Pseudoscience*, ed. Michael Shermer, 2 vols (Santa Barbara, CA, 2002), pp. 17–22; Story, *Space-Gods Revealed*; Barry Thiering and Edgar Castle, eds, *Some Trust in Chariots: Sixteen Views of Erich von Däniken's Chariots of the Gods* (New York, 1972); Clifford Wilson, *Crash Go the Chariots: An Alternative to Chariots of the Gods* (New York, 1972) and *The Chariots Still Crash* (New York, 1975). There are

other books and articles debunking von Däniken.

For a good overview of the state of knowledge concerning the Nasca lines rejects von Däniken and pseudohistorians' claims about alien airfields, see Anthony E. Aveni, *Between the Lines: The Mystery of the Giant Drawings of Ancient Nasca, Peru* (Austin, TX, 2000) esp. pp. 112–13.

80 Heyerdahl quoted in Story, *Space-Gods Revealed*, pp. 47–8. The description of how the *moai* were carved, moved and mounted is on pp. 48–68.

81 Von Däniken, *Chariots of the Gods*, pp. 17–20 and *Odyssey of the Gods*, pp. 140–46; Story, *Space-Gods Revealed*, pp. 27–33; Stiebling, *Ancient Astronauts*, pp. 91–4 and McIntosh, *Piri Reis Map*, pp. 56–62.

82 Robert S. Ellwood, Jr, 'UFOs and the Bible', in Story, *Space-Gods Revealed*, pp. 121–2, reprinted from *Aerial Phenomenon Research Organization Bulletin* (September–October 1971); 'George Adamski', in Jerome Clark, *Extraordinary Encounters: An Encyclopedia of Extraterrestrial and Otherworldly Beings* (Santa Barbara, CA, 2000) and Pia Andersson, 'Ancient Astronauts', in *UFOs and Popular Culture: An Encyclopedia of Contemporary Myth* ed. James R. Lewis (Santa Barbara, CA, 2000), pp. 20–21.

83 'Donald E. Keyhoe Archive', at www.hallrichard.com/keyhoe.htm (accessed 21 October 2008) and 'Earth versus the Flying Saucers', in Lewis, *UFOs and Popular Culture*, pp. 110–11.

84 The page references are to the English translation (New York, 1964).

85 The page references are to the English translation (New York, 1970).

86 Robert Charroux, *Phantastische Vergangenheit: die unbekannte Geschichte der Menschen seit hunderttausend Jahren* (Berlin, 1966) and Louis Pauwels and Jacques Bergier, *Aufbruch ins dritte Jahrtausend; von der Zukunft der phantastischen Vernunft* (Berne, 1970).

87 Von Däniken, *Chariots of the Gods* (1999 edn), pp. 189–90, Chardin should come before Charroux alphabetically; Von Däniken, *Gods from Outer Space*, pp. 7, 10; Story, *Space-Gods Revealed*, pp. 5–6.

88 Von Däniken, *Gods from Outer Space*, p. 14 and Stiebing, *Ancient Astronauts*, p. 92.

89 'Zecharia Sitchin' at http://en.wikipedia.org/wiki/Zecharia_Sitchin (accessed 21 October 2008); Zecharia Sitchin, *The Twelfth Planet: Book 1 of the Earth Chronicles* (New York, 1978), p. viii; 'Nephilim', in *The Anchor Bible Dictionary*, ed. David Noel Freedman (New York, 1992).

90 Zecharia Sitchin, *The End of Days: Armageddon and Prophecies of the Return* (New York, 2007) and for the hoax see http://2012trial. blogspot.com (accessed 21 October 2008), for the refutation of the hoax see 'This is a Hoax: Zecharia Sitchin charged by Federal grand jury on '2012' issues', at www.zone_radio.com/news/planetx.htm.

91 Eric Wojciehowski, 'Ancient Astronauts: Zecharia Sitchin as a Case Study', in *The Skeptic Encyclopedia of Pseudoscience*, vol. II, pp. 532–3; 'Zecharia Sitchin' at Wikipedia; Michael S. Heiser, 'The Myth of the 12th Planet in Sumero-Mesopotamian Astronomy: A Study of the Cylinder Seals', at www.michaelsheiser.com/va_243%20page.htm. Also see Heiser's website, www.sitchiniswrong.com (accessed 21 October 2008).

92 Johann Gottfried von Herder, *Outlines of a Philosophy of the History of Man*, trans. T. Churchill [1784] (New York, 1966), p. 345.

93 See www.world-mysteries.com/pex_4.htm (accessed 21 October 2008).

94 Colavito, *Cult of Alien Gods*, ch. 12, 'Dusting for Fingerprints'; Fagan,

Archaeological Fantasies, pp. xv–xvi, 20–21, 27–42, 63, 94–103, 124–8, 220, 236–56, 366; and James and Thorpe, *Ancient Mysteries,* pp. xvi, 59–76, 133–4, 174, 215, 223, 227–30.

95   For a brief summary and critique of Hancock's ideas see James and Thorpe, *Ancient Mysteries,* pp. 59–60, 66–71.

96   James and Thorpe, *Ancient Mysteries,* pp. 133–4, 223, 227–30.

97   Michael A. Cremo and Richard L. Thompson, *Forbidden Archaeology: The Hidden History of the Human Race* (Los Angeles, CA, 1998) and J. Douglas Kenyon, 'Exposing a Scientific Cover-Up', in *Forbidden History,* ed. J. Douglas Kenyon, pp. 22–8.

98   For a good overview of these pseudohistorical and pseudoscientific methodologies see Garrett G. Fagan, 'Alternative Archaeology', in *The Skeptic Encyclopedia of Pseudoscience,* vol. 1, pp. 9–16.

99   Robert M. Schoch with Robert Aquinas McNally, *Voices of the Rocks: A Scientist Looks at Catastrophes and Ancient Civilizations* (New York, 1999); *Voyages of the Pyramid Builders: The True Origins of the Pyramids from Lost Egypt to Ancient America* (New York, 2003) and *Pyramid Quest: Secrets of the Great Pyramid and the Dawn of Civilization* (New York, 2005).

100 Letter of Jan Sammer to Leroy Ellenberger, 6 August 1977, available at www.varchive.org and Vine Deloria's books *God is Red: A Native View of Religion* (New York, 1973) and *Red Earth, White Eyes: Native Americans and the Myth of Scientific Fact* (New York, 1995); Charles H. Hapgood, *Earth's Shifting Crust,* p. 7 and *The Path of the Pole,* p. xx.

CHAPTER 6: PROFESSORS GONE WILD: THE *BLACK ATHENA* CONTROVERSY

1   Mark Twain, *The Innocents Abroad* [1869] (New York, 1984), p. 505.

2   Martin Bernal, *Black Athena: The Afroasiatic Roots of Classical Civilization,* volume I:*The Fabrication of Ancient Greece 1785–1985* (New Brunswick, NJ, 1987), p. 119. Hereafter cited as *BA1*.

3   *BA1,* ch. 4, 'Hostilities to Egypt in the 18th Century'.

4   Jacques Berlinerblau, *Heresy in the University: The 'Black Athena' Controversy and the Responsibilities of American Intellectuals* (New Brunswick, NJ, 1999), pp. 90–91.

5   Ibid., pp. 82–90.

6   Ibid., p. 89.

7   Ibid., p. 90.

8   Ibid., p. 58.

9   Martin Bernal, *Black Athena: The Afroasiatic Roots of Classical Civilization,* volume II: *The Archaeological and Documentary Evidence* (New Brunswick, NJ, 1991), p. 12. Hereafter cited as *BA2*. Also Martin Bernal, *Black Athena: The Afroasiatic Roots of Classical Civilization,* volume III: *The Linguistic Evidence* (New Brunswick, NJ, 2006), which does not mention a fourth volume in its preface or introduction, see pp. xv–xvi and 1–27. Hereafter referred to as *BA3*. The website of the Rutgers University Press refers to *BA3* as 'this long–awaited third and final volume'.

10 Charles Freeman, *Egypt, Greece and Rome* (New York, 1996), p. 73 and Anthony S. Mercatante, *Facts on File Encyclopedia of World Mythology and Legend* (New York, 1988), entry for 'Neith'. There are also

various references to Anat and Neith in Marjorie Loach, *Guide to the Gods* (Santa Barbara, CA, 1992). Also see Robert E. Norton, 'The Tyranny of Germany over Greece', in Mary R. Lefkowitz and Guy Maclean Rogers, eds, *Black Athena Revisited* (Chapel Hill, NC, 1996), p. 415. Hereafter referred to as BAR.

11 Berlinerblau, *Heresy*, p. 34.

12 Ibid., pp. 35–8.

13 Antonio Gramsci, *Selections from Cultural Writings* (Cambridge, MA, 1985), p. 124.

14 Gerda Lerner, 'Comment [on *Black Athena*]', *Journal of Women's History*, IV (Winter 1993), p. 90.

15 Molly Myerowitz Levine, 'Anti-Black and Anti-Semitic? Have Classical Historians Suppressed the Black and Semitic Roots of Greek Civilization?', *Bible Review*, VI (1990), p. 35.

16 Michael Poliakoff, 'Roll Over Aristotle: Martin Bernal and His Critics', *Academic Questions*, IV (1991), pp. 12–28.

17 John R. Lenz, 'Ancient Histories and Modern Humanities [review of BA2]', *Free Inquiry*, XIII (Fall 1993), pp. 54–5.

18 Emily Vermeule, 'The World Turned Upside Down [review of BA2]', *New York Review of Books* (26 March 1992), p. 41 and John Baines, 'Was Civilization Made in Africa? [review of BA2 and *Civilization or Barbarism* by Cheikh Anta Diop],' *New York Times Book Review* (11 August 1991), p. 12.

19 Paul O. Kristeller, 'Comment on *Black Athena* [review of BA1 and BA2]', *Journal of the History of Ideas*, LVI (January 1995), pp. 125 and 127.

20 Berlinerblau, *Heresy*, p. 6.

21 Ibid., p. 5.

22 Ibid., pp. 1–3.

23 Geralyn S. Lederman, 'Review of *Heresy in the University: The 'Black Athena' Controversy and the Responsibilities of American Intellectuals* by Jacques Berlinerblau', *Bryn Mawr Classical Review* (5 May 2000), available at http://ccat.sas.upenn.edu/bmcr/2000/2000-05-05.html, p. 3 (accessed 22 October 2008).

24 Robert S. Boynton, 'The Bernaliad: A Scholar-Warrior's Long Journey to Ithaca', *Lingua Franca*, V/VI (November 1996), p. 44.

25 Walter Cohen, 'An Interview with Martin Bernal', *Social Text*, XXXV (1993), p. 21.

26 Martin Bernal, 'Responses to Critical Reviews of *Black Athena: The Afroasiatic Roots of Classical Civilization*, volume I: *The Fabrication of Ancient Greece 1785–1985*', *Journal of Mediterranean Archaeology*, III/I (1990), pp. 120–21.

27 Mary Lefkowitz, 'The Afrocentric Interpretation of Western History: Lefkowitz Replies to Bernal', *Journal of Blacks in Higher Education*, XII (Summer 1996), p. 90.

28 Margaret Washington, 'Revitalizing an Old Argument', *Journal of Women's History* (Winter 1993), p. 106.

29 Bernal, '*Black Athena* and the APA', *Arethusa*, Special Issue (Fall 1989), p. 31.

30 See below, pp. 233–6.

31 Bernal, '*Black Athena* and the APA', p. 32.

32 Bernal, 'Responses to Critical Reviews', p. 133.

33 Molly Myerowitz Levine, 'Bernal and the Athenians in the Multicultural World of the Ancient Mediterranean', in *Classical Studies in Honor of*

David Solberg, ed. Ranon Katzoff (Ramat Gan, 1996), p. 35.

34 Molly Myerowitz Levine, 'The Use and Abuse of *Black Athena*', *American Historical Review*, XCVII (April 1992), p. 454; 'Bernal and the Athenians', p. 16 and Mary R. Lefkowitz and Guy Maclean Rogers, 'Preface', in *BAR*, p. xii.

35 David Gress, 'The Case Against Martin Bernal', *New Criterion*, VIII/4 (1989), p. 39.

36 Gress, 'Case Against Martin Bernal', p. 42.

37 James D. Muhly, '*Black Athena* versus Traditional Scholarship', *Journal of Mediterranean Archaeology*, III/1 (1990), pp. 104–5.

38 Gress, 'Case Against Martin Bernal', p. 39.

39 Lederman, 'Review of *Heresy in the University*' and Berlinerblau, *Heresy*, p. 3.

40 W.E.B. DuBois, 'The Propaganda of History' [1935], in *Writings* (New York, 1986), p. 1029.

41 *BAI*, p. 8.

42 Ibid., p. 9.

43 Bernal, 'Response to Critical Reviews', p. 130.

44 Vermeule, 'World Turned Upside Down', p. 42. See also Jasper Griffin, 'Who Are These Coming to the Sacrifice [review of *BAI*]', *New York Review of Books* (15 June 1989), p. 26.

45 Lerner, 'Comment [on *Black Athena*]', p. 91.

46 Berlinerblau, *Heresy*, p. 71.

47 John C. Coleman, 'Did Egypt Shape the Glory that was Greece?', in *BAR*, p. 292.

48 Berlinerblau, *Heresy*, pp. 181–2.

49 Ibid., pp. 72–3.

50 Guy MacLean Rogers, 'Quo Vadis', in *BAR*, p. 452. See also Coleman, 'Did Egypt Shape the Glory that was Greece?', p. 292 where he says, 'A case that is implausible but cannot be ruled out as impossible, as so often happens with archaeology, is not a strong one; and implausible claims in several areas of study do not strengthen the overall proposition.'

51 Examples are John Baines, 'Aims and Methods of *Black Athena*', in *BAR*, p. 47 and 'Was Civilization Made in Africa', p. 12; Griffin, 'Who are These Coming', p. 26 and Vermeule, 'World Turned Upside Down', p. 47.

52 Jean Bodin, *Method for the Easy Comprehension of History* (New York, 1969), p. 85; first written in 1565.

53 Frank M. Turner, 'Martin Bernal's *Black Athena*: A Dissent', *Arethusa*, Special Issue (Fall 1989), pp. 97–109 and Robert Palter, '*Black Athena*, Afrocentrism, and the History of Science', in *BAR*, pp. 209–66. Both deal extensively with this aspect of *Black Athena*.

54 *BA2*, p. 2.

55 Berlinerblau, *Heresy*, pp. 91–2 and 107–8.

56 Turner, 'Martin Bernal's *Black Athena*: A Dissent', pp. 108–9.

57 John Ray, 'Levant Ascendent: The Invasion Theory of the Origins of European Civilization [review article including *BA2*]', *Times Literary Supplement* (16 October 1991), p. 3.

58 Turner, 'Martin Bernal's *Black Athena*: A Dissent', pp. 103–4 and Bernal, '*Black Athena* and the APA', p. 26.

59 See esp. the essays of Coleman Jenkyns, Norton, Palter and Rogers in *BAR*.

60 Suzanne Marchand and Anthony Grafton, 'Martin Bernal and His

Critics', *Arion*, v (1997), p. 3.

61 Marchand and Grafton, 'Martin Bernal and His Critics', pp. 4–7.

62 *BAI*, p. 206.

63 Von Herder, *Outlines of a Philosophy of the History of Man*, p. 149.

64 Martin Bernal, 'Response [to Cheryl Johnson-Odim, Gerda Lerner, Ann Michelini, Margaret Washington and Madeline C. Zilfi]', *Journal of Women's History*, IV (Winter 1993): 'Response [to Gerda Lerner]', p. 120.

65 Baines, 'Was Civilization Made in Africa', p. 12 and 'Aims and Methods of *Black Athena*', in *BAR*, p. 46; Jonathan Hall, '*Black Athena:* A Sheep in Wolf's Clothing', *Journal of Mediterranean Archaeology*, III/2 (1990), p. 251; Molly Myerowitz Levine, 'Use and Abuse of *Black Athena*', p. 451; Muhly, '*Black Athena* vs. Traditional Scholarship', p. 104; Ray, 'Levant Ascendent', p. 3; Guy McLean Rogers, 'Multiculturalism and the Foundations of Western Civilization', in *BAR*, pp. 434–40.

66 Berlinerblau, *Heresy*, pp. 152 and 157; Bernal, 'Response [to Gerda Lerner]', p. 120 and Gress, 'Case Against Martin Bernal', p. 39.

67 Bernal, 'Responses to Critical Reviews', p. 119. Also see Bernal's comments in 1993 to Cohen, 'Interview', p. 7.

68 Berlinerblau, *Heresy*, pp. 148–9.

69 Bernal, '*Black Athena* and the APA', pp. 30–1.

70 Ann N. Michelini, 'Comment [on *Black Athena*]', *Journal of Women's History*, IV (Winter 1993), pp. 97–8 and Lerner, 'Comment on *Black Athena*', p. 90.

71 Bernal, 'Response [to Cheryl Johnson–Odim, Gerda Lerner, Ann Michelini, Margaret Washington and Madeline C. Zilfi], p. 123.

72 Berlinerblau, *Heresy*, p. 184.

73 For example, see Scott Trafton, *Egypt Land: Race and Nineteenth-Century American Egyptomania* (Durham, NC, 2004); Richard Poe, *Black Spark, White Fire: Did African Explorers Civilize Ancient Europe?* (Rocklin, CA, 1997); and most famously George G. M. James, *Stolen Legacy: The Greeks were not the Authors of Greek Philosophy, but the People of North Africa, Commonly Called the Egyptians* (New York, 1954).

74 Ibn Khaldûn, *The Muqaddimah: An Introduction to History* [1377] (Princeton, NJ, 1967), p. 35.

75 The following paragraphs and comments on Bernal are based on these sources: Mary R. Lefkowitz, 'Ancient History, Modern Myths', in *BAR*, pp. 20–22; Frank J. Yurco, '*Black Athena*: An Egyptological Review', in *BAR*, p. 98; Morris, 'Legacy of *Black Athena*', in *BAR*, pp. 172 and 174 and Rogers, 'Multiculturalism', pp. 442–3; Boynton, 'Bernaliad,' p. 44; Griffin, 'Who Are These Coming', p. 27; Poliakoff, 'Roll Over Aristotle: Martin Bernal and His Critics', p. 23; John Ray, 'How Black was Socrates? The Roots of European Civilization and the Dangers of Afrocentism [review of *Not Out of Africa* and *Black Athena Revisited*]', *Times Literary Supplement* (14 February 1997), p. 4; Levine, 'Bernal and the Athenians', pp. 19–24 and 'Use and Abuse of *Black Athena*', pp. 440, 451–2, 458–60.

76 Cheikh Anta Diop, *The African Origin of Civilization: Myth or Reality* (Chicago, IL, 1974) and Molefi Kete Asante, *The Afrocentric Idea* (Philadelphia, PA, 1987) are two classic works of Afrocentricism. Stephen Howe, *Afrocentrism: Mythical Pasts and Imagined Homes* (London, 1998) and Clarence E. Walker, *We Can't Go Home Again: An*

Argument About Afrocentrism (Oxford, 2001) are critical evaluations of Afrocentric extremism.

77 Bernal, '*Black Athena* and the APA', p. 32 and 'Response to Critical Reviews', p. 133. But, as Mary Lefkowitz has pointed out, Bernal tells a different story in *Black Athena: The Afroasiatic Roots of Classical Civilization*, volume III: *The Linguistic Evidence* (New Brunswick, NJ, 2006), p. 548. See Lefkowitz, *History Lesson*, p. 163, n2.
78 Palter, '*Black Athena* and Science', in BAR, p. 209; Cohen, 'Interview', p. 9 and Eric Dyson, 'On Black Athena: An Interview with Martin Bernal', *Z Magazine*, V (1992), p. 56.
79 Stanley Crouch, *Always in Pursuit: Fresh American Perspectives* (New York, 1998), p. 27.
80 Martin Bernal, 'European Images of Africa: Tale of Two Names: Ethiopia and N——', in *Images of Africa: Stereotypes & Realities*, ed. Daniel M. Mengara (Trenton, NJ, 2001), p. 40.
81 Yurco, '*Black Athena*: An Egyptological Review', pp. 95–6.
82 Boynton, 'Bernaliad', p. 46.
83 Jasper Griffin, 'Anxieties of Influence [review article including *Not Out of Africa* by Mary Lefkowitz and *Black Athena Revisited*, ed. Mary Lefkowitz and Guy MacLean Rogers]', *New York Review of Books* (20 June 1996), p. 70, also p. 68 and Boynton, 'Bernaliad', p. 46.
84 Levine, 'Use and Abuse of *Black Athena*', p. 445.
85 Molefi Kete Asante, '*Black Athena Revisited*: A Review Essay', *Research in African Literatures*, XXIX/1 (1996), p. 206.
86 Cheryl Johnson-Odim, 'Comment: The Debate Over *Black Athena*', *Journal of Women's History*, IV (Winter 1993), p. 85 and Boynton, 'Bernaliad', p. 44.
87 BAI, pp. xvi–xx.
88 Lerner, 'Comment on *Black Athena*', p. 92 and Griffin, 'Anxieties', p. 69.
89 BAI, pp. 401–2.
90 Frank M. Snowden, Jr, 'Bernal's "Blacks" and the Afrocentrists', in BAR, pp. 89–91 and Bernal, '*Black Athena* and the APA', p. 32.
91 BAI, pp. 109 and 460 n.165.
92 Martin Bernal and David Chioni Moore, *Black Athena Writes Back: Martin Bernal Responds to His Critics* (Durham, NC, 2001), pp. 392–3; BAI, pp. 401, 435 and Poliakoff 'Roll Over Aristotle', p. 23.
93 Martin Bernal, 'The Afrocentric Interpretation of History: Bernal Replies to Lefkowitz', *Journal of Blacks in Higher Education*, XI (Spring 1996), pp. 87 and Martin Bernal, 'Afrocentrism and Historical Models for the Foundation of Ancient Greek', in *Ancient Egypt in Africa*, ed. David O'Connor and Andrew Reid (London, 2003), p. 28.
94 Bernal, 'Afrocentric Interpretation', p. 87.
95 Mary Lefkowitz, 'The Afrocentric Interpretation of Western History: Lefkowitz Replies to Bernal', *Journal of Blacks in Higher Education*, XII (Summer 1996), p. 89 and *Not Out of Africa: How Afrocentrism Became an Excuse to Teach Myth as History* (New York, 1996), pp. 148, 153.
96 Mario Liverani, 'Bathwater and Baby', in BAR, p. 424.
97 Berlinerblau, *Heresy*, pp. 134 and 140–3; Jacob H. Carruthers, 'Outside Academia: Bernal's Critique of the Black Champions of Ancient Egypt', *Journal of Black Studies*, XXII (June 1992), pp. 459–65 and Manu Ampin, 'The Problem of the Bernal–Davidson School', in *Egypt Child of Africa* in *Journal of African Civilizations*, XII (Spring 1994),

pp. 191–204.

98 Berlinerblau, *Heresy*, p. 12.

99 Rogers, 'Quo Vadis', pp. 452–3 and Bernal, 'Passion and Politics: A Reply to Guy Rogers', in *Black Athena Writes Back*, pp. 198–218.

100 Mary Lefkowitz, *History Lessons' A Race Odyssey* (New Haven, CT, 2008), pp. 134, 138 and 181–3.

101 T. S. Eliot, 'Little Gidding', *Four Quartets* (London, 1945), section III.

102 Lefkowitz, 'Ancient History, Modern Myths', p. 19.

103 Johnson-Odim, 'Debate Over *Black Athena*', p. 85; Jonathan Hall, '*Black Athena*: A Sheep in Wolf's Clothing', pp. 247, 252; Lefkowitz, 'Ancient History, Modern Myths', p. 20 and Stanley M. Burstein, 'The Debate Over *Black Athena*', *Scholia*, V (1996), p. 16.

104 Burstein, 'Debate Over *Black Athena*', p. 16; Lerner, 'Comment on *Black Athena*', pp. 93–4; Levine, 'Bernal and the Athenians', pp. 2 and 4; Liverani, 'Bathwater and Baby', p. 421; Rogers, 'Multiculturalism', p. 443 and Michelini, 'Comment on *Black Athena*', p. 95.

105 Poliakoff, 'Roll Over Aristotle', p. 16, also see p. 18.

106 Lerner, 'Comment on *Black Athena*', pp. 90–91.

107 Coleman, 'Did Egypt Shape the Glory that was Greece', p. 293; Liverani, 'Bathwater and Baby', p. 425 and Jay H. Jasanoff and Alan Nussbaum, 'Word Games', in *BAR*, pp. 201, 203.

108 Griffin, 'Anxieties', p. 68 and Ray, 'Was Socrates Black?', p. 3.

109 Sir Thomas Browne, *Pseudodoxia Epidemica*, in *The Works of Sir Thomas Browne*, vol. II (Chicago, IL, 1964), p. 40.

110 Griffin, 'Anxieties', p. 70.

111 Marchand and Grafton, 'Martin Bernal', p. 3.

112 Berlinerblau, *Heresy*, pp. 8–9.

113 Ibid., pp. 13–20 and 179; Bernal, *BAI*, pp. 6–7; Boynton, 'Bernaliad', p. 46 and Lefkowitz and Rogers, 'Preface', in *BAR*, p. xi.

114 Berlinerblau, *Heresy*, pp. 17, 57; Johnson-Odim, 'Comment on *Black Athena*', pp. 84–5 and Turner, 'Bernal's *Black Athena*: A Dissent', pp. 97–9.

115 Gress, 'Case Against Martin Bernal', p. 38; Stuart W. Manning, 'Frames of Reference for the Past: Some Thoughts on Bernal, Truth, and Reality', *Journal of Mediterranean*, pp. 264–9 and Muhly, '*Black Athena* versus Traditional Scholarship', pp. 83–5.

116 Mary R. Lefkowitz, 'Ethnocentric History from Aristobulus to Bernal', *Academic Questions*, VI (Spring 1993), pp. 17.

117 *BAI*, p. 73.

118 Bernal, 'Responses to Critical Reviews', p. 128; Boynton, 'Bernaliad', pp. 47–8 and Gress, 'Case Against Martin Bernal', p. 40.

119 Rogers, 'Multiculturalism', pp. 440–42; Berlinerblau, *Heresy*, p. 17 and Bernal, *Black Athena Writes Back*, pp. 206–8.

120 Ron Robin, *Scandals and Scoundrels: Seven Cases that Shook the Academy* (Berkeley, CA, 2004), ch. 7, 'Science Fiction: Sokal's Hoax and the "Linguistic Left"', pp. 195–218.

Select Bibliography

Adavasio, J. M., with Jake Page, *The First Americans: In Pursuit of Archaeology's Greatest Mystery* (New York and London, 2002)

Allen, Jr, Ernest, 'When Japan was "Champion of the Darker Races": Satokata Takahashi and the Flowering of Black Messianic Nationalism', *Black Scholar*, XXIV/1 (1994), pp. 23–46

——, 'Religious Heterodoxy and Nationalist Tradition: The Continuing Evolution of the Nation of Islam', *Black Scholar*, XXVI/3–4 (1996), pp. 2–34

Ashe, Geoffrey, et al., *The Quest for America* (New York, 1971)

Austin, Algernon, *Achieving Blackness: Race, Black Nationalism, and Afrocentrism in the Twentieth Century* (New York, 2006)

Bailey, James, *The God-Kings & the Titans: The New World Ascendancy in Ancient Times* (New York, 1973)

Bailey, Jim, *Sailing to Paradise: The Discovery of the Americas by 7000 BC* (New York, 1994)

Barkun, Michael, 'From British-Israelism to Christian Identity: The Evolution of White Supremacist Religious Doctrine', *Syzygy: Journal of Alternative Religion and Culture*, I/1 (1992), pp. 52–8

——, *Religion and the Racist Right: The Origins of the Christian Identity Movement* (Chapel Hill, NC, 1994)

Bauer, Henry H., *Beyond Velikovsky: The History of a Public Controversy* (Urbana, IL, 1984)

Benedict, Jeff, *No Bone Unturned: The Adventures of a Top Smithsonian Forensic Scientist and the Legal Battle for America's Oldest Skeletons* (New York, 2003)

Berlinerblau, Jacques, *Heresy in the University: The 'Black Athena' Controversy and the Responsibilities of American Intellectuals* (New Brunswick, NJ, 1999)

Bernal, Martin, *Black Athena: The Afroasiatic Roots of Classical Civilization*, vol. 1: *The Fabrication of Ancient Greece* (New Brunswick, NJ, 1987)

——, *Black Athena: The Afroasiatic Roots of Classical Civilization*, vol. 2: *The Archaeological and Documentary Evidence* (New Brunswick, NJ, 1991)

——, *Black Athena: The Afroasiatic Roots of Classical Civilization*, vol. 3: *The Linguistic Evidence* (New Brunswick, NJ, 2006)

Bernal, Martin, and David Chioni Moore, *Black Athena Writes Back: Martin Bernal Responds to His Critics* (Durham, NC, 2001)

Beynon, Erdmann Doane, 'The Voodoo Cult Among the Negro Migrants in Detroit', *American Journal of Sociology*, XLIII (May 1938), pp. 894–907

Boland, Charles Michael, *They All Discovered America* (Garden City, NY, 1961)

Boynton, Robert S., 'The Bernaliad: A Scholar-Warrior's Long Journal to Ithaca', *Lingua Franca* (November 1996), pp. 43–50

Bradley, Michael, *The Iceman Inheritance: Prehistoric Sources of Western Man's Racism, Sexism and Aggression* [1978] (New York, 1991)

Bramwell, James, *Lost Atlantis* (New York, 1938)

Burstein, Stanley M., 'The Debate over *Black Athena*', *Scholia*, V (1996), pp. 3–16

Campbell, Bruce F., *Ancient Wisdom Revived: A History of the Theosophical Movement* (Berkeley, CA, 1980)

Campbell, Colin, 'The Cult, the Cultic Milieu and Secularization', in *A Sociological Yearbook of Religion in Britain: 5*, ed. Michael Hill (London, 1972), pp. 119–36

Castleden, Rodney, *Atlantis Destroyed* (London, 1998)

Charroux, Robert, *One Hundred Thousand Years of Man's Unknown History* (New York, 1970)

Chatters, James C., *Ancient Encounters: Kennewick Man and the First Americans* (New York, 2001)

Churchward, James, *The Lost Continent of Mu* [1926] (Saffron Walden, 1987)

Clegg III, Claude Andrew, *An Original Man: The Life and Times of Elijah Muhammad* (New York, 1997)

Cohen, Walter, 'An Interview with Martin Bernal', *Social Text*, XXXV (1993), pp. 1–24

Colavito, Jason, *The Cult of Alien Gods: H. P. Lovecraft and Extraterrestrial Pop Culture* (Amherst, NY, 2005)

Collins, Andrew, *Gateway to Atlantis: The Search for the Source of a Lost Civilization* (New York, 2000)

Cremo, Michael A., and Richard L. Thompson, *Forbidden Archaeology: The Hidden History of the Human Race* (Los Angeles, 1993)

Crouch, Stanley, 'Do the Afrocentric Shuffle', in *The All-American Skin Game, or, The Decoy of Race* (New York, 1995), pp. 33–44

Curl, James Stevens, *Egyptomania: The Egyptian Revival: A Recurring Theme in the History of Taste* (Manchester, 1994)

Däniken, Erich von, *Chariots of the Gods: Unsolved Mysteries of the Past* [1970] (New York, 1999)

——, *Gods from Outer Space: Return to the Stars or Evidence of the Impossible* (New York, 1970)

Davies, Nigel, *Voyagers to the New World* (New York, 1979)

Deacon, Richard, *Madoc and the Discovery of America: New Light on an Old Controversy* (New York, 1966)

Dewar, Elaine, *Bones: Discovering the First Americans* (New York, 2001)

Donnelly, Ignatius, *Atlantis: The Antediluvian World* [1882] (New York, 1976)

——, *Ragnarok: The Age of Fire and Gravel* [1883] (New York, 1970)

Downey, Roger, *Riddle of the Bones: Politics, Science, Race, and the Story of Kennewick Man* (New York, 2000)

Dreyer, Edward L., *Zheng He: China and the Oceans in the Early Ming Dynasty, 1405–1433* (New York, 2007)

Dyson, Eric, 'On Black Athena: An Interview with Martin Bernal', *Z Magazine*, 5 (1992), pp. 56–60

Ellis, Richard, *Imagining Atlantis* (New York, 1998)

Essien-Udom, E. U., *Black Nationalism: A Search for an Identity in America* (Chicago, IL, 1962)

Evanzz, Karl, *The Messenger: The Rise and Fall of Elijah Muhammad* (New York, 1999)

Fagan, Garrett G., ed., *Archaeological Fantasies: How Pseudoarchaeology Misrepresents the Past and Misleads the Public* (London, 2006)

Fauset, Arthur Huff, *Black Gods of the Metropolis: Negro Religious Cults of the Urban North* (Philadelphia, PA, 1944)

Feder, Kenneth L., *Frauds, Myths, and Mysteries: Science and Pseudoscience in Archaeology*, 5th edn (Boston, MA, 2006)

Fell, Barry, *America BC: Ancient Settlers in the New World* (New York, 1976)

Forrest, Bob, *A Guide to Velikovsky's Sources* (Santa Barbara, CA, 1987)

Galanopoulos, A.G. and Edward Bacon, *Atlantis: The Truth Behind the Legend* (Indianapolis, IN, 1969)

Gardell, Mattais, *In the Name of Elijah Muhammad: Louis Farrakan and the Nation of Islam* (Durham, NC, 1996)

Gardner, Martin, *Fads and Fallacies in the Name of Science* (New York, 1957)

Gilbert, James, *Redeeming Culture: American Religion in an Age of Science* (Chicago, IL, 1997)

Godbey, Allen H., *The Lost Tribes a Myth – Suggestions toward Rewriting Hebrew History* [1930] (New York, 1974)

Godwin, Joscelyn, *Arktos: The Polar Myth in Science, Symbolism, and Nazi Survival* (Kempton, IL, 1996)

Goldsmith, Donald, ed., *Scientists Confront Velikovsky* (Ithaca, NY, 1977)

Gordon, Cyrus H., *Before Columbus: Links Between the Old World and Ancient America* (New York, 1971)

——, *Riddles in History* (New York, 1974)

Goudge, H. L., *The British Israel Theory* (London, 1933)

Grant, John, *Discarded Science* (Wisley, Surrey, 2006)

Grazia, Alfred de, Ralph E. Juergens and Livio C. Stecchini, eds, *The Velikovsky Affair: Scientism vs. Science* (New Hyde Park, NY, 1966)

Gress, David, 'The Case Against Martin Bernal', *New Criterion*, VIII/4 (1989), pp. 36–43

Guiley, Rosemary Ellen, *Harper's Encyclopedia of Mystical & Paranormal Experience* (New York, 1991)

Hall, Jonathan, ' *Black Athena*: A Sheep in Wolf's Clothing', *Journal of Mediterranean Archaeology*, III/2 (1990), pp. 247–54

Hancock, Graham, *Heaven's Mirror: Quest for the Lost Civilization* (New York, 1998)

——, *The Mars Mystery: The Secret Connection Between Earth and the Red Planet* (New York, 1998)

——, *Fingerprints of the Gods* (New York, 1999)

——, *Underworld: The Mysterious Origins of Civilization* (New York, 2002)

——, and Robert Bauval, *The Message of the Sphinx: A Quest for the Hidden Legacy of Mankind* (New York, 1996)

Hapgood, Charles H., *Maps of the Ancient Sea Kings: Evidence of Advanced Civilization in the Ice Age*, revd edn [1966] (New York, 1979)

——, *The Path of the Pole* [1970] (Kempton, IL, 1999)

Harold, Francis B., and Raymond A. Eve, eds, *Cult Archaeology and*

Creationism: Understanding Pseudoscientific Beliefs about the Past (Iowa City, IA, 1987)

Harris, Hendon M., *The Asiatic Fathers of America (Two Books in One Volume)* (Taipei, 1975)

Heyerdahl, Thor, *American Indians in the Pacific: The Theory behind the Kon-Tiki Expedition* (London, 1952)

——, *Early Man and the Ocean: A Search for the Beginnings of Navigation and Seaborne Civilization* (Garden City, NY, 1979)

Holand, Hjalmar R., *Norse Discoveries and Explorations in America, 982–1362* [1940] (New York, 1969)

Huddleston, Lee Eldridge, *Origins of the American Indians: European Concepts, 1492–1729* (Austin, TX, 1967)

Irwin, Constance, *Fair Gods and Stone Faces* (New York, 1963)

Iversen, Erik, *The Myth of Egypt and Its Hieroglyphs in European Tradition* [1963] (Princeton, NJ, 1993)

James, George G. M., *Stolen Legacy: The Greeks Were Not the Authors of Greek Philosophy, but the People of North Africa, Commonly Called the Egyptians* (New York, 1954)

James, Peter, and Nick Thorpe, *Ancient Mysteries* (New York, 1999)

Jenkins, Philip, *Mystics and Messiahs: Cults and New Religions in American History* (New York, 2000)

Jolly, David C., 'Was Antarctica Mapped by the Ancients?', *Skeptical Inquirer* XI (Fall 1986), pp. 32–43

Jordan, Paul, *The Atlantis Syndrome* (Stroud, Gloucestershire, 2001)

Kaplan, Jeffrey, ed., *Encyclopedia of White Power: A Sourcebook on the Radical Racist Right* (Walton Creek, CA, 2000)

——, *Radical Religion in America: Millenarian Movements from the Far Right to the Children of Noah* (Syracuse, NY, 1997)

Lee, Martha F., *The Nation of Islam: An American Millenarian Movement* (Syracuse, NY, 1996)

Lefkowitz, Mary R., *Not Out of Africa: How Afrocentricism Became an Excuse to Teach Myth as History* (New York, 1996)

——, *History Lesson: A Race Odyssey* (New Haven, CT, 2008)

——, and Guy Maclean Rogers, eds, *Black Athena Revisited* (Chapel Hill, NC, 1996)

Levine, Molly Myerwitz, 'Anti-Black & Anti-Semitic? Have Classical Historians Suppressed the Black and Semitic Roots of Greek Civilization?', *Bible Review*, VI (1990), pp. 32–41

——, 'Multiculturalism and the Classics', *Arethusa*, XXV (1992), pp. 215–20

——, 'The Use and Abuse of *Black Athena*', *American Historical Review*, XCVII (April 1992), pp. 440–60

——, 'Bernal and the Athenians in the Multicultural World of the Ancient Mediterranean', in *Classical Studies in Honor of David Solberg*, ed. Ranon Katzoff (Ramat Gan, 1996), pp. 1–56

Lewis, James R., UFOS *and Popular Culture: An Encyclopedia of Contemporary Myth* (Santa Barbara, CA, 2000)

Lincoln, C. Eric, *The Black Muslims in America* (Boston, MA, 1961)

Livingstone, David N., 'The Preadamite Theory and the Marriage of Science and Religion', *Transactions of the American Philosophical Society*, LXXXII/3 (1992)

McIntosh, Gregory C., *The Piri Reis Map of 1513* (Athens, GA, 2000)

Marchand, Suzanne and Anthony Grafton, 'Martin Bernal and His Critics', *Arion*, V (1997), pp. 1–35

Menzies, Gavin, *1421: The Year China Discovered America* (New York, 2002)
——, *1434: The Year a Magnificent Chinese Fleet Sailed to Italy and Ignited the Renaissance* (New York, 2008)
Morrison, David, 'Velikovsky at Fify: Cultures in Collision on the Fringe of Science', *Skeptic*, IX/1 (2001), pp. 62–76
Muhly, James D., '*Black Athena* versus Traditional Scholarship', *Journal of Mediterranean Archaeology*, III/1 (1990), pp. 83–110
Palmer, Trevor, *Perilous Planet Earth: Catastrophes and Catastrophism through the Ages* (Cambridge, 2003)
Parfitt, Tudor, *The Lost Tribes of Israel: The History of a Myth* (London, 2003)
Pauwels, Louis and Jacques Bergier, *The Morning of the Magicians* (New York, 1963)
Peebles, Curtis, *Watch the Skies! A Chronicle of the Flying Saucer Myth* (Washington, DC, 1994)
Peradotto, John and Molly Myerowitz Levine, eds, 'The Challenge of Black Athena', *Arethusa*, Special Issue (Fall 1989)
Poliakoff, Michael, 'Roll Over Aristotle: Martin Bernal and His Critics', *Academic Questions*, IV (1991), pp. 12–28
Popkin, Richard, 'The Pre-Adamite Theory in the Renaissance', in *Philosophy and Humanism: Renaissance Essays in Honor of Paul Oskar Kristeller*, ed. Edward P. Mahoney (New York, 1976), pp. 50–69
——, *Isaac La Peyrère (1596–1676): His Life, Work, and Influence* (Leiden, 1987)
Pringle, Heather, *The Master Plan: Himmler's Scholars and the Holocaust* (New York, 2006)
Ramage, Edwin S., *Atlantis: Fact or Fantasy?* (Bloomington, IN, 1978)
Ramaswamy, Sumathi, *The Lost Land of Lemuria: Fabulous Geographies, Catastrophic Histories* (Berkeley, CA, 2004)
Ransom, C. J., *The Age of Velikovsky* (Glassboro, NJ, 1976)
Ridge, Martin, *Ignatius Donnelly: The Portrait of a Politician* (Chicago, IL, 1962)
Saler, Benson, Charles A. Ziegler and Charles B. Moore, eds, UFO *Crash at Roswell: The Genesis of a Modern Myth* (Washington, DC, 2007)
Schoch, Robert M. and Robert Aquinas McNally, *Voyages of the Pyramid Builders: The True Origins of the Pyramids from Lost Egypt to Ancient America* (New York, 2003)
——, *Pyramid Quest: Secrets of the Great Pyramid and the Dawn of Civilization* (New York, 2005)
Seaver, Kirsten A., *Maps, Myths, and Men: The Story of the Vinland Map* (Stanford, CA, 2004)
Sheaffer, Robert, *The* UFO *Verdict: Examining the Evidence* (Amherst, NY, 1986)
Shermer, Michael, *Why People Believe Weird Things: Pseudoscience, Superstition, and Other Confusions of Our Time* (New York, 1997)
——, ed., *The Skeptic Encyclopedia of Pseudoscience*, 2 vols (Santa Barbara, CA, 2002)
——, and Alex Grobman, *Denying History: Who Says the Holocaust Never Happened and Why Do They Say It?* (Berkeley, CA, 2000)
Silverberg, Robert, *Mound Builders of Ancient America: The Archaeology of a Myth* (Greenwich, CT, 1968)
Sitchin, Zecharia, *The 12th Planet* [1976] (New York, 1978)
——, *The Stairway to Heaven* [1980] (New York, 1983)
——, *The Wars of Gods and Men* (New York, 1985)

Spence, Lewis, *History of Atlantis* [1926] (London, 1995)
Sprague de Camp, L., *Lost Continents: The Atlantis Theme in History, Science, and Literature* [1954] (New York, 1970)
Stacy-Judd, Robert, *Atlantis: Mother of Empires* [1939] (Kempton, IL, 1999)
Stanfield, William D., 'Creationism, Catatrophism, and Velikovsky', *Skeptical Inquirer*, XXXII (January/February 2008), pp. 46–50
Stiebing, Jr, William H., *Ancient Astronauts, Cosmic Collisions and Other Popular Theories about Man's Past* (Buffalo, NY, 1984)
Story, Ronald, *Guardians of the Universe?* (New York, 1980)
——, *The Space-Gods Revealed: A Close Look at the Theories of Erich von Däniken* (New York, 1976)
Story, Ronald D., *The Encyclopedia of Extraterrestrial Encounters: A Definitive, Illustrated A–Z Guide to All Things Alien* (New York, 2001)
Talbott, Stephen L., et al., eds, *Velikovsky Reconsidered* (New York, 1974)
Thiering, Barry and Edgar Castle, ed., *Some Trust in Chariots: Sixteen Views on Erich von Däniken's Chariots of the Gods* (New York, 1972)
Thomas, David Hurst, *Skull Wars: Kennewick Man, Archaeology, and the Battle for Native American Identity* (New York, 2000)
Thompson, Gunnar, *American Discovery: The Real Story* (Seattle, WA, 1992)
Turner, Richard Brent, *Islam in the African-American Experience*, 2nd edn (Bloomington, IN, 2003)
Van Sertima, Ivan, *They Came Before Columbus* (New York, 1976)
Velikovsky, Immanuel, *Worlds in Collision* (Garden City, NY, 1950)
——, *Ages in Chaos* (Garden City, NY, 1952)
——, *Earth in Upheaval* (Garden City, NY, 1955)
——, *Peoples of the Sea* (Garden City, NY, 1977)
——, *Ramses II and His Time* (Garden City, NY, 1978)
——, *Stargazers and Gravediggers: Memoirs to Worlds in Collision* (New York, 1983)
Wauchope, Robert, *Lost Tribes & Sunken Continents: Myth and Method in the Study of American Indians* (Chicago, IL, 1962)
Washington, Peter, *Madame Blavatsky's Baboon: A History of the Mystics, Mediums, and Misfits Who Brought Spiritualism to America* (New York, 1993)
White, John, *Pole Shift: Predictions and Prophecies of the Ultimate Disaster* (New York, 1992)
Williams, Gwyn A., *Madoc: The Making of a Myth* (Oxford, 1987)
Williams, L. Pearce, 'Why I Stopped Reading *Black Athena*', *Academic Questions*, VII (1994), pp. 37–9
Williams, Stephen, *Fantastic Archaeology: The Wild Side of North American Prehistory* (Philadelphia, PA, 1991)
Wilson, Clifford, *Crash Go the Chariots: An Alternative to Chariots of the Gods?* (New York, 1972)
——, *The Chariots Still Crash* (New York, 1976)

Acknowledgements

> Many and powerful as were the attractions which drew us toward the settlements, we looked back even at that moment with an eager longing toward the wilderness of prairies and mountains behind us. For myself I had suffered more that summer from illness than ever before in my life, and yet to this hour I cannot recall those savage scenes and savage men without a strong desire again to visit them.
> FRANCIS PARKMAN (1823–1893), THE OREGON TRAIL

Francis Parkman was describing his feelings at the end of the journey that formed the basis for his book *The Oregon Trail*. As I finish this book, I too feel a reluctance to depart from the subject I have spent the last few years investigating. Like Parkman, I ventured into a wilderness but the wilderness that I explored was one of the mind, ideas and books. I was exploring the wilderness of pseudo-science and pseudohistory. At times my task was quite fun and at others it was rather depressing. Although writing a book is largely a solitary process, most authors get plenty of help along the way and I was certainly no exception. Now is the time to thank the people who helped and I hope that I don't forget anyone. First, I want to express my thanks to Jeremy Black for helping to get this book placed with a publisher. Jeremy has been a good friend for many years and I suspect will end up in the *Guinness Book of World Record* in two places: the number of books he has written himself and the number of other people's books he has helped to get published without even being a literary agent. As I have worked on this book, many people have helped to make it better. The inter-library loan staffs at the University of Central Arkansas and Athens State University have always been extremely helpful in getting me access to materials needed for my research. Lisa Mitten, the book review editor for the humanities at *Choice*, has been very supportive over the years in sending me books to review on topics related to the sometimes quirky subject matter of this book. As I finished the book, various people read and commented on all or some of the chapters. I would like to thank all of them for helping it to be a better book with their suggestions about content and style – Ebenezer Bowles, Frazier Douglass, Al Elmore, Tim Jones, Tony Moyers, Bill Robison and Bruce Thomas. I would also like to thank Michael Leaman, the publisher at Reaktion Books, for offering me a contract and being patient when I needed to move the deadline back two years. His own comments on the book also helped to improve it further. Other members of the staff at Reaktion Books, in particular Ian Blenkinsop and Robert Williams, have been uniformly efficient and cordial during the process of preparing this book for publication. Their efforts have made this book better and are genuinely appreciated. Finally, I would like to thank my wife Twylia. She's been patient as I spent night after night in my study after a day of deaning while I struggled to get this book done in time to meet my extended deadline. I would say that she deserves sainthood for putting up with me, my writing, and my sometimes weird sense of humour, but since she's a Methodist that's not going to happen except in my heart.

Index